PHILOSOPHERS OF THE WARRING STATES

PHILOSOPHERS OF THE WARRING STATES

A Sourcebook in Chinese Philosophy

TRANSLATED WITH
COMMENTARY BY
KURTIS HAGEN AND
STEVE COUTINHO

broadview press

BROADVIEW PRESS – www.broadviewpress.com
Peterborough, Ontario, Canada

Founded in 1985, Broadview Press remains a wholly independent publishing house. Broadview's focus is on academic publishing; our titles are accessible to university and college students as well as scholars and general readers. With over 600 titles in print, Broadview has become a leading international publisher in the humanities, with world-wide distribution. Broadview is committed to environmentally responsible publishing and fair business practices.

© 2018 Kurtis Hagen and Steve Coutinho

Library and Archives Canada Cataloguing in Publication

Philosophers of the warring states : a sourcebook in Chinese philosophy / translated with commentary by Kurtis Hagen and Steve Coutinho.

Includes bibliographical references.
ISBN 978-1-55481-067-3 (softcover)

1. Philosophy, Chinese—To 221 B.C. 2. Philosophy, Chinese—To 221 B.C.—Translations into English. I. Hagen, Kurtis, editor, translator II. Coutinho, Steve, 1963-, editor, translator

B126.P455 2018   181'.11   C2018-904328-8

Broadview Press handles its own distribution in North America:
PO Box 1243, Peterborough, Ontario K9J 7H5, Canada
555 Riverwalk Parkway, Tonawanda, NY 14150, USA
Tel: (705) 743-8990; Fax: (705) 743-8353
email: customerservice@broadviewpress.com

Distribution is handled by Eurospan Group in the UK, Europe, Central Asia, Middle East, Africa, India, Southeast Asia, Central America, South America, and the Caribbean. Distribution is handled by Footprint Books in Australia and New Zealand.

Broadview Press acknowledges the financial support of the Government of Canada for our publishing activities.

Canada

Copy-edited by James Thomas

Book design by Chris Rowat Design

PRINTED IN CANADA

Contents

Preface

In recent years the academic discipline of philosophy has begun expanding its boundaries at an accelerating pace, and the number of courses in philosophical traditions outside the 'West' continues to increase. This anthology of early Chinese philosophy is an attempt to help meet some of the needs of this expansion, as philosophy professors seek texts that will enable them to make the rich traditions of Chinese philosophical thought accessible to Western students.

Ivanhoe and Van Norden's *Readings in Classical Chinese Philosophy* has provided an excellent sourcebook of contemporary translations of essential texts. But the editors explicitly disavow the role of providing a "philosophical primer" with introductions and interpretations. The purpose of our anthology, however, is precisely to provide such a primer with introductions and extensive explanatory *philosophical* commentaries throughout the text. We do not think that ancient texts are monoliths with fixed meanings that can simply and straightforwardly be 'translated' into modern English. Indeed, our goal is to provide a structured guide to *actively interpreting* ancient Chinese philosophical texts, not only for the student, but also for the professor of philosophy (who may or may not have expertise in Chinese language or philosophy).

In this, we are deeply influenced by the hermeneutics of Hans-Georg Gadamer. Readers familiar with the work of Roger Ames will recognize that we are also influenced by his advice and his methodology, though we are not dogmatic adherents, and do not always draw the same conclusions. Reading Chinese philosophy from a Western perspective is a comparative 'hermeneutic' project: that is, a living interaction between cultural traditions that involves interpreting one culture from the perspective of another: merging disparate cultural and linguistic threads, strands, currents, and streams, placing them side by side, interweaving them, kneading them together where they blend, and teasing them gently apart where they resist. The goal of this ongoing and ever-unfinished interpretive practice is to *learn how* to better interpret these ancient texts, to allow their more hidden significances to continue to emerge and unfold. We invite students to participate in this interpretive project, using as guidance the introductions, commentaries, and explanations of key philosophical terms that we provide.

The introductory chapter provides a small amount of historical background; this will also help make sense of the early texts as they sometimes make reference to these historical figures and events in developing their arguments. Further detail is presented where necessary in the comments in each chapter. The philosophical overview attempts to show that there is an organic coherence to the development of the various philosophical views that arose in response to these historical conditions.

Chapter 2 provides a detailed glossary of the essential philosophical concepts of early Chinese philosophy. Chinese philosophical concepts do not match neatly with Western philosophical concepts, and so the possibility for misunderstanding and inappropriate imposition of concepts is great. To read ancient Chinese texts responsibly, the reader must be vigilant not to *presuppose* the universality of concepts they find most intuitive. The reader should therefore spend some time with this chapter, noting important concepts and how they interrelate. Those who are familiar with Western philosophy should be on the lookout for where there may be differences in significance between terms that might appear superficially similar. There is, of course, a huge amount of material in the glossary that cannot be fully understood on first reading. But the student will be better placed to understand the texts and concepts that arise in the texts if they make some attempt to familiarize themselves with some basic concepts first. We have identified these fundamental concepts with an asterisk. The reader should continue to refer to explanations in the "Key Philosophical Terms" chapter when encountering them in the texts until the concepts become familiar.

We've selected essential chapters and passages from the nine most influential texts of early Chinese philosophy, beginning just before the 'official' start of the Warring States period, and ending just after. The evocative title of this anthology should not mislead readers into assuming that the texts were written as complete documents within the official dates of this period. Confucius, for example, was born much earlier, and the syncretistic imperialists recorded in the *Zhuang Zi* wrote much later. But all their writing was influenced, directly or indirectly, by this historical and cultural context. We have made generous selections of the most important chapters, and other relevant passages. The seasoned reader will notice that we have not followed traditional chapter structure. The original texts were written and compiled in a non-thematic, holistic style that tends to make them less accessible to students from cultural contexts outside of China. First-time readers often complain this creates an obstacle to understanding and appreciation of the philosophical content of the texts. This also tends to be a problem for professors who need to introduce the material in an orderly way, within the course of a single semester. We have therefore taken the liberty of arranging the texts thematically. Traditionalists might at first find this a little jarring, but we intend it as a 'skilful means' to enable the professor to introduce the novice to the complexities of early Chinese philosophy as efficiently as possible. We believe that even the most experienced of traditional teachers will warm to this arrangement as it quickly yields its pedagogical benefits.

Each chapter begins with an overall introduction to the text and its philosophy. Some chapters also have introductions to thematic subsections, where the complexity of content makes this necessary. The texts are interspersed liberally with comments that highlight concepts of particular philosophical significance. We draw out their implications, offer philosophical interpretations—our own and those of other scholars—and, where relevant, note how the discussions relate to the philosophical claims of other texts in the anthology. Since the purpose of this text is to provide modern interpretations to bring Chinese and Western philosophies into closer dialogue, we do not translate traditional commentaries, though we do make reference to traditional interpretations that contribute to this contemporary discourse.

ORDER OF STUDY

While Chinese philosophical texts are usually studied chronologically, we do not believe that this is the best way to make the ideas accessible to a novice audience. We suggest beginning the class with the "Fundamentals of Legalism" section of the *Han Fei Zi*. This presents the basic ideas behind ruling by laws and punishments. Although the text was written late, it encodes ideas that predate other thinkers, perhaps even by millennia. The reader can then begin studying the *Da Xue* ("Expansive Learning"), which provides an excellent introduction to the politics of ruling by virtue, the Confucian alternative to the legalist realpolitik of rule by law. Since a fuller appreciation of the *Analects* presupposes an already existing familiarity with Confucian concepts, we suggest returning to the *Analects* after reading the *Meng Zi* and the *Xun Zi*. Finally, we recommend revisiting the Mystical Imperialism strand of the *Zhuang Zi* after studying the rest of the *Han Fei Zi*, at the end of the course.

QUOTATION-MARK CONVENTIONS

We use double quotation marks ("*x*") to name texts, to refer to words, and to mention translations into English. For example: "*yi*" has been translated as "rightness." We use single quotation marks ('*x*') for more subtle purposes: to refer to concepts, to give meanings of terms (when not intended as straightforward translation equivalents), and to highlight unusual senses of words while using them. For example: "*yi*" has a sense of 'being right and fitting,' and can express the sense of one's highest 'ideals.' The terms in single quotation marks are not being used as translation equivalents, but are explicating the sense of the Chinese term, while being used in their English senses (and not just mentioned as words).

ELLIPSES

Missing text is indicated with ellipses in brackets: "[…]." Literary ellipses to indicate pauses or lists implied in the text, but where no text is actually missing, are indicated without brackets: "…."

GENDER-NEUTRAL LANGUAGE

While early Chinese texts were written in a patriarchal culture, the concepts need not be interpreted in a patriarchal way for contemporary philosophical purposes. However, where the original texts clearly make historical reference to gendered roles, we preserve these meanings. But where the ideas concern ideals that need not be gendered, we have attempted to make the language gender-neutral as much as possible. We have therefore, sometimes made use of the 'singular "they"' to facilitate this.

BINOMES

We believe that the current convention of using binomes (disyllabic single words: Laozi, Zhuangzi, Kongzi, etc.) for the names of philosophers is misleading and unfortunate. In modern Mandarin, "*kongzi*" means "space," "*laozi*" means "father" (and can be a colloquial way of referring to yourself), "*zhuangzi*" can mean "village" or "stump." This strikes us as quite inappropriate. In fact, these names are honorifics with the word "Zi" functioning as a title. "Kong Zi" means "Master Kong," and "Zhuang Zi" means "Master Zhuang." We therefore present their names as full titles with honorifics: the "Zi" should be pronounced as a separate syllable with its own emphasis.

The modern convention is also to present many early Chinese concepts as binomes: "*tianming*," and "*wuwei*," for example. Though these terms eventually became single words, as they are in modern Mandarin, they were not single words in Zhou dynasty Chinese, but were two-word phrases. We therefore write them as phrases: "*tian ming*," and "*wu wei*." We make exceptions for reflexives (which have the prefix "*zi*"), and simple negations (with the prefix "*bu*").

ANCIENT CHINESE MEASURES

Ancient Chinese measures were neither exact nor standardized (until the Qin dynasty), and do not correspond closely with modern Western measures. A *li*, for example, is a flexible measure, perhaps the distance you could cover in 5 or 10 minutes walking: one *li* uphill would be much shorter than one *li* downhill. In philosophical texts their purpose is to evoke approximate and relative size or distance; and context is usually sufficient to follow the philosophical argument. We have usually chosen to render these terms using 'imperial' measures ("foot," "mile," "inch," "stone," "fathom," and "league," for example), though these should be understood in their ancient and less precise senses. In some cases, we have left the Chinese measure untranslated as the context seems clear enough to give a general impression of the size intended.

BIBLIOGRAPHY

The Bibliography aims to be as useful as possible. It lists not only works cited, but also extensive materials for students who would like to further their study of ancient Chinese philosophy.

AUTHORSHIP

Kurtis Hagen translated the *Da Xue, Analects, Meng Zi, Xun Zi, Zhong Yong*, and most of the *Han Fei Zi*. Steve Coutinho translated the *Mo Zi, Lao Zi, Zhuang Zi*, and chapter 6 of the *Han Fei Zi*. Although we each remain responsible for our translations of these texts, we had editorial input into each other's translations. We co-wrote the Introduction and "Key Philosophical Terms" chapters. Where we share opinions and recommendations we refer to ourselves in the plural. In other places, we make individual comments in the first person with our initials in parentheses for clarification (KH) or (SC).

Acknowledgments

Steve Coutinho would like to thank Muhlenberg College for a sabbatical in the Fall of 2012, a Summer Research Grant in 2013, and for the Hoffman Fellowship for the academic year, 2014/15, that released time to work on the manuscript.

Kurtis Hagen would like to thank SUNY Plattsburgh for a one-year sabbatical in 2013–14.

We would also like to thank Sor-hoon Tan (National University of Singapore), Amy Olberding (University of Oklahoma), Stephen Angle (Wesleyan University), Li Chenyang (Nanyang Technological University, Singapore), and Chong Kim-chong (the Hong Kong University of Science and Technology), for taking time to pore over the hefty manuscript and offer their invaluable feedback and suggestions.

We would finally like to thank Stephen Latta and the editorial staff at Broadview Press for their unwavering support, and for their patience and understanding while unfortunate personal circumstances resulted in very long delays to completion of the manuscript.

1

Introduction

To understand China (*Zhongguo* 中國) we must understand not only its present, but its past; and not only its history, but its philosophy. China has always understood itself in terms of its philosophical history, tracing its self-understanding back to the philosophical reflections recorded in the ancient texts of the Zhou dynasty.

Philosophical thinking began to flourish in China about 2,500 years ago, during a period of high culture and civil unrest known as the Warring States period of the Eastern Zhou dynasty. But at that time, there was no single country of 'China.' The central plains surrounding the Yellow River basin consisted of many 'states' (*guo* 國), the size of small European countries. Zhou, Zheng, and Song were in the center, Jin in the north, Qin in the west, Lu and Qi in the east, and Chu in the south, and many other smaller states throughout the region. Like their counterparts in Europe, while they shared much in common there were also regional differences that manifested in cuisine, style of dress, customs, and linguistic dialect. Differences in culture were looked down on: those furthest away from the central states (*zhong guo* 中國) were considered most 'barbaric' by those living in the 'center.' The states, however, coexisted under dynastic rule. The earliest named dynasty is the Xia, which lasted from approximately 2100 BCE to 1600 BCE. The Shang is the earliest for which we have reliable historical records. It was founded in 1600 BCE and lasted till 1046 BCE, when it was defeated by the state of Zhou.

The Zhou dynasty was founded by King Wen, his brother, the Duke of Zhou, and his son, King Wu. It was King Wu who led the decisive battle that had defeated the Shang dynasty, which was said to have become corrupt after ruling for 550 years. They took their victory as indicating that they had received the command (*ming* 命) to rule from *Tian* (天 the Heavens, the Cosmos). But they had also adopted and developed much of the culture of the previous Shang rulers. In 771 BCE western tribes attacked the Zhou, and forced the rulers to move their capital to the east. Thus, 771 BCE marks the division between the 'Western Zhou' and the 'Eastern Zhou.'

The first part of the Eastern Zhou is known as the "Spring and Autumn" period (771–476 BCE). During this time the culture of the ruling house of Zhou flourished. The ruling aristocracy devoted themselves to the practice of archery, charioteering, mathematics, and calligraphy. Scribes devoted themselves to the preservation and transmission of ancient classical texts including the *Shu Jing* (The Book of History), and the *Shi Jing* (a collection of ancient poetry). Classes of teachers and scholars, known as the "Ru," studied the carefully preserved accounts of the origins of dynasties, their values, and the exploits of their heroes and villains. Over the centuries, the authority of the house of Zhou began to dwindle as battles began to increase between states, and the entire region became increasingly volatile. Although political instability began much earlier, the traditional starting date of the Warring States is given as the year 475 BCE.[1] The house of Zhou fell in 256 BCE, and the Warring States came to a brutal end after the defeat of the great southern state of Chu in 223 BCE, with the fall of the state of Qi and the founding of the Qin dynasty by the first emperor, Qin Shi Huang Di, in 221 BCE.

It was in this historical context of warring states, which began well before the period known officially as the "Warring States," that the scholars and teachers studying the histories and observing the behavior of those around them began to reflect philosophically. This has traditionally been referred to as the period of the "Hundred Schools" of philosophical thought. The Grand Historian of the Han dynasty, Sima Tan, classified the various thinkers under six broad categories, which he referred to as "*jia*" ('schools,' or 'families' of thought). These were the *Ru Jia*, or school of Ru; the *Mo Jia*, or school of Mo Zi; the *Fa Jia*, or school of 'Law'; the *Ming Jia*, or Linguistic school; *Yin Yang Jia*, or school of *Yin* and *Yang*; and his own preferred school, the *Dao (De) Jia*, the school of the Way (and Virtuous Potency). He characterized their concern as articulating ways to bring about social order, or good government (*zhi* 治). Their goal was to understand nature, life, and society, so that we could live together harmoniously (*he* 和). Their political theories were grounded in reflections on what it means to be human, our psychologies, emotions, the nature of

---

1   The Warring States period is sometimes regarded as starting as late as 403 BCE, giving a large gap between it and the end of the preceding Spring and Autumn period. The date 475 BCE derives from Sima Qian. In any case, the point is that, regardless of where one marks the beginning of this period, in actuality the whole classical period, from Confucius to the unification of China in 221 BCE, can be fairly characterized as a period marked by warring between states.

ethical ideals, the nature of understanding, the limits of knowledge, the nature of language, how to live a healthy and flourishing life, how natural processes function, where things come from, and the place of humans in the Cosmos. They articulated competing proposals, each offering their own guidance (*dao* 道): accounts of the "way" things should be, the way to return to a flourishing life and social harmony. The most influential of the early texts came from the schools of *Ru, Mo, Fa,* and *Dao.*

The first thinker and teacher, "*Ru,*" to attain prominence was Confucius, with his extraordinarily idealistic philosophy, based on the cultivation of our human capacity to be virtuous (*ren* 仁) and devotion to doing what is appropriate (*yi* 義). He rejected the prevalent tendency to rely on laws and administer punishments in order to control people. Confucius argued that we must cultivate our highest ethical character in our social and familial relationships. Our strongest obligations begin with the family and reverberate outwards into the social world. Subsequent thinkers either developed his way or reacted against it, and formulated their own alternatives. The Mohists (*Mo Jia*) were equally idealistic, but formulated a more egalitarian and impartial *dao,* based on a utilitarian understanding of the virtues. The Mohists also argued that without uniformity of values and clarity of conceptual and evaluative distinctions (*shi fei* 是非, 'right and wrong'), social harmony was unattainable. After them, Mencius followed the thought of Confucius along one course, seeing humans as naturally virtuous, and after him, Xun Zi steered it along another, seeing virtue as needing to be artificially inculcated. By the end of the Warring States period, Han Fei Zi responded to the Ruism of Confucius by articulating a philosophy of Legalism (*Fa Jia*) that presupposed a very cynical view of human nature as selfish and untrustworthy. The Ruists, Mohists, and Legalists were all concerned with how to cultivate human order and social flourishing. They focused on culture, ethical behavior, political hierarchies, laws and punishments, and language. The Daoists (*Dao Jia*), however, criticized all of these 'humanistic' proposals as shortsighted and counterproductive obsessions with the artificial constructs of the human realm. They attempted to redirect our attention towards a more expansive *dao* rooted in *tian* (天), nature or the Cosmos.

RUISM

The Confucians belonged to a social group called "Ru" preserving a tradition that predates Confucius himself. The word "*ru*" (儒) originally meant 'scholar,' and the Ruists who preceded Confucius were scholars of the ritual traditions. Confucius saw himself as a follower and preserver of this tradition, but at the same time he was an innovator[2] who transformed what had previously been a ritual scholasticism into a profound social and ethical philosophy. And despite the fact that later Ruists saw themselves as followers of Confucius, they also developed new and competing interpretations of his *dao*. Soon after the death of Confucius, the term "*Ru*" came to denote not just any Ru scholar, but specifically thinkers who sought to follow and broaden his *dao*. By the Han dynasty, the Grand Historian, Sima Tan, referred to this school of ethico-political thought as the "*Ru Jia*," the 'family of Ru.' Indeed, the modern Mandarin term for "Confucianism" to this day is still "*Ru Jia*." In English, scholars increasingly refer to Confucians and Confucianism as "Ruists" and "Ruism."

In broadest terms, what is distinctive about the Confucians is that they sought to create social harmony (*he* 和) by means of traditional norms of ritualized, appropriate conduct (*li* 禮, ritual propriety). They maintained that the influential character (*de* 德) of exemplary persons (*junzi* 君子), who model ritual propriety and appropriate conduct, would have a transformative influence on society. They stressed working hard for the benefit of others, and maintained that when rulers exhibited *ren* 仁 (humanity, or empathetic effort), others would do so as well. They viewed the family as an analogy for society, with the ruler filling the role of a father to the people. They promoted a social hierarchy in which each member had his or her roles and responsibilities, and in which upward social mobility was based on merit.

The most influential early Ruist philosophical texts are the *Analects* of Confucius, *Meng Zi*, *Xun Zi*, *Da Xue*, and *Zhong Yong*. The Neo-Confucian philosopher Zhu Xi extracted the *Da Xue* and *Zhong Yong* from the *Li Ji* (*Book of Rites*), grouped them with the *Analects* and *Meng Zi*, and dubbed them the "Four Books." Although scholars believe the *Da Xue* and the *Zhong Yong* date from the Han dynasty, we have included them in this anthology because they have become highly influential texts that throw light on early Confucian philosophy.

TENSIONS WITHIN RUISM

The *Analects*, which is regarded as the most reliable repository of Confucius' words and ideas, contains many pithy sayings and some short stories. It is terse, Confucius' positions are rarely elaborated, and its principles of organization are less than obvious. One must read a fair

---

2   Some scholars appeal to *Analects* 7.1 to suggest that Confucius did not view himself as an innovator. See comment to 7.1 and the introductory section to the chapter, "The *Analects* of Confucius."

number of passages together to develop a sense of Confucius' project, to understand the key concepts, and only then begin to see how these fit together into a philosophical vision. And even then, fundamental questions may be left unanswered.

Ambiguities in Confucius' teachings led to the development of different lines of interpretation. The most prominent interpreters of the classical period were Meng Zi (c. 372–c. 289 BCE) and Xun Zi (c. 325–c. 235 BCE). In the *Meng Zi* and *Xun Zi*, Confucian concepts are discussed explicitly, richly fleshed out, and developed in depth. Only through studying later Confucian texts does the student gain sufficient experience with Confucian philosophy to effectively approach the *Analects*. For this reason, although we ordered these three texts chronologically, we strongly suggest that the *Analects* be studied *after* the *Meng Zi* and the *Xun Zi*, or at least some thereof. The following subsections consider the root tensions that led to contrasts between the Ruist interpretations of Meng Zi and Xun Zi.

Human Dispositions (*xìng* 性)

The most discussed difference between Xun Zi and Meng Zi involves their evaluation of *xing* 性 (natural dispositions).[3] Confucius had said that people are similar in their dispositions (*xing*), but he did not specify whether these dispositions were good or bad.[4] Meng Zi attempted to ground Confucian values in natural salutary human dispositions, which are conceived of as the 'sprouts' from which full-grown virtues naturally develop, given the fertile soil of a healthy family context. Thus, Meng Zi declared human dispositions to be good. Perhaps he perceived a need for a solid grounding for Confucianism in order to defend it against rival philosophies that, by his time, had begun to flourish.

Xun Zi agrees that people have the capacity to become good. However, he believes that Meng Zi's characterization of *xing* is not only mistaken, it is potentially disastrous. Prior to enculturation, Xun Zi argued, people's desires are without limit. Further, since there is no natural restriction on the pursuit of these desires, people would compete for scarce goods without restraint, and chaos would ensue. What was needed, he surmised, was some means of shaping personal character in a productive way. Fortunately, the sages had developed just such a way, and embodied that

---

3 This is often discussed in the secondary literature under the rubric of "human nature," but that phrase presupposes an essentialism that is open to dispute.

4 The character *xing* 性 occurs only twice in the *Analects*, one time just to say that Confucius rarely spoke about it (*Analects* 5.13). In the other passage, Confucius says the people are similar in *xing*, but differ in their practices (*Analects* 17.2).

way in ritualized norms and practices. If people assume that they would develop virtues without the need of any special artifice, then even those who aspired to moral improvement would not appreciate the importance of the creations of the sage kings. If Meng Zi's view held sway, Xun Zi reasoned, the role of ritual propriety, and even the importance of sustained and determined learning, would be disregarded. The result would be chaos and societal implosion.

Feeling versus Thinking

While Meng Zi views human goodness as growing out of natural *feelings*, Xun Zi locates our capacity to become good in our *understanding and intelligence (zhi* 智/知) (*Xun Zi* 21.1b and 22.5b). Indeed, Xun Zi's distrust of our unrestrained emotions is the basis for declaring our initial dispositions to be detestable. Xun Zi maintains that what sets us apart from mere animals is a sense of appropriateness (*yi* 義), which allows us to make distinctions and thereby form societies (*Xun Zi* 9.16a). Meng Zi and Xun Zi both emphasized the role of *xin* 心 (the heart–mind),[5] but for Xun Zi *xin* is closer to 'mind' than to 'heart.' Goodness, Xun Zi emphasizes, is a product of artifice (*wei* 偽) rather than natural feelings and dispositions.

This difference is a matter of degree of emphasis. After all, Meng Zi does seem to suggest that one ought to *reflect* on one's feelings in a particular situation so as to appropriately influence one's feelings in another (see *Meng Zi* 1A7, p. 140). And yet failure to exhibit the appropriate moral feeling is described as "losing one's root feelings (*ben xin* 本心)" (*Meng Zi* 6A10). Further, while Meng Zi does include the sprout of wisdom (*zhi* 智) as one of his 'four sprouts,' and it is not entirely clear to what degree wisdom is to be thought of as intellectual as opposed to emotional, one clue is that wisdom starts as a natural "sense (literally 'heart,' *xin* 心) of right and wrong" (*Meng Zi* 2A6).

Emphasizing *ren* 仁 (humanity) versus Emphasizing *li* 禮 (ritual propriety)

Two of the most fundamental and distinctive characteristics of Confucius' philosophy are his emphasis on *ren* 仁 (humanity) and *li* 禮 (ritual propriety). A key difference between Meng Zi's philosophy and that of Xun Zi can be framed around Meng Zi's emphasis on *ren* and Xun Zi's emphasis

---

5   Though it is convenient to refer to *xin* as the 'heart–mind,' it is often better thought of as 'thinking and feeling.'

on *li*. Meng Zi does include *li* (ritual propriety) as one of the four virtues, which has its sprout in a natural attitude of deference. However, Meng Zi does not particularly emphasize *li* (or *zhi* 智, wisdom), for that matter, emphasizing *ren* and *yi* instead. To some degree, Meng Zi's emphasis on *ren* correlates with his emphasis on feeling, while Xun Zi's emphasis on *li* correlates with his emphasis on thinking. That is, *ren* (humanity)—which is associated with *ai* (care for others)—can be thought of as a response that comes from a kind of sentiment. In contrast, *li* (ritual propriety) is a product of the *intelligence* of sages and exemplary people, and it requires thoughtfulness in each new interpretation and application.

Again, this is a matter of degree of emphasis. While Xun Zi emphasizes the importance of learning, and the role of intelligence in generating an effective system of ritual propriety, the function of ritual propriety is, in significant measure, to constructively influence one's feelings and emotional dispositions.

Two Views of Self-Cultivation

Meng Zi and Xun Zi both believed human beings could become virtuous. While Meng Zi says, "human dispositions are good," he explicitly states that this means that people have the *potential* to become good (*Meng Zi* 6A6). Xun Zi would wholeheartedly agree. Indeed, he maintained that even an ordinary person has the potential to become a sage. The crux of their dispute was over what grounds that possibility and *how* to realize that potential. Meng Zi naturalizes virtues: he traces their origins to natural tendencies and emotions that we are born with as humans. Xun Zi, however, rejects the notion that natural tendencies are good, declaring them to be detestable. It is human intelligence and artifice that are the source of all valuable achievements, ethical and aesthetic.

In practice, however, the difference between the two is less pronounced: both require that we develop our virtues. For Meng Zi, our cultivation of virtues requires constant attention and nurturing to *allow* those natural tendencies to grow and flourish to their fullest potential. We must take great care to create and maintain the optimal conditions for growth and can never neglect them, or they will atrophy. For Xun Zi, our cultivation of virtues is not simply a matter of allowing something that is already there to grow, but is a deliberate and active *transformation* of character such that one becomes able to resist natural selfish impulses and choose, instead, to follow a wise and well-tested course. Thus, Xun Zi encourages learning, and stresses the role of ritual propriety.

MOHIST PHILOSOPHY

The Mohists were straightforward common-sense thinkers who had little patience with the aesthetic flourishes of Ruist cultivation and articulated a more systematic and utilitarian philosophy in response. Their social *dao* was grounded in a justification of the origins of social structures: a mythical reconstruction of a primal human state that requires a universal, hierarchical power structure if the state is to achieve its goals: population, wealth, and order. As with the Confucians, Mo Zi's concern is with cultivating one's person: cultivating moral qualities as embodied by one's superiors.

Though their conception of an ideal society differed from that of the Ruists, they shared much of the same moral language, "humanity" (*ren* 仁) and "rightness" (*yi* 義), but with a more utilitarian interpretation of the meanings of those terms. A person with humanity, for example, works to increase the benefit (*li* 利) to all people, and to eliminate the harm, and to do so is to act rightly (*yi*).

The Mohists disapproved of expenditures on luxuries, and criticized the Ruists for what they perceived to be their useless extravagance in state ceremonies. Since they explain usefulness in terms of benefit to the ordinary people, any extraneous expenditure that does not benefit people is wasteful. And if it exploits the energies of the people preventing them from producing basic material goods, it becomes a direct harm. This is because they measured benefit only in terms of basic human necessities: food, clothing, shelter, and rest. But, they did not recognize that ceremonies can have a special sort of *significance* for what they *represent*. It is *meaningful* to the participants and audience alike. Rituals also serve other practical purposes, such as bringing the community together, and establishing community norms.

Mohists are particularly known for their policy of *jian'ai* (兼愛) 'impartial concern,' which they believe can be seen rationally to be the only policy that can guarantee a harmonious society. They rejected the Ruist notion that our love and concern should be greatest for our family and friends and diminish by degrees as emotional distance increases. They regard partial treatment of others as a kind of harm, since it involves choosing to benefit some at the expense of others. They were moved instead by a vision of mutuality and universal harmony, which they based on a version of the Golden Rule: "Act on behalf of others as you would act on behalf of yourself."

The Mohists appear to be the first school to be concerned with identifying modes of epistemic justification, that is, the acceptable ways in which knowledge claims may be justified. They identify three principles: collate historical evidence ("examination"), identify observational evidence ("the source"), and experiment to identify whether a policy has positive or negative effects ("application").

DAOIST PHILOSOPHIES

The majority of thinkers during the Warring States period were concerned with how to cultivate human order and flourishing in a social context. This was to be achieved through *humanistic* means: language, technology, society, laws, culture, and ethics. Confucians emphasized social hierarchies and ethical cultivation; the Mohists advocated clear laws, regulations, and standards; the Legalists emphasized laws and punishments. According to the *Lao Zi* and the *Zhuang Zi*, these philosophies had too narrow and short-sighted a focus. The Daoist texts recommended that we shift our awareness from the restricted perspective of the human (*ren* 人) point of view to the all-encompassing overview of the whole Cosmos (*tian* 天).

Daoist philosophy begins from such an all-embracing cosmology and derives an existential and political philosophy from it. The cosmological philosophy attempts to understand the nature and existence of the Cosmos as a whole and thus plays at the border between cosmology and metaphysics. That is, it comes *close* to suggesting the necessity of a realm beyond the empirical world of experience on which that world depends for its existence. Readers *expecting* to find a metaphysics that presupposes a 'transcendent' realm will indeed find such a metaphysics. But a more cautious reading will enable us to construct an alternative discourse for discussing such ultimate questions.

Building on this cosmology, the Daoists developed a philosophy of life. There were even strands of Daoist thought that attempted to incorporate their meditative and cosmological insights into their political theories. Two distinctive and contrasting political tendencies can be found in the Daoist texts. A quasi-anarchistic small-scale society is described in some passages of the *Lao Zi*, and also in the Utopian strands of the *Zhuang Zi*. At the other end of the spectrum, there are passages that advocate a holistic (or 'Syncretistic') political philosophy in which a single ruler is able to take control of a vast state system through esoteric forms of inner cultivation, and delegation of practical duties.

The majority of the *Zhuang Zi* text presents its own distinctive strand of Daoist thought. It can be found in the *Inner Chapters*, and in passages throughout the rest of the anthology. This 'Zhuangzian' *dao* is existential in spirit, dwelling on the significance of life and the inevitability of death. It is rooted in a deep and perhaps paradoxical understanding of our place in the world: both that we are an integral part of the processes of nature, and at the same time only a minuscule constituent of a vast and disinterested Cosmos; fully at home, and yet temporary visitors. From our everyday perspective, we take the dramas of our social lives very seriously. We judge the value of our existence according to the standards of success that have been ingrained in us since childhood. But when we adopt a more cosmic perspective, our concerns and worries diminish in significance.

Two interpretations of the *Zhuang Zi* have been influential. From a religious point of view, they have often been treated as mystical doctrines that posit an absolute, metaphysical *Dao* that lies beyond the reach of language. From a philosophical point of view (not only modern, but extending as far back as Guo Xiang in the Jin dynasty), scholars have tended to treat the text as an exercise in relativism, epistemological, ontological, and ethical. Our evaluative judgments of right and wrong (*shi fei* 是非) can only be made from some perspective: there can be no such thing as an overarching perspective from which to make a final judgment between them. More recently, some scholars have constructed an interpretation that is comparable with the way of life recommended by the ancient Skeptics: because no final judgment can be made, we should simply avoid making any judgments at all. My own preference (SC) is to steer clear of all three, to avoid absolutism, relativism, and Skepticism. Instead, I see the Zhuangzian worldview and way of life as a nature-oriented form of pragmatism involving mind–body discipline and cultivation of tranquility; it is existential in spirit and comparable, but not identifiable, with the way of life recommended by the ancient Stoics. The linguistic and epistemological claims must be situated within this overall existential stoic context for their full significance to emerge. As I see it, the abstruse discussion of *shi fei* judgment is deployed in service of a more practical philosophy that enables us to find our home in an unfathomably vast and infinitely varied world whose endless changes seem indifferent to human fortune.

LEGALIST PHILOSOPHY

When considering how to create a social structure that promotes social harmony, the first thought is often that we need to control people with laws, which in turn have to be enforced with punishments. This kind of view gets a fuller formal treatment in the writings of Han Fei Zi, towards the end of the Warring States period. But the ideology it represents was certainly practiced long before this. Although Confucius lived 250 years before Han Fei Zi, the practice of using punishments to enforce social rules predates Confucius by centuries, if not millennia. Indeed, it is instructive to view Confucianism as, in part, providing a radical alternative to legalistic approaches to governing. For this reason, we strongly recommend studying "The Fundamentals of Legalism," in Chapter 12 (*Han Fei Zi*), before studying Confucianism.

The most famous of the early Chinese Legalist philosophers was Han Fei Zi, who emphasized the role of rewards and punishments that are like two reins held by the ruler to maintain control of a state. According to Legalist philosophy, people are naturally selfish and unruly, and they are motivated primarily by desire and fear. On this view, they need to be strictly guided and constrained by laws and punishments for their own benefit. Han Fei Zi maintained that social order and compliance with laws are assured when the ruler has awe-inspiring power and authority, backed up by the motivating factors of rewards and punishments. Explicitly rejecting Confucian and Mohist emphasis on virtue and care, as well as the strategy of winning over the hearts and minds of the people, Han Fei Zi argues that a well-functioning society can only be maintained by means of strict application of inviolable laws and administrative methods.

Prominent among Han Fei Zi's Legalist methods was entertaining proposals from ministers. When a proposal is accepted, the minister must achieve the promised results. If the results are achieved the minister is praised and rewarded. If they are not achieved the minister is punished severely.

Han Fei Zi had admirable ideals: individuals and factions should not be able to benefit at the expense of the general public. Not even the emperor should rule for personal benefit. But his psychology of self-interested individuals leaves him unable to place any trust in people. He thus attempts to create a system of universal inviolable law and absolute control. But these two ideals stand in uneasy relationship to the ruler. If the law is inviolable, then is the emperor really ultimately in control?

It is worth noting that the end of the classical period comes when the Legalist state of Qin finally succeeds in conquering all of its rivals and unifying China under the Qin dynasty. In this short-lived dynasty, Legalism was the official guiding philosophy. Although Confucianism officially regains favor in the ensuing Han dynasty, in practice governments mixed Confucian strategies with Legalist ones throughout most of subsequent Chinese history.

HAN DYNASTY SYNCRETISM

By the beginning of the Han dynasty, thinkers had already begun examining the proposed theories of the various schools of thought. Xun Zi had already warned against being too one-sided in one's understanding, and proposed that the best way would be one that was broad and inclusive. Perhaps under the influence of Xun Zi, a tendency towards syncretism developed, that is, an attitude of analyzing a variety of competing philosophies, and seeking to identify what was best in each, while eliminating their faults. These could then be combined into a holistic philosophical system. The Syncretists are represented in this anthology by the 'Mystical Imperialist' strand of the *Zhuang Zi*. They adopted various policies from each of the competing schools, including the Ruists, Mohists, and Legalists, and sought to unify them under an overarching meditative practice deriving directly from the Daoists.

2

Key Philosophical Terms

INTRODUCTION

In this chapter, we provide a glossary of fundamental concepts of early Chinese philosophy. Chinese philosophy arose in a different cultural context from Western philosophy, and the fundamental issues that motivate the two traditions do not precisely match. Indeed, a careful examination of usages shows that the meanings, significances, and conceptual associations of the fundamental concepts of Zhou dynasty Chinese philosophy tend to differ quite significantly from those of Western philosophy.

This means that there are no easy sets of equivalent terms that we can appeal to from Western philosophy. For each Chinese term there will generally be a number of English words that overlap with its range of meaning, but none that fully match the ranges of associations of the Chinese term. For example, the word "*yi*" is an ethical term that has no exact match in English. It has a sense of 'rightness,' 'honor,' 'duty,' 'appropriateness,' and 'conscientiousness.' But none of these is an exact equivalent of the Chinese term. Moreover, different significances will also come into play to different degrees in different contexts: in some contexts the sense of 'honor' might be most relevant; in other contexts, 'appropriateness.'

This creates problems not only for the translator, but also for the reader, as translation choices can lead us to draw inappropriate inferences, especially when we rely on the meanings and implications of the words in our own language. This is problematic when important terms are translated with fixed equivalents, as tends to be done with most existing translations. (For example, "*Tian*" = "Heaven"; "*yi*" = "righteousness"; "*e*" = "evil"; "*ren*" = "benevolence," etc. These were the translation choices favored by the missionaries who first introduced Chinese philosophy to

English-speaking audiences, and who compiled the earliest Chinese–English dictionaries from the perspective of their own Christian conceptual framework.) The problem is that the modern reader inevitably *identifies* the meanings of these translation equivalents with the ancient Chinese terms, and will be tempted to draw inferences that make sense in English, or in a Christian theological context, but not necessarily in the original Chinese. This is especially problematic for the practice of philosophy, which proceeds in part by drawing inferences based upon the terms in which philosophical claims are articulated.

A major motivation for our translation, then, is to grapple with this translation problem. Rather than attempting the impossible task of finding perfect equivalents for each concept, we have attempted to be more responsive to conceptual and contextual differences in the original texts. In this glossary, we provide explanations of the philosophical significances of each term, attempting to account for ranges of meanings, and differences of significance between different philosophical texts.

In the translations themselves, we draw from a range of translation choices for each Chinese term, depending on the specific meaning in each context, but we provide the Chinese term in parentheses to clarify which Chinese concept is being rendered this way. This enables the reader to develop a richer sense of the meaning ranges of the Chinese philosophical concepts in the original texts. We also sometimes find it appropriate to leave the term untranslated, especially after enough familiarity has been built up through prior exposure in the text.

Basic Concepts

On a first reading, the student should pay particular attention to the more basic concepts, which we have marked with an asterisk, below. The reader should continue to refer to this glossary as they encounter new vocabulary. This will enable them to gradually build up a rich and intuitive sense of the meanings and significances of each ancient Chinese philosophical term.

*biàn 辯: *disputation*
The philosophers of the Hundred Schools argued with each other over who had the best way of life, or the best understanding of which values would help us realize our ideals. These arguments were referred to as 'disputations' (*bian* 辯). But since the correct understanding of values involves making the right 'distinctions' (*bian* 辨) both characters were often used in philosophical contexts with the sense of 'philosophical

disputes over correct distinctions.' The Daoists express deep dissatisfaction with the endless arguments and often profess not to know how to resolve the disputes, giving rise to the attempt to construct a *dao* beyond disputation and distinction-making.

cháng 常: *regular; constantly recurring; always*

In its everyday sense, *"chang"* means 'regular' and refers to what ordinarily occurs on a regular basis. In Daoist texts, its primary philosophical sense refers to the regularity of natural processes: most paradigmatically, the diurnal and seasonal cycles, and the cycles of living and dying. In the texts of the Warring States period, it can be translated as 'constant' so long as this is understood in the sense of 'regularly recurring changes' that constitute the natural processes of transformation of the Cosmos.

It is nevertheless often interpreted as 'eternal' in commentaries on the *Lao Zi*, in the sense of 'enduring for infinite time.' This popular understanding seems to be derived from *later* commentaries, either Buddhist or influenced by Buddhist thought.[1]

chéng 誠: *authenticity*

A Confucian concept emphasized particularly in the *Zhong Yong*, *"cheng"* is the Confucian counterpart of *"zhen"* (真) in Daoist philosophy. It is a sincere manifestation of one's deepest motivations; and these must harmonize with the dynamic tendencies of the Cosmos itself. While the Daoist ideal of *zhen* is ethically neutral, the Confucian virtue of *cheng* is primarily ethical.

dà 大: *great; vast; expansive*

Ordinarily, *"da"* means 'big,' but in philosophical contexts it has a much deeper range of significances. When applied to people, it has an honorific sense of 'greatness,' indicating prestige or power. In the Confucian text, *Da Xue*, "Expansive Learning," it indicates the learning of a ruler that must rise above practical issues.

Ontologically, it has a verbal sense implying increasing in size, growth, and expansion. In the Mohist texts it indicates that which is of greater importance in ethical judgments. In the *Zhuang Zi*, it gets extended even further to suggest the overcoming of all petty limitations. At the limit it is used to express the magnitude and magnificence of the Cosmos itself.

---

1   The Indian concept of *"nicca"* or 'permanence' enters the Chinese language as *"chang"* and is co-opted to translate it, and *"buchang"* to translate *"anicca."* But this sense is not present in pre-Qin usage. The word *"heng"* 恒, incidentally, has the sense of "lasting" or "enduring"; but *"chang"* has the sense of "constantly recurring." Some commentators confuse these two terms, incorrectly transposing these senses.

The contrasting term of "*da*" is "*xiao*" (小), which literally means 'small,' but can have an evaluative sense of 'petty' or 'insignificant.' In the *Autumn Floods* chapter of the *Zhuang Zi*, it develops the sense of that which becomes increasingly small and imperceptible.

*dào 道: *way or path; to guide; guiding moral discourse*
It would not be controversial to say that "*dao*" is perhaps the most fundamental concept of Chinese philosophy. Literally, it means 'road' or 'path,' but the metaphor gets extended to mean the 'way' that is followed, or the ways in which processes occur or things happen. Though used as a noun, the term has primary connotations of process rather than substance: the ways in which events happen or in which things take place. During the pre-Qin period, each school offered its own prescription, its own *dao*, its way to bring human lives to a state of flourishing. But there was no agreement over the prescription: there was lively disputation (*bian* 辯) over which of the ways were preferable and effective.

"*Dao*" can refer to the way, or ways, the world develops, the propensities and regularities of the Cosmos (*tian* 天). But it can also refer descriptively to the way or ways humans are; and it can also refer normatively to the way that humans ought to be. The Daoists emphasized *tian dao*, the way of the Cosmos, while the other philosophers focused their attention on the human. Indeed, Confucius is said not to have discussed *tian dao* (*Analects* 5.13).

"*Dao*" has the verbal sense, 'to guide,' or 'to show the way.' This guidance may take place non-verbally, as in the functioning of the natural world, or it might be put into words as a guiding discourse. For example, the first line of the *Lao Zi* can be read as, "*Dao* can guide (*dao*), but not as any ordinary (*chang* 常) *dao*" (*Lao Zi* 1); while Meng Zi defines "*dao*" as "conjoining *ren* 仁 (humanity) with *ren* 人 (humans, people), and putting it into words" (*Meng Zi* 7B16).

According to Xun Zi, the way of people (*ren dao* 人道) requires artifice (*wei* 偽) for its construction. As Chen Daqi, a twentieth-century Chinese scholar, explains:

> The standards of ritual and propriety for ordering a country and cultivating oneself originate from exemplary people and are produced by sages. It is people themselves who invent and establish them, they do not exist naturally. Because *tian* cannot be patterned after, people must establish [ritual and propriety] themselves. Xun Zi does not establish the way of people (*ren dao*) based on the way

of *tian* (*tian dao*). This is the great distinguishing character of Xun Zi's theory. The way of people is what people create. This view can be called artificialism.

(D. Chen 1954, 5)

Thus, *ren dao*, at least for Xun Zi, is both the way for people to follow, and a way created, articulated, and extended by exemplary people. It is the latter that Confucius stresses in *Analects* 15.29: "People are able to broaden *dao*, it is not *dao* that broadens people." And Xun Zi puts it this way, "*Dao* is not the way (*dao*) of *tian* 天, neither is it the way (*dao*) of the earth. It is that by which the people are led (*dao*); it is the path (*dao*) of the exemplary person" (*Xun Zi* 8.3).

In Daoist thought, by contrast, "*dao*" is that which goes beyond the confines of the human; it is that which is most expansive, and all-encompassing: the way of the Cosmos, the natural world, as a whole. It is also that which in the final analysis must be appealed to in order to account for the existence and nature of all things. Because of the cosmological concerns of the Daoists, and the fundamental role played by *dao*, it becomes a 'limiting' concept: as such, it verges on the borderline between a cosmological explanation and a transcendent one. While some passages in Daoist texts suggest an origin that transcends the world of experience, others suggest a holistic interdependence between them. How these two sets of passages should sit together is problematic. Do they represent the views of different strands of Daoist thought? Or do they represent a tension that could get resolved either way? Or do they represent an ineliminable tension that is not to be resolved at all?

*dé 德: *virtue; potency of character; compelling/influential character*
For Confucians, *de* is a compelling moral influence, stemming from excellence of character, which can have a transformative effect on others. For example, Xun Zi writes, "The resonance of the virtuous charisma (*de* 德) [of persons of *ren* (humanity)] is sufficient to transform [the common people]" (*Xun Zi* 10.5). Confucius makes the same point, saying, "An exemplary person's (*junzi* 君子) influential character (*de* 德) is the wind; a petty person's influential character is the grass. When the wind flows over grass, it is sure to bend" (*Analects* 12.19). In the following passage, Xun Zi clarifies how this works: "Exemplary persons (*junzi*) achieve the epitome of compelling character (*de* 德). Though silent, they serve as an analogy. Though not bestowing gifts, they are held dear. Though showing no anger, they are held in awe" (*Xun Zi* 3.9b). And Confucius

explains, "Lead [the common people] with virtue (*de* 德), keep them in line with ritual propriety (*li* 禮), they will develop a sense of shame and furthermore will reform themselves" (*Analects* 2.3).

"*De*" (德) is explicitly contrasted with physical coercion (*li* 力). Xun Zi writes, "The exemplary person (*junzi*) uses virtuous character (*de*); the petty person uses coercive force (*li* 力)" (*Xun Zi* 10.6; cf. *Xun Zi* 15.6a). The non-coercive nature of potency of character makes it more effective than physical power, and also allows it to play a role in providing political legitimacy. Meng Zi says, "Those who use their influential virtue (*de* 德) and put *ren* (humanity) into practice are kingly" (*Meng Zi* 2A3; cf. *Xun Zi* 15.6a).

In Daoist philosophy, *de* has a more naturalistic sense. It is an inner potency through which anything, or anyone, has its character and especially through which it influences what is going on around it. In people, it manifests as a charismatic potency that has a mesmerizing power over others. But its influence has nothing to do with the Confucian virtues, and may be ethically neutral, or even ambiguous. It is often associated with people who have been rendered outcast by Confucian standards: those who have been 'deformed' by punishment, or who have been born with 'strange' or 'extraordinary' (*ji* 畸) bodies.

fǎ 法: *standards; models; measures; laws*
Standards or models are objective means of determining correctness. In Mohist philosophy, "fa" refers to concrete models that serve to guide our actions, a straight-edge rule, or compasses, for example. When applied politically, it means clear statements determining the correct evaluation of an action and how to respond to it: what is acceptable behavior to be rewarded and unacceptable behavior that is to be punished. The Legalists agree that such standards must be clear, and that rewards and punishments must be unequivocal, if they are to serve as incentives. Han Fei Zi argues that the resulting laws must be independent even of the desires of the ruler, and must apply universally without exception.

fǎn 反: *returning*
The idea of 'returning,' as embodied in the image of revolving or rotating around a central axis, plays a fundamental role in Daoist philosophy. It is appealed to throughout Daoist texts as the modus operandi of the natural world. While the central axis may be still, it is continuous with the movement around it. *Dao* is thus processive, and the stillness of its axis does not need to be interpreted as something altogether other-worldly or transcendent. It is, rather, like the stillness and emptiness at the center

of a vortex. Thus, in contrast with Parmenides' Being, even when still, the way is not motionless. The circular and cyclical movements of nature lie at the heart of the recycling and replenishing functions that enable living processes to continue flourishing. In the *Zhuang Zi*, this process cosmology of returning is expressed with the close synonym, "*fu*" (復).

he 和: *harmony*
Harmony is a fundamental goal of the pre-Qin philosophers. The Daoists strive to cultivate a harmonious spirit that is in accord with the functioning of the natural world, while the Confucians aspire after social harmony. For the Confucians, ritual propriety (*li* 禮) is the key to its achievement. A follower of Confucius, Master You, says "Of the uses of *li* 禮 (ritual propriety), producing harmony (*he* 和) is the most valuable." He goes on to imply that harmony cannot be achieved without the guidance of ritual propriety (*Analects* 1.12). Similarly, according to Xun Zi, rituals are devised such that, by following them, "people can most reasonably live together in a harmonious (*he* 和) and unified community" (*Xun Zi* 19.9c). For Confucians, harmony doesn't just happen. According to the *Zhong Yong*, "Harmony (*he* 和) is the spreading of the way (*da dao* 達道) throughout the world (*tian xia* 天下)" (*Zhong Yong* 1).

Confucius said, "Exemplary persons harmonize (*he* 和), rather than homogenize (*tong* 同)" (*Analects* 13.23). Harmonizing involves blending different ingredients such that they complement each other and produce a satisfying overall result. The following excerpt from the *Zuo Zhuan*, about two people who are always in agreement, emphasizes the point:

> Master Yan said, "You and Ju are the same (*tong* 同), how can you be in harmony (*he* 和)?"
> The Marquis asked, "Are harmony and sameness different?"
> [Master Yan] replied, "They are different. Harmony is like making soup. Taking water, fire, vinegar, sauce, salt, and plums, one cooks fish and meat by heating it with firewood and blending (*he* 和) it to coordinate the flavors, adding ingredients or diluting with water to achieve just the right effect. When exemplary persons partake of this, it stabilizes their thoughts and feelings (*xin* 心). [...] If one adds water to water, who will want to eat it? If one plays nothing but the same note on a lute, who will want to listen to it? This shows the inadequacy of sameness."[2]

---

2 *Chun Qiu Zuo Zhuan* ("The Zuo Commentary on the Spring and Autumn Annals"), Book 10 ("Duke Zhao"), Year 20; cf. Ames and Rosemont 1998, 254–58n216.

Although Confucians tend to focus on harmony among human beings, they also recognize a more inclusive sense of harmony, such as when Xun Zi writes, "Each of the myriad creatures obtains conditions in harmony (*he* 和) with what it needs to live; each obtains the nourishment by which it achieves maturity" (*Xun Zi* 17.2b). The Daoist ideal is more inclusive still, attempting to embrace the variety of things and multiplicity of differences in a grand and effortless concord. The Cosmic perspective simultaneously contains all differences in their uniqueness, and yet blends them in a boundariless whole.

In contrast, while the Mohists shared the goal of social harmony within a state, and harmony throughout the world, their understanding in practice was very different. For the Mohists harmony requires uniformity or sameness (*tong* 同). The Mohists, like the Legalists, were afraid that difference contains the potential for social disruption and so should not be tolerated. Uniformity is to be imposed from above and deviation is to be punished severely.

huà 化: *transformation*

In ancient Chinese cosmology, the world is not conceived of simply as an entity, or as a collection of entities. Rather, its processive, seasonal, temporal aspects are brought to prominence. To understand the world is, first and foremost, to understand how it changes and transforms over time. Indeed, the myriad things "*wan wu*" (萬物) are on occasion referred to as the myriad transformations "*wan hua*" (萬化). Transformations are conceived of as cyclical, movements of revolution or rotation, oscillating in a *yin yang* pattern between two poles, heating and cooling, lightening and darkening, and so on, thereby generating seasonal changes and stages in the development of living processes.

jūnzǐ 君子: *exemplary person; person of noble character*

Before Confucius, the term *junzi* 君子—literally, the son (*zi* 子) of a lord (*jun* 君)—had meant 'a noble' (a member of the nobility) or 'gentleman' (a member of the gentry). Confucius, however, used it to refer to someone who had the 'noble' and exemplary qualities of character that someone carrying those honorific titles ought to possess. To be a *junzi*, in the Confucian sense, is to be an 'exemplary person,' a model of conduct worthy of emulation. As the term is used in the *Analects*, *junzi* are focused on what is appropriate (*yi* 義; see *Analects* 4.10, 4.16, 15.18, 16.10, pp. 90, 92, 88, 89), on ritual propriety (*li* 禮; see *Analects* 6.27, 12.5, 15.18, pp. 94, 108, 88), and on exhibiting *ren* 仁 (humanity). Confucius asks rhetorically, "If 'exemplary persons' (*junzi* 君子) abandon *ren* 仁, how can they fulfill their title?" (*Analects* 4.5). As the virtues of ritual propriety, appropriateness, and *ren* (humanity) develop, they provide *junzi* with the potency of character (*de* 德) necessary to effectively serve as models (*fa* 法) to others. (Notice how these terms form a 'concept cluster' such that they are best understood together, in reference to each other.)

Xun Zi emphasizes the role of *junzi* as models of proper conduct in the following passages:

> *Junzi* speak seldom but serve as exemplary models (*fa* 法).
>
> (*Xun Zi* 6.9)

> The learning of *junzi* enters through their ears, adheres to their heart (*xin* 心), spreads to their four limbs, and is embodied in their actions. Every word, every subtle movement, may be taken as a model and pattern.
>
> (*Xun Zi* 1.9)

> *Junzi* measure themselves with a stretched cord [i.e., strictly] [...] Thus, they may be taken as models worthy of emulation everywhere.
>
> (*Xun Zi* 5.7)[3]

And the *Da Xue* ("Expansive Learning") states:

> It is only after seeing the example of a *junzi* that they begin to cover up their degeneracy (*bu shan* 不善) with disgust, and make appearances of excellence (*shan* 善).
>
> (*Da Xue* 6)

Through their compelling conduct, exemplary persons continually reaffirm, and potentially subtly revise, norms of appropriate conduct. (*Analects* 9.3 provides a good example.) This is the sense in which, "The exemplary person (*junzi* 君子) is the beginning of ritual and propriety (*li-yi* 禮義)" (*Xun Zi* 9.15), and, "'The way' (*dao* 道) [...] is the path (*dao* 道) of exemplary persons" (*Xun Zi* 8.3).

lǐ 禮: *ritual propriety*
Etymologically combining the image of a sacrificial vessel with that of an altar, this character originally indicated sacrificial rites. However, as

---

3 See also *Xun Zi* 3.9b and *Analects* 12.19, both quoted above in the section on *de* 德 (potency of character), p. 33; cf. also *Analects* 8.2, and *Xun Zi* 22.4a, pp. 79 and 217.

with the idea of the *junzi*, its significance was extended to include proper conduct generally, involving judicious observance of social norms, or fulfilling an ethical role by faithfully discharging the responsibilities associated with that role. *Li* can be thought of as 'ritualized roles and responsibilities' and 'ritualized appropriate conduct.' A genuine performance of ritual propriety involves a deep sense of reverence that turns every act, in its minutest detail, into something of profound, even spiritual, significance. A.C. Graham describes *li* as follows:

> [*Li* 禮] embraces all rites, customs, manners, conventions, from the sacrifices to ancestors down to the detail of social etiquette. *Li* in social intercourse corresponds to a considerable extent with Western conceptions of good manners: the Confucian gentleman moves with an effortless grace within the framework of fixed convention, informing every action with consideration and respect for the other person.
>
> (Graham 1989, 11)

Li is also the means by which one cultivates one's character. Constantly returning to *li*, Confucius says, is the way to achieve *ren* 仁 (humanity). When asked for specifics, he replied, "Do not look in a way which is not *li* 禮, do not listen in a way that is not *li*, do not speak in a way that is not *li*, do not move in a way that is not *li*" (*Analects* 12.1). Confucius is suggesting that one should, in all circumstances, act with the attention and care characteristic of the performance of a sacred rite. This does not mean following a precise code of action, although *li* does include norms that provide guidance. Nor does it mean that one should always be somber. Rather, in all circumstances, one should be conscientiously attentive to detail, and sensitive to what is most appropriate to the situation. Consider the following passage from the *Odes*, which Xun Zi quotes twice: "Ritual ceremony, completely according to the standard; laughing and talking, completely appropriate." According to Yang Liang's commentary, "By quoting this he makes clear that, for the person of *li*, every movement is fitting and appropriate" (Wang 2012, 358). Xun Zi also quotes Confucius, who in *Analects* 17.11 says, "In singing the praises of *li* 禮 (ritual propriety), how could I be referring merely to jade and silk offerings?" Xun Zi comments, "If it is not timely and fitting, if it is not respectfully sociable, if it is not cheerfully enjoyed, although it may be beautiful, it is not ritual propriety" (*Xun Zi* 27.11).

In sum, to conform to ritual propriety is to be attentive to details and the particularities of one's situation *as well as* adhering to the norms set, maintained, and perhaps modified by exemplary precedent. And, importantly, to do so with an appropriate attitude—usually one that is respectful and deferential.

Xun Zi often combined *li* with *yi* 義 (appropriateness) as a single expression *li-yi* 禮義. As Robert Eno points out, "The compound is fundamentally a linkage of explicit conventional rules and a more abstract ethical notion [...] The linkage is often understood as a way of enlarging the prescriptive range of ritual, allowing individuals to act according to what seems ethically right even if it is not in absolute accord with convention" (Eno 1990, 273n71). (For more on the expression *li-yi*, see "*yi* 義: appropriateness," below).

ming 命: *circumstances; Circumstance; command; allotment; lifespan*
"*Ming*" is an extraordinarily complex term with a broad range of meanings that are more closely associated in Chinese than they are in English. Its basic sense is the 'call' or 'command' of a ruler. As a verb, it means 'to call' or 'to name,' that is, to command or ordain that a certain name be applied to something. As such, it can be interpreted as a kind of 'performative utterance': a speech act that doesn't just describe, but actively brings about a change by its very performance. For example, a speech act can make something so by naming it so, as when a ruler bestows title and rank on a person in the act of saying so. In a political sense, the authority to rule was said to reside in the command of the Heavens, *tian ming* 天命.

But the term, "*tian ming*" has a more general sense that extends beyond the political. The Cosmos, *tian*, is responsible for all things; it 'calls' (命) them into being, calls them to be what they are. In this sense, "*ming*" is the 'bringing to life' of the myriad things, and by extension 'life' itself. Each thing and each creature has its 'allotted existence' and the conditions into which it is born. These conditions, brought about independently of us by the world itself, are beyond our control. For example, Xun Zi defines "*ming*" as follows: "The conditions one encounters are called 'the circumstances of one's life (*ming* 命)'" (*Xun Zi* 22.1b). Meng Zi said, "What occurs when nobody brought it about is due to circumstances (*ming* 命)" (*Meng Zi* 5A6; cf. 7A1; 7A3; 7B33, pp. 128, 129, 129). And Confucius said, "If the way (*dao* 道) is about to be put into practice, it is due to the prevailing circumstances (*ming* 命). If the way is about to be laid to waste, it is due to the prevailing circumstances" (*Analects* 14.36). Although "*ming*" refers to forces beyond human control that does not mean one's actions make no difference at all. As Meng Zi points out, "a person who understands *ming* does not stand beneath a wall that is poised to collapse" (*Meng Zi* 7A2).

In the most general sense, "*ming*" can be understood as 'Circumstance': the conditions of the Cosmos as a whole, the way the world simply is. In this broad sense, it is almost synonymous with "*tian*." The Zhuangzian Daoists emphasize harmonizing ourselves with the way of the Cosmos, and reconciling ourselves with the circumstances that we can do nothing about: life, death, and the ultimate conditions into which we are thrown. "To tend to your heart–mind so that sadness and joy do not sway or move it; to understand what you can do nothing about and to rest content with Circumstance (*ming* 命), this is the height of potency" (*Zhuang Zi*).

The Mohists mistakenly criticized the Ruist doctrine of *ming*, as they took it to imply a kind of helpless fatalism. One strand of Daoist thought (in the *Lie Zi*, not translated in this anthology) also takes the term in the same way. In these two texts it can be translated as "fate."

ming 名: *linguistic terms; words; names*

In its ordinary sense, "*ming*" means 'name,' and as a verb it means 'to be named,' but in philosophical contexts, it has a technical sense of 'linguistic terms' in general. It refers to the linguistic means by which we distinguish and categorize the many phenomena. But naming is understood to be a linguistic function that imposes not only distinctions and divisions, but also hierarchical evaluations. We distinguish not only cows from horses, but also strong and weak, high and low, noble and base. Names, or linguistic terms, are not just neutral labels, but evaluative terms that must be earned: they either bestow honor or imply critique. A noble must live up to the title and manifest nobility of character; a father must live up to the title of 'father' and manifest parental virtue. Even a drinking vessel must live up to the evaluative implications of its name (consider the implications of calling a cup a 'chalice,' for example). If they do not, we cannot rightly honor them with those designations.

The *Lao Zi* notes a close connection between naming and desiring: we distinguish things evaluatively, and desire the specific aspects and qualities of the world that we evaluate as more beautiful or excellent. Linguistic conventions thus stimulate our desires.

ming 明: *clarity; insight*

In its most basic sense, "*ming*" means 'bright' or 'clear'; as a noun it means 'clarity.' In the *Mo Zi*, it refers to the clarity of linguistic distinctions. The Mohists insist there must be no confusion about when our linguistic terms apply, no vagueness, no ambiguity. We must not only be able to clearly distinguish cows from horses, but more importantly we must be clear about the distinction between noble and base, and especially right (*shi* 是) and wrong (*fei* 非). Only then can we have a hope for a flourishing society.

In the *Zhuang Zi*, "*ming*" refers to a deep understanding or 'insight' that arises as we clear our mind, or 'spirit' (*shen* 神) through the meditative practices of attenuating (*xu* 虛) (thinning out of distractions) and stilling (*jing* 靜) (becoming more calm and tranquil). In contrast to the Mohists, the Zhuangzian Daoists maintain that cultivating clarity of insight entails becoming aware that the distinctions between things are not as sharp as we might believe.

qì 氣: *energy; breath*
In Chinese cosmology, *qi* is understood as a fundamental, and even primordial, stuff. Conceived of as a kind of vapor, it can refer to atmospheric energies, the wind and the clouds for example, that propel atmospheric conditions. More generally, it is understood as the energy that makes up and invigorates all existing things; it has physical extension, and yet also has a tenuous spirit-like fluidity, capable of rarefying into gaseous form, or condensing into a solid. In living things it is associated with the breath, and with blood, and is thought of as a form of life energy. *Qi* and *shen* (spirit) are closely related, though not necessarily in any strictly defined ontological relationship. The *Zhuang Zi* refers to *shen qi* ('spirit-like energy') in describing the attentive concentration involved in superlative levels of dexterity. And Meng Zi claims to excel at nurturing his expansive *qi*, which he describes as a product of *yi* (appropriateness) and *dao* (*Meng Zi* 2A2).

qíng 情: *conditions; emotions*
"*Qing*" is a fundamental term in Chinese ontology and cosmology. It has a more general sense of 'conditions,' and a more specific sense referring to the inner conditions of specified types of things (especially "*ren qing*" (人情), 'human conditions' or 'the distinctive conditions of being human'). It is closely related to "*xing*" (性) 'dispositional tendencies,' and can be thought of as referring to the specific conditions that ground those dispositional tendencies. The two concepts are so closely related that in some contexts the distinction between them may be blurred.

In another sense, it also refers to the natural conditional responses of humans to their circumstances: our likes (*hao* 好) and dislikes (*wù* 惡), not as a matter of personal taste, but as a matter of basic human motivation. It thus also refers to human emotional responses to our experiences, and in those contexts can be translated as 'emotions.' We have a natural tendency to take pleasure in what is beneficial and to be repelled by what is harmful. We then approve (*shi* 是) what we like and reject (*fei* 非) what we dislike, and impose these distinctions on our experience of the world. *Ren qing*, human inner conditions, thus ground our tendency to divide, categorize, and evaluate phenomena, and ultimately are the source of our logical distinctions and judgments (regarding what is so and what is not).

*rén 人: human; person; humans; people; others
One of the fundamental issues that motivates early Chinese philosophy is the relation between the human, *ren* 人, and the natural world or Cosmos, *tian* 天. The word "*ren*" means 'human,' or 'person'; it is gender neutral and indeterminate with regard to number. So, it is misleading to translate it as "man," or "a man." Rather, it means human and humans, person and people.

Early Confucianism is a kind of humanism; it traces the source of value to our humanity, and its goal is to cultivate what invests human life with deep significance: virtue and culture. Certainly, we are born as human beings, but fulfilling our humanity is both a duty and an achievement. To be fully human, we must be actively involved in constructing and shaping our own humanity. This sort of cultivation is a never-ending process: humanity is always a work in progress. There is no perfected end point that is the finalized ideal, but something more beautiful that precedes and exceeds us is always ahead of us and out of our reach.

The Daoists consider human-oriented endeavors of such magnitude to be counterproductive and disastrous, artificial fabrications that set us in conflict with the natural way. Transforming our natural behaviors and following artificially constructed orders and patterns involves a loss of genuineness that leads to a kind of hypocrisy.

*rén 仁: humanity; human-heartedness
To be *ren* 仁 is to be human in the fullest sense (*Meng Zi* 7B16). It is the consummate Confucian virtue. At one point, Confucius captures the essence of *ren* as "caring for other people" (*ai ren* 爱人). At another point Confucius characterizes *ren* in terms of five virtues: "respect, magnanimity, trustworthiness (*xin* 信), diligence, and kindness" (*Analects* 17.6). *Ren* is thus a term of deep, complex, and fundamental significance, encompassing a broad range of virtues. Randall Peerenboom characterizes *ren* as "a duty to act appropriately in relation to others," or in other words "excellence in interpersonal relations" (Peerenboom 1993b, 44, 42).

Meng Zi affirms the close connection between *ren* and *shu*, 恕 (empathetic consideration), saying: "There is nothing closer to *ren* 仁 than striving to put empathetic consideration (*shu* 恕) into practice" (*Meng Zi* 7A4). He also views "a sense of compassion" as "the sprout of *ren*" (*Meng Zi* 2A6). Indeed, Confucius says, "The ability to take what is close as an analogy can be called *ren*'s compass" (*Analects* 6.30), which is a good description of *shu* (empathetic understanding). Furthermore, when asked about *ren*, Confucius answers: "Dwell in reverence. Carry out affairs with respect. Support others with your whole heart (*zhong* 忠)" (*Analects* 13.19; cf. 4.5, 6.22, 15.9, and 15.10, pp. 88, 84, 85, 80). Thus, when Confucius says that his *dao* is unified with a single thread, and his follower Master Zeng explains, "The *dao* of the Master is to do his utmost (*zhong* 忠) with sympathetic understanding (*shu* 恕), and that is all" (*Analects* 4.15), we might interpret these as two aspects of the virtue *ren* 仁.

Master Zeng, a follower of Confucius, says: "Aspirants (*shi* 士) must be strong and determined, for their burden (*ren* 任) is heavy and their way (*dao* 道) is long. They take *ren* 仁 as their own responsibility (*ren* 任). Is this not heavy? And they carry it until their dying day. Is this not long?" (*Analects* 8.7). It should be noted, that while *ren* involves taking on a burden, it also results in benefits that are all the more rewarding for being truly earned. Confucius said, "Undergoing difficulties, and only then reaping the rewards can be called *ren*" (*Analects* 6.22).

Chen Jingpan has characterized *ren* as "an earnest desire and benefi-cent action, both active and passive, for the well-being of the one loved" (J. Chen 1990, 252). Indeed, *ren* is often associated with the concept of love (*ai* 愛) (see *Analects* 12.22, p. 95), and so it has been often translated as "benevolence." Though we should be careful not to conceive of it as a merely psychological state. Meng Zi does indeed define "*ren* 仁" as 'human feelings' or 'the heart of being human' (*ren xin* 人心), but this goes beyond mere kindly feelings and is embodied in virtuous conduct.

The real problem with "benevolence," or with "empathetic effort," as translations of *ren* is that they sound supererogatory, admirable yet some-how optional. These terms do not convey the intimate and inseparable connection between being *ren* 仁 and being truly human (*ren* 人). Meng Zi says, "To be *ren* 仁 is to be a person (*ren* 人)" (*Meng Zi* 7B16). For this reason, we translate "*ren*" here as "humanity." The character *ren* 仁 is com-posed of two radicals (*ren* 人, meaning person, and *er* 二, meaning two). Thus, *ren* is being a consummate human being in relation with others, expressing one's humanity by striving to help others out of genuine care.

The Mohists also promote the virtue of *ren*, but they understand it in more utilitarian terms. A person with humanity works to bring about the greatest benefit to the greatest number of people. The Daoists, on the other hand, are deeply critical of the cultivation of such a virtue. They see such cultivation as artificial, and therefore hypocritical, and more importantly they believe that by imposing it on ourselves we are thereby damaging our natural tendencies. The culmination of this line of critique can be found in the Utopian Daoist chapters of the *Zhuang Zi*.

shàn 善: *excellent; good*

"*Shan*" is an evaluative term that describes quality of character or ability. It has a basic sense of 'good,' but also has a sense of 'being good at,' or 'excellence.' Etymologically, the graph is related to *mei* (美, 'beautiful') and *yi* (義, 'highly appropriate/honorable conduct'), and so has strong ethical and aesthetic connotations. Although translatable as "good," it is notable that it does not play as central a role in Chinese philosophy as the concept of 'the Good' does in Western philosophy.

shén 神: *spirit*

"*Shen*" has a range of meanings similar to "spirit" in English. And yet, in philosophical contexts, this word fails to do it justice. It may be used to refer to our more rarefied capacities for sensation and reflection: intelligence, or perhaps even 'genius.' It may also be used adjectivally to refer to the rarefied qualities of these capacities. This usage is much harder to find an equivalent for in English. In these contexts, it has a sense that may be conveyed by words such as "marvelous," "divine," or "wondrous." In Daoist texts, "*shen ming*" (神明) is an epistemological term naming a particular kind of awareness that is rooted in our natural intuitive abilities. It is thought of as a wondrous clarity of insight into the holistic interconnectedness of the natural transformations of the Cosmos, one that sees through the artificiality of distinctions.

Traditional Chinese 'folk psychology' (i.e., culturally transmitted beliefs about the nature and origins of our minds, souls, or mental functions) does not presuppose a single 'soul,' but several spirits ("*hun po*" 魂魄) in addition to *shen*. In sleep, they scatter and disperse: their adventures become our dreams. When we awaken they come together; to concentrate attentively is to hold them together and keep them integrated.

shēng 生: *life; living; birth; producing; growing; existing*

In its primary sense, "*sheng*" is a biological term; as a verb it means 'to live,' 'to be born,' and 'to give birth'; as a noun, it refers to the process of living, or to the process of producing life. In philosophical contexts, its significance extends beyond the biological, and refers to producing and existing in general. Even in its extended sense, however, the biological metaphor continues to function vividly in its meaning. Etymologically, the character represents an image of a plant emerging from the soil. Conceptually, it has close resonances with *"chu"* (出), 'to emerge,' which coincidentally, also shares a similar etymology.

When used to refer to the life of living things (in contrast to its more general sense of 'existence'), it is closely related to *"xing"* (性), 'natural dispositions,' the tendencies that impel the living processes.

"Sheng" is contrasted with *"si"* (死), which refers to the process of dying. While it is often translated as "death," the sense of an extended process of dying is much more emphatic than in English. Metaphorically, the process of dying is associated with entering, *"ru"* (入) (re-entering the soil), and returning, *"gui"* (歸).

shèng rén 聖人: *wise person; sage; wise ruler; virtuous ruler*
A *"sheng ren"* is an extraordinarily wise person, one who has a profound understanding of the world, of people, and of life and death. A sage would therefore understand the best ways to deal with the circumstances of life, to manage affairs, to deal with other people, and even to govern a state. This sort of understanding goes beyond ordinary knowledge and skills, and usually arises only after sustained self-cultivation and spiritual discipline, though it is possible for someone to be born with an extraordinary degree of wisdom. The Ruist sage, in particular, must cultivate an ethical attitude and virtuous behavior. These sorts of qualities are important for anyone who should be entrusted with rulership of any kind. But since these qualities are hard, if not impossible, to attain, it tends to represent an ideal ruler, rather than a real person.

The Utopian Daoists, however, are suspicious of cleverness, artifice, and hegemony, and so tend to regard sagely 'wisdom' suspiciously as a kind of shrewdness; they also regard the virtues that are artificially cultivated as hypocritical.

In pre-Qin philosophical texts, the context of usage of *"sheng"* (聖) is primarily political, and the term refers to a pre-eminently wise and virtuous ruler, worthy of the deepest reverence. (It gets extended to incorporate the senses of 'holy' or 'saintly' when adopted into explicitly religious contexts, but it does not strictly have these senses in the philosophical texts of the Warring States.)

shì 士: *aspirant; scholar-official; officer-aspirant; moral apprentice*
The Confucian category *"shi"* (士) is, in its non-normative sense, a social rank. It indicates someone who does or may hold a governmental post requiring some degree of learning. In non-philosophical contexts, it can

refer to a soldier or military officer. But for Confucians, a *shi* is a kind of moral apprentice. It is a person who endeavors to become exemplary, following norms of ritual propriety and emulating exemplary conduct. When Meng Zi is asked, "What is the task of a *shi* 士?," he replies, "To elevate one's aspirations (*zhi* 志)" (*Meng Zi* 7A33).[4] Confucius likewise implies that *shi* either do or should "aspire to *dao*" (*Analects* 4.9; cf. 15.9, p. 85). Xun Zi characterizes *shi* as follows: "The *shi* desire, on their own, to improve their character (*shen* 身)" (*Xun Zi* 2.7). Xun Zi also says, "One whose conduct stems from cherishing what is exemplary is a *shi*" (*Xun Zi* 2.10). Also, according to the *Xun Zi*, Confucius is said to have remarked, "Those who are called *shi*, although they are not able to fully exhaust the methods of the way, they do necessarily have standards to which they conform. Although they cannot be admirable and effective in everything they do, they definitely have places [in which they excel] [...]" (*Xun Zi* 31.2). For these reasons, we translate "*shi*" in Confucian philosophical contexts as "aspirant."

Becoming an aspirant is the first step in a continuum of moral improvement. Xun Zi remarks, "Where does learning begin, and where does it end? [...] Regarding what is appropriate and honorable (*yi* 義), it begins with becoming an aspirant (*shi* 士) and ends with becoming a sage (*sheng ren* 聖人)" (*Xun Zi* 1.8). A category in between an aspirant and a sage is an exemplary person (*junzi* 君子).

shì 勢: *position of authority; influential status; potential; propensity; strategic advantage*
"*Shi*" is a complex term that has no simple equivalent in English. Politically, it is used by the legalists to refer to the status and authority of a leader, a power of strength and influence that is backed by the legal codes and punishments. This sort of influence contrasts dramatically with the virtuous potency (*de* 德) promoted by Confucius. Etymologically, "*shi*" appears to be derived from an agricultural metaphor: the productive condition of cultivated land. It refers to the array of potential qualities over a terrain, potentials that can change over time. It is adopted by military strategists to refer to a position of strategic advantage that arises in a terrain of changing conditions and potentials.

shì fēi 是非: *evaluative judgment; affirmation and denial; right and wrong; approval and disapproval*
"*Shi fei*" is an abstract concept referring to 'evaluative' judgment regarding what is the case (*shi* 是) and what is not the case (*fei* 非). It can be

---

4   Notice that the character *zhi* 志 (aspiration) has the character *shi* 士 (aspirant) as a component.

translated either as a phrase: "affirmation and denial," "right and wrong"; or it can be understood as an abstract term: 'judgment' or 'evaluation.'

The word "*shi*" (是) means 'this.' It can be used as a complete sentence as an affirmation, 'It is this.' As a verb, it means 'to affirm'; and as a sentence modifier, it means 'It is the case that ...' In general, it expresses positive evaluation at its most abstract. "*Fei*" (非) is the contradictory of "*shi*," and means 'It is not,' 'It is not the case that,' and as a verb, means 'to deny.' In general, it expresses negative evaluation at its most abstract.

But, in addition to this logical function, the terms also have a more explicit evaluative sense. To affirm something is also to approve of it; and to deny something is to reject it. They thus also have a sense of 'rightness' and 'wrongness,' not just in the sense of 'correctness' and 'incorrectness,' but in their moral or ethical senses.

The Mohists emphasize the importance of making our distinctions so clear (*ming* 明), through the application of distinguishing criteria, that there can be no doubt about what is and what is not, which in turn removes doubt about what behavior is to be approved and what behavior is unacceptable.

Zhuangzi expresses deep suspicion about the possibility of such *shi fei* judgments. There are different interpretations of the precise nature of his critique: whether *shi fei* distinctions can be made as *clearly* and distinctly as the Mohists require; whether we can ever be *sure* that we have made the right distinctions; whether there is only *one* right way to make such distinctions; or whether there is *any such thing* as the right distinction at all.

shù 恕: *empathetic consideration; magnanimous understanding; forgiveness*

"*Shu*" is at one point identified by Confucius as the one virtue that unites his *dao*. Its primary meaning is 'forgiveness,' but philosophically it gets extended to mean 'broad-minded generosity of spirit.' It is a virtue cultivated by superiors in dealing with their subordinates, and in this sense is the counterpart to *zhong* (忠) (see below). They put themselves in the shoes of their subordinates, attempt to understand why they might not be as accomplished, and treat them with generosity and understanding. Confucius reinterprets the term and extends it even further: using our own relationships with others as a measure in all relationships, we should refrain from treating others in ways that we would not want ourselves to be treated. This is sometimes referred to as the 'Silver Rule.'

__tiān__ 天: *the Cosmos; the forces of nature; the natural world; the heavens; the sky*

The primary meaning of "*tian*" is 'sky,' or 'the heavens,' as distinguished from the earth (*di* 地) below. Prior to Confucius, the term had a sense of the sky as a 'divine' celestial force. There were temples and altars at which official state sacrifices to this celestial divinity took place. But in philosophical discussions, it develops a more abstract sense: the sky is conceived of as the overarching context under which, or within which, all things exist. It becomes a way of understanding the whole cosmic context of all existing things, and thereby also includes the earth below. It thus develops the sense of 'Nature,' or the natural world as a whole, and is thought of as that which produces all things, calls them into being as they are (see *ming* 命). It thereby gives 'life' to them, or brings them into 'existence': *sheng* 生. In this sense, *tian* is what is responsible for all things, and therefore what is beyond human control. It thereby also has connotations that distinguish it from what humans (*ren* 人) do.

Although *tian* is the natural world, it is still regarded by most philo-sophical schools with a sense of awe and reverence as something deeply 'spiritual.' As ultimate context, it extends deep into the past and is the repository of all things ancestral (*zong* 宗): its powers are 'ancestral' powers.

While Confucius's thought acknowledges the status of *tian*, it remains a thoroughly 'humanistic' philosophy. Confucius often uses exclama-tions involving the word *tian* (such as in *Analects* 11.9 and 14.35), but does not describe "*tian*" (see *Analects* 5.13, p. 105). He even discourages questions about *tian* and about the spirits, insisting that the focus of our concern should be our life in the world and in our current social context. Xun Zi's "Discourse on *Tian*" (*Xun Zi*, Chapter 17) emphasizes that "Nature's course (*tian xing* 天行) has regularities" (*Xun Zi* 17.1), but is mostly about clarifying the role of people in bringing to completion what *tian* has made possible.

Ogyū Sorai, a Tokugawa-period Japanese Confucian thinker, provides a useful description of *tian*:

> Tian 天 needs no explanation. Everybody knows what it is. Gaz-ing at its vast and hazy blueness, it seems dusky dim, far and high. We cannot fully fathom it. The heavenly bodies are fastened to it. Wind and rain, cold and heat, travel through it. It is where the myr-iad phenomena receive their conditions (*ming* 命), and is the an-cestor of the hundred spirits. The most revered, it is unparalleled. Nothing could be higher than it. Thus, the ancient sage-kings and

enlightened rulers all ordered the world modeling *tian*. Venerating *tian*, the way was thereby put into practice in their government and teachings. Thus is the way of the sages.[5]

But this gives rise to a conceptual tension. If *tian* is all-encompassing, doesn't it also include the human: can we really distinguish the human from the natural? Doesn't everything human already follow *tian*? This problem becomes especially pressing for Daoist philosophy, whose critique of humanist philosophies seems to presuppose some kind of distinction.

The binomial expression "*tian ming* 天命" may be taken to mean both what is dictated (*ming*) by *tian* and also natural (*tian*) conditions (*ming*). In a political context it indicates a ruler's mandate to rule.

wéi 為: *do; make; become; function as*

"*Wei*" is a fundamental grammatical term whose ranges of meaning reveal a deep-rooted pragmatist ontology. It means 'to do,' 'to act,' 'to make,' 'to become,' and 'as,' and can also function nominally to refer to doing, acting, and making. It also means 'to function as,' and can often be translated with the copula, 'to be,' suggesting that the equivalent of 'being' in ancient Chinese was conceived with pragmatic significance as a kind of acting or *functioning*: things *are* what they *do*, what they act *as*.

It is also sometimes used in the same sense as the word "*wei*" 謂 meaning 'to call' or 'to deem as.' This suggests a close conceptual connection between how something functions (what something is) and how it is understood to be (what it is called). Humans act in accordance with an understanding of how things function; and what things are is in part a function of how we understand and interact with them. When we deem (*wei* 為) things to be useful, beautiful, or valuable, we interact with them as such, manipulate them as such, and they thereby become (*wei* 為) useful, beautiful, or valuable things.

wěi 偽: *artifice; intentional activity*

A term of philosophical importance closely related to "*wei*" 為 (do, make) is "*wei*" 偽, in which "為" is combined with the 'human' radical "亻" to form a character that means 'artificial activity' or 'artifice.' Artifice is what humans add to the natural world through their acting, doing, and making. They transform the natural world according to their intentions to create artificial objects. The Confucian philosopher, Xun Zi, considers this to be the origin of order, structure, and beauty in the world. Without deliberate

---

5 Inoue and Kanie 1970, 79; cf. Najita 1998, 114.

transformation according to the planning of the wisest humans, natural tendencies simply result in unruly and messy behavior, which can eventually devolve into ugliness and conflict.

The Daoist philosophical attitude is quite the reverse: human intentional ordering is no match for the spontaneous harmony of the natural world. Natural processes arise from their own inmost tendencies, and as such are considered to be 'genuine' (*zhen* 真; see below). For the Daoists, then, *wei* 偽 is not a solution but a problem: it is forced or contrived behavior that draws us away from our own most natural and spontaneous tendencies, and so is a manifestation of insincerity or even disingenuousness. It is criticized as a manipulation of the world by the crafty for their own purposes.

**wén* 文: *culture*

Human transformative activity is not random, but accords with artificial structures, patterns and values, and these function to transform not only our environments, but also ourselves. Everything we do is imbued with a sense of proper form—a right way to be performed—which is transmitted from generation to generation. The right way to eat, to sleep, to communicate, are all clothed in a particular style of a particular community, passed down from its predecessors. The forms we imitate and embody from the very first moments of our lives eventually become transparent, seem effortless and natural. It is not usually until we come face to face with cultural difference, with people whose behaviors we find odd, surprising, and even unnatural, that we realize the contingency of culture: that it is artificial, its particularities and peculiarities highly variable, and that far from being natural it must be inculcated and cultivated over many years. All these transforming activities—linguistic and performative—combine to construct the human world in all of its multiple manifestations. The social patterns, the physical constructs and machines we use, the abstract constructs through which our lives are given significance, and the values by which they are judged, these are all constitutive of culture, *wen*.

wú 無: *absence; nothing; lacking*

The most literal meaning of "*wu*" as a verb is 'to not have,' 'to lack,' and more generally it can function as a negative quantifier, 'there is no...' to describe the absence of something. In philosophical texts, when used as an abstract noun, it can refer to absence in the most general sense, or non-existence. It can be translated as "nothing," but we must be careful not to simply assume that it has the same significance as Western philosophical concepts of 'non-being.' Ordinarily, we think of absence in negative terms, but in Daoist philosophy this devaluation is overturned.

'Absence' has both cosmological and pragmatic significance. The capacity of a tool to function requires space for movement. We tend to pay attention to what is present, *you* 有 (see below), to value it as a possession, but without absence there would be no room for it to grow. In a way, this is the mirror image of Parmenides' metaphysical argument that Being must be full (altogether without absence) and therefore can manifest no movement at all. On the contrary, if presence is to allow for transformation and growth, then it must be surrounded by, and filled with, absence.

"*Wu*" is often used in conjunction with another word to form a special kind of 'negation.' But just as absence is not the absolute negation of presence, so its 'negating' function is not a straightforward negation. It functions, rather, as a reversal of significance: recommending that we minimize our predilection for some activity. For example, "*wei*" 為 (actively constructing) is modified to form the notion of "*wu wei*" 無為, minimizing active control over our circumstances, so that phenomena may develop according to their own natural tendencies. "*Ming*" 名, naming, is modified to form "*wu ming*" 無名, refraining from dividing up and evaluating phenomena by applying artificially constructed categories. In a similar way, "*yu*" 欲, the desires that are stimulated by cultivating dissatisfaction, is modified to become "*wu yu*" 無欲, the process of diminishing the stimulation of those artificial desires to an optimal minimum.

*xīn 心: *heart; mind; heart–mind; thoughts and feelings; intention; awareness*
"*Xin*" is the heart, and is traditionally thought of as located in the solar plexus area at the center of the torso. It is taken to be the locus of all our mental and spiritual life: emotions, moods, thoughts, plans, intentions, perceptions, understanding, conscious awareness, and wisdom. In Western thinking, the heart is thought of as the seat of the emotions, while the mind is thought of as the seat of cognition and rational thinking. The two are often in conflict. But while these are not always harmonious, there is no presupposed conflict between the head and the heart in Chinese thinking. For Xun Zi, however, the sense of thinking and objective planning takes precedence, while the emotions are more closely associated with our natural tendencies (*xing* 性).

xìng 性: *natural dispositions; natural tendencies*
The character "性" is composed of two radicals: "忄" (an alternative radical for 'heart') and "生" ('life'). It suggests that *xing* may be thought of as

that which lies at the heart of natural life processes. *Xing* are the natural tendencies that propel the growth and development of each kind of thing, each kind having its own distinctive tendencies. It is often translated as "nature," though it appears to have greater fluidity than a strictly essentialist concept of nature.

Xun Zi gives a clear characterization: "The means by which life is as it is—this is called '*xing* 性' (natural disposition). [...] That which requires no work, but is naturally so of itself—this is called '*xing* 性.' The likes and dislikes, delights and aggravations, and the sorrows and joys that are part of *xing* are called 'emotions' (*qing* 情)" (*Xun Zi* 22.1b). Elsewhere he writes, "Natural dispositions (*xing* 性) are given by *tian* (nature). They cannot be learned nor acquired through work" (*Xun Zi* 23.1c). Similarly, according to the *Zhong Yong*, "What *tian* endows (*tian ming* 天命) [in people] is called *xing* 性 (natural disposition)" (*Zhong Yong* 1).

yì 義: *appropriateness; honorable; consummate conduct; integrity; rightness; conscientiousness*
"*Yi*" is a fundamental ethical concept. For the Ruists, it is used to express the admirable quality of one's highest ideals, or the ethical quality of actions that one strives for, that exemplify the most honorable conduct. The written character evokes close etymological associations with 美 (*mei*, beauty) and 善 (*shan*, excellent, good). Confucius contrasts it with *li* 利, the personal gain that tempts us away from living up to our highest ideals. We might think of it as 'doing what is right,' not necessarily in the singular sense of '*the* right thing,' but whatever will enable us to manifest the nobler aspects of our character. As Huang Chun-chieh put it, "In China, *yi* has never been a universal rule of conduct eternally fixed in the cognitive heavens, but instead has always been a matter of flexible judgment rendered to make ourselves fit for ever-changing situations" (C.-C. Huang 1993, 60). As the *Zhong Yong* states, "Appropriateness (*yi* 義) is what is fitting (*yi* 宜)" (*Zhong Yong* 20).

For Confucians, *yi* is integral to their core ethical concept cluster— *ren, yi, li, zhong, shu*, etc.—and is closely paired with *li*. Ritual propriety (*li* 禮) provides a normative context in which one acts. Acting with *yi* 義 (appropriateness) involves the exercise of a kind of moral intelligence within that context which both reaffirms the context and interprets it relative to each situation as it arises. Concrete exemplifications of *yi* are both informed by *li*, and, in turn, influence what will count as ritually proper—even if this 'influence' is largely in the form of reaffirmation. Thus, *yi* provides a subtle check on *li*, and provides a mechanism for conservative change and adjustment to circumstances, as well as a degree of personal assessment. The *Book of Rites* states: "*Li* is the fruit of appropriateness (*yi*). If it harmonizes with what is appropriate and is concordant, then although it was not among the rites of the ancient kings, it may be instituted by virtue of its appropriateness" (*Li Ji*, "Li Yun").

Kwong-loi Shun has described the relation between *li* and *yi* as follows:

> A person with *li* is not only skilled in and disposed to follow the rules of *li* but is also prepared to depart from such rules when appropriate. This preparedness involves the operation of *yi*, and commitment to propriety. Even when a rule of *li* should be followed, *yi* still has a role to play in that one should ideally follow the rule with an awareness of its appropriateness to the situation and, in that sense, *make the observance of the rule not a mechanical action but a display of one's own assessment of the situation.*
>
> (Shun 1997, 65, emphasis added)

In this light it is understandable that in the *Xun Zi*, *li* and *yi* often occur in the phrase *li-yi* 禮義 (ritual and propriety). *Li-yi* is both ritualized conduct regarded as appropriate, and a sense of appropriateness informed by traditional norms. As I (KH) wrote in *The Philosophy of Xunzi*, "A performance of *li* without *yi* is no performance of *li* at all. [...] On the other hand, one cannot put *yi* into practice in a social vacuum. *Yi* requires *li* as a medium in which to operate" (Hagen 2007, 156).

Nevertheless, as fitting as the word "appropriate" is in some contexts, it doesn't seem to capture the high degree of excellence implied by the term "*yi*," nor its normative weight. After all, Meng Zi tells us that he would choose *yi* over life itself (*Meng Zi* 6A10). And so, when *yi* seems to indicate a type of conduct, phrases such as 'impeccable conduct,' or 'consummate conduct' convey the quality of being notable for its excellence, and thus exemplary. When the context implies that *yi* is referring to a virtuous disposition, as it often does in the *Meng Zi* in particular, words such as 'integrity' are intended to convey *commitment to impeccably honorable conduct*, and 'conscientiousness' to convey *painstaking attentiveness to normative considerations.*

The Mohists also appeal to *yi* as a basic ethical concept. However, for Mo Zi, its primary meaning is simply *whatever* we hold as our highest ideals, and the Mohists see this, not just as contextual and flexible, but as varying radically from person to person. When people act from personal ideals, they will often come into conflict. The solution is to impose a single sense of 'rightness' from above, and the sense of rightness that they promote is a consequentialist one of whatever will promote the greatest benefit of the people.

yī 一: *one; unify; integrate; wholeness*
In its most basic sense, "*yi*" is simply the number 'one.' Because it is such a basic concept, it is tempting to presuppose that its philosophical significance is universal and a priori. It is too easy to assume that "*yi*" must be equivalent to the Western metaphysical concept of 'the One.' This reading is so familiar to us that it may be hard to see the cultural inappropriateness of imposing the concept, but there is no unambiguous textual, contextual, or historical justification for this reading.

In the *Lao Zi*, its primary philosophical significance is that of integration: cosmic and organic processes of merging together, and holding together. These are the natural processes of the ontogenesis of 'things.' The maturity of integration results in observed 'things.' The converse process is disintegration. In another sense, when applied to the myriad things altogether, "*yi*" emphasizes the continuity between things and their resulting organic wholeness. This is also understood as spreading through time, a continuous flow from past to present. It is tempting to presuppose that such an undifferentiated continuity implies sameness, but this is not necessarily the case.

Phenomenologically, it can also have a sense of unification of awareness, or singular concentration.

⁎yīn yáng 陰陽: *yin and yang; shady and bright*
Etymologically, "*yin*" and "*yang*" refer to the shady and sunny aspects of hills and mountains. As place names, they mean 'shady side' and 'sunny side' respectively. Philosophically, these terms get extended and become metaphors for the contrastive qualities of natural phenomena and processes. It is tempting to describe them as 'forces of nature,' but this is a little too easy, and somewhat misleading. Rather, they are naturalistic metaphors through which natural forces and phenomena can be understood.

Reflecting the shady and sunny contrasts that begin to become evident in some hilly and mountainous areas, "*yin*" connotes 'shade,' 'darkness,' 'coolness,' and 'wetness,' while "*yang*" connotes 'brightness,' 'warmth,' and 'dryness.' Note that these are only contrasts, not opposites. Some parts are shadier and cooler than others, but no part is completely dark or cold (whatever that might mean). Extending these qualities metaphorically, analogically, and metonymically, "*yin*" connotes 'night,' 'sleep,' 'winter,' and 'earth,' while "*yang*" connotes 'day,' 'wakefulness,' 'summer,' and the 'sky.' If *yin* is 'falling' and 'returning,' then *yang* is 'rising' and 'progressing'; if *yin* is 'gentle' and 'yielding,' then *yang* is 'firm' and 'strong.' These also become applied to socially coded gender differences:

yin is understood as feminine and nurturing, while *yang* is understood as masculine and controlling.

But as matters of degree, *yin* and *yang* become relative to context. The Moon is *yin* compared to the Sun, because it is not as bright; but it is *yang* compared to the night sky. If the summer is *yang*, then spring would be *yin* in comparison; but in comparison with the *yin* of winter, spring emerges as *yang*. From this it is clear that interpreting them as naming objective 'forces of nature' cannot be right.

Yin and *yang* are mutually supportive contrasts with no precise boundary between them; each yields to the other in a dynamic balance. But while they are held in balance, Daoist philosophy draws our attention to the nurturing and regenerative role of *yin*, which we ordinarily tend to overlook in our preference for brightness, energy, and progress.

yǒu 有: *something*; *presence*; *existence*; *having*

The most literal meaning of "*you*" is 'to have,' and in a more abstract sense it means 'to have around,' 'to be there,' 'to exist'; in this verbal sense it is very close in meaning to the Spanish "*hay*." In philosophical texts, it gets used as an abstract noun, and is often translated as "being" or "existence." Philosophically, it can refer to all the varieties of things that exist. It very often tends to be used as an abstract verbal noun: having around, being around, being there. It can also refer to what we have or possess.

In Daoist texts, the philosophical context of these abstract nominal senses is often the ontological question where everything comes from. But we should be careful not to infer from this context that "*you*" has the same range of meanings as the Western ontological term "Being." In fact, "being" also expresses identity (that two things are in fact identical: Kong Zi's being Confucius, for example) and essence (what the characteristic qualities of a thing are: Kong Zi's being human), while "*you*" cannot be used to express these linguistic senses. We therefore caution against the hasty assimilation of these two philosophical terms.

zhēn 真: *genuine*; *genuineness*

"*Zhen*" is the counterpart of "*wei*" (僞 'artifice'; see above); it connotes the innermost characteristics or qualities of something. It can be thought of as what is most genuine. The contrast between *zhen* (the genuine) and *wei* (the artificial) is correlated with the contrast between *tian* (the natural) and *ren* (the human). This, of course, should not be understood as a direct opposition between mutually exclusive qualities: humans can also be genuine. There is nevertheless a tension between the two, and this tension underlies a key difference between Ruist and Daoist ideals.

The Ruists believe we can cultivate human authenticity and sincerity, *cheng* 誠, which can be thought of as the Confucian counterpart of *zhen*. The Daoists, however, contend that this is insufficient, and even hypocritical: artificial authenticity cannot be genuine. While *zhen* and *ren* are not mutually contradictory, sincere genuineness involves undoing artifice and returning to a more deep-rooted core of naturalness.

Though "*zhen*" can be translated as "true" in modern Chinese, we should be careful not to assume that the pre-Qin usage is equivalent to concepts of 'Truth' that arise in Western ontology and philosophy of language.

zhēn rén 真人: *the genuine(ly) human*

The Daoists see quite a dramatic contrast between the natural, *tian*, and the human, *ren*; and they are alarmed at the extent to which we value and cultivate the latter while remaining relatively oblivious to the former. We even disapprove of the apparent messiness of nature and prefer instead to construct artificial environments, and artificial dispositions in ourselves. But in doing so, we remove ourselves from what is most natural and most genuinely human. One central problem raised in the *Inner Chapters* of the *Zhuang Zi* is: how do we now recover what is most genuinely human?

A person who has done that would be a *zhen ren*, genuinely human person. Such a person rises above the petty obsessions of the workaday human world, and instead seeks out the Cosmic context in which that world is embedded, and from which the worries and anxieties of that world seem distant and less pressing. Those who are genuinely human develop a kind of tranquility that results from cultivating a Cosmic perspective on the trials and tribulations of everyday life. The attitude of the genuine human may be compared with that of the Western Stoic ideal. This ideal human is also sometimes referred to as a *zhi ren* (至人), a person who has reached the pinnacle of humanity.

zhōng 忠: *wholehearted commitment; loyal resolve; doing one's utmost*

"Zhong" is a central Confucian virtue; the term expresses a wholehearted resolve and commitment in the service of *dao*. It is the virtue cultivated by the subordinates in relation to those who are worthy of admiration and devotion, and as such is the counterpart of *shu* 恕. In family relations, *zhong* manifests as *xiao* (孝) the virtue of being a good child or descendent.

PART I

Ru Jia: The School of Ru (Confucianism)

3

Da Xue 大學: "Expansive Learning"

INTRODUCTION

The *Da Xue* is included in the Warring States text, the *Li Ji* (*The Book of Rites*). Though traditionally attributed to Confucius and his student Zeng Zi, its true authorship is disputed. The Neo-Confucian philosopher, Zhu Xi (1130–1200), extracted the *Da Xue* from the *Li Ji*, along with the *Zhong Yong*, and grouped them with the *Analects* of Confucius and the *Meng Zi* (*Mencius*), to form "The Four Books." He maintained that the study of Confucianism ought to begin with the *Da Xue*. We agree that it does indeed provide an excellent introduction for the novice to Confucian philosophy.

The core of the text contains a 'Canon,' which succinctly articulates the central Confucian notion that self-cultivation, training oneself to realize one's full human potential, is key to transforming society. The underlying idea is that self-cultivation leads to the development of an influential virtuous character (*de* 德) that resonates with others in such a way as to inspire in them the desire to act appropriately and develop their own character. Confucians believe that this process is critical to achieving a harmonious social order.

The title of this work, *Da Xue* 大學, has been famously translated "Great Learning." But its contents may be most succinctly summarized: *learning to be great*, as Wing-tsit Chan has translated the phase (W.-T. Chan 1963, 86). The word "*xue* 學" means "learning" in a broad sense that includes cultivating personal excellence of character. The idea is this: Concentrating on the root—one's own inner character—is the most important ("great") learning, for this is the means of attaining personal excellence. And, further, great achievements in the world are rooted in the achievement of excellence in personal character.

While the word *da* 大 does mean "great," it also has the sense of expanding out and reaching everywhere. Indeed, the *Da Xue* is about precisely this: virtue at the individual level expands outwardly to influence increasingly larger circles until the whole world is ordered. For this reason, we render "*da xue*" as "expansive learning."

Now, to cultivate one's character, one must consider the actual circumstances of the world itself—both through introspection and empirical observation—with calm, rigorous honesty. In other words, one begins the process of expansive learning, and in turn the process of ordering the world, by engaging in philosophical inquiry.

THE CANONIC CORE OF THE *DA XUE*

Note: Bracketed numbers here serve as reference markers corresponding to some of the elucidations provided in the commentarial portion of the *Da Xue*, which follows the Canonical Core.

The *dao* of expansive learning (*da xue* 大學) resides in illuminating (*ming* 明) illustrious potency of character (*ming de* 明德) [1], treating the common people as close relatives (*qin* 親),[a] and stopping only when one has achieved the utmost excellence (*shan* 善). When one understands that this is the stopping point, one may be resolved. Being resolved, one can achieve tranquility. Being tranquil, one can achieve peace of mind. With peace of mind, one is able to be reflective. Being reflective, one is able to obtain [excellence]. All phenomena have roots (*ben* 本) and extremities (*mo* 末, "branches"); affairs have ends and beginnings. If one understands what comes first and what comes later, then one is approaching the *dao* [of expansive learning].

> *Comment:* The metaphor of root and branches, "*ben mo*," can be found in other Ruist texts, as well as Mohist, Legalist, and Daoist texts. The concern is what we should tend to the root in order to achieve success in affairs (the branches). The text here seems to suggest that there is a hierarchy between what comes before and what comes after, and to Western-trained ears this in turn suggests a strict foundationalism. But the relation between root and branches is a thoroughly organic one, and so the reader would be wise to investigate the fuller argument to see if the metaphor might not better be interpreted more holistically.

In antiquity, those who wanted their distinct influential virtue (*de*) to shine forth in the world first put their states in order. Wishing to put their states in order, they first proceeded to regulate their families. Wishing to regulate their families, they first proceeded to cultivate their personal character (*shen* 身). Wishing to cultivate their personal character, they first proceeded to properly align (*zheng* 正) their feelings (*xin* 心). Wishing to properly align their feelings, they first proceeded to make their thoughts and intentions (*yi* 意) authentic (*cheng* 誠) [6].

> *Comment: Cheng* 誠 is often translated "sincerity." But the commentary suggests that here the passage means, "One ought not deceive oneself." (See §6 of the Commentary, below, p. 63.) The word "*xin*" 心 means "heart," and was associated with thinking as well as feeling. Sometimes context suggests that one element is being emphasized more than the other. That the "feeling" element is dominant here is suggested by the examples in §7 of the Commentary (p. 63).

Wishing to make their thoughts and intentions authentic, they first proceeded to extend their understanding. Extending understanding resides in examining things and phenomena (*gewu* 格物).

> *Comment:* A controversy developed in later Confucianism. While it would be to some degree anachronistic to insert Neo-Confucian concepts into the discussion here, it is worth considering, in general terms, whether the "examining of things and phenomena" refers to an examination of the external world, or an examination and cultivation of one's mind.

Only when one has examined things and phenomena is one's understanding adequate. And only when one's understanding is adequate can one's thoughts and intentions be authentic (*cheng* 誠). Only after one's thoughts and intentions are authentic can one properly align one's feelings. Only after one has properly aligned one's feelings can one cultivate one's personal character [7]. Only after one cultivates one's personal character can one regulate one's family [8]. Only after one regulates one's family can one put the state in order [9]. And only after one has put the state in order can there be peace in the world [10].

What all people have in common, from the emperor down to the common people, is that they consider self-cultivation to be the root (*ben* 本). For the fundamental to be in a shambles and yet the details dependent upon it to be well ordered is unheard of. There has never been a case in which the profoundly important and the insignificant were interchangeable. This is called "understanding the root" and "the fulfillment of understanding."

SELECTIONS FROM THE COMMENTARY ON THE *DA XUE*

1 The Proclamation of Kang says, "Their self-mastery exhibits an illustrious (*ming* 明) potency of character (*de* 德)." The *Tai Jia* says, "He attended to and examined his illustrious command (*ming* 命) [to rule] provided by *tian* 天." The Emperor's Canon says, "His self-mastery exhibits an illustrious and lofty *de*." These are all [examples of] making oneself illustrious.

> *Comment:* The character *ming* 明, which is composed of the radicals for the Sun and the Moon, means bright and clear, and also can mean "to make clear." The phrase "illustrious potency of character" (*ming de* 明德) is meant to suggest a compelling character that shines bright and clear, and in doing so, manifests outwardly a clear and compelling example, illustrative of consummate conduct.

3 [...] As a ruler of others, one rests in *ren* 仁 (humanity). As a minister, one rests in respectfulness. As a child, one rests in filiality. As a father, one rests in loving kindness. And, fellow countrymen in their relations rest in trustworthiness (*xin* 信).

The *Odes* say, "[...] The refined person: like cutting and filing, like carving and polishing" [...] "Like cutting and filing" means learning the way. "Like carving and polishing" means self-cultivation. [...]

Junzi 君子 (exemplary persons) value their own worth (賢其賢), and they treat those to whom they are close dearly (親其親). Petty persons enjoy their own amusement (樂其樂), and benefit from profit taking (利其利). [...]

4 The Master [Confucius] said, "In presiding over public disputes, I am like any other. What is necessary is to ensure that no such disputes occur" (*Analects* 12.13, see p. 94).[b]

> *Comment:* One prevents disputes from occurring by using norms of ritual propriety to help people develop their character. Cultivated persons find ways of resolving disagreements before they become disputes needing to be formally arbitrated. As is suggested in *Analects* 2.3 (p. 94), people led by ritual propriety will develop a sense of shame and reform themselves.

Those who are unfeeling are not to make exhaustive accusations. Holding the aspirations of the common people in great awe is called "understanding the root."

6 The phrase "make their thoughts and intentions (*yi* 意) authentic (*cheng* 誠)" means not deceiving themselves, just as when one detests foul odors, and is fond of lovely colors. This is being comfortable with oneself. Thus, *junzi* are sure to be cautious in their solitude. Idle petty persons, being degenerate (*bu shan* 不善), have nothing they will not do. It is only after seeing the example of a *junzi* that they begin to cover up their degeneracy with disgust, and make appearances of excellence (*shan* 善). When others observe them, it is as though they see through to their very lungs and liver. So what use is [pretending]? This is why it is said "authenticity (*cheng* 誠) from within takes shape on the outside." Thus, *junzi* are sure to be cautious in their solitude.

> *Comment:* What one does in private, and even what one merely thinks about, affects one's character. And one's character shows through when one acts publicly. Thus, one's character cannot be hidden, it "takes shape on the outside." (Cf. *Analects* 2.10, p. 92.) And thus, one must be "cautious in one's solitude" because private thoughts and actions have real effects in the world, mediated through the character that they reinforce.

Zeng Zi said, "What all see and condemn is grave indeed." Wealth enriches the home, virtue (*de* 德) enriches the person, and expansive feelings (*xin* 心) make the body content. Thus, *junzi* are sure to be authentic in their thoughts and intentions (*yi* 意).

7 "Cultivating personal character" resides in the proper alignment of one's feelings (*xin* 心). If one has anger and resentment as part of one's character, one will not be able to achieve this alignment. If one is fearful, one will not be able to achieve it. If one's feelings are not in alignment, then although one looks, one will not see; although one listens, one will not hear; although one eats, one will not know the flavor. This is why it is said that self-cultivation resides in the proper alignment of one's feelings.

8 [...] To say that regulating one's family resides in cultivating one's person means: people are partial regarding those they are close to and love, regarding those they disdain and despise, regarding those they are in awe of and respect, regarding those who are modest and engender pity, and regarding lazy pleasure-seekers. Thus, there are few people in the

world who, though fond of something, apprehend its flaws, and though repulsed by something, appreciate its merits. Thus, as the saying goes: "No one knows one's own child's defects. No one knows a seedling's great [potential]." Because of this, if one does not cultivate one's person, one will not be able to regulate one's family.

9 To say that ordering the state surely involves first unifying one's family means that there are no people who, though unable to instruct their own families, are capable of instructing others. *Junzi* do not abandon their families to become instructors of the state. Being filial is how one serves one's lord. Brotherly respect is how one serves elders. Loving kindness is how one serves the masses. [. . .]

> *Comment:* Confucians posit an analogy between the political and the familial: a ruler should be as a good parent, a loyal minister as a good son. And, as they see it, it is in the context of a family that the virtues necessary for proper governance, such as caring for others and loyalty, naturally arise and are cultivated.

The *Odes* say: "Befitting an elder brother, befitting a younger brother." After one has been a true elder brother and a true younger brother, only then is one able thereby to educate the people of the state. [. . .]

10 To say that pacifying the world resides in ordering one's state means: When those above are like good parents, the people will gladly be filial. And when those above behave with brotherly guidance (like an elder brother should) the people will gladly respond with brotherly respect (as a younger brother would). For when those above ensure that orphans are provided for, the people will not forsake [those in need]. It is on this basis that *junzi* have a way (*dao* 道) of assessing and of setting standards (*xie ju* 絜矩).

> *Comment:* The reference to elder and younger brothers is clearly a male-oriented way of making the point. Today we would make it with reference to older and younger "siblings." Such male orientation is not uncommon in the Confucian classics; for example, *Xun Zi* 14.7 refers to fathers as being "the most exalted in the family" (see comment to *Xun Zi* 21.1, p. 201). Historically, this is undeniable. However, although the idea of different roles for different people, and the value of harmony over sameness, are central to Confucianism, for contemporary *philosophical* purposes we can interpret more inclusively without causing much distortion in the system as a whole.

What those above detest, do not impose on those below. With what those below detest, do not serve to those above. What is detested in the past, do not repeat over and over. What will be detested in the future, refrain from doing from the beginning. What is detested on the right, do not give to the left. What is detested on the left, do not give to the right. This is what is meant by the *dao* of assessing and of setting standards (*xie ju* 絜矩). [...]

> *Comment:* The expression 絜矩 (*xie ju*) means: to assess (something) and then set appropriate standards. What the text is conveying is that the way this assessment is done, and the basis for the standards set, is something very much like empathetic consideration (*shu* 恕). See *Analects* 6.30 and 15.24, both on p. 83.

The Proclamation of Kang says: "A mandate (*ming* 命) [to rule] is not necessarily long enduring (*chang* 常)." With the *dao* of excellence (*shan* 善), one will gain it. If one is not excellent, one will lose it.

The book of Chu says: "In the state of Chu, nothing except excellence was regarded as precious." [...]

ENDNOTES

[a] This line may involve a corruption of the text. Cheng Yi emended the text by changing *qin* 親 (parents, relatives; to be emotionally close to) to *xin* 新 (new; renew). The meaning of the phrase then becomes, "renewing the common people." This is plausible. On the other hand, the idea of "treating the common people as close relatives" is expressed in Commentary §§9 and 10, and is consistent with the Confucian analogy between the country as a whole and a family. However, *Meng Zi* 1A7 (p. 140) may seem to suggest the opposite.

[b] This statement also constitutes the entirety of *Analects* 12.13.

4

The *Analects* of Confucius

INTRODUCTION

Confucius

Confucius, or Kong Zi[1] (Master Kong), traveled among the various warring states in an effort to persuade rulers to implement his ideas, but met with little success. Believing himself to be a failure, Confucius settled into teaching a number devoted students. These include Yan Hui, his most admired student, as well as Zilu, Zigong, Zixia, Zizhang, Ranyou, Master Zeng, and Master You, all of whom play a role in the *Analects*.

Confucius was an exceptionally demanding teacher, expecting both effort and insight from his students. His purpose was not to instruct fixed doctrines, but to instill values, and provide subtle clues to guide students to their own insightful self-cultivation. Of his methodology, he said that if he held up a corner and the student couldn't come back with the other *three*, he would not go on with the lesson. His style of discourse, unlike that of Socrates, was not designed to define and delineate meanings by being as precise as possible, but to be open and suggestive, and inspire profound interpretation.

The *Analects* reveals Confucius to be a deeply concerned humanitarian determined to realize his vision of a harmonious social order by

---

1 His family name was Kong, his given name, Qiu; his 'style' name, Zhongni. In the texts, Confucius is referred to as "Kong Zi," meaning 'Master Kong,' or simply as "Zi," 'Master,' or "Fu Zi," '*the* Master.' The Latinized name "Confucius" (Kong-Fu-Zi-us) is widely recognized in the West, and so we use that name to refer to the originator of the philosophy that Westerners generally refer to as "Confucianism." Confucius, it should be noted, saw himself as part of a tradition of teacher-scholars or "Ru." The Han dynasty historian Sima Tan referred to this school as "Ruism." ("Mencius" is likewise a Latinized version of "Meng Zi" (Meng-Zi-us), but since the name "Mencius" is not already widely recognized, we use the more authentic "Meng Zi.")

encouraging his students and the leaders he advises to take personal responsibility in doing their utmost for others, guided by ritual propriety (*li* 禮) and a high standard of appropriateness (*yi* 義). But the text also reveals Confucius as a complete human being—sometimes encouraging, sometimes playful, often critical, and sometimes even scornful. We see him confident in the face of danger, and distraught at the loss of a protégé. When speaking of himself, Confucius' words are modest. But the message of the *Analects* is to be found as much in the way Confucius conducts himself as it is in the literal content of what he says. And so, for example, when he seems to claim not to be an innovator (as he is made out to do in most translations of *Analects* 7.1), and yet uses terms like *ren* 仁 (humanity) and *junzi* 君子 (exemplary person) in new ways, his practice speaks louder than his modest self-descriptions.

Indeed, one of Confucius' methods was to teach by example. For this reason, passages that describe details of Confucius' own conduct are significant, because they are not just about chance quirks of personality without philosophical relevance. Rather, they ought to be regarded as conscious choices in behavior that reflect Confucius' view of exemplary conduct.

Confucius' Philosophy

Confucius' mission was to foster conditions conducive to social harmony (*he* 和). He was also intent on enabling people to cultivate their human potential to the fullest, that is, to realize *ren* (humanity). These projects are intertwined since, he believed, self-cultivation is critical to achieving social harmony. Self-cultivation, or "learning," broadly understood, was not primarily about acquiring book knowledge, though it does involve in various ways becoming cultured, and thus requires coming to understand one's tradition. But what was central was developing character, rather than the ability to pass a test (although in later times exams on Confucianism did become the basis for qualification for government service). As we saw in the *Da Xue*, if those in positions of authority cultivated themselves, their developed virtuous charisma (*de* 德) would motivate others to follow suit (see also *Analects* 12.17, 12.19, and 13.13, all on p. 93). At the same time, rulers who cultivate the ultimate virtue of *ren* (humanity) would institute appropriate policies that would contribute concretely to social harmony—though Confucius was less explicit than the *Da Xue* about this latter dynamic.

As philosophers, when we study the *Analects*, we are interested in understanding (and also analyzing and critiquing) Confucius' worldview, which requires understanding his conceptual framework. And thus we must, to whatever degree possible, become comfortable with the interrelated cluster of concepts most central to his thinking. For example, in Confucius' usage, the term *junzi* 君子 signifies exemplary persons who, being committed to impeccable conduct (*yi* 義), follow and exemplify norms of ritual propriety (*li* 禮) in order to develop what he regards as the consummate virtue, *ren* 仁. *Ren* involves loyal devotion (*zhong* 忠) to the service of others, guided by empathetic consideration (*shu* 恕). This all-too-brief description illustrates the interconnectedness of several of the key concepts that are stressed in the *Analects*. These 'humanistic' concepts form the core of Confucius' concerns. Although Confucius had a sense of reverence for cosmic matters, he thought that it was not a good use of our time to be concerned about such distant things. Confucius' project has multiple dimensions: ethical, social, political, cultural, aesthetic, etc. But they should not be conceived as separate projects: rather they are interrelated aspects of a single *dao*. The distinction between the ethical and the social and political is purely conceptual. At the time of Confucius, no explicit distinction was made at all.

Confucius says that, if given a chance at governance, the first thing he would do is *zheng* 正 *ming* 名 (name properly), which involves assuring both that terminology is used correctly to describe and evaluate behavior, and conversely, that we act properly according to the norms associated with our titles, which often indicate roles such as 'father,' 'son,' 'ruler,' or 'minister.' There is only one passage in which the term "*zheng ming*" (正名) occurs in the *Analects* (13.3). But what we read Confucius doing throughout the *Analects* is precisely this: defining roles and striving to live up to his own requirements. The centrality of *zheng ming* to Confucius' project also provides us with another reason to focus carefully on his key philosophical terms.

The Text

Although not written by Confucius himself, the text known as the *Analects of Confucius* contains what is widely considered the most reliable depiction of his remarks, along with those of his closest students. These students are thought to have written accounts of their interactions with Confucius, with others contributing accounts at later times. This material was ultimately compiled and edited by a series of editors. This process is likely to have occurred over a period of at least 200 years, the longer passages probably being written later. The *Analects* may therefore contain more than one strand of Confucianism.

Often, the brief passages found in the *Analects* are enigmatic, highly contextualized, and hard for the novice to interpret. If, however, we first study the more detailed discussions of the *Da Xue* (Chapter 3), the *Meng Zi* (*Mencius*) (Chapter 5), and the *Xun Zi* (Chapter 6), before the *Analects*, this enables us to develop a general sense of early Confucianism that can inform our interpretation of the sometimes more ambiguous comments of Confucius. For this reason, we recommend returning to the study of the *Analects* after studying these later texts.

The casual reader will also notice that the books of the *Analects* do not seem to be arranged by theme. Passages in each chapter touch on multiple concepts, but without extensive explanation of any particular one. And passages in a single chapter do not develop a single continuous discourse on one theme. This creates an obstacle for those who need a structured introduction to this complex text. In order to introduce students to Confucian concepts in a more pedagogically effective way, we have selected and arranged the passages more thematically. Once key concepts have become familiar, the student will then more easily be able to see the interrelations between the concepts and how they cohere. Readers should not be misled into believing that each passage is about only one theme.

Also, because passages that may be mutually revealing are grouped together, it is easier to derive interpretations based on multiple passages. For example, consider the meaning of the following:

> Zigong asked, "What do you think of me?"
> The Master said, "You are an implement (*qi* 器)."
> Zigong asked, "What implement?"
> The Master responded, "A jeweled sacrificial vessel."
> (*Analects* 5.4)

Our understanding of this passage can be informed by considering *Analects* 2.12, which reads: The Master said, "*Junzi* are not [mere] implements (*qi* 器)." The word "*qi*," 'implement,' is used here presumably to mean something like 'functionary,' someone utilized to perform a narrow set of duties. In the context of *Analects* 2.12, one may infer that telling Zigong that he is an implement is a kind of criticism. However, when it comes to what kind of implement he is, Confucius acknowledges that Zigong is an exquisite one.

In reading the *Analects*, it may be helpful to remember that, as *Analects* 5.4 exemplifies, Confucius sometimes playfully teased his students. He was also sometimes sarcastic. So, it is useful to keep such possibilities in mind as one interprets the meaning of his comments.

(Since passages have been rearranged, indices are provided at the end of this chapter.)

CONFUCIUS ON PERSONAL CONDUCT AND CHARACTER

Learning, Tradition, and Progress

Proper conduct, and the development of the character to consistently exhibit it, both start with learning—for which Confucius expressed much fondness. And a significant object of learning relevant to Confucius' concerns is traditional norms and practices. Indeed, Confucius stressed tradition so much that he is not uncommonly characterized as striving to return to a kind of golden age of the past.[a] But there are serious problems with interpreting that traditionalism too strongly. First, Confucius was *selective* about which parts of the tradition he would follow, and he was eclectic in his choices. For example, in *Analects* 15.11 (p. 73), Confucius advocates adopting the calendar of the Xia dynasty, the carriages of the Shang, and the ceremonial caps of the Zhou.[2] Further, Confucius seemed to draw inferences from contemporary observation, as well as tradition, and was willing to adapt tradition pragmatically, as in *Analects* 9.3 (p. 76).

7.8 The Master said, "I will not instruct those who are not fervently striving to learn. I will not provide pronouncements to those who are not struggling to articulate their thoughts. I will not further instruct those who, having been provided with one corner, do not respond with three others based upon it."

5.28 The Master said, "In any ten-family town, there will surely be some as good as I in loyal resolve (*zhong* 忠) and honoring commitments (*xin* 信). But there will be none as fond of learning."

7.1 The Master said, "Conveying, but not initiating (*zuo* 作), I am faithful to, and fond of, antiquity. I liken myself to Old Peng."

> *Comment:* The character "*zuo* 作" generally has the sense of "to start, to make or create, or cause to arise." Although it is here usually understood to mean "innovate," it could equally be understood as "initiate" or "institute," that is, to cause his *dao* to be put into practice on a large scale. As far as innovation goes, while Confucius does not see himself as the originator of the *dao* that he has adopted, this passage need not be read as suggesting that he makes no contribution to it. Indeed, that would be clearly false. Confucius *has* innovated. It is possible, as some

---

2 See *Xun Zi* 21.4 (p. 203) for a comment on Confucius' eclecticism. Xun Zi himself shows similar eclecticism in *Xun Zi* 22.1a (see p. 208).

scholars suggest, that Confucius is just being modest. But the passage may reflect Confucius' coming to terms with his inability to attain the kind of position that would allow him to put his *dao* into practice in government. So, he has accepted the realities of his circumstance; he "understood *tian ming*" (see *Analects* 2.4, below, p. 86) and embraced his role as teacher and model. By this means he hopes to take his stand by establishing others (*Analects* 6.30, p. 83), his students. As for "Old Peng," his identity is uncertain. But one plausible account is that he was an exemplar who lived during the preceding dynasty "who was fond of transmitting ancient tales" (Slingerland 2003, 64).

2.11 The Master said, "[Those who] rekindle the old with an understanding of the new can be taken as teachers."

> *Comment:* Confucius' emphasis on tradition is well known. But Confucius also seems to acknowledge that, to be applicable, tradition has to accommodate contemporary realities. His philosophy is not about returning to the past, it is about making traditional wisdom relevant to the present. This is a point Xun Zi makes as well: "Those who are good at articulating the ancient must show its applicability to the present" (*Xun Zi* 23.3b). Xun Zi also characterizes Confucius as follows: "Confucius exhibited *ren* 仁 (humanity) and wisdom (*zhi* 知), and moreover was not beguiled. [...] He promoted [his *dao*], and put it to use, without being obsessed by old customs" (*Xun Zi* 21.4).

7.28 The Master said, "There may be others who accomplish things despite their ignorance, but I lack this ability. I just hear of many things, select what has been effective, and follow that. And I observe many things, and come to understand them. Having knowledge is second best."

> *Comment:* Confucius seems to be being sarcastic. Being able to accomplish things despite ignorance would indeed be impressive, but it is not plausible. In that sense, truly, the knowledgeable are "second to none." (There are, however, some passages in the Daoist anthologies that extol the virtues of unlearning, and unknowing, which they believe will bring us back to a more genuine core of human life, purified of artifice. If any of these predate Confucius, then it is possible that he is referring to their mysterious doctrines.) The second sentence expresses what can be called "selective traditionalism," which is augmented by continuous observation and reasoning, and adaptation to contemporary conditions,

as suggested in *Analects* 2.11 (directly above). Confucius' selective traditionalism is exemplified in 15.11, directly below.

15.11 Yan Hui asked about statecraft. The Master said, "Follow the calendar of the Xia dynasty; ride in carriages of the Yin; wear the ceremonial cap of the Zhou. And for music, let it be the *shao* and *wu*. Put aside the music of the Zheng, and keep away from crafty people. The music of the Zheng is depraved, and crafty people are dangerous."

2.15 The Master said, "If one learns without thinking, one may be deceived. If one thinks without learning, one takes a dangerous chance."

15.31 The Master said, "I once went through a whole day without eating, and a whole night without sleeping, to just think. But it was of no benefit. I would have been better off learning."[3]

5.9 The Master asked Zigong, "Between yourself and Yan Hui, who will do better?"
   Zigong answered, "How could I dare hope to match Hui? Having heard one thing he thereby understands ten. When I learn one thing I thereby understand only two."
   The Master said, "You are not as good. You and I are not as good."

Comment: Notice how Confucius appears to playfully criticize his student, tempering his criticism in a surprising way. Compare *Analects* 5.4, quoted in the introduction above (p. 70).

15.16 The Master said, "For those who do not constantly ask themselves, 'What to do? What to do?'—I simply don't know what to do with them."

Comment: As the preceding passages suggest, Confucius' ideal students would not at all be mindless followers of clear and easily applied rules and norms, but rather thoughtful persons constantly striving to understand for themselves and adapt their behavior in appropriate ways to the complex nuances of real situations. Here again Confucius seems somewhat playful in the way he makes his point.

7.22 The Master said, "Walking with a couple of people, there is sure to be a teacher for me among them. I identify their good points, and follow them; and what is not good I reform [in myself]."

---

3 *Xun Zi* makes a similar comment, followed by elaboration, in *Xun Zi* 1.3, p. 158.

4.17 The Master said, "When I encounter someone of merit, I worry whether I measure up to them. When I encounter someone flawed, I inwardly examine myself."

1.4 Zeng Zi said, "Every day I examine myself on three things. When planning for others have I not exhibited loyal devotion (*zhong* 忠)? In my interactions with my friends have I not been true to my word? And in what I pass on, have I not practiced it myself?"

5.27 The Master said, "I've had enough! I have not yet met anyone who, having become aware of their own faults, then takes themselves to task."

16.11 Confucius said, "[Regarding the boast,] 'Upon seeing moral aptitude (*shan* 善), I feel inadequate; seeing moral ineptitude, I recoil as if touching boiling water'—I have met such people, and have heard such claims. [Regarding the boast,] 'Dwelling in seclusion to pursue my aspirations, I put appropriateness (*yi* 義) into practice to realize my *dao*.' I have heard such claims, but have not yet met such a person."

> *Comment:* Even if people meeting this latter description exist, neither Confucius nor anyone else is likely to be influenced by them—after all, Confucius has never even met such a person. So, what difference could they make? And so, how could they realize their *dao* in the world? On one level, Confucius hasn't met such people because, even if they exist, they are reclusive. On another level, Confucius seems to be implying— perhaps half-jokingly—that the notion of a recluse realizing their *dao* doesn't even make sense: one cannot have *yi* as an ideal and live in seclusion, because *yi* is a social ideal.

2.23 Zizhang asked, "Can one know of events ten generations removed?" The Master answered, "The Yin dynasty was based on the ritual patterns (*li* 禮) of the Xia, what was added and subtracted can be known. The Zhou dynasty is based on the ritual patterns of the Yin, what was added and subtracted can be known. If there is a dynasty which inherits Zhou culture, although a hundred ages may pass, [Zhou culture] can be known [by them]."

> *Comment:* Zizhang's question is ambiguous. He is often interpreted as meaning: "Can the distant *future* be known?" If that is correct, Confucius seems to recognize the ambiguity in the way the question is put and answers as if it is about the past. In this way Confucius gently suggests to Zizhang that fortune-telling is not a topic of interest to him. In any case,

the passage conveys the message that apt adaptation of tradition is the way to produce cultural accomplishments worthy of being remembered.

15.29 The Master said, "People are able to broaden *dao* 道, it is not *dao* which broadens people."

Comment: The first part is relatively clear: *Dao* may be influenced by human efforts. But why does Confucius say that *dao* does not broaden people? Isn't *dao* supposed to facilitate social harmony by helping people become better? Perhaps a clue can be taken from *Analects* 12.1, in which Confucius says, "Becoming *ren* stems from oneself, how could it stem from others?" Just as one cannot become *ren* through the efforts of others, so too one cannot be improved simply because the *dao* prevails. Rather, one must choose to improve oneself and make the necessary efforts. Of course, this is not to say that *dao* does not play an important supporting role. Of course it does, as do other people in one's life. Confucius is just making a point: people need to take responsibility for their own self-cultivation, and for contributing to *dao*. They cannot expect *dao* to do it for them.

Ritual Propriety (*li* 禮)

For Confucius, a key aspect of tradition was ritual and the ritualized norms of impeccable conduct associated with one's roles, both expressed under the rubric of *li* 禮 (ritual propriety). Although Confucius advocated following these traditional norms, he emphasized that it was the underlying attitude that was of central importance, rather than the form of the ritual itself.[4] This is an attitude of deep reverence that invests the action and event with profound significance. And, as for the form, he was willing to endorse justified modifications. Still, such modifications would not be adopted lightly. As Xun Zi expresses in *Xun Zi* 17.11, traditional norms of ritual propriety act as reliable markers; it is risky to ford a river ignoring the tried and marked path.

3.4 Lin Fang asked about the root of ritual propriety (*li* 禮). The Master answered, "What a great question! In the observance of ritual propriety, it is better to be frugal than extravagant. In mourning, it is better to grieve than to be meticulous."

---

4 In addition to the passages in this section, *Analects* 19.1 and 3.26 (pp. 87 and 101) also support this point.

Comment: Note that Confucius does not give rules about what must be done or not done. Instead, he provides more fundamental criteria by which to judge how to act. And the judgments are not absolute but comparative. He would *rather* be frugal than extravagant. The above translation follows the current trend, interpreting the final sentence along the same lines as Legge, Lau, Slingerland, as well as Ames and Rosemont—all apparently following Zhu Xi. An alternative reading would be: "In mourning, it is better to grieve than to take it too lightly." According to James Legge, this was how the early commentators took it.[b] This early interpretation seems like a plausible alternative.

19.14   Ziyou said, "One should mourn as long as one truly grieves and then stop."

9.3   The Master said, "A hemp cap is called for by *li* (norms of ritual propriety), but nowadays a silk one is worn as a matter of frugality. On this matter I follow the common practice. To bow before ascending is called for by *li*, but nowadays people bow after ascending. This is arrogant. Although diverging from the common practice, I bow before ascending."

Comment: In this case, *li* seems to refer to traditional ritual norms. However, Confucius indicates that he does not always follow these norms, but rather makes judgments regarding their fittingness to the context. One may assume that traditional norms are given the benefit of the doubt. But when there is a compelling justification for their modification, Confucius endorses change with his own behavior.

11.1   The Master said, "Country folk are the first to make advancements in ritual propriety and music. *Junzi* (nobility)[5] make advancements later. If I apply these, I follow the first advancements."

17.11   The Master said, "In singing the praises of *li* 禮 (ritual propriety), how could I be referring merely to jade and silk offerings? In singing the praises of music, how could I be referring merely to bells and drums?"

Comment: Xun Zi comments on this passage saying, "If it is not timely and fitting, if it is not respectfully sociable, if it is not cheerfully enjoyed, although it may be beautiful, it is not ritual propriety (*li* 禮)" (*Xun Zi* 27.11).

---

5   Occasionally Confucius uses the term "*junzi*" in its original non-normative sense.

3.12 "Sacrifice as if present" [means] sacrifice to the spirits as if the spirits were present. The Master said, "If I do not participate in the sacrifice, it is as though no sacrifice were made."

> *Comment:* The sense of "participating" intended here, presumably, involves being psychologically, not just physically, present. That is, the ritualistic gesture of an offering has no value unless one has also adopted the proper attitude of attentiveness and sincere reverence, as if one was actually in the presence of one's departed ancestor. The "as if" suggests that the actual presence of spirits is not assumed. Rather, what is important in these rituals is the deep significance invested by the authenticity of one's attitude, not the actuality of supernatural beings. (Cf. *Xun Zi* 17.8, p. 184.)

10.1 When Confucius was in his home village, he was so courteous and deferential that it seemed as if he was unable to speak. But at the ancestral temples, and at court, he spoke with great eloquence, though solemnly.

> *Comment:* Confucius himself exemplifies ritual propriety in this and the following passage. In fact, Book 10 of the *Analects*, of which these two passages are representative, contains many detailed descriptions of Confucius' actions and proclivities. These serve as examples of behaviors and attitudes worth reflecting on and emulating, and interpreting. This open and exemplary attitude to understanding and embodying the virtues stands in stark contrast to that of Socrates, who tries to refine and close off explicit definitions of concepts in order to get closer to the Truth.

10.11 Even for a helping of coarse greens or vegetable soup, he was sure to make an offering, and to do so respectfully.

Ritual Propriety, Music, and Harmony

Following ritualized norms of propriety earnestly and respectfully enables people of different stations to interact smoothly and productively, thereby maintaining social harmony.

1.12 Master You said, "Of the uses of *li* 禮 (ritual propriety), producing harmony (*he* 和) is the most valuable. This is what makes the *dao* of the ancient kings admirable. Every accomplishment, large and small, stems from it [i.e., from their ability to harmonize]. But when things are not working, if one appreciates the value of harmony, but attempts to harmonize without guiding one's efforts using *li*, this also will not work."

> *Comment:* Master You is suggesting that following a *direct* approach to attaining harmony, by acting according to what one believes will produce harmony, is not going to be effective. One must adopt an *indirect* approach: by taking exemplary performance of ritual propriety as one's goal, harmony is produced as a matter of course. As an analogy, trying to achieve happiness in a direct way, that is, by doing what one thinks will make oneself happy (shopping, indulging in trivial entertainment, and so on) will fail. A better strategy for achieving happiness would be to take an indirect approach—strive to help others. Happiness will be a natural by-product. (Cf. *Meng Zi* 4A17, p. 130.)

13.23 The Master said, "*Junzi* (exemplary persons) harmonize (*he* 和), rather than homogenize (*tong* 同). Petty persons homogenize, rather than harmonize."

> *Comment:* The word "*tong*," most basically, means to be similar or the same. Here the point is that *junzi* value differences and take proper advantage of them, rather than trying to make everyone the same.[6] A dialogue from the *Zuo Zhuan* illustrates the point well: "Are harmony and sameness different?" asked the Marquis. "Yes, they are," said Yan Zi. "Harmony is like soup! Water, fire, vinegar, pickle, salt, and plums are used to cook fish. When the firewood is lit, the chef harmonizes them, balancing the flavors, increasing where insufficient and reducing what is excessive. [...] If you add water to water, who would be able to taste it? If lutes played only one note, who would want to listen to them? This is why mere sameness is unacceptable."[7]
>
> Ritual propriety involves the harmonious coordination of differences, just as does cooking and music (as we see in the following passage).

7.32   When the Master was with others who sang a song well, he was sure to ask them to repeat it, and then harmonize (*he* 和) with them.

---

6   Contrast with *Mo Zi* "Conforming with Superiors," p. 251, and see "*he* 和: harmony" in Chapter 2 ("Key Philosophical Terms"). In comparing the translation of the *Zuo Zhuan* passage given here with the one in the "Key Philosophical Terms" chapter, notice how translations may legitimately differ.

7   *Chun Qiu Zuo Zhuan* ("The Zuo Commentary on the Spring and Autumn Annals"), Book 10 ("Duke Zhao"), Year 20; cf. Ames and Rosemont 1998, 254–58n216.

8.2 The Master said, "Respect (*gong* 恭) without *li* 禮 (ritual propriety) will wear one out. Caution without *li* results in timidity. Bravery without *li* leads to chaos. Uprightness without *li* becomes crooked. When *junzi* are earnest toward their parents, the people will be inspired to *ren* 仁 (humanity). When old friends are not forsaken, the people will not be perfunctory [in fulfilling their responsibilities]."

16.5 Confucius said, "Three types of enjoyment are beneficial, and three are harmful. The enjoyment of coordinating with ritual propriety (*li* 禮) and music, the enjoyment of speaking (*dao* 道) of the moral efficacy (*shan* 善) of others,[8] and the enjoyment of having many worthy friends are beneficial enjoyments. Enjoyment of pomposity, escapism, and leisure are harmful enjoyments.

7.6 The Master said, "Align your aspirations with *dao*, depend upon your compelling virtuous character (*de* 德), comply with *ren* 仁 (humanity), and take respite in the arts."

> *Comment:* The six arts were: the rites, music, archery, charioteering, calligraphy, and mathematics.

19.25 Chen Ziqin said to Zigong, "You are deferential to Confucius, but how could he be superior to you?"

Zigong responded, "*Junzi* must be cautious in what they say, for they may be regarded as wise or as unwise based on a single remark. That the Master cannot be rivaled is like the impossibility of ascending on a ladder into the heavens (*tian* 天). If the Master were in charge of a state or clan, it would be said: 'He helped them stand, and they stood. He guided (*dao* 道) them, and they followed (*xing* 行). He made peace, and they flocked to him. He stimulated them to activity, and they were harmonious (*he* 和).' His birth would be celebrated, and his death mourned. How could such a person be rivaled?"

3.3 The Master said, "What would an inhumane (*bu ren* 不仁) person (*ren* 人) do with ritual propriety (*li* 禮)? What would an inhumane person do with music?"

> *Comment:* There is a parallel between ritual and music. Both are elaborately structured human social activities that have the power to arouse

---

8   Often interpreted as "speaking well of people," this may also be understood as "speaking of what others do well." (One meaning of *dao* is "discourse.")

and direct sentiment. Used properly, they can facilitate the achievement of social harmony. But what use would an inhumane person, with no interest in producing harmony, have for ritual and music? Would they be of no use or might they be put to perverse use?

Ritual Propriety and Realizing *ren* 仁 (humanity)

Confucius' use of the term *ren* 仁 (humanity) was novel, and he was repeatedly asked about its meaning. His answers vary considerably, being tailored for the benefit of each specific interlocutor.[9] The following passages express a relation between *li* (ritual propriety) and *ren*, and perhaps tell us at least as much about *li* as they do about *ren*. (There will be more on the meaning of *ren* in the following subsection.)

15.10 Zigong asked about becoming *ren* 仁. The Master said, "Craftspeople desiring to excel at their work are sure to sharpen their tools. While residing in this state, you should serve ministers who are worthy, and befriend scholar-officials (*shi* 士) who exhibit *ren*."

> *Comment:* This passage expresses the importance of one's environment. Being in contact with good people has a salutary effect, like the contact of the sharpening stone with a tool. (Cf. *Xun Zi* 23.8, p. 229.)

14.1 Xian asked about "shame."
The Master said, "It is shameful to be concerned about salary when the *dao* does not prevail in your state. But it is also shameful to be concerned about salary when the *dao* does prevail in your state."
"If I refrain from being overbearing, boasting, resentful, and covetous, can this be called '*ren*' (humanity)?"
The Master said, "You could call it 'difficult,' but I don't know about calling it 'humanity.'"

17.6 Zizhang asked Confucius about *ren* 仁. Confucius said, "One who can put five [traits] into practice in the whole world may be regarded as *ren*."
Zizhang asked, "May I inquire about these [traits]?"
The Master replied, "[The five traits are:] respect, magnanimity, trustworthiness (*xin* 信), diligence, and kindness. If you are respectful, you will not be mistreated. If you are magnanimous, you will have the

---

9 See *Analects* 6.22, 6.30, 12.1, 12.2, and 12.22 (pp. 84, 83, 81, 81, and 95) for varying responses to questions about *ren*.

masses on your side. If you are trustworthy, people will rely on you. If you are diligent, you will achieve results. And if you are kind, this will suffice for you to be able to direct others."

Comment: Given that Confucius advises consistently turning to *li* to become *ren* (*Analects* 12.1, directly below), and that *li* is closely related to respect and deference, it is not surprising that respect is the first trait here associated with *ren*. Notice also the inclusion of diligence on the list, for effort is also closely associated with *ren*.

12.1 Yan Hui asked about *ren* 仁.

The Master responded, "Practicing self-restraint and returning repeatedly to *li* 禮 (ritual propriety) is the way to become *ren*. If one does this for a single day, the civilized world would defer to the one's *ren*.[10] Becoming *ren* stems from oneself, how could it stem from others?"

Yan Hui asked, "May I inquire about its specific details?"

The Master replied, "Do not look in a way which is not *li*, do not listen in a way that is not *li*, do not speak in a way that is not *li*, do not move in a way that is not *li*."

Yan Hui said, "Slow though I am, please permit me to conduct my affairs according to these teachings."

Comment: Similarly, Xun Zi writes, "One must not abandon ritual and propriety (*li-yi* 禮義) for even a moment" (*Xun Zi* 9.16a). Here *li* (ritual propriety) is paired with *yi* (painstaking attentiveness to normative considerations). Also, the *Zhong Yong* states: "*Dao* should not be departed from, even for an instant, if it could be departed from it would not be *dao*. Thus, the *junzi* is cautious even when not being watched, and is concerned even when no one is listening. Nothing is more visible than what is hidden; nothing more apparent than what is minute. Thus, the *junzi* is cautious in his solitude" (*Zhong Yong* 1; cf. *Da Xue* 6, p. 63). Consider how reflecting on these passages might influence one's interpretation of *Analects* 12.1.

12.2 Zhonggong asked about *ren* 仁.

The Master said, "When dealing with the public, do so as though receiving important guests; in putting the people to work, do so as though performing a great sacrificial ritual. Do not press on others what you yourself do not desire, and you will incur no resentment in the state or in your family."

---

10 Cf. *Analects* 12.17, 13.6, and 13.13, all on p. 93.

Zhonggong replied, "Slow though I am, please permit me to conduct my affairs according to these teachings."

Comment: Recognizing that receiving important guests involves ritualized greetings, this passage seems to echo the advice of the previous passage, that becoming *ren* involves repeatedly returning to ritual propriety. And it also suggests an interpretation of that passage. That is, it suggests that "do not move in a way that is not *li*" may best be understood as "always exhibit the salient characteristics of ritual propriety," namely, respectful attention to the details of the situation and to the desires of others.

This passage is also relevant to the following section, as it is suggestive of the idea that *shu* (empathetic consideration) is "*ren*'s compass" (see *Analects* 6.30, p. 83, below). Note that "Do not press on others what you yourself do not desire" is very close to the definition of *shu* 恕 (empathetic consideration) given in *Analects* 15.24, p. 83, below.

Doing One's Utmost with Empathetic Consideration: *ren* 仁, *zhong* 忠, and *shu* 恕

As the following (and some previous) passages suggest, *ren* 仁 requires hard work. It involves diligence (*Analects* 17.6, p. 80, above); it is a heavy responsibility (*ren* 任) (8.7, p. 83); it implies undergoing difficulties; and it requires strength (13.27, p. 84). In *Analects* 13.19 (p. 83), *ren* is explicitly likened to *zhong* 忠, wholehearted commitment. It is also closely associated with the idea of empathetic consideration (*shu* 恕), as in 19.6 and 6.30 (both on p. 83, below) as well as 12.2 (p. 81, above). Perhaps, then, it is *ren* 仁 that is the "connecting thread" referred to in *Analects* 4.15, directly below, understood as doing one's utmost with empathetic consideration. The reader is advised to study the "Key Philosophical Terms" chapter entries on *zhong* and *shu* carefully, while reflecting on the following passages.

———————

4.15 "Dear Zeng!" The Master said, "My *dao* 道 is unified with a connecting thread."

"Yes," said Master Zeng.

After the Master had left, his students asked, "What did he mean by that?"

Master Zeng replied, "The *dao* of the Master is to do one's utmost (*zhong* 忠) with empathetic consideration (*shu* 恕), and that is all."

15.24 Zigong inquired, "Is there a single phrase that one can use as a basis of conduct until the end of one's life."

The Master said, "It is 'empathetic consideration' (*shu* 恕): Do not impose on others what you do not wish for yourself."

13.19 Fan Chi asked about *ren* 仁. The Master said, "Dwell in reverence. Carry out affairs with respect. Support others with your whole heart (*zhong* 忠). Even if one goes to the tribes of the east and the north, one must not give up."

> Comment: The tribes of the east and the north (the Yi and the Di) were regarded as uncouth barbarians. But even among them, Confucius stresses, one must be respectful and do one's best.

8.7 Master Zeng said, "Aspiring scholars (*shi* 士) must be strong and determined, for their burden (*ren* 任) is heavy and their way (*dao* 道) is long. They take *ren* 仁 (humanity) as their own responsibility (*ren* 任). Is this not heavy? And they carry it until their dying day. Is this not long?"

13.12 The Master said, "Even with kingly rulers, only after generations would *ren* be prevalent."

6.30 Zigong said, "If someone were to establish wide-ranging improvements for the common people, and were able to deliver the masses [from their impoverished condition], what would you say? Could such a person be called '*ren* 仁'?"

The Master responded, "What has this to do with *ren*? Surely such a person would be a sage! Even [the great sage-kings] Yao and Shun would be daunted by this. As for those who are *ren*: desiring to establish themselves, they establish others; desiring to become prominent themselves, they promote others. The ability to take what is close as an analogy can be called *ren*'s compass."

> Comment: Although the character *shu* is not used here, something close to this idea is characterized as *ren*'s compass. Similarly, we find the idea echoed in the following passage, in which "reflecting on what is near at hand" may include empathetic introspection.

19.6 Zixia said, "Learn broadly with steadfast aspiration. And inquire with a sense of urgency while reflecting on what is near at hand. *Ren* 仁 resides precisely in this."

6.22 Fan Chi asked about wisdom (*zhi* 知).

The Master said, "Conscientiousness (*yi* 義) in serving the common people, and showing respect for ghosts and spirits while keeping them at a distance, can be called wise."

Then Fan Chi asked about *ren* 仁.

The Master answered, "As for *ren*, undergoing difficulties, and only then reaping rewards can be called *ren*."

13.27 The Master said, "Being strong and resolute, like a tree, and slow to speak—this is close to *ren* 仁."

6.12 Ranyou said, "It is not that I do not admire your way. It is that my strength is insufficient."

The Master responded, "Those whose strength is insufficient drop from exhaustion in mid-course (*zhong dao* 中道). You, however, have simply drawn a line."

15.6 Zizhang asked about *xing* 行 (proper conduct).

The Master said, "[1] Regarding speech, do your utmost (*zhong* 忠) to honor your commitments (*xin* 信); [2] regarding conduct (*xing* 行), be unwaveringly respectful—and even if you are in the land of the Man and the Mo ['barbarians'], things will go well (*xing* 行). But if you do not do your utmost to honor your commitments, and are not unwaveringly respectful in your conduct, how could things go well (*xing* 行) even in your own neighborhood? When standing, see these two before you, forming a trio with you. In your chariot see them resting on the yoke. Only then will things proceed well (*xing* 行)."

Zizhang wrote this on his sash.

Comment: The use of the character *xing* 行 may involve a sort of pun. The third, fourth, and fifth occurrences of *xing* seem to express a different meaning than the second occurrence—the first occurrence being entirely ambiguous. (For another example of Confucius taking advantage of an ambiguity in a question, see 2.23, p. 74.) Alternatively, *xing* may be taken as "proper conduct" throughout: "Regarding proper conduct (*xing*), be unwaveringly respectful—and even if you are in the land of the Man and the Mo [barbarians], it will be proper conduct (*xing*)." Note that the Confucians regarded the tribal people of the outer regions as less than civilized. They referred to them with contemptuous titles: "*man* 蠻" (implying 'creatures') for the tribal peoples of the south, "*mo* 貊" (implying 'beasts') for those of the north-east. These are usually translated into English as "barbarians."

4.1 The Master said, "[The presence of] *ren* 仁 makes a community attractive. If one chooses not to dwell among the *ren*, how will one acquire wisdom?"

4.3 The Master said, "Only those who have *ren* 仁 are able to [properly] admire [some] people and detest others." (Cf. *Da Xue* 8 and 10, pp. 63 and 64.)

14.28 The Master said, "Among the ways (*dao* 道) of *junzi*, there are three for which I lack ability: Those who are *ren* 仁 are not anxious; the wise are not at a loss; and the courageous are not apprehensive."
    Zigong responded, "Master, this is precisely your own way (*dao* 道)."

15.36 The Master said, "Facing *ren* 仁 [an opportunity to express humanity], do not yield [even] to your teacher."

7.30 The Master said, "Is *ren* 仁 really all that far away? When I desire it, it is here."

> *Comment:* After all the stress on the effort involved in exhibiting *ren*, it is important to remember that doing our best for others with sympathetic understanding of their desires, based on careful and honest introspection of our own, is always within our power. Indeed the desire to cultivate the highest virtue, no matter how difficult it is, is itself *already* a manifestation of the highest virtue.

From aspirants (*shi* 士) to exemplary persons (*junzi* 君子)

One does not become exemplary overnight. One must go through a lengthy process of self-cultivation. At early stages, in which one strives to distinguish oneself, one is called a "*shi* 士." (aspirant)—one who aspires (*zhi* 志) to be a *junzi* (exemplary person), but is not there yet. And even when one has become exemplary, there is always room for more learning and "fine-tuning" (*Analects* 19.7, p. 89, below).

15.9 The Master said, "Among aspirants (*shi* 士) with aspiration (*zhi* 志), and people with humanity (*ren* 仁), none would strive to save their lives if *ren* 仁 was thereby impaired. Some, however, would give up their lives if *ren* could thereby be achieved."

Comment: Sometimes referred to more neutrally as "scholar-officials," the *shi* 士 were a class of individuals capable of having a role in governance. But, analogous with the term *junzi* (prince, exemplary person), Confucius uses the term "*shi*" in an ethical sense to refer to someone who is a kind of exemplary person in training: one who *aspires* (*zhi* 志) to be fit for true governance and the implementation of *dao*.

4.9 The Master said, "A scholar (*shi* 士) who aspires (*zhi* 志) to the way, but is ashamed of ugly clothes and wretched food, is not worth talking to."

2.4 The Master said, "When I was fifteen, I aspired to learn. At thirty, I took a stand. At forty, I had no doubts. At fifty, I understood the circumstances of *tian* (*tian ming* 天命). At sixty, I had an ear for things. At seventy, I followed my heart's desire without overstepping what is proper."

Comment: The phrase translated "had an ear for things" is obscure. Perhaps it suggests that, more than just a feel for the general flow of things, Confucius could judge with accuracy more subtle matters. In *Analects* 16.1 (in "Confucius' Political Philosophy," p. 98, below), for example, Confucius quickly sees through a deception.

13.20 Zigong asked, "What must one be like to merit being called an 'aspirant' (*shi* 士)?"

The Master said, "Those who conduct themselves with a sense of shame (*chi* 恥), and who do not bring disrepute on their ruler's directives while away on diplomatic missions to distant regions, merit being called aspirants."

Zigong said, "May I venture to ask what is next best?"

The Master said, "One who is judged to be filial (*xiao* 孝) toward his clan and ancestors, and judged to exhibit brotherly affection in his neighborhood."

Zigong said, "May I venture to ask what is next best?"

The Master said, "One who's speech is sure to be lived up to (*xin* 信), and who's conduct is sure to bring results—bullheaded petty persons though they may be, they may nevertheless be taken as next best."

Zigong said, "What do you think of those currently serving in government?"

The Master said, "Ugh! How could that shallow lot be worth considering?"

19.1 Zizhang said, "On perceiving danger, they face up to the circumstances (*ming* 命); on perceiving an opportunity for gain, they think of what is honorable (*yi* 義); while performing a sacrifice, they attend to being respectful; when in mourning, they dwell on their grief (cf. *Analects* 3.4, p. 75)—this is all it takes to be an acceptable aspirant (*shi* 士)."

> *Comment:* A *shi*, as a kind of moral apprentice, examines and deliberates on the most appropriate and salient considerations in each of these cases, but is not expected to always actually perform flawlessly.
>
> The first clause is often read as: "In facing danger, they put their lives (*ming* 命) on the line," which amounts to the same thing.

12.20 Zizhang asked, "What must an aspiring officer (*shi* 士) be like in order to merit being called 'distinguished'?"

The Master said, "What do you mean by 'distinguished'?"

Zizhang replied, "Sure to be famous whether [serving] in a state or in a noble family."

The Master said, "That is fame, not distinction. [Genuine] distinction involves being honest, true, and fond of consummate conduct (*yi* 義). One who is discerning regarding what is said, observant of countenance, and considerate of those of lower station is sure to be distinguished in a state or in a noble family. Becoming famous [on the other hand] involves putting on a show of *ren* 仁 (humanity) while one's conduct is quite the opposite. Having no qualms with this, such a person is sure to be famous whether [serving] in a state or in a noble family."

9.11 Yan Yuan, heaving a deep sigh, said:

> Looking up, it looms ever higher.
> Delving deep, the tougher it becomes.
> You see it before, and suddenly it is after.

The Master excels at inspiring people to follow. He broadens us with culture (*wen* 文) and restrains us with propriety (*li* 禮). We could not give up even if we wanted to, and yet,

> Even though we have exhausted our abilities, it seems to tower before us;
> Even though we desire to follow it, we simply have no way of doing so.

15.33 The Master said, "If our understanding can reach it, but we cannot maintain it with humanity (*ren*), then although we may attain it we will certainly lose it. If we understand it, and are able to maintain it with humanity, but do not rule with dignity, then the people will not be respectful. If we understand it, can maintain it with humanity, and rule over the people with dignity, but do not deploy them with propriety, then we have not begun to excel."

17.13 The Master said, "Respectable villagers are thieves of virtue (*de* 德)."

> *Comment:* This passage reminds us that being exemplary is not about show. It requires sincere commitment. This passage also reminds us that Confucius was a reformer. Being a "respectable villager" amounts to conformity to popular expectations that may not be genuinely admirable. (For Meng Zi's explanation of "respectable villagers," see *Meng Zi* 7B37, p. 134.)

15.18 The Master said, "*Junzi* make conscientiousness (*yi* 義) their basic character, put it into practice by observing ritual propriety (*li* 禮), express it with modesty, and accomplish it by honoring their commitments (*xin* 信). Such are *junzi* indeed!"

4.5 The Master said, "Being wealthy and eminent is what people desire.[11] But [*junzi*] will not settle into such circumstances if not attained by means of their way (*qi dao* 其道). Being impoverished and despised is what people detest. But [*junzi*] will not abandon such circumstances if they are[c] attained by means of their way. If '*junzi*' abandon *ren* 仁 (humanity), how can they fulfill their title? *Junzi* do not depart from *ren* even for the duration of a meal. Even if they are in a rush, they are sure to accord with [*ren*]. Though stumbling and tumbling to the ground, they are sure to do so in accord with [*ren*]."

> *Comment:* The subject of the second and forth sentences of this passage is unspecified. Many interpreters take it to be Confucius himself. Taking the subject to be the *junzi* also yields a plausible reading that coheres well with the rest of the passage.
>
> The precise meaning of the last couple of sentences is uncertain, and translations vary. It may be a humorous way of emphasizing the point of this passage: *junzi* find a way to be *ren*, and to live by their principles, *no matter what.*

---

11 To compare Xun Zi's view regarding what people desire and detest, see "Xun Zi on Motivation" (p. 161) and passage *Xun Zi* 23.1e, p. 223. Notice that exemplary persons don't seem to be exceptional in what they desire and detest. But there are things they are unwilling accept, despite their desires. (Cf. also *Xun Zi* 1.14, p. 161, and *Meng Zi* 6A10, p. 121.)

16.10 Confucius said, "*Junzi* are concerned with nine things:

> In terms of what is seen, they are concerned with being illuminating (*ming* 明); in what is heard, with cogency.
> In facial expression, with warmth; in manner, with respectfulness.
> In speech, with wholehearted commitment (*zhong* 忠); in service, with reverence.
> When in doubt, they are concerned with inquiry; when indignant, with [not] making matters worse.
> And, seeing an opportunity for gain, they are concerned with what is honorable (*yi* 義)."

1.1 The Master said, "To learn something and practice it over time—is this not satisfying? To have friends visit from afar—is this not a joy? To be unappreciated and yet unperturbed—is this not [characteristic of] a *junzi*?"

19.7 Zixia said, "The various artisans reside in their workshops in order to fully develop their crafts. *Junzi* engage in learning in order to extend their way (*dao* 道)."

Virtuous Character and Ethical Sensibility

As discussed above, *ren* (humanity) involves working hard for the benefit of others, striving to understand their perspective. In addition, *li* (norms of ritual propriety) provide patterns to facilitate *ren* conduct, and also to develop the *disposition* to so conduct oneself. But we need to develop a certain kind of ethical sensibility, if we are to be able to attune our normative conduct to varying circumstances in appropriate ways. We cultivate a moral sense of what is fitting and approvable in different contexts. And, on a deeper level, this sort of sensibility is also required for us to be able to evaluate and adjust those very norms themselves.

13.18 The Duke of She spoke to Confucius, saying: "There is a man among my people who is so personally upright (*zhi* 直) that when his father stole a sheep he informed the authorities."

Confucius responded, "Among my people, being upright is different from this. Fathers cover for sons, and sons cover for fathers. Being upright resides precisely in this."

Comment: This is quite a surprise to modern Western ears, and on first hearing sounds contrary to our deepest ethical sensibilities. But, Confucians emphasize the family roots of ethical sensibility, and also find here our strongest ethical obligations and loyalties. The further from the family we get, the less weight those obligations retain. Family members have a profound obligation not to treat their own as though they were strangers. The Mohists, however, find the Confucian attitude to be hypocritical, and criticize them severely for it. They emphasize the equivalence of all people, whether related to us or not, and draw from this a principle of equitable concern for everyone (*jian'ai*).

4.10 The Master said, "In a *junzi*'s view of the civilized world (*tian xia* 天下), there is nothing that is [always] suitable, and nothing that never is. They favor what is appropriate (*yi* 義)."

> *Comment:* Passages like this may be taken to support the view that *yi* is not absolute, but contextual. If therefore, we translate "*yi*" as "rightness" or "duty," we should be clear that these do not have to be understood in a singular or exclusive sense, but are intended to be open and pluralistic.[12] In *Analects* 18.8, Confucius says, "To me, nothing is simply permissible, and nothing is simply impermissible."[13]

11.22 Zilu asked, "Upon learning something, should one put it [straight-away] into action?"

The Master said, "So long as your father and elder brothers live, how could you do so?"

[Later] Ranyou asked the same question. The Master said, "Upon learning something, put it into action."

Zihua said, "When Zilu asked you 'Upon learning something, should one put it into action?' you said, '[Not] so long as your father and elder brothers live.' But when Ranyou asked the same question, you said, 'Upon learning something, put it into action.' I am confused. May I ask for an explanation?"

The Master said, "Ranyou holds back [too much], so I urged him forward. Zilu is [as active as] two people, so I held him back."

1.11 The Master said, "While one's father lives, pay heed to his [stated] intentions. After one's father has passed on, pay heed to his [past] conduct. A son who refrains from amending (*gai* 改) the ways (*dao* 道) of his father until the third year may be called 'filial' (*xiao* 孝)."

---

12 See the introduction to the "Key Philosophical Terms" chapter, as well as key philosophical term "*yi*."

13 The full passage can be found on p. 103.

1.13 Master You said, "What brings honoring one's commitments (*xin* 信) close to consummate conduct (*yi* 義) is that one's words can be relied on. What brings respectfulness (*gong* 恭) close to ritual propriety (*li* 禮) is that it keeps one far removed from shame and humiliation. A reliable person who does not neglect intimates is surely worthy of veneration."

2.24 The Master said, "To offer sacrifices to ancestors that are not one's own is to engage in flattery. To see what is honorable (*yi* 義) and not act is to lack courage."

7.3 The Master said, "Failure to cultivate a compelling character (*de* 德), failure to practice what has been learned, inability to move into action upon awareness of what is honorable (*yi* 義), and inability to improve inadequacies—these are what concern me."

> Comment: This has generally been taken to mean that Confucius worried that *he himself* may not live up to these requirements. This fits with a Confucian notion, also found in the *Xun Zi*, that one ought to be strict with oneself and more lenient with others. Xun Zi writes, "*Junzi* measure themselves with a stretched cord. In their contacts with others they use a bow frame. Because they measure themselves with a stretched cord, they may be taken as a model worthy of emulation everywhere. By using a bow frame in their contact with others, they are thus able to be magnanimous and tolerant."[d] Nevertheless, the above translation maintains the ambiguity of the original, leaving open the interpretation that Confucius worries about others failing in these ways as well. All of this is in contrast to worrying about petty or selfish matters, such as what is profitable.

14.12 Zilu asked about accomplished persons (*cheng ren* 成人).

The Master said, "If one is as wise as Zang Wuzhong, as free from desires as Gongchuo, as courageous as Zhuang Zi of Bian, as proficient as Ranyou, and also cultured by ritual propriety (*li* 禮) and music, then one can surely be regarded as an accomplished person."

The Master continued, "But must an accomplished person today necessarily be like this? At the sight of profit, those who think of what is honorable (*yi* 義); at the sight of danger, those who would offer their lives; when in want for a long time, those who do not forget the words they lived by in better times—they surely may also be considered accomplished persons."

> Comment: Clearly, a person would not have to have all the qualities stated in Confucius' first statement to qualify as accomplished, as he is listing

examples of qualities of accomplished people. Similarly, it seems that a person would only have to have one of the qualities listed in his second statement to qualify. The reference to "people today" seems to suggest that, given the disadvantages of the times, there should be a lower than traditional standard for what is considered an accomplishment. And clearly, meeting the conditions of either the first description or the second would suffice. Further, the characterizations are non-exhaustive—they are merely examples of clear cases. The implication is that there are a number of ways of being accomplished. In this passage, Confucian pluralism and contextualism are amply evident.

4.16 The Master said, "*Junzi* epitomize honorable conduct (*yi* 義). Petty persons epitomize profit seeking (*li* 利)."

7.16 The Master said, "I may eat coarse rice, drink water, use my bent arms as a pillow, and still be joyful to the core. Dishonorably (*buyi* 不義) acquired wealth and honors are to me like fleeting clouds."

7.12 The Master said, "If I could approve (*ke* 可) of seeking wealth, then even if it meant serving as an attendant with whip in hand, I would do it. If it is not approvable, I will pursue that of which I am fond (*hao* 好)."

> *Comment:* The last phrase seems to allude to Confucius' love of learning (see *Analects* 5.28, 8.13, pp. 71 and 104, for Confucius' attitude toward learning). If so, the meaning seems to be that Confucius will pursue *learning* instead of wealth. It is not that one should pursue *whatever* one pleases. At least, what one pursues must be genuinely approvable.

2.10 The Master said, "If you observe their means, look at their motives, and investigate wherein they find comfort, where can people hide? Where can people hide?"[14]

CONFUCIUS' POLITICAL PHILOSOPHY

Virtuous Rulership

Central to Confucius' political philosophy is the compelling virtuous character (*de* 德) of *junzi*, expressed through conduct that comports with the norms of ritual propriety (*li* 禮).

---

14 Cf. *Da Xue* 6, p. 63.

2.1 The Master said, "One who governs through virtuous potency (*de* 德) is like the Pole Star: it simply resides in its place and the multitude of stars circle it in deference."

12.17 Ji Kang Zi asked Confucius about governing (*zheng* 政). Confucius replied, "Governing (*zheng* 政) is being proper (*zheng* 正). If you lead by being proper, who would dare not be?"

> *Comment:* To be *zheng* 正 (proper, straight) is to be unbiased and morally upright, and here suggests being *a model of rigorously proper conduct*. This passage could also be read as saying, "Governing is *making* proper," that is, improving the character of the people is fundamental to governing. One does this, in part, by being a model of proper behavior oneself.
>
> This passage can be seen as an example of what Xun Zi will later call "apt naming" (*Xun Zi* 22.2g, p. 213), which is an aspect of his theory of *zheng ming*, the proper use of terms. (For Xun Zi's theory of *zheng ming* see p. 208.)

12.19 Ji Kang Zi asked Confucius about governing (*zheng* 政) saying, "What do you think about killing those who lack the way (*dao* 道) in order to obtain people who have it?"

Confucius responded, "If you are after governance (*zheng* 政), what use is there in killing? Simply desire to be good (*shan* 善) yourself, and the common people will be likewise. A *junzi*'s influential character (*de* 德) is the wind; a petty person's influential character is the grass. When the wind flows over grass, it is sure to bend."

13.6 The Master said, "If one comports oneself properly, the people will work well (*xing* 行), without even being commanded. But if one does not comport oneself properly, even commands will not be followed."

> *Comment:* Neither *li* 禮 (ritual propriety) nor *de* 德 (influential character) appear in this passage (or in *Analects* 13.13, directly below). However, the idea expressed here suggests a strong link between ritually proper conduct (*li*) and influential character (*de*). This illustrates the holistic interconnectedness of Confucian concepts.

13.13 The Master said, "If one is proper in one's own character (*zheng qi shen* 正其身), what problem will one have governing? If one is *not* able to be proper in one's own character, how can one make other people proper?"

Comment: Similarly, Meng Zi will later say, "Never have those who bent themselves been able to straighten others" (*Meng Zi* 3B1).

Notice that "make other people proper" here parallels "governing," suggesting an equation between the two, an idea confirmed by *Analects* 12.17, p. 93, above: "Governing is being/making proper."

2.3 The Master said, "If you lead (*dao* 道) them with [Legalistic] government (*zheng* 政), keep them in line with punishments, the common people will avoid trouble but have no sense of shame. If you lead them with virtue (*de* 德), keep them in line with ritual propriety (*li* 禮), they will develop a sense of shame and furthermore will reform themselves."

Comment: Note that the cultivation of the emotion of shame is seen as central to ensuring self-control over ethical actions.

12.13 The Master said, "In presiding over public disputes, I am like any other. What is necessary is to ensure that no such disputes occur."[15]

Comment: Considering 2.3 and 12.13 together suggests that people who have reformed themselves through ritual propriety are more likely to be able to resolve disagreements amicably themselves.

14.41 The Master said, "When those above are fond of ritual propriety (*li* 禮), the common people are easily governed."

4.13 The Master said, "If one is able to govern a state by means of ritual propriety and deference (*li rang* 禮讓), what difficulties would there be? If one is unable to govern a state by these means, what purpose would ritual propriety (*li*) serve?"

6.27 The Master said, "*Junzi* are well versed in cultural patterns (*wen* 文), which they regulate (*yue* 約)[16] with ritual propriety (*li* 禮). And they can thereby avoid transgressions."

1.2 Master You said, "There are few people who are filial (*xiao* 孝) and brotherly who delight in defying authority. Not delighted to defy authority, yet delighted to incite rebellion—there is not a single example of

---

15 This statement also occurs in *Da Xue* 4, p. 62.

16 *Yue* 約 means to bind with rope, to restrain. But it also means simple and concise, thus the binding may be thought of as being for the purpose of keeping something organized, as well as being preventative. In addition, *yue* also means "agreed upon," which suggests some degree of conventionality, as well as the acquiescence of the participants.

this. *Junzi* devote themselves to the root. When the root is established, *dao* 道 will grow. Are not filial and brotherly [virtues] the root of *ren* 仁 (humanity)?"

> *Comment:* To achieve harmony, or at least to avoid rebellion, the key is to make sure the people maintain filial and brotherly virtues. Family feelings are the root from which we grow into fully developed persons (*ren* 仁) who extend their fraternal concerns to others. Cf. *Meng Zi* 7B16: "To be *ren* 仁 is to be a person (*ren* 人)."

1.5 The Master said, "Guide (*dao* 道) a small state by living up to one's words (*xin* 信) while respectfully managing affairs, by caring for others while being moderate in [one's own] expenses, and by utilizing the common folk as seasonally appropriate."

12.22 Fan Chi asked about *ren* 仁. The Master said, "Care for others (*ai ren* 愛人)."

Fan Chi asked about knowledge (*zhi* 知). The Master said, "Know others."

> *Comment:* According to a story in the *Xun Zi*, Confucius' protégé, Yan Hui, answers a question saying, "The person of wisdom knows himself; the person of *ren* 仁 (humanity) loves himself." Confucius gives this answer his highest approval, higher even than this answer: "The person of wisdom knows others; the person of *ren* 仁 loves others" (*Xun Zi* 29.7). Perhaps Confucius thought that the insight in Yan Hui's statement would be lost on Fan Chi.

Fan Chi did not understand. The Master elaborated, "By raising up the straight and laying aside the crooked, one can make the crooked straight."

Fan Chi withdrew and went to see Zixia. He said, "I just saw the Master and asked him about wisdom. The Master said, 'By raising up the straight and laying aside the crooked, one can make the crooked straight.' What did he mean?"

Zixia exclaimed, "What a wealth of meaning in these words! When the sage-king Shun possessed the world, selecting from the masses, he promoted [the virtuous] Gao Yao, and those who lacked *ren* were kept at a distance. When the sage-king Tang possessed the world, selecting from the masses, he promoted [the virtuous] Yi Yin, and those who lacked *ren* were kept at a distance."

13.9 The Master traveled to Wei, with Ranyou driving his carriage. The Master commented, "What a large population!"

Ranyou asked, "When there is already a large population, what more can be done for them?"

The Master said, "Help them prosper."

Ranyou asked, "When they are already prosperous, what more can be done for them?"

The Master said, "Edify (*jiao* 教) them."

Comment: Notice the priority placed on economic well-being. The imperative to help people prosper, Confucius seems to imply, precedes the imperative to educate them.

11.26 Zilu, Zengxi, Ranyou, and Zihua were seated with Confucius. The Master said, "Though I am a little older than you, don't hold back with me. You always complain, 'No one appreciates me!' Well, if someone did appreciate you, how would you use the opportunity?"

Zilu immediately replied, "Given a (small) state of a thousand chariots, surrounded by great states, menaced by foreign armies, and suffering famine, within three years I could instill courage and a sense of direction." The Master smiled at him.

"Ranyou," The Master asked, "How about you?"

Ranyou replied, "Given a small state of 60 or 70—or even only 50 or 60—square *li*,[17] within three years I could make sure the needs of the common people were satisfied. As for ritual propriety (*li* 禮) and music, this would have to wait for a *junzi*."

"Zihua," said the Master, "How about you?"

Zihua replied, "I am not saying that I am capable of it, but I sincerely wish to have a chance to learn from it—to have duties in the Royal Ancestral Shrine, such as serving as a master of ceremonies at diplomatic meetings, dressed in ceremonial garb."

"Zengxi," said the Master, "How about you?"

Finishing a tune on his zither, Zengxi put it aside with a clang and stood up, replying, "I would answer differently from the other three."

The Master said, "What harm is there in that? Surely everyone is just expressing their aspiration."

Zengxi said, "In late spring, when the spring clothes are completed, I would like to go with five or six young men, and six or seven boys, to bathe in the Yi River, enjoy the breeze at the Rain Alter, and return home singing."

---

17 In Modern Chinese, *li* is a unit of measure, approximately one-third of a mile. In ancient times it was not used precisely. Sometimes we loosely translate it as "miles" or "leagues."

The Master sighed, saying, "I am with Zengxi!"

After the other three departed, Zengxi remained. He asked, "What did you think of what the others said?"

The Master said, "They also each expressed their aspiration, and that is all."

Zengxi said, "Why did you smile at Zilu?"

The Master replied, "One governs a state with ritual propriety (*li* 禮), yet his words were not deferential (*rang* 讓). This is why I smiled at him."

"Was Ranyou the only one who did not speak of governing a state?"

"How could 60 or 70—or even 50 or 60—square *li*, not be a state?"

"Was Zihua the only one who did not speak of governing a state?"

"If conducting diplomacy in the Royal Ancestral Shrine does not involve the feudal lords, then what is it? Further, if Zihua is going to limit himself to minor roles, who can manage the larger ones?"

15.1 Duke Ling of Wei asked Confucius about military formations. Confucius replied, "I am familiar with the use of instruments for ritual sacrifice. But military matters I have not yet studied." The next day he left.

> *Comment:* Confucius seems to be saying, in an indirect way, "The ritual sacrifice of animals is one thing. But the sacrifice of human lives in war is something I will have no part in." According to the *Zuo Zhuan*, Confucius was almost persuaded to stay when told that the intention was to defend the state from attack.[e]

13.29 The Master said, "After the common people have been edified (*jiao* 教) by good people for seven years, then one may on this basis proceed to include [the study of] military affairs."

13.30 The Master said, "Engaging in battle (*zhan* 戰) without having instructed (*jiao* 教) the common people is throwing them away."

> *Comment:* By itself, this passage may seem to suggest that Confucius thought simply that one should instruct people in how to fight before sending them into battle. However, the preceding passage, and the following consideration, render this simple interpretation questionable. After making a very similar comment, Meng Zi says, "Even if one defeated [the powerful state of] Qi in a single battle (*zhan* 戰), and gained complete possession of Nanyang, it would still be unacceptable." Meng Zi then provides a confusing explanation to an already perplexed interlocutor, which ends as follows: "A person with *ren* 仁 (humanity) would not even take something from one [state] to give to another; much

less would he kill people to acquire [territory]. A *junzi* serves his lord by striving to guide him to accord with *dao* 道, and to aspire only to *ren* 仁 (humanity)—and that is all."[f] It is hard to know exactly what Confucius meant—or what he was trying to *do*—when he made the above comment. He may have been trying to forestall a particular act of aggression with an ambiguous statement that might be persuasive even to a ruler who interprets it simplistically. In any case, the following passage may better inform our understanding of Confucius' view of the use of military power.

16.1 The Ji clan intended to attack (*fa* 伐) Zhuanyu [a vassal state within the state of Lu]. Ranyou and Zilu [two of Confucius' students] met with Confucius and said, "The Ji clan intends to deal with Zhuanyu."

Confucius responded, "Ranyou! Is this not your fault? In ancient times, the former kings put Zhuanyu in charge of [ritualistic observations regarding] Mount Dongmeng. Moreover, it is within the boundaries of the state [of Lu], and functions as the minister to the altars of soil and grain. Why attack it?"

Ranyou said, "Our lord wants to do this, but we do not."

Confucius responded, "Ranyou! Zhouren [the legendary historian] had a saying: 'To display your strength, put forth your ranks. If you are not able, then give it up.'"

> *Comment:* Confucius is suggesting that Ranyou and Zilu should either use their influence to prevent this unjustified attack, or resign.

"Of what use is a minister who fails to hold [his lord] back from peril, and provides no support when he stumbles? Moreover, what you've said is specious. If a tiger or rhinoceros escapes from his cage, or if a tortoise shell or piece of jade is destroyed in its case, who is at fault?"

> *Comment:* You can't blame a tiger or a rhinoceros, or a piece of jade. The fault must lie with those who are charged with keeping wild animals in their cages, or with protecting fragile objects.

Ranyou said, "But Zhuanyu is fortified and near Bi [the Ji clan's stronghold]. If we don't seize it now, it will surely be a source of trouble for future generations."

Confucius said, "Ranyou! Something *junzi* abhor is disavowing a desire and yet making excuses in favor of it. I have heard that [true] leaders of states or clans:

They do not worry about poverty, but inequity.
They do not worry about [insufficient] population, but insecurity.
For if there is equity, there will be no poverty.
If the population is harmonious (*he* 和), they will not be few in number.
And if they are secure, there will be no instability.

And so, if distant peoples do not submit, cultivate civil virtues (*wen de* 文德) and thereby attract them. Once drawn in, make them secure. But now, with you and Zilu as ministers, distant peoples do not submit, and cannot be drawn to you. You are not able to ensure the protection of your state, which is fracturing and crumbling to pieces. So, you plan to take up arms within your own state. I fear that Ji Sun's troubles reside not in Zhuanyu, but within the screen of reverence [of the Lu court]."

> *Comment:* The last line is yet another way of saying that the problem here is the failure of Ranyou and Zilu.

14.42 Zilu asked about *junzi*. The Master said, "They cultivate themselves with deep reverence."
Zilu said, "Just this, and that's it?"
The Master said, "They cultivate themselves and thereby bring peace to others."
Zilu said, "Just this, and that's it?"
The Master said, "They cultivate themselves and thereby bring peace to all people. *They cultivate themselves and thereby bring peace to all people!* Even [the great sage-kings] Yao and Shun would be daunted by this."

> *Comment:* Confucius seems to believe that aggression is not necessary if one can draw people by the potency (*de* 德) of their character.

Roles, Responsibilities, and Names

In *Analects* 13.3 (directly below) Confucius suggests that making names proper (*zheng ming* 正名) is more fundamental than even ritual propriety. Although this is the only passage in the *Analects* in which the term "*zheng ming*" occurs, the idea is exemplified in other passages (see below).[18] As Chad Hansen has written, "[T]he rectification of names [*zheng ming*] can be regarded as a genuine Confucian teaching in the sense that without it, the ethical system of Confucius would be considerably less coherent."[8]

---

18 Xun Zi devotes a whole chapter to the concept of *zheng ming* (*Xun Zi* 22, "Proper Terminology").

13.3 Zilu inquired, "If the lord of Wei were to entrust you with the governance of his state, what would you do first?" The Master answered, "It would certainly be to make names proper (*zheng ming* 正名)."

Zilu replied, "That is what you would do? Your way is certainly circuitous. What is there to make proper?"

The Master responded, "What an oaf you are, Zilu! With respect to that of which they are ignorant, *junzi* remain quiet.

> If names are not made proper, then what is said will not be followed.
> If what is said is not followed, affairs will not be successfully accomplished.
> If affairs are not successfully accomplished, ritual propriety and music will not flourish.
> If ritual propriety (*li* 禮) and music do not flourish, then punishments and penalties will be off the mark.
> If punishments and penalties are off the mark, the common people have no place to put hand or foot.

Thus, the *junzi*'s words are sure to warrant speaking. And what is said is sure to warrant being put into practice. There is nothing lax in the *junzi*'s attitude toward language."

> *Comment:* This passage suggests that proper naming is a precondition of ritual propriety. And if ritual propriety and music are not in ascendance, people will not be thereby guided in their moral development. So, to punish them for what is really a failure of government would be unfair.

12.11 Duke Jing of Qi asked Confucius about governing (*zheng* 政). Confucius replied, "Rulers rule (*jun jun* 君君); ministers minister (*chen chen* 臣臣); parents parent (*fu fu* 父父); and children likewise fulfill the roles proper to children (*zi zi* 子子)."

The Duke responded, "Excellent! Truly, if rulers do not rule, ministers do not minister, parents do not parent, and children do not fulfill their roles, then even if there were plenty of grain, how would I obtain any to eat?"

> *Comment:* This passage expresses the concept of *zheng ming* 正名, properly according (*zheng*) to the name (*ming*): people are to live up to the morally imbued meaning of the titles that name their roles.
>
>   Strictly speaking, "*fu fu*" literally says "fathers father," but "to father" has the wrong meaning in English, whereas "parents parent" better captures the idea of fulfilling the responsibilities suggested by the name.

6.25 The Master said, "A '*gu*' that is not a *gu*—is it a *gu*? Is it a *gu*?"

Comment: A *gu* is a particular kind of goblet that is used in certain rituals. Confucius worries about something that does not have the qualities of a *gu* being used and called one, especially in a ritual context. This is analogous to a "father" who is not a father, that is, who does not have the moral qualities of a father (see *Analects* 12.11, directly above), or a "superior" who does not have superior qualities (*Analects* 3.26, directly below). For a modern-day parallel, imagine being given a plastic champagne glass at a wedding: "You call that a 'champagne glass'?"

3.26 The Master said, "Holding high office (*shang* 上) without being broad-minded, performing ritual propriety (*li* 禮) without reverence (*bu jing* 不敬), attending funerals without lamenting—How could I contemplate such things."

Comment: This passage makes it clear that there is an indispensable psychological dimension to ritual propriety. It is certainly not mere "good form." This passage also tells us something about *zheng ming*, the proper use of names. The reason Confucius does not know what to make of such behavior is that it is not in tune with the relevant terms. True ritual propriety requires reverence, and "irreverent reverence" is contradictory. Similarly, to be worthy of being "*shang*" one *must* be broad-minded; it does not make sense for a "superior" to be petty. In this light, consider Confucius' comment in *Analects* 4.5: "If '*junzi*' abandon *ren* 仁 (humanity), how can they fulfill their title?" (See also *Analects* 1.11, 12.17, and 15.18, pp. 90, 93, and 88.)

When *dao* Does Not Prevail

Just as Confucius disparages wealth dishonorably acquired (see *Analects* 7.16, p. 92, and surrounding passages, above), he suggests that one should only achieve political prominence when the *dao* 道 prevails in one's state. When it does not, Confucius suggests, one should remain obscure, staying out of trouble while one, presumably, focuses on ordering one's own family and local community (see Chapter 3, the *Da Xue*). However, though he lived in a troubled time, Confucius himself continued to remain engaged and struggled to be influential, as did Meng Zi and Xun Zi. Confucius was once described as "the one who knows it is impossible, but keeps at it" (*Analects* 14.38).

5.2 The Master said of Nan Rong, "When *dao* 道 obtains in the state, he will not be cast aside. When it does not, he will escape punishment." With this, the Master gave his niece to marry Nan Rong.

5.7 The Master said, "*Dao* 道 is making no headway. I shall go drift off to sea in a raft. The one who will follow me, I suppose, is Zilu." Upon hearing this, Zilu was delighted. The Master commented, "Zilu's fondness for daring surpasses mine, but he lacks what it takes to acquire timber [for the raft]."

> Comment: Interpretations vary, especially regarding the last line. Perhaps it just means that Zilu "doesn't have the right stuff," since other passages suggest that Zilu is brave, but lacks talent. Zhu Xi takes it to be about Zilu's judgment—for not recognizing that Confucius was not *really* going to take to the seas in a raft. But the association with timber and rafts, which Zhu Xi denies, is worth considering. The above translation allows for the connection between timber and rafts, while also permitting Zhu Xi's interpretation that Zilu lacked good sense. In any case, Confucius is both praising and teasing, as he often does. Note also that the passage begins with a sarcastic remark that doesn't reflect Confucius' true intention, even when taken figuratively. He is not really giving up.
>
> Compare *Analects* 17.19, in which Confucius seems to contemplate giving up speaking. For other passages that reveal Confucius' sense of humor, see *Analects* 4.5, 5.4, 5.21 (directly below), 7.28, 7.35, and 15.16 (pp. 88, 70, 102, 72, 107, and 73). In another passage, responding to the criticism that he is not renowned for any particular accomplishment, Confucius jokes, "What should I take up? Charioteering? Archery? I'll take up charioteering!"[h]

5.21 The Master said, "When *dao* 道 obtained in his state, Ning Wu Zi was wise. But when it did not, he was a fool. His wisdom can be matched, but his foolery cannot be rivaled."

> Comment: Ning Wu Zi had been a prominent and respected minister, but in order to become inconspicuous and thereby avoid coming to harm, he skillfully feigned incompetence when his state descended into chaos. (Cf. *Analects* 18.8, p. 103, below.)

18.6 [...] [Jie Ni, a recluse, says to Zilu] "The whole world is frothing and flowing [just like the river Confucius and Zilu are meaning to ford], and who can change it? Further, rather than follow a teacher who avoids [certain] people [like yours does], why not follow teachers who avoid the age altogether [like us]?" He said all this without a pause from raking.

Zilu reported this [to Confucius].

The Master, taken aback, said, "I cannot flock together with birds and beasts. If not with people, with whom shall I associate? [Besides,] if the *dao* 道 obtained in the world, I would not [need to] help change it."

18.7 [...] Zilu said, "To fail to perform one's public duty is to lack *yi* 義 (dutifulness). The relationships between young and old cannot be neglected. How then can the *yi* of ruler and minister be neglected? Wishing to be pure in character throws the ethics of human relationships into chaos. The public duty of the *junzi* is to put *yi* into practice. That the *dao* 道 is not progressing—this is already understood."

> *Comment:* Zilu had been taken in for the night and treated in a ritualistically appropriate manner by a recluse living with his two sons. The old recluse seemed to understand the importance of "the relationships between the young and old" and could have contributed to society, yet he chose to live in isolation.

18.8 Bo Yi, Shu Qi, Yu Zhong, Yi Yi, Zhu Zhang, Liuxia Hui, and Shao Lian all escaped into seclusion [for principled reasons]. The Master remarked, "Bo Yi and Shu Qi would neither compromise their aspirations, nor suffer disgrace to their character. Regarding Liuxia Hui and Shao Lian: while they compromised their aspirations and suffered disgrace, their words were principled, and their conduct was well considered. [They are regarded highly] for just this, and nothing more. As for Yu Zhong and Yi Yi, they lived in seclusion where they could speak freely. They kept their persons pure, and their renunciation of office was carefully weighed. I, however, am different than these people. To me, nothing is simply permissible, and nothing is simply impermissible."

> *Comment:* While Confucius is known for his commitment to the highest ideals, here he seems to criticize the high-minded scholars who preferred to live in seclusion rather than compromising their ideals. He suggests, perhaps unexpectedly, a more lax attitude towards what is acceptable and what is not. This is surprising because it seems to go beyond the openness, flexibility, and pragmatic conceptualism of his ideals regarding what is acceptable.

8.13 The Master said, "Love learning with staunch commitment (*xin* 信), and defend until death the way of excellence (*shan dao* 善道). Do not enter an unstable state, and do not remain in a chaotic one. Be prominent when *dao* obtains in the world; be inconspicuous when it does not. To be impoverished and despised in a state in which *dao* obtains is shameful. To be wealthy and eminent in a state in which it does not is also shameful."

> *Comment:* The enjoinder to "love learning with staunch commitment" contains an ambiguity, or dual meaning. On the one hand, the commitment is to eagerly pursue learning, on the other it is to live up to the lessons learned—the character *xin* 信 is composed of a person standing next to words.

4.18 The Master said, "In serving one's parents, remonstrate gently with them. Seeing that your advice is not followed, continue to be respectful and not oppositional. And exert yourself without resentment."

> *Comment:* Considering that the parent–child relationship is taken to be analogous to that of ruler and minister, this passage may be regarded as suggestive of how ministers should deal with rulers who are making bad choices. It may be useful in this context to also consider that Xun Zi will write: "Tradition has it: 'One should follow the way, not follow one's lord'" (*Xun Zi* 13.2) and also, "When a ruler is involved in schemes and affairs which go too far, and one fears they will endanger the state, high officials and senior advisers are able to approach and speak to the ruler. Approving when one's advice is used, and leaving when it is not, is called 'remonstrance'" (*Xun Zi* 13.2). In addition, the *Li Ji* says, "Norms of ritual propriety applicable to ministers indicate that one should not remonstrate conspicuously. After remonstrating three times, if one's advice is ignored then one should flee."[i] A key difference is that Confucians do not sanction abandoning one's parents.

CONFUCIUS' WORLDVIEW AND ATTITUDE TOWARDS SPIRITUAL MATTERS

Confucius had little to say about cosmic and ultimate matters, such as the nature of *tian* 天, though he did evoke *tian* in several exclamations. The significance of those exclamations is debatable, but it seems fair to say that Confucius was more concerned about prevailing conditions and the role of humans in these conditions than he was about understanding cosmic matters. This is sometimes referred to as Confucius' "humanism." In addition to passages involving *xing* and *tian*, as well as *ming* 命 (prevailing conditions), the passages below also include a number of statements from which one may develop a tentative interpretation of Confucius' spiritual sensibility.

Eventually, increasing reverence for Confucius would propel him to the status of a spiritual sage and spiritual leader, and the devotion exhibited by his students would lead them to be understood as "disciples." But establishing a religion was the furthest thing from Confucius' mind. His devotion to the culture of Zhou required mastering all the traditions: poetry, music, ritual, etc. But when asked explicitly, he always downplayed the specifically religious aspects concerning spirits and the afterlife. What was important for Confucius was cultivation of the reverential attitude and the human ideals they represented in the governing of a state.

———————

5.13 Zigong said, "We hear about the Master's cultural embellishments, but no discussion of natural dispositions (*xing* 性) nor the way of the Cosmos (*tian dao* 天道)."

Comment: The only other passage of the *Analects* that mentions *xing* 性 (natural dispositions) is 17.2, directly below. Of the passages that evoke *tian* below, most are exclamations. They don't tell us anything about the *way* of *tian*. For Confucians, *dao* refers to "the path (*dao*) of the *junzi*," as Xun Zi put it, rather than the way of *tian* (*Xun Zi* 8.3, see the "Key Philosophical Terms" chapter, *dao*).

17.2 The Master said, "In their natural dispositions (*xing* 性), human beings are similar; it is by habit that they diverge."

Comment: Humans share much in common, but unlike other animals they also diverge quite dramatically in their behavior. Confucius accounts for this in terms of the difference between the natural dispositions with which we are all born and the cultural practices that we are subsequently brought up in.

However, humans also differ regarding their ethical behavior: some behave virtuously, others behave reprehensibly. What role do natural dispositions play regarding this difference? Confucius' lack of specificity here leads to the great split in Confucianism between Meng Zi, on the one hand, who said that *xing* is good, that people are born with the sprouts of virtue, and Xun Zi, on the other hand, who insists that natural human dispositions are detestable—that is, we have selfish desires and require norms of ritual propriety to help us reform our character.

6.28 The Master had an audience with Nanzi, and Zilu was upset. The Master swore at him, saying, "If I have done something wrong, let *tian* 天 condemn it! Let *tian* condemn it!"

Comment: Nanzi was the wife of Lord Ling of Wei. She was accused of sexual impropriety, which is why Zilu was upset. However, we do not have enough evidence to know whether the accusation was justified, or whether she was being maligned as a woman with political ambitions.

8.19 The Master said, "Great (*da* 大) indeed was Yao as a ruler. How lofty! *Tian* (the heavens) is exceptional in its vastness (*da* 大), and Yao was exceptional in emulating it. How expansive! The people could find no words to express it. How lofty were his accomplishments! How brilliant were his cultural compositions!"

11.9 When Yan Hui died, the Master exclaimed, "Oh! *Tian* 天 has bereaved me! *Tian* has bereaved me!"

Comment: Yan Hui was Confucius' most admirable student, with the most noble character, and commitment to self-improvement. Confucius' admiration is so great, that he even denies being Yan Hui's equal. But Yan Hui died at a very young age (possibly around the age of 40, or younger).

14.35 The Master said, "Nobody appreciates (*zhi* 知) me, do they?"
Zigong asked, "Why do you say that nobody appreciates you?"
The Master replied, "I do not fault *tian* 天, nor do I blame others. Applying my studies, I strive to become prominent. But only *tian* appreciates me."

Comment: Zhi 知 means "to know" or "to understand." The word "appreciate" is intended to capture these meanings, but also to more specifically suggest, in this context, "realizing the value of." Confucius believes that, given the nature of things, the ways he advocates will be effective. In this sense *tian* appreciates him. But rulers fail to realize the value in his teachings, and so fail to implement his way.

7.23 The Master said, "*Tian* 天 has engendered the potency of character (*de* 德) in me. What can the likes of Huan Tui do to me?"

9.5 Besieged in Kuang, Confucius said, "King Wen (文) has long since passed away. Yet is not his culture (*wen* 文) present even now [in me]? If *tian* 天 favored the loss of this culture, then after Wen's death, it would not have been possible to participate in it. But *tian* provided that this culture would not be lost. So what can the people of Kuang do to me?"

> *Comment:* In other words, if the culture of King Wen has survived this long, can the petty group surrounding Confucius in Kuang really put an end to it? The forces and propensities supporting the continuation of Wen's great cultural achievements are much greater than Kuang's military forces. Compare *Analects* 14.36, directly below, which is similar except that Confucius appeals to *ming* 命.

14.36 Gongbo Liao slandered Zilu to Ji [Kang Zi]. Zifu Jingbo informed Confucius, saying, "Master [Ji Kang Zi] has surely been misled by Gongbo Liao, but I still have the power to have [Gongbo's] corpse displayed in the market place or at court."

The Master said, "If the way (*dao* 道) is about to be put into practice, it is due to the prevailing conditions (*ming* 命). If the way is about to be laid to waste, it is due to the prevailing conditions. What can Gongbo Liao do about these conditions?"

7.35 When the Master was very ill, Zilu asked to offer a prayer. The Master said, "Are such things done?"

Zilu replied, "They are. The Eulogies say, 'Pray you to the upper and lower spirits, and the Earth Spirit.'"

The Master said, "I have been praying a long time already."

> *Comment:* Though somewhat enigmatic, it seems that Confucius may be drawing a contrast between merely asking for something in time of need, and conducting oneself with a proper attitude over a period of time. If this is right, Confucius is suggesting that the proper way to pay respects to the spirits (however those are conceived) is through one's conduct, work, and attitude throughout one's life, not an isolated and desperate request for divine intervention.
>
> This passage may also serve as an example of *zheng ming* (making terminology proper), for Confucius seems to be adjusting the meaning of "praying."

9.12 When the Master was gravely ill, Zilu arranged for some of the Master's students to act as though they were his ministers. During a remission, the Master said, "It has been quite some time, has it not, that this deception has been afoot! Acting as though I have ministers, although I have none, whom am I going to deceive? Will I deceive *tian* 天? Besides, I would rather die in the arms of a few students than in the arms of ministers. Although I may be laid to rest without receiving a grand funeral, it is not as though I would be left to die by the side of the road!"

11.12 Zilu asked about serving ghosts and spirits. The Master answered, "You are not yet able to serve people. How can you serve ghosts?" Zilu said, "Dare I ask about death?" The Master answered, "You do not yet understand life. How can you understand death?"

16.8 Confucius said, "There are three things that *junzi* find awe-inspiring: *tian ming* 天命 (circumstances of *tian*), eminent people (*da ren* 大人), and the words of sages. Petty persons, lacking an understanding of *tian ming*, fail to regard it with awe, they disrespect eminent people, and they presumptuously ridicule the words of sages."

17.19 The Master said, "I would rather say nothing!"
    Zigong inquired, "If you say nothing, then how will we, your lowly students, be able to convey [your way]."
    The Master replied, "What does *tian* 天 say? The four seasons proceed through it. The myriad things are engendered by it. Yet what does it say?"

> *Comment:* The view of *tian* expressed here seems comparable to Xun Zi's depiction of *tian* in *Xun Zi* 17.1 (see p. 178). But Confucius' point is not about the nature of *tian*. It is about actions speaking louder than words (cf. *Analects* 1.11 and 2.10, pp. 90 and 92). As we shall see, though, the Daoists do take the wordlessness of the Cosmos very seriously, and idealize a wordless *dao*.

20.3 Confucius said, "If one does not understand circumstance (*ming* 命), one lacks what it takes to be a *junzi*. If one does not understand ritual propriety (*li* 禮), one has no means by which to take a stand. And if one does not understand words, one has nothing by which to understand other people."

12.5 Sima Niu lamented, "All others have brothers, I alone do not."

Zixia responded, "I have heard: life and death are circumstantial (*ming* 命), wealth and nobility reside in *tian* 天. *Junzi* are unfailingly reverent. In their engagements with others they are respectful and observe ritual propriety (*li* 禮). Throughout the world, all are their brothers. Why would a *junzi* worry about not having brothers?"

Comment: Sima Niu is advised not to worry about his lack of brothers, for such things are out of one's control. But being respectful and observing ritual propriety has generally predictable, positive results, including worldly success (see *Xun Zi* 4.6 and 4.8, p. 162) and also robust relationships with others—like having many brotherly relationships. Thus, generally speaking, by behaving as a *junzi* one will achieve the equivalent of having brothers, and more.

SEQUENCE OF PASSAGES

Confucius on personal conduct and character
  Learning, tradition, and progress
  7.8, 5.28, 7.1, 2.11, 7.28, 15.11, 2.15, 15.31, 5.9, 15.16, 7.22, 4.17, 1.4, 5.27, 16.11, 2.23, 15.29
  Ritual propriety (*li* 禮)
  3.4, 19.14, 9.3, 11.1, 17.11, 3.12, 10.1, 10.11
  Ritual propriety, music, and harmony
  1.12, 13.23, 7.32, 8.2, 16.5, 7.6, 19.25, 3.3
  Ritual propriety and realizing *ren* 仁 (humanity)
  15.10, 14.1, 17.6, 12.1, 12.2
  Doing one's utmost with empathetic consideration: *ren* 仁, *zhong* 忠, and *shu* 恕
  4.15, 15.24, 13.19, 8.7, 13.12, 6.30, 19.6, 6.22, 13.27, 6.12, 15.6, 4.1, 4.3, 14.28, 15.36, 7.30
  From aspirants (*shi* 士) to exemplary persons (*junzi* 君子)
  15.9, 4.9, 2.4, 13.20, 19.1, 12.20, 9.11, 15.33, 17.13, 15.18, 4.5, 16.10, 1.1, 19.7
  Virtuous character and ethical sensibility
  13.18, 4.10, 11.22, 1.11, 1.13, 2.24, 7.3, 14.12, 4.16, 7.16, 7.12, 2.10
Confucius' political philosophy
  Virtuous rulership
  2.1, 12.17, 12.19, 13.6, 13.13, 2.3, 12.13, 14.41, 4.13, 6.27, 1.2, 1.5, 12.22, 13.9, 11.26, 15.1, 13.29, 13.30, 16.1, 14.42

Roles, responsibilities, and names
13.3, 12.11, 6.25, 3.26
When *dao* does not prevail
5.2, 5.7, 5.21, 18.6, 18.7, 18.8, 8.13, 4.18
Confucius' worldview and attitude towards spiritual matters
5.13, 17.2, 6.28, 8.19, 11.9, 14.35, 7.23, 9.5, 14.36, 7.35, 9.12, 11.12, 16.8,
17.19, 20.3, 12.5

INDEX OF KEY PHILOSOPHICAL TERMS AND CONCEPTS IN THE *ANALECTS*

---

* Parentheses indicate that the key philosophical term is not explicitly used in the passage, though its idea is nonetheless implied.

† Bold type indicates particularly informative passages.

INDEX OF PASSAGES

17.13	88		18.8	103		19.14	76
17.19	108		19.1	87		19.25	79
18.6	102		19.6	83		20.3	108
18.7	103		19.7	89			

ENDNOTES

[a] See Slingerland 2003, xxii; Schwartz 1985, 64–66; Ivanhoe 2000, 1–4.

[b] See Legge 1960, vol. 1, 156.

[c] There seems to be an extra "not" in the text, probably an interpolation.

[d] *Xun Zi* 5.7, not included in this anthology.

[e] See Legge 1960, vol. 5, 826.

[f] *Meng Zi* 6B8, not included in this anthology.

[g] Hansen 1983, 181n.

[h] *Analects* 9.2, not included in this anthology.

[i] *Li Ji*, Quli B (*Book of Ritual Propriety*, Chapter 2).

5

Meng Zi (Mencius)

INTRODUCTION

Meng Zi (372–289 BCE), often referred to in the West by the Latinized name "Mencius," is reputed to have been a direct student of Confucius' grandson, Zisi, though this is generally regarded by scholars to be improbable. He has been called "the second sage." He not only defended Confucianism against early critics, such as the Mohists, but he also developed a particular interpretation of Confucius' philosophy. Possibly in an effort to best defend Confucianism against challenges, Meng Zi's most distinctive contribution is his attempt to ground the Confucian virtues in natural human dispositions. According to Meng Zi, because we naturally have "sprouts" of virtue, it is important to nurture our natural dispositions so that they are not harmed, and so that they may fully develop into virtues. However, we must be careful, for we may unwittingly harm them ourselves. The process begins with natural familial love and affection, which we are to extend to cover increasing circles. However, Meng Zi rejects the Mohist idea that we can or should exhibit "impartial care" (*jian'ai* 兼爱) to all people equally.

When we act, Meng Zi encourages us both to conscientiously consider norms of proper conduct and to think empathetically. As our character grows, we become capable of exercising a positive influence. And rulers who cultivate their feelings will institute *ren* governance, one that exhibits empathetic effort on behalf of the people, which Meng Zi implies will have positive effects for all concerned.

Below, passages from the *Meng Zi* are divided into three major categories: human nature, ethical philosophy, and political philosophy. (Since passages are not arranged in the traditional order, indices are provided at the end of the chapter.)

MENG ZI'S VIEW OF HUMAN NATURE

The Sprouts of Virtue

Meng Zi maintains that people naturally possess at least the beginnings of caring feelings and altruistic dispositions. The word translated "sprout" is *duan* 端, meaning "beginning points," which Meng Zi interprets botanically in accordance with its etymology. The "four sprouts" are nascent feelings that have the propensity to grow and blossom into virtues, namely, *ren* (humanity), *yi* (integrity/conscientiousness), *li* (ritual propriety), and *zhi* (wisdom). Meng Zi suggests that people generally grow to be "largely reliable" (*Meng Zi* 6A7), so long as they are not deprived of basic needs. His defense of this view is most clearly and famously depicted in passage 2A6 (p. 116, below), which involves a stranger passing a child who is about to fall into a well. The stranger, it is suggested, would be moved to react, spontaneously, to prevent the child from falling into the well. According to Meng Zi, since everyone would be *spontaneously* moved to do this, not moved out of some self-interested calculation, this shows that there are natural altruistic dispositions in everyone. However, Meng Zi maintains, it is possible for these dispositions to be damaged, and this is how one can account for wicked individuals—though if their virtuous dispositions were entirely destroyed, Meng Zi would hesitate to call them "people."

Meng Zi's view that natural dispositions are good is later vigorously challenged by a fellow Confucian, Xun Zi (see *Xun Zi*, Chapter 23, p. 218).

4B19 Meng Zi said, "Scant difference distinguishes humans (*ren* 人) from beasts. The masses neglect this difference; *junzi* 君子 (exemplary persons) preserve it. [The sage-king] Shun, having insight into the things of the world, and scrutinizing human relationships, acted *from ren* 仁 (humanity) and *yi* 義 (integrity/conscientiousness). It is not that he enacted them."

> *Comment:* In other words, *ren* and *yi* are not simply human constructions. Rather, exemplary human activity is a product of *ren* and *yi*, which are internal qualities that develop naturally in human beings. Sages exhibit these qualities most fully and clearly.

6A6 Gongdu Zi said, "Gao Zi says, 'Natural disposition (*xing* 性) is without either goodness or badness.' Others say, 'Dispositions (*xing*) can be made good, and can be made bad. And thus, when inspired by King Wen and King Wu the common people were prone to goodness, and when inspired by King You and King Li they were prone to violence.' And still others say, 'There is both goodness and badness in natural dispositions. And thus, [even] during the reign of the sage-king Yao there was [Shun's evil brother] Xiang. And the [wicked] Blind Man was the father of [the sage-king] Shun. And, [the good] Viscount Qi of Wei and Prince Bigan had [the evil] King Zhòu as both their nephew and their ruler.' Now, you say, 'Natural dispositions are good (*xing shan* 性善).' So, are all these others wrong?"

Meng Zi said, "People's emotional disposition (*qing* 情) can become good. That is why I call it good. As for it becoming bad, it is not the fault of the raw material (*cai* 才). All people have a heart (*xin* 心) of compassion, a sense of shame, feelings of respect, and a sense of what to affirm and what to reject. A heart of compassion is associated with *ren* 仁 (humanity), a sense of shame with *yi* 義 (integrity/conscientiousness), feelings of respect with *li* 禮 (ritual propriety), and a sense of what to affirm and what to reject is associated with *zhi* 智 (wisdom).

> Comment: The word *xin* 心 means "heart," and is associated with feeling (as well as thinking). Here it is translated as "heart," "sense," and "feeling."

"*Ren, yi, li,* and *zhi* are not melded into us from the outside. We have them intrinsically. We just don't think about it. And thus some say, 'Strive, and you will attain it. Give up, and you will lose it.' The reason some people are many times better than others is that [the lesser ones] are unable to make full use of their endowments (*cai* 才). The *Odes* say,

> *Tian* 天 spawns the teeming masses, and
> Where there are creatures, there are norms.
> The people hold to what feels natural,
> And thus cherish this admirable potency of character (*de* 德).

"Confucius commented, 'The writer of this Ode really knows the way (*dao* 道)!' Thus, where there are beings, surely there are norms. And the people hold on to what feels natural, and thus cherish this admirable *de*."

7A15 Meng Zi said, "What people are able to do without learning is virtuous ability. What they know without mulling over is virtuous knowledge. There are no infants who do not know how to love their parents. And when they grow up, they know how to respect their elder brothers. The tender feeling we have toward our closest relatives is *ren* 仁. The respect we show toward our elders is appropriate (*yi* 義). There is nothing else to do but make these manifest throughout the world."

Comment: The goodness of natural dispositions arises from the natural feelings one has for one's family members, beginning in infancy. This passage also suggests that these natural feelings ought to be extending beyond where they occur spontaneously. This is central to Meng Zi's ethical philosophy (see *Meng Zi* 7B31, p. 127, below). However, Meng Zi criticizes the Mohist idea of impartial care (see *Meng Zi* 3B9 and 7A26, both on p. 133, below).

4B12 Meng Zi said, "A great person is someone who does not lose the heart of a newborn babe."

2A6 Meng Zi said, "All people have compassionate feelings.

Comment: The phrase translated "compassionate feelings" (不忍人之心) can be understood more literally as "a heart that cannot bear [the suffering of] others."

"The first kings, having compassionate feelings, also had compassionate governance. Using compassionate feelings to put into practice compassionate governance, they brought order to the world as though carrying it in the palms of their hands. Here is the reason that I say that all people have compassionate feelings: Suppose a person suddenly saw a child about to fall into a well. Any such person would have feelings of concern and compassion. It is not a matter of wishing to ingratiate oneself with the child's parents. It is not a matter of wanting praise from fellow villagers, companions, or friends. It is surely not a matter of being bothered by the sound [of the child's cry]. Looking at it this way, without a sense of compassion, one is not a person. Without a sense of shame, one is not a person. Without a sense of deference, one is not a person. Without a sense of approval and disapproval (*shi fei* 是非), one is not a person.

"A sense of compassion is the sprout of *ren* 仁 (humanity); a sense of shame is the sprout of *yi* 義 (integrity/conscientiousness); a sense of deference is the sprout of *li* 禮 (ritual propriety); a sense of right and wrong is the sprout of wisdom (*zhi* 智). People have these four sprouts (*duan* 端) just as they have four limbs. Those who have these four sprouts and yet say they are personally incapable [of exhibiting the corresponding virtues] injure themselves. Those who say that their ruler is incapable injure their ruler. Generally, having the four sprouts in us and knowing how to completely expand and fulfill them is like igniting a flame, or a spring breaking through [the ground]. If one can fulfill them, this will suffice to be the protector of the four seas. If one does not fulfill them, one will not even be able to serve one's parents."

> *Comment:* For Meng Zi, *yi* 義 may be understood in terms of conscientiousness and integrity in the sense that it indicates painstaking attentiveness to normative considerations with a commitment to impeccably honorable conduct. It implies a high normative standard of "appropriateness."

4A27 Meng Zi said, "The fruit of *ren* 仁 is serving one's parents. The fruit of *yi* 義 is following one's elder brother. The fruit of wisdom (*zhi* 智) is understanding these two things, and never departing from them. The fruit of ritual propriety (*li* 禮) is the regulation of these two with cultured refinements. The fruit of music is enjoying these two things. If they are enjoyed they give life. If they give life, how can one stop? Not being able to stop, one's feet skip to it and hands wave to it without even knowing."

6A1 Gao Zi said, "Natural disposition (*xing* 性) is like a willow tree; *yi* 義 is like cups and bowls. Using natural disposition (*xing*) to form people manifesting *ren* 仁 and *yi* is like using a willow tree to make cups and bowls."

Meng Zi replied, "Can you follow the disposition of the willow in making it into cups and bowls? [No.] Only after it is mutilated can it be made into cups and bowls. If one must mutilate a willow to make cups and bowls out of it, must one also mutilate people to make them *ren* and *yi*? Surely, your doctrine will lead the people of the world to ruin *ren* and *yi*."

> *Comment:* One can make cups and bowls out of a willow tree, but not because being a cup or bowl is an inherent part of the nature of a willow. It is a matter of shaping them (cf. *Xun Zi* 19.5b and 23.1b, pp. 195 and 221). Meng Zi is arguing that Gao Zi's analogy does not hold, that it has absurd implications. Further, trying to make dispositions proper by external imposition will have disastrous results. Meng Zi makes this clear in 2A2 (p. 126, below), in which a man pulls on his seedlings to help them grow, thereby inadvertently harming them.

6A2 Gao Zi said, "Natural disposition (*xing* 性) is like flowing water. If one channels it to the east, it flows east. If one channels it to the west, it flows west. The natural disposition (*xing*) of people has no affinity for either good or bad, just as water has no affinity for east or west."

Meng Zi replied, "Water truly has no affinity for east or west, but is it indifferent to up and down? The goodness of natural human disposition is like the tendency of water to go down. There are no people who possess [a natural tendency] to be bad, and there is no water that has [a natural tendency] to go up. Now, if one slaps water and splashes it up, one can force it over one's head. If one forces it into a channel, one can make it stay up on a mountain. But how is this the natural disposition of water? It is the circumstances that bring about these conditions. People can be made to be bad because their disposition is analogous to this."

6A3 Gao Zi said, "*Sheng* 生 is what is meant by '*xing*' 性 (natural disposition)."

> *Comment*: The word "*sheng*" 生 is ambiguous. Its plausible meanings here include "life" and "what is inborn." Note that the character "生" is a component of the character "性." Both characters have similar pronunciations (in both modern and classical Chinese), and they were sometimes both written "生." Gao Zi may be appealing to this to give prima facie plausibility to his claim.

Meng Zi replied, "Is '*sheng* is what is meant by "*xing*"' analogous to white being called 'white'?"
[Gao Zi] said, "Yes."
[Meng Zi said,] "The white of white feathers is like the white of white snow, and the white of white snow is like the white of white jade. Yes?"
[Gao Zi] said, "Yes."
[Meng Zi said,] "So, [are you saying that] a dog's natural disposition is like that of an ox, and the natural disposition of an ox is like that of a person?"

> *Comment*: If "*sheng*" means 'life' it would seem right to say that it operates like the word "white"—a live dog and a live ox and a live person all share the same quality of being alive. But if "*sheng*" means 'what is inborn,' which is more plausible as a definition of "*xing*" (natural disposition), then it seems that it does not operate like the word "white"—the inborn nature of a dog is not the same as that of an ox or a person.
>
> Gao Zi may have been taking advantage of the ambiguity in the meaning of "*sheng*," wanting to imply that all living things share the same *xing* (which, on his view, meant lacking any specific disposition) while relying on the plausibility of the notion that all living things share the same *sheng* in the sense of "living." By asking if *xing* is analogous to white,

Meng Zi is forcing Gao Zi to clarify what he means so that the falsity of what Gao Zi intends to imply is clear.

6A7 Meng Zi said, "In years of abundance, young men are largely reliable. In years of famine, they are largely unruly. This is not due to their natural raw material. It is due to special circumstances that drown their natural feelings (*xin* 心).

> *Comment:* Unlike in years of want, in years of abundance young men are not pressed by circumstances into inappropriate conduct. And thus, their natural goodness tends to shine through, and they are therefore largely reliable. But, since their character has not fully developed, if they are pressed by circumstances they may stray from the path.

"Consider barley: Sow the seeds and cover them. The soil is the same. The time of planting is also the same. They burst through with life, and by the time of the summer solstice they all have ripened. Even if there is some difference, it is because there is unevenness in the soil's fertility, in the amount of moisture received, as well as in cultivation. Thus, what is of the same type will develop to be similar. This is only doubted when it comes to people—why is that? The sages are of the same type as we are. Thus, Long Zi said, 'If someone makes a sandal for a foot of which he has no specific knowledge, I know he will not make a basket.' Sandals resemble each other because throughout the world feet are alike.

"There is a commonality in what is enjoyed as flavorful to the palate. [The master chef] Yi Ya was first in realizing what is enjoyable to our tastes. If flavor was by nature particular to each person, just as dogs and horses are different from humans in kind, then why does everyone in the world enjoy the flavors of Yi Ya? Since the whole world strives to be like Yi Ya in achieving flavor, the palates of the world must be similar to each other. This is also so of the ear. Since the whole world strives to be like Shi Kuang in producing music, ears throughout the world must be similar to each other. And this is also so of the eye. Nobody in the world fails to recognize the handsomeness achieved by Zidu. To fail to recognize Zidu's handsomeness is to be blind.

"Thus, I say, 'There is a commonality in what is enjoyed as flavorful to the palate. There is commonality in what is heard as musical to the ear. There is commonality in the appearance of beauty to the eye. 'Is it only in the achievements of heart (*xin* 心) that there is no such commonality? What are the commonalities of the heart? They are coherence (*li* 理) and *yi* 義 (integrity/conscientiousness). The sages were simply first in realizing the commonalities in our hearts. Thus, coherence and *yi* delight our hearts just as the meat of hay-fed animals delights our palates."

> *Comment:* Xun Zi seems to agree that people are similar in their tastes and desires, and he even appeals to similar analogies (see *Xun Zi* 4.10, 4.11, and 19.1b, pp. 164 and 191). Meng Zi suggests here that we all, like the sages, find pleasure in coherence and the honorable conduct that stems from painstaking attention to normative considerations. In contrast, Xun Zi suggests that our common desires are selfish. And while Xun Zi believes that *yi* distinguishes human beings from animals, he does not conceive of *yi* as arising from emotional dispositions, as Meng Zi does.

6A8 Meng Zi said, "Ox Mountain's trees were once beautiful. But due to its proximity to a great state, they were felled by hatchets and axes. How can it now be regarded as beautiful? There were days and nights of respite, and the rain and dew provided moisture, so it is not as though there were no sprouts growing on it. But then cattle and sheep were brought there and ate them. This is why it seems barren. When people see it barren, they assume it was never wooded. But how can this be the dispositional nature (*xing* 性) of the mountain?

"Even considering humans (*ren* 人), how could they lack a heart of *ren* 仁 (humanity) and *yi* 義 (integrity/conscientiousness)? The means by which people lose their virtuous heart (*liang xin* 良心) can indeed be likened to the relation between axes and trees. Being hacked day after day, can they thereby become beautiful?

"With days and nights of respite, and the calming of the morning air (*qi* 氣, energies), the affections and aversions of people are not far apart. But if such occasions are rare, then one's daily activities shackle and destroy [these natural human feelings]. If one shackles them repeatedly, the night *qi* will not be sufficient to preserve them. If the night *qi* is not sufficient to preserve them, one will degenerate to a level not far from birds and beasts. People who see this beastliness will infer that there never was any endowment of positive disposition in them. [But] how could this be the natural emotional conditions (*qing* 情) of people?

"Thus, there is nothing that will not mature if nurtured; and nothing that will not diminish if deprived of nurturance. Confucius said, 'Hold on, and you will retain it; let go, and you will lose it. Its comings and goings have no special season, and no one knows its original place.' Perhaps this is a reference to one's heart."

6A10 Meng Zi said, "Fish is something I desire. Bear's paw [a delicacy] is also something I desire. If I had to choose, I would forgo the fish, and take the bear's paw. Life is also something that I desire, and so too is integrity (*yi* 義). If I had to choose, I would forgo life and take integrity. Life is something I desire, but there is something that I desire more than life. Thus, I will not act with moral indifference to attain it. Death is something I loathe, but there is something that I loathe more than death. Thus, there are grave perils that I will not avoid. If there were no human desire stronger than the desire for life, then there would be nothing that people would not do to avoid grave peril. It follows that there are means of living that generally will not be employed; there are things that [people] will not do to avoid peril. Thus, people desire something more than life and loathe something more than death. Not only the worthy (*xian* 賢) have this heart. All people have it. The worthy are just able to not lose it.

"[Suppose] that if one got a basket of food and a bowl of soup one would live, but if not one would die. If these were given with contempt, even a street person would not accept it. Even a beggar, if given it with a kick, would disregard [the food]. But when it comes to a lavish salary, people accept it without consideration of ritual propriety (*li* 禮) or integrity (*yi*). Yet what does a lavish salary provide one? Is it for the elegance of a palatial room, for wives and concubines, or for the indebtedness of needy acquaintances? In the former case, the food is refused even at the cost of death; and yet, in the latter case a lavish salary is accepted for an elegant palatial room, for wives and concubines, and for the indebtedness of needy acquaintances. Is this really a matter of not being able?[1] This is called losing one's root feelings (*ben xin* 本心)."

3A4 [...] Meng Zi said, "[...] When well fed, with warm clothes, living in ease and ignorance, people approach the level of brutes. The sage [Shun] was concerned about this. So he put Xie in charge of education. Xie taught human relationships, namely: [1] There are feelings of affection between father and child. [2] There are appropriate norms (*yi* 義) for rulers and ministers. [3] There are different roles for husbands and wives. [4] There is a hierarchy among older and younger siblings. And, [5] there is faithfulness (*xin* 信) between friends and colleagues. [These are collectively known as "the five relations."] [The sage-king] Yao said, 'Recompense their labors and draw them near, assist them in becoming straight, help and protect them, enable them to achieve things themselves, and then one may also stimulate them to compelling character (*de* 德).'" [...]

---

1 Cf. *Meng Zi* 1A7(iii), p. 141.

3A5 The Mohist Yi Zhi, through Xu Bi [a follower of Meng Zi], requested a meeting with Meng Zi. Meng Zi said, "I would certainly like to meet with him, but now I feel suddenly ill. I will go see him when I've recovered. He need not come here." ·

Another day, Yi Zhi again asked to see Meng Zi. Meng Zi said, "I can [not] meet with him now. But if he is not straightened out, the way will not be apparent. So I will straighten him out. I have heard that Yi Zhi is a Mohist. And Mohists, when it comes to regulating funerals, take frugality as their *dao*. Yi Zhi thinks this will change the world. How could he take it to be not affirmable and not valuable? And yet, since he gave his own parents a lavish burial, he served his parents with what he regards as ignoble."

Xu Bi told this to Yi Zhi.

Yi Zhi said, "For Confucians, following the way of the ancients is [as the *Book of Documents* says] 'like protecting a newborn babe.' What do these words mean? I take this to mean caring (*ai* 愛) without difference in degree, and this is carried out beginning with one's parents."

Xu Bi told this to Meng Zi.

Meng Zi said, "Does Yi Zhi genuinely believe that the love people feel for their brother's children is just like their love for other children in the neighborhood? Yi Zhi has seized upon only this: When a child is about to fall into a well, it is not the child's fault.

Comment: Presumably the last line is a reference to the story in *Meng Zi* 2A6, p. 116, above.

"All of *tian*'s creatures [i.e., people] are engendered with a single root, and yet on Yi Zhi's account there are two roots. In very early times, there were peoples who did not bury their parents. When parents died, they were discarded in ditches. Later, passing by, someone observed foxes and such eating them, and flies and gnats biting them. His forehead broke out into a sweat; he turned away and could not look. Now, he did not sweat for the sake of show. His inner heart (*xin* 心) expressed itself in his face and eyes. And he returned home for a basket and shovel to cover them up. If covering them was truly right (*shi* 是), then when filial sons and persons who are *ren* 仁 bury their parents, this surely is also proper."

Xu Bi told this to Yi Zhi. Stunned for a moment, Yi Zhi said, "I stand corrected."

Is *yi* 義 Internal or External?

As a corollary to the idea that natural human dispositions are good, Meng Zi maintains that *yi* 義 (integrity/conscientiousness)—which he believes develops from a natural sense of shame—is internal. In other words, *yi* is an internal feeling, sense, or disposition not simply a standard determined by external circumstances.

6A4 Gao Zi said, "[Desire for] food and sex are natural dispositions (*xing* 性). *Ren* 仁 (humanity) is internal, not external. But *yi* 義 (integrity/conscientiousness) is external, not internal."

Meng Zi asked, "Why do you call *ren* internal and *yi* external?"

[Gao Zi] replied, "When I treat others as elders it is because *they* are older, not because they are elders of *mine*. Similarly, I treat something as white because *it* is white. It follows that whiteness is external. This is why I call [*yi*] external."

[Meng Zi] responded, "[*Yi* and elderliness] are different from whiteness. The whiteness of a white horse is no different from the whiteness of a white [i.e., gray-haired] person. But is there no difference between the elderliness of an old horse and that of an elder? Furthermore, is it the elder who behaves conscientiously (*yi*), or is it the one who treats him as an elder who behaves conscientiously?"

[Gao Zi] said, "I love my younger brother, but I do not love the younger brother of the man from Qin. In this case, I am the one who is pleased (*yue* 悅). [That is, I serve as the explanation (*shuo* 說).] So, I call [love, which is associated with *ren*,] internal. [On the other hand,] I treat the elderly man from Chu as an elder, and also treat my own elders as elders. In this case the elders are pleased (*yue* 悅). [That is, the elders serve as the explanation (*shuo* 說).] Thus I call it external."

[Meng Zi] responded, "Enjoying (*shi* 耆) a roast provided by someone from Qin is no different from enjoying my own roast, [which shows that what you describe] can also be so of things. So, then, is the enjoyment of a roast also external?"

Comment: The character *yue* 悅 (to be pleased) in this passage is often read as *shuo* 說 (explain). But there may be a visual punning going on here, and so both meanings are provided in the translation above. Just as one treats elders with equal respect regardless of whether or not they are one's own elders, as Gao Zi has pointed out, so too one's enjoyment— being *pleased* with the taste—of a roast is the same whether or not it is one's own roast. Surely, Meng Zi implies, that does not prove that the explanation/enjoyment lies in the roast. This is supposed to show that Gao Zi's example fails to establish that *yi* is external.

6A5   Meng Ji Zi asked Gongdu Zi, "Why do you say that *yi* 義 is internal?"

[Gongdu Zi] replied, "[My] conduct (*xing* 行) [comes from] *my* respect. This is why I call it internal."

[Meng Ji Zi] asked, "If a fellow villager is one year older than your elder brother, which one do you respect?"

[Gongdu Zi] answered, "I respect my older brother."

[Meng Ji Zi] asked, "To whom do you serve wine first?"

[Gongdu Zi] said, "I serve the villager first."

[Meng Ji Zi] said, "So, you respect one, and yet treat the other as an elder. Thus, [*yi*] depends on what is external. It does not come from what is inside."

Comment: Meng Ji Zi suggests that while *respecting* someone may be internal, *treating* with respect, which he seems to consider analogous to *yi* 義, is external. And indeed, impeccable conduct, such as performing a display of respect by serving a fellow villager before your older brother (which the examples imply is *not* a reflection of actual respect), does not come from inside, but is rather dictated by the external situation.

Gongdu Zi was not able to respond, and reported the incident to Meng Zi.

Meng Zi said, "[Ask him,] 'Do you respect your uncle or your younger brother?' He will say, 'I respect my uncle.' Ask him, 'If your younger brother is playing the role of an ancestor during a ritual, then whom do you respect?' He will say, 'I respect my younger brother.' Then you ask, 'Where is your respect for your uncle?' He will say, 'It depends upon the circumstances.' You add, 'It depends upon the circumstances: in ordinary circumstances, respect goes to one's brother; in exceptional circumstances, respect goes to the villager.'"

Comment: In Meng Zi's view, the fact that it 'depends on the circumstances' does not show that *yi* is external. In both ordinary and exceptional cases, consummate conduct is driven by an internal sense of appropriateness (*yi*). It is just that this internal sense is informed by the situation. This would also apply to serving a villager before one's brother.

[Meng] Ji Zi heard about this and said, "Respect for my uncle is respect. Respect for my younger brother is [also] respect. [Who respect goes to] depends on what is external. It does not come from what is inside."

Gongdu Zi said, "On winter days one drinks hot water. On summer days one drinks cool water. Does this mean drinking and eating are also external?"

Comment: Here Gongdu Zi clarifies Meng Zi's point: In different circumstances, one *feels* differently. In the winter, one drinks hot water because one is internally motivated to do so. The fact that there is an obvious relation to external circumstances does not diminish the internal motivation. (Notice that this passage shows that Gongdu Zi was able to grasp Meng Zi's point and express it in his own way.)

MENG ZI'S ETHICAL PHILOSOPHY

In explicit contrast to the philosophy of Mo Zi, Meng Zi believed we naturally care more for some people—those emotionally close to us, such as family members—than we do for others. And, he thought, this is how it ought to be. However, although our good dispositions start with and remain strongest with family members, it is possible to take our kind feelings for those close to us and extend those feeling to others, though the intensity of these feelings will not be the same. This care with diminishing degrees stands opposed to Mo Zi's "impartial care." Although Meng Zi thought people naturally have within themselves "sprouts" of goodness, he still recognized the need for moral cultivation. After all, these naturally good dispositions were just "sprouts," not fully grown virtues. It is only through empathetic consideration that one can and should extend one's natural feelings.

Preserving and Nourishing One's Heart

Since Meng Zi views natural dispositions as good, it makes sense that he would advocate preserving those good tendencies. At the same time, since we are born with only the "sprouts" of virtues, not fully developed virtues, it also makes sense that a nurturing process would be important. This involves extending natural care for one's immediate family to wider circles, though there will remain differences in degrees of care. But Meng Zi warns that this cultivation must be such that innate dispositions are allowed to develop naturally, in accordance with their nature—after all, we don't want to mutilate our virtuous nature (as suggested in *Meng Zi* 6A1, p. 117, above). Meng Zi encourages us to focus on what is within our power, namely, doing what is proper and exhibiting *ren* (humanity), understood through empathetic consideration (*shu*).

––––––––––

2A2 [...] Gongsun Chou said, "May I ask, Master, wherein you excel?"

Meng Zi said, "I understand words, and I am good at nurturing my expansive *qi* 氣 (vital energy)."

Gongsun Chou said, "May I ask what you mean by expansive *qi*?"

Meng Zi said, "It is difficult to express in words. This *qi* is supremely expansive and powerful. If only it is nurtured and unharmed, it would fill the space between the heavens and the earth. This *qi* is a natural product of *yi* 義 (integrity) and *dao*, without which it starves. It is born of and grows (*sheng* 生) from the accumulation of consummate conduct (*yi* 義). It is not simply seized by repeating an appropriate (*yi* 義) motion. If one's conduct involves a feeling of dissatisfaction, it will starve. That is why I say that Gao Zi does not understand *yi*, since he treats it as external. One must attend to it, but not force one's feelings to conform. One must not neglect it, but one must not help it grow either. Do not be like the man from Song. Being worried that his seedlings would not grow, he pulled on them. He wearily returned home, and reported, 'Today I'm exhausted. I was helping my seedlings grow.' His son hurried to see. The seedlings were withered. There are few in the world who do not help seedlings grow. Those who see no benefit, giving up entirely, fail to weed their crops. Those who [try to] help them grow, pull on seedlings. This not only provides no benefit, it also harms them." [...]

4B26 Meng Zi said, "The people of the world talk of natural disposition (*xing* 性) only as a cause (*gu* 故), which is taking benefit (*li* 利) as the root.

> *Comment: Gu* 故 ("cause") implies basic conditions of outward manifestations and behavior, and Meng Zi contrasts it with his richer concept of living–emotional–ethical conditions expressed by *xing* 性.[2] Thinking in terms of mere cause and effect, Meng Zi suggests, treats consequences ("benefit") as what is most important, which leads so-called "wise men" to try to bring about their desired result by forcing things (see below).

––––––––––

2   *Gu* 故 can also mean old, and many interpreters read *gu* as suggesting some version of that meaning here. *Gu* is thus translated as, for example, "what is primordial" (Van Norden) or "the former theories" (Lau). These interpreters typically also interpret the last clause of the sentence differently. There is ample room for differences in interpretation here.

"What is deplorable in clever people is that they [try to] pound their way through. If they followed the way [the great sage] Yü channeled water, then there would be nothing to fault in their cleverness. Yü channeled the waters such that there was no interference. If the clever also channeled [natural dispositions] such that there was no interference, then they would also be great. The heavens (*tian* 天) are high, and the stars are distant. If one seeks their causes (*gu* 故), one can sit and determine the solstice of a thousand years hence."

> *Comment:* The solstices can be determined in advance because, presumably, their causes do not involve interference. If we allow our nature to develop naturally (channeled to allow it to express its natural disposition), then people will reliably become good (see *Meng Zi* 6A7, p. 119, and 1A7(v), p. 144). Before Yü, so the story goes, an attempt was made to control floods with dams. But that only made things worse. For good results, in other words, one must work with one's natural dispositions. Watering sprouts is one thing, pulling on them is another (see 2A2, p. 126, above).

7B31 Meng Zi said, "For all people (*ren* 人), there are things which are [morally] unbearable. *Ren* 仁 (humanity) is extending (*da* 達) this [attitude] to what one can bear. For all people, there are things they will not do. *Yi* 義 (conscientiousness) is extending this [attitude] to whatever one does." [...][3]

7B35 Meng Zi said, "For nourishing one's heart, there is nothing so effective as reducing desires. If people have but few desires, although there will be [good aspects of their nature] that are *not* preserved, they will be few. If people have many desires, although there will be [good aspects of their nature] that *are* preserved, they will be few."[4]

4B28 Meng Zi said, "*Junzi* 君子 (exemplary persons) are different from others in that they preserve their heart. They preserve their heart using *ren* (humanity) and ritual propriety. Those who are *ren* love others. Those who possess ritual propriety respect others. Those who love others are loved everywhere by others. Those who respect others are respected everywhere by others.

"If treated in a churlish and arrogant manner, a *junzi* will surely engage in self-reflection, saying, 'I must not exhibit *ren* (humanity); I must be

---

3 Cf. *Meng Zi* 7A15, p. 115.
4 Cf. *Meng Zi* 7A17, p. 132. See *Xun Zi* 22.5a (p. 166) for a criticism of reducing desire.

lacking in ritual propriety. How else could such a thing occur?' Upon self-reflection, if *ren* has been exhibited, and ritual propriety is possessed, and yet this treatment continues, the *junzi* will surely engage in further self-reflection, saying, 'I must not have done my utmost.' But upon self-reflection, if one has done one's utmost, and this treatment continues, the *junzi* says, 'These are nothing but wild people. How are they different from beasts? And so how could I expect more from them than from beasts?'

"Thus, *junzi* have lifelong concerns, but are without a single morning of anxiety. Regarding what one should be concerned about, consider the following example: Shun was human. I am also human. Shun provided a model for the world that can be passed down through the generations. I have not done better than to influence my fellow villagers. This is a legitimate concern. What is one to be concerned about? Simply about being like Shun. But regarding anxiety, *junzi* have none. If something is not *ren* 仁 (an expression of humanity), one does not do it. If it is inconsistent with ritual propriety, one does not proceed with it. Even if something troubling occurs, *junzi* are not anxious."

2A7   Meng Zi said, "How could an arrow maker and an armor maker be equal in *ren* 仁 (humanity)? The arrow maker's only worry is that people will *not* be harmed [by his arrows], while the armor maker's only worry is that people *will* be harmed [despite his armor]. So too with the healer and the coffin maker. Thus, one must be cautious about one's craft. [...]

"Those who have *ren* 仁 (humanity) are like archers. Archers assume the proper form, after which they release their shot. If their shot does not hit the mark, they do not blame those who hit it, but rather simply seek the cause within themselves."[5]

7A1   Meng Zi said, "Those who use their hearts to the fullest understand their natural disposition (*xing* 性). If one understands one's natural disposition (*xing*), one understands *tian* 天. Preserving one's heart and nurturing one's natural disposition (*xing*) is the means by which one serves *tian*. Don't let concerns for how long you will live unsettle you. Cultivate your own person (*shen* 身) and accept what comes. This is the way to take a stand amid the circumstances (*ming* 命)."

> Comment: Meng Zi characterizes *tian* and *ming* as follows: "That which is done through nobody's doing is the work of *tian* 天. What occurs when nobody brought it about is due to circumstances (*ming* 命)" (*Meng Zi* 5A6). The following passages provide more details about *ming*.

---

5   Cf. *Meng Zi* 4B28, p. 127.

7A2 Meng Zi said, "There is nothing that is not [influenced by] circumstance (*ming* 命), but one should yield to and accept only one's *proper* [result]. Thus, a person who understands *ming* does not stand beneath a wall that is poised to collapse. Those who die having lived their *dao* 道 to the fullest receive their proper *ming*. Those who die in shackles do not."

7A3 Meng Zi said, "'Strive, and you will attain it. Give up, and you will lose it.' In this case, one is sure to attain it because what one strives for resides in oneself. 'There is a *dao* 道 to striving for it, but attaining it depends on circumstances [beyond one's control] (*ming* 命).' In this case one is not sure to attain it because what one strives for is external."

> *Comment:* The first saying is also quoted in 6A6, which suggests that it is *ren* 仁 (humanity), *yi* 義 (integrity/conscientiousness), *li* 禮 (ritual propriety), and *zhi* 智 (wisdom) that are within one's power to attain. 'External' things, such as social status and wealth, depend on the contingencies of circumstance in addition to one's own efforts. Still, there is a proper way to strive to attain these. (Consider *Analects* 7.12, 7.16, p. 92, and compare *Analects* 8.13, p. 104.)

7B33 Meng Zi said, "For [the sage-kings] Yao and Shun, it was a matter of natural disposition (*xing* 性). [The great kings] Tang and Wu turned to it. Movements and manner revolving around ritual propriety achieve the highest influential character (*de* 德). Weeping in mourning for the dead is not done for the sake of [impressing] the living. Conducting oneself with unswerving virtue (*de* 德) is not to advance one's career. Words that are sure to be lived up to (*xin* 信) are not meant to [gain a reputation for] proper conduct. *Junzi* conduct themselves according to the proper model (*fa* 法) and simply leave the rest to circumstance (*ming* 命)."

7B16 Meng Zi said, "To be *ren* 仁 is to be a person (*ren* 人). *Dao* is the doctrine which puts these two together."

What to Do?

For Confucians, what constitutes proper conduct is mediated by norms associated with the various roles one occupies. At the same time, life presents challenging cases to which we are not expected to react robotically. We have to both think and feel in order to come up with a fitting course of action. The following passages address this issue.

4A17 Chunyu Kun said, "Men and women are not to touch hands when giving and receiving. Is that not ritual propriety (*li* 禮)?"

Meng Zi replied, "It is."

Chunyu Kun said, "If one's sister-in-law is drowning, should one help her with one's hand?"

Meng Zi replied, "To fail to help one's drowning sister-in-law is to be a beast. That men and women do not touch hands when giving and receiving is a matter of ritual propriety. When one's sister-in-law is drowning, helping her with one's hand is a matter of *quan* 權 (exigency)."

Chunyu Kun said, "Now the whole world is drowning. Why do you, Master, not help?"

Meng Zi responded, "When the whole world is drowning, one helps it with *dao* 道. When a sister-in-law is drowning, one helps her with a hand. Do you want me to help the world with my hand?"

> *Comment:* Meng Zi seems to be making the point that the relevant norm of ritual propriety applies only to *giving and receiving gifts*. *Quan* 權 literally means "to weigh," and here it would seem to mean weighing the importance of competing considerations—which in the case of a drowning sister-in-law is not difficult. *Quan* also has a sense of adaptability and flexibility, which also makes good sense in this context, even if one regards the touching of hands as more generally prohibited. And it has the related meaning "temporary measure." This suggests understanding *quan* here as being able to adapt to the special circumstances and, as a temporary measure, act in a way that may not be ordinarily proper. (See also *Meng Zi* 6A5, p. 124, and contrast *Meng Zi* 3B1, directly below; also consider *Analects* 1.12, p. 77, the point of which is that for large complex issues at least, following what seems expedient will not work. For Meng Zi's account of Mo Zi and Yang Zi's attitude toward helping the world, and also for additional remarks from Meng Zi about *quan*, see 7A26, p. 133.)

3B1 Chen Dai said, "Your refusal to meet with the feudal lords seems petty. If you were to meet with one, he could, at best, become kingly; and, at least, he might become a hegemon. Besides, the *Records* say, 'bend a foot so as to straighten three yards.' This seems like something you could do."

Meng Zi said, "[...] To say 'bend a foot so as to straighten three yards' is to speak of profit (*li* 利). In terms of profit, wouldn't it also be acceptable to bend three yards to straighten a foot? [...] Even a charioteer is ashamed to collaborate with an archer [to cheat in hunting]. Although if he collaborated they would attain a large pile of prey, he would not do it. How then would it be for me to bend the way to ingratiate these [lords]? Besides, you are mistaken. Never have those who bent themselves been able to straighten others."

4B6 Meng Zi said, "The great person will not abide by 'ritual propriety' (*li* 禮) that is not ritual propriety, nor abide by 'honorable conduct' (*yi* 義) that is not honorable (*yi* 義)."

> *Comment:* The second part suggests that one should be genuinely responsive to actual circumstances, not merely conform to standardized formulations or social expectations. After all, Meng Zi regards *yi* as internal. The first part of Meng Zi's comment is more ambiguous. Perhaps it is best understood as analogous to the second part, keeping in mind Xun Zi's remark, "If it is not timely and fitting, if it is not respectfully sociable, if it is not cheerfully enjoyed, although it may be beautiful, it is not ritual propriety" (*Xun Zi* 27.11).
>
> Note that this passage (and 4A17, p. 130, above) suggests that, like Confucius and Xun Zi, Meng Zi was also concerned about *zheng ming* 正名 (the proper use of terms). (Cf. *Analects* 6.25, p. 101, and 13.3, p. 100; *Meng Zi* 1B8, p. 147; as well as *Xun Zi*, Chapter 22, p. 208.)

4B8 Meng Zi said, "Only when there are things one will not do can one thereby have [significant] actions."

4B11 Meng Zi said, "The great person does not necessarily fulfill promises, and does not necessarily succeed in endeavors, being intent exclusively on what is *yi* 義 (appropriate/honorable)."

7A9 Meng Zi said to Song Goujian, "Are you fond of traveling [to counsel various rulers]? I'll give you some advice about this. If others appreciate you, maintain serene aloofness; if they don't appreciate you, also maintain serene aloofness."

Song Goujian replied, "How can one maintain this serene aloofness?"

Meng Zi said, "One maintains serene aloofness by honoring [one's own] compelling character (*de* 德) and finding joy in *yi* 義 (consummate conduct). Thus, scholar-officials do not fail to exhibit *yi* even in straitened circumstances, nor do they depart from the way (*dao* 道) when they become prominent. Because they do not fail to exhibit *yi* in straitened circumstances, they realize themselves. And because they do not depart from the way (*dao* 道) when they become prominent, the common people do not lose confidence in them. When the ancients realized their aspirations, blessings flowed to the common people. And when they did not realize their aspirations, their cultivated character was visible to the people of the time. In straitened circumstances they improved (*shan* 善) their own character alone; in prominence, they simultaneously improved the whole world."

7A17 Meng Zi said, "Do not do what is not to be done. Do not desire what is not to be desired. Be like this, and that is all."

7A33 Prince Dian [the son of the king of Qi] asked, "What is the task of an aspirant (*shi* 士)?"
    Meng Zi said, "To elevate one's aspirations (*zhi* 志)."
    The Prince asked, "What do you mean by that?"
    Meng Zi said, "[Aspire] solely to being *ren* 仁 (humane) and *yi* 義 (honorable). To kill a single blameless person is not to be *ren*. To take what is not yours is not *yi*. Where should one reside? In *ren*. On what road [should one travel]? On *yi* (honorable conduct). Residing in *ren* and following *yi* constitutes the fulfillment of the great person's tasks."

7A4 Meng Zi said, "The myriad things are all already provided for us. There is no greater joy than examining oneself sincerely. There is nothing closer to *ren* 仁 (humanity) than striving to put empathetic consideration (*shu* 恕) into practice."

> *Comment:* The idea that unites these three sentences is that people who strive after worldly possessions are on a fool's errand. On the one hand, as the first sentence suggests, the necessities of life are already provided for us. On the other hand, the greatest pleasure comes not from material things. Rather, our greatest joy and self-realization (achieving *ren*) comes from reflecting on and exhibiting an empathetic character. Socrates famously said, "The unexamined life is not worth living." Perhaps Socrates and Meng Zi were sharing an insight here.

7A37 Meng Zi said, "To provide [someone] with food without care is to treat them like a pig. To care for [someone] without respect is to treat them like a pet. A show of respect precedes the offering of a gift. But a show of respect that is not genuine cannot entrap *junzi*."

> *Comment:* Confucians are concerned not just about what to do, but also about what attitude to do it with.

7A40 Meng Zi said, "*Junzi* have five modes of instruction. [1] They enlighten the people with education like a timely rain. [2] They develop compelling virtuous character (*de* 德). [3] They inculcate positive qualities. [4] They respond to inquiries. And, [5] they exhibit personal refinement and self-discipline. These are the five modes of instruction of *junzi*."

> *Comment:* Ultimately, personal ethics is not only for one's own merit; it is to positively influence others.

Critique of Yang Zi and Mo Zi

7A26 Meng Zi said, "Yang Zi chose egoism (*wei wo* 為我, literally, being 'for oneself'). If he could benefit (*li* 利) the whole world by plucking a single hair, he would not do it. Mo Zi was for 'impartial care' (*jian'ai* 兼愛). If being pummeled from head to heel would benefit the world, he would do it. Zimo held to a middle course. Holding to the middle is closer to it. But holding to the middle without the proper balance (*quan* 權) is just like holding to one [extreme]. What is deplorable about holding on to one [extreme] is that it is detrimental to *dao* 道, singling out one [consideration] and casting aside a hundred others."[6]

3B9 Gongdu Zi said, "Outsiders all say you are fond of arguing. May I ask why?"

Meng Zi said, "How could I be fond of arguing? I simply have no choice. Ever since the beginning of the world, there have been times of order and times of chaos. [...]

"The discourse of the world today—if it doesn't smack of Yangism, it smacks of Mohism. Yang Zi's motto is 'for myself.' This denies one's ruler. Mo Zi's motto is 'impartial care' (*jian'ai* 兼愛). This denies one's father. To be without a father or a ruler is to be a beast. Gong Ming Yi said, 'There are rich meats in your kitchens, and well-fed horses in your stables. Yet the common people appear famished, and starved corpses are found in the countryside. This is leading beasts to feast on humans.'[7] The ways (*dao* 道) of Yang and Mo are repeated incessantly, while the way of Confucius is not expressed. These pernicious doctrines deceive the people, crowding out and obstructing *ren* 仁 (humanity) and *yi* 義 (integrity/conscientiousness). The result of *ren* and *yi* being crowded out and obstructed is 'leading beasts to feast on humans,' and people eventually will be eating each other. I am fearful about this. So I defend the

---

6 Cf. *Xun Zi* 21.4 (p. 203).
7 This sentence is also found in *Meng Zi* 1A4. See also *Meng Zi* 4A14, p. 151.

way of the ancient sages, oppose the views of Yang and Mo, and repel extreme sayings so that pernicious doctrines do not arise. For if such doctrines arise in one's heart, they will harm one's practices. And if they arise in one's practices, they will harm governance. When sages arise again, they will concur with what I have said. [...]

"The Duke of Zhou resisted the denial of father and ruler. I also wish to properly align people's hearts, extinguish pernicious theories, oppose misguided conduct, and repel extreme sayings, thereby following the three kings. How could I be fond of arguing? I simply have no choice. Being able to speak against Yang and Mo is being a follower of the sages."

Critique of "Respectable Villagers"

7B37 Wan Zhang asked, "When Confucius was in Chen, he said, 'Why don't we return home? My young followers are rash and inattentive to nuance; forging ahead, they do not forget their original [ways].' Why was Confucius thinking about his rash aspirants (*shi* 士) back in Lu while he was in Chen?"

Meng Zi said, "Confucius said, 'If one is not able to associate with those who strike the center (*zhong* 中) of the way (*dao* 道), one will surely be with either the rash or the scrupulous. The rash ones keep forging ahead; the scrupulous ones won't do certain things.'ᵃ Of course Confucius wanted followers who strike the center of the way (*dao*). But, not being sure he could get them, he thought of those who were next best."

Wan Zhang said, "May I venture to ask what it takes to be called 'rash'?"

Meng Zi said, "Qin Zhang,[8] Zeng Xi, and Mu Pi are examples of what Confucius refers to as 'rash.'"

Wan Zhang said, "Why are they called 'rash'?"

Meng Zi said, "They pompously proclaim their aspirations,[9] saying, 'The ancients! The ancients!' But if one calmly reflects on their conduct, they don't live up to it. Not able to acquire rash [followers], [Confucius] would want to obtain and associate with aspirants who fastidiously refrain from impure conduct; these are the scrupulous ones. They are next best. Confucius said, 'The only ones who pass by my door without entering, about which I have no regrets, are the respectable villagers. Respectable villagers are thieves of virtue (*de* 德).'"[10]

Wan Zhang said, "What is a 'respectable villager'?"

---

8 Qin Zhang might be Confucius' follower Zi Zhang. In any case, Zi Zhang is a follower who fits the description.

9 Cf. *Analects* 11.26, p. 96.

10 See *Analects* 17.13, p. 88.

Meng Zi said, "[Respectable villagers say,] 'What is all this pompous talk [of the rash aspirants]? Their words do not match their conduct. And their conduct does not match their words. They say, "The ancients! The ancients!" And, [on the other hand,] what is it with the conduct [of the scrupulous aspirants], so aloof? They live in the present age, so they should act according to the present age. Being good (*shan* 善) according to the age is to be approved (*ke* 可).' Pleasing everyone of the present age, like a eunuch—these are the respectable villagers."

Wan Zhang said, "In any village, everyone praises the respectable villagers. And wherever they go they are regarded as honest folk. Why does Confucius regard them as thieves of *de* 德?"

> *Comment:* Moral relativism is the view that morality is relative to the moral evaluations of some group. (If what determines morality is one's culture, it is called "cultural relativism.") Here Wan Zhang, in effect, raises the question: What is wrong with moral relativism?

Meng Zi said, "One can cite nothing for which to reproach them. Criticizing them is without any sting. They partake in the common customs, and conform to [the norms of] a crooked age. In their community, they seem to be wholeheartedly committed (*zhong* 忠) and faithful (*xin* 信). They seem to conduct themselves with integrity and temperance. And the masses are all pleased with them. And they even see themselves as right. And yet one is not able to enter into the *dao* of Yao and Shun with such a person. That is why they are called 'thieves of *de* 德.'

> *Comment: De* 德 signifies influential virtuous character, through which standards of proper conduct are expressed and encouraged. (Cf. *Analects* 12.19, p. 93; see also the "Key Philosophical Terms" chapter.) But "respectable villagers" simply reflect the corrupted conventional expectations of their time, rather than taking a stand for what is genuinely proper. (See *Analects* 9.3, p. 76, for an example of Confucius taking a stand, through his actions, on which common practices are to be followed and which are to be rejected.)

"Confucius said, 'I detest what is not what it seems: I detest weeds for fear they will be confused with seedlings. I detest clever [conduct] for fear it will be confused for *yi* 義 (integrity/honorable conduct). I detest clever speech for fear it will be confused with faithfulness (*xin* 信). I detest the tunes of Zheng for fear they will be confused with [genuine] music. I detest purple for fear it will be confused with [royal] red. I detest respectable villagers for fear that they will be confusedly thought to exhibit virtue (*de* 德). *Junzi* return to standards (*jing* 經) and that is all. If the standards (*jing* 經) are proper (*zheng* 正) then the common people will be uplifted. If the common people are uplifted, there will be no depravity and deceit.'"[11]

> *Comment:* In contrast to moral relativism, Meng Zi suggests that there are proper standards to be followed. A proper standard will be effective in uplifting people and thereby eliminating depravity. When *junzi* repeatedly return to such standards, which were formalized in ritualized norms, the standards are recursively reinforced.

MENG ZI'S POLITICAL PHILOSOPHY

Like Confucius before him, Meng Zi traveled and gave advice to various rulers, trying to convince them to adopt his Confucian strategy of *ren* 仁 governance, one that exhibits empathetic effort. In doing so, he often appealed to the king's sense of self-interest. Rulers had a strong desire to become "kingly," which has both a selfish, self-aggrandizing side and a socially responsible one. Everyone wants to be regarded as good, and rulers especially want a noble legacy. But to achieve that, as well as other benefits, Meng Zi implies, they would have to work harder for the benefit of the people.

Meng Zi locates the legitimacy of a ruler in their treatment of the people. This leads him to endorse a position that comes close to a right to revolution. In addition, while he implies that rulers tend to engage in warfare unnecessarily, and for selfish and misguided reasons, he does not seem to be a strict pacifist. He does not seem opposed to self-defense, for example. And he approves of the military endeavors of the great Kings Wu and Tang. Some interpreters believe this amounts to an endorsement of the doctrine of humanitarian intervention (with Confucian characteristics).[b] However, the conditions under which Meng Zi would condone military interventions seem to be so restrictive and implausible in the real world that, arguably, it would be inappropriate, and perhaps even perverse, to appeal to Meng Zi in support of any offensive war, even if it were based on humanitarian concerns.[c] After all, even though he seems to approve of the military activities of the semi-mythic sage-kings, he consistently opposes actual cases in his own time, and asserts that there were no honorable wars during the 300-year Spring and Autumn period (*Meng Zi* 7B2).

---

11   Cf. *Analects* 12.1 (p. 81), which suggests that repeatedly returning to ritual propriety (*li* 禮) is the way to uplift one, not just out of depravity, but to *ren* 仁 (humanity).

Meng Zi did in fact serve as adviser to two well-known heads of state, King Hui of Liang, and King Xuan of Qi. The following dialogues demonstrate how a Confucian idealist might remonstrate with a ruler, especially the more ethically challenged King Xuan.

Dialogues with King Hui of Liang

1A1 Meng Zi had an audience with King Hui of Liang. The king said, "Venerable sir, you traveled all this way thinking nothing of the great distance, surely you will have some means by which to profit (*li* 利) my state."

"Your Majesty," Meng Zi replied, "Why must you speak of profit. Indeed, I have *ren* 仁 (humanity) and *yi* 義 (integrity/honorable conduct) [to offer], and that is all. When a king says 'What will profit my state?' then high officials will say, 'What will profit my family?' and scholar-officials (*shi* 士) as well as common people will say 'What will profit myself?' Everyone becomes greedy, and the state will be imperiled.

"The murderer of a ruler of a state of 10,000 chariots is surely from a clan of 1,000 chariots. The murderer of a ruler of a state of 1,000 chariots is surely from a clan of 100 chariots. To have 1,000 chariots out of 10,000, or to have 100 out of 1,000 is no small amount. But if one puts *yi* last and profit first, one will not be satisfied without taking things by force. There has never been a case of one who has *ren* who was remiss towards his parents. There has never been a person who has *yi* who put his ruler last. Your Majesty should also speak only of *ren* and *yi*. What need is there to speak of profit?"

> *Comment:* In *Meng Zi* 6B4 (not included in this anthology), Meng Zi encounters the pacifist philosopher Song Zi who is off to see the kings of Chu and Qin with the intent of preventing war between them by persuading them that war is unprofitable. To this Meng Zi responds, "Your intention is great indeed, but your slogan will not do." Rather than focusing on profit, Meng Zi insists that the rulers should be persuaded to refrain from war because they are drawn to *ren yi* 仁義 (humanity and integrity/honorable conduct). With this approach, Meng Zi argues, other people will be influenced to act from similar motives.

1A4 King Hui of Liang said, "I wish to calmly receive instruction."

Meng Zi replied, "Is there a difference between killing someone with a staff and doing so with a knife?"

The king answered, "There is no difference."

Meng Zi asked, "Is there a difference between using a knife and using governance (*zheng* 政)?"

The king answered, "There is no difference."

Meng Zi said, "There are rich meats in your kitchens, and well-fed horses in your stables. Yet the common people appear famished, and starved corpses are found in the countryside. This is leading beasts to feast on humans.[12] People are repulsed even when animals eat each other. [A king is supposed to be] the father and mother of the people. Yet, if one governs such that one ends up leading beasts to feast on humans, in what way is one serving as the father and mother of the people? Confucius declared, 'Let the originator of tomb figurines have no descendants!' merely because objects *resembling* humans were used. How then should one regard causing the common people to starve to death?"

1A5 King Hui of Liang said, "No state in the world was as strong as [Liang], as you know. Yet, in my time as king, we were defeated by Qi in the east, where my eldest son died; we lost 700 *li* of land to Qin in the west; and we were humiliated by Chu in the south. I feel ashamed by this, and I wish to devote the rest of my life wholly to cleansing myself of this shame. How can I do this?"

Meng Zi replied, "One hundred square *li* is sufficient for one to be kingly. If you practiced *ren* 仁 (humanity) in governing the people—sparing punishments, reducing taxes, so that the fields will be deeply plowed and well cultivated—the strong would use their respite to cultivate their filial piety and faithfulness. In the home they would serve their parents and elder siblings, and in the community they would serve their elders and superiors. Such people could be enjoined to fashion simple staffs with which they would beat back even the well-armed and armored soldiers of Qin and Chu. States such as those deprive their people of the time to plow deeply and to thereby nurture their parents, who freeze and starve, causing families to scatter. Such states drown their own people. If a [genuine] king were to conduct punitive expeditions against them, who would treat him as an enemy? Thus it is said, 'Those who are *ren* (humane) have no enemies.' I urge Your Majesty to have no doubts about this."

> *Comment:* This passage seems to sanction punitive expeditions, but does it really? In fact, what Meng Zi is trying to do here is simply to convince

---

12   This sentence is also found in 3B9, where it is attributed to Gong Ming Yi. Cf. *Meng Zi* 4A14 (see p. 151).

the King to adopt humane governance. And he is framing his argument to address the King's aspiration. Presumably Meng Zi does believe what he is saying. But it is doubtful that he holds much hope that the King will ever fully satisfy the conditions that would make a punitive expedition of the kind he describes permissible or feasible. (If this is right, there is a sense in which Meng Zi is misleading the King.) Before engaging in a punitive expedition, the King would have to establish a moral differential between himself and those whom he would punish such that his people, armed only with makeshift weapons, would easily rout the well-armed troops of his adversaries. While that is highly unlikely to occur, Meng Zi presumably believes that there is an important sense in which he is *not* misleading the King. Namely, in addition to being true of an ideal case, his method of humane governance is the best way for a less-than-perfect king to maintain a strong and stable state, and to secure for himself a favorable reputation, truly wiping away any shame.

1A6 Meng Zi had an audience with [the new] King Xiang of Liang [who succeeded his father, King Hui]. Upon leaving, [Meng Zi] commented to others, "Observing [the King] from a distance, he did not seem like the ruler of the people. When I approached him, I did not see anything majestic in him. The King brusquely asked 'How does one pacify the world (*tian xia* 天下)?'

"I answered, 'Pacify by unifying.'

"[He asked,] 'Who would be able to unify it?'

"I answered, 'Someone who does not enjoy killing people could unify it.'

"[He asked,] 'Who would be able to give it?'

Comment: The King seems to be reasoning as follows: If leadership of the known civilized world, literally "all under the heavens" (*tian xia*), is not taken by force, then those who currently hold sway over various parts would have to willingly give up power. But who would do that? Meng Zi's answer shows that it is not so much that other rulers will give it, but that the common people will.

"[I replied,] 'No one in the world would not give it. Does Your Majesty know about seedlings? The seventh and eighth months are dry, and seedlings whither. When the heavens (*tian* 天) spontaneously generate dense clouds, and rain falls in abundance, the seedlings are rejuvenated. With something like this, who could hold it back? Now, among the shepherds of the civilized world, there are none who do not enjoy killing people. If there were one who did not enjoy killing people, then the common people of the world would all stretch their necks to see him. If he is truly like this, the common people will be drawn to him just as water streams downward. Surging forward, who could hold it back?'"

> *Comment:* The issue of how to pacify the people suggests that Meng Zi's references to "killing people" express, at least in part, a condemnation of warfare, since war is a common means by which "pacification" is attempted. At the same time, it probably also implies killing with bad governance, as mentioned in *Meng Zi* 1A4, p. 137, above. Meng Zi is accusing the rulers of his time of perverse "shepherding." And he is implying that it is through compassion and empathetic governance that universal peace and personal greatness—which is presumably the king's ultimate desire—is achieved.

Dialogues with King Xuan of Qi

1A7(i) King Xuan of Qi asked, "May I hear of the matter between Huan of Qi and Wen of Jin?"

Meng Zi replied, "None of Confucius' followers discussed this matter, and since there was nothing passed on about it, I have no information. So, shall we discuss kingliness (*wang* 王) [instead]?"

> *Comment:* Sometimes the word "*wang*" 王 (king) is simply used as a polite way of addressing a king, equivalent to "Your Majesty." However, when not used in this way, it often implies a king that truly lives up to that title, being "kingly." (This can be thought of in relation to *zheng ming* 正名, the proper use of terms, where terms have normative meanings; people who fill those roles ought to fulfill the associated responsibilities.) The implication of this is that Xuan currently lacks genuine kingliness. But Meng Zi is confident that the sprouts of his humanity are not entirely lost.

1A7(ii) The King said, "What sort of compelling character (*de* 德) enables kingliness?"

Meng Zi said, "A king who safeguards the people can be thwarted by no one."

The King said, "Would a man such as I be able to safeguard the people?"

"Yes."

"How do you know that I can?"

Meng Zi said, "I have heard from Hu He that, as Your Majesty sat in the hall, someone led an ox past the hall. You saw it and asked, 'What is this ox for?' He replied, 'It is to be sacrificed to consecrate the bell.' Your Majesty said, 'Release it. I cannot bear its trembling in fear, like an innocent person headed to the execution grounds.' The man responded, 'Does that mean we will forgo the consecration of the bell?' You said, 'How can we forgo that? Exchange it with a sheep.' I don't know if this really happened."

"It did."

"These feelings (*xin* 心) suffice for kingliness. While the hundred families all regarded you as begrudging the [loss of an ox], I'm convinced that it is rather that you could not bear [to see the ox being led to its death]."

The King said, "Yes! There was a genuine reason for what the people thought. But though Qi is a small state, how could I grudge the loss of a single ox. It was rather that I could not bear it trembling in fear, like an innocent person headed to the execution grounds. That is why I had it exchanged for a sheep."

Meng Zi said, "It is not surprising that the people thought you begrudged the ox. You exchanged something small for something large. How would they know [your true motivation]? If you were grieved because it was like an innocent person headed to the execution grounds, what difference does it make whether it is an ox or a sheep?"

The king laughed, saying, "Honestly, what was I thinking? It is not that I grudged its value, and yet I exchanged it for a sheep. It is understandable that the people say I grudged [the expense]."

Meng Zi said, "There is no harm in it. This is the method of [cultivating] *ren* (humanity). You had seen the ox, but had not seen the sheep. The attitude of *junzi* 君子 (exemplary persons) toward animals is: seeing them alive, they cannot bear to see their death; hearing their cries, they cannot bear to eat their flesh. That is why *junzi* stay away from the kitchen."

Comment: Partly, *junzi* stay away from the kitchen because they could not bear to eat an animal whose cries they had heard. However, keeping this distance, as well as the King's substitution of the sheep for the ox, is also a "method of cultivating *ren*." This is because, presumably, to do otherwise would interfere with the development of their emotional sensitivity, perhaps even engendering callousness. From this perspective, the King's action actually made sense.

1A7(iii) The King replied, "The *Odes* say, 'Other people have feelings (*xin* 心), and I plumb their depths.' This describes you. I was the one who did it, and yet when I searched myself, I was not able to grasp my own feelings. As you have said, my heart (*xin* 心) does contain feelings of commiseration. But why do these feelings conform with kingliness?"

Meng Zi said, "Suppose someone were to assert: 'I am strong enough to lift 1,500 pounds, and yet not strong enough to lift a single feather,' or 'I see clear enough to scrutinize the tip of an autumn hair, but not to see a cartload of firewood.' Would Your Majesty accept that?"

"No!"

"Then, how can your compassion (*en* 恩) possibly be sufficient to extend to animals, and yet not succeed in reaching the people? So then, if a feather is not lifted, it is because one has not applied one's strength to it. If a cartload of firewood is not seen, it is because one has not directed one's sight to it. If the people are not being protected, it is because you have not applied your compassion toward them. Thus, that Your Majesty is not kingly is a matter of not doing, it is not a matter of inability."

The King said, "How does someone who *does not* do something differ in appearance from someone who *cannot* do it?"

Meng Zi said, "If you tell others that you cannot take Mount Tai under your arm and leap over the North Sea, this is genuinely inability. But if you tell people that you cannot break off a twig for an elder, this is simply not doing; it is not a case of inability. Your Majesty's not being kingly is not in the same category of leaping over the North Sea with Mount Tai under your arm. It is in the category of not breaking a twig.

"Respect your own elders, and others will do likewise toward theirs; act tenderly toward your own youngsters, and others will do likewise toward theirs. Then you can hold the world in the palm of your hand. As the *Odes* say, 'A model to his wife, extended to his brothers, he thereby governed his family and state.' This just expresses how these feelings (*xin* 心) influence everyone else. And thus, if you extend your compassion, this will suffice for you to be protector of the four seas. But if you don't, you will not even be able to protect your wife and children. That by which the ancients surpass all others is nothing other than this: they were adept (*shan* 善) at extending what they did, and that is all.

"Now, how can your compassion possibly be sufficient to extend to animals, and yet not succeed in reaching the people? Weighing, we come to know light from heavy. Measuring, we come to know long from short. This is so of all things, and especially of the feelings (*xin*). Your Majesty, I suggest you to take measure of it. But Your Majesty delights in weapons and armies. You endanger soldiers and ministers. You incur the resentment of the feudal lords. Does this please your heart?"

1A7(iv) The King said, "No. How could I find pleasure in that? It is that I am pursuing my great desire."

Meng Zi said, "May I hear of your great desire?"

The King smiled, but did not respond.

Meng Zi said, "Do you not have enough savory foods for your mouth? Do you not have a sufficient supply of light and warm clothes for your body? Or, are the colorful displays insufficiently pleasing to your eye? Is there not enough music for your ears to hear? Are there not enough obsequious servants before you to carry out your commands? Any of Your Majesty's various ministers would be able to supply these things, so how could [your great desire] be for them?"

The King said, "No. It is not for such things."

Meng Zi said, "So then, Your Majesty's great desire can be surmised. You desire to expand your territory, to have the states of Qin and Chu at your court, to rule the central kingdoms, and to pacify the barbarian tribes. Seeking what you desire in this way is like climbing a tree to catch a fish."

The King said, "Is it that bad?"

Meng Zi said, "It is more perilous than that. If you climb a tree to catch a fish, although you will not catch any, there will be no calamity. But by seeking what you desire in this way, you will exhaust yourself emotionally and physically in the process, and it is sure to end in disaster."

The King asked, "May I hear more?"

Meng Zi asked, "If the people of Zou are at war with the people of Chu, who do you think would win?"

The King said, "The people of Chu would win."

Meng Zi said, "So then, the small certainly cannot defeat the large. The few certainly cannot defeat the many. The weak certainly cannot defeat the strong. Now, the land within the four seas, in units of thousands of square *li*, measures nine. Of this, the state of Qi occupies only one. How is using one to subdue eight different from Zou defeating Chu?

"Why not return to what is truly the root? If Your Majesty governs in a way that expresses *ren* 仁 (humanity), the officials of the world would all want to take their place in Your Majesty's court. The farmers would all want to plow Your Majesty's fields. Merchants would all want to house their wares in Your Majesty's markets. Travelers would all want to go by way of Your Majesty's roads. And anyone under the heavens that bore ill will toward their ruler would want to share their complaints with you. Under these conditions, who could prevent [you from achieving your ends]?"

1A7(v) The king said, "I am a blockhead, and would not be able to carry this forward. I would like you to help me to keep my intentions in line and enlighten me with your teachings. Although I am not sharp, please let me try it."

Meng Zi said, "Only a true aspirant (*shi* 士) is able to maintain a constant heart (*xin* 心) without a reliable means of subsistence. The people lack a reliable means of subsistence, and thus are unable to maintain constant hearts. Lacking constant hearts, they become uninhibited, depraved, and extreme, and they will stop at nothing. To punish them when they then fall into crime is entrapment. How could a person who has *ren* 仁 (humanity) entrap his people?

"For this reason, an enlightened ruler organizes the people's means of support, and is sure to engender respect sufficient to serve their parents, and humility sufficient to serve their wives and children. In good years they eat their fill, and in bad years they are at least able to avoid death. Then, they will go galloping toward the good (*shan* 善), and thus getting the people to follow is easy.

"The current organization of the people's means of support is neither sufficient for the people to serve their parents nor support their wives and children. In good years they suffer, and in bad years they cannot avoid death. In such a situation, the people strive only to escape death, and fear they will not be able. How will they find the leisure to cultivate ritual propriety (*li* 禮) and a sense of appropriateness (*yi* 義)?

"If Your Majesty desires to put this into practice, then why not return to the root. On each residence of 5 *mu*, plant a mulberry tree, and fifty-year-olds can wear silk. If you don't miss the breeding time for chickens, pigs, and dogs, then seventy-year-olds can eat meat. If you don't miss the planting time for fields of 100 *mu*, then even families of eight will not go hungry. If you take care with the curriculum in the schools, explaining the appropriateness (*yi* 義) of filial piety and fraternal respect, then the elderly would not be carrying heavy loads down the roadways. When the elderly wear silk clothes and eat meat, and the black-haired masses are neither hungry nor cold—there has never been a case of such conditions without kingliness."

1B3 King Xuan of Qi asked, "Is there a proper way (*dao* 道) to have relations with neighboring states?"

Meng Zi replied, "There is. Only those who are *ren* 仁 (humane) can use a great [state] to serve a small one. For example, King Tang served the kingdom of Ge, and King Wen served the Kun tribes. Only the wise are able to use the small to serve the large. Thus, King Tai served Xun

Yu, and Guo Jian served Wu. It is one who rejoices in *tian* 天 who uses a large [state] to serve a small one. It is one who is in fear of *tian* who uses a small state to serve a large one. One who rejoices in *tian* protects all under *tian* [i.e., the known civilized world]. One who fears *tian* protects their own state. The *Odes* say: 'Fearing *tian's* power, one protects one's state.'"

Comment (on international relations): Meng Zi's view of international relations involves quasi-moral hierarchical relations between states that parallel the hierarchical relations between family members. A genuine father, like a genuine ruler of a great state, lovingly looks after the interests of those lower in the hierarchy. And a son, like a small state, serves his father by following his loving guidance.

Comment (on tian*):* What inferences can we make about Meng Zi's view of *tian* 天, and on what our attitude toward it ought to be? First, one who rejoices in *tian* seems nobler than one who fears it. The one who fears it merely takes precautions against it, and thus is moved (that is, feels coerced) to protect his state. But one who rejoices in *tian*, feeling more secure and appreciative of the conditions *tian* has brought, is moved (inspired) to protect everybody. So, while acting out of fear of *tian* has some good results, it is not as good or noble as acting out of delight in *tian*. This tells us something about what our attitude toward *tian* ought to be. But it doesn't tell us much about the nature of *tian* itself. *Tian* is powerful, the Ode suggests, but does Meng Zi think it acts with intentionality? Is there some sort of moral or quasi-moral dimension to *tian*? Elsewhere Meng Zi says, "[…] *Tian* 天 does not speak, it informs by means of the 'course of things' (*xing* 行) and by events (*shi* 事), that is all […] The *Taishi* says, '*Tian* 天 perceives from the perspective of the common people. *Tian* hears from the perspective of the common people'" (*Meng Zi* 5A5).

The King said, "What great words! But I have a problem. I'm fond of valor."

Meng Zi said, "Your Majesty, please do not be fond of petty valor, wielding a sword with an angry glare, saying, 'He is loathsome, I dare him to resist me!' This is the valor of the vulgar, for use against an individual antagonist. Your Majesty, I implore you to enlarge [your valor]. The *Odes* say:

The King, in awe-inspiring fury,
thereupon marshaled the military,
to block the army advancing toward Ju,

and thereby bolster the blessings of the Zhou,
in response to the whole world.

"This was the valor of King Wen. With a single bout of fury, he brought peace to the people of the whole world. The *Documents* say: '*Tian* descended among the people, and brought forth rulers and teachers, saying only that they were to help Shang Di bestow blessings. "Only I inspect the whole world for guilt or innocence." How could anyone in the world dare to transgress against its aspirations (*zhi* 志)?' If one person in the whole world acted unjustly, King Wu was ashamed. This was the valor of King Wu. And King Wu also, in a single bout of fury, brought peace to the people of the whole world. Now, if Your Majesty too, in a single bout of fury, brought peace to the people of the whole world, the people's only worry would be that you were not fond of valor."

> *Comment:* What inferences can we draw from this passage regarding Meng Zi's view of using the military? On the one hand, it may seem like he is suggesting that the military should be used to create peace. However, there is a strikingly difficult condition that must be met. One must be able, in a single stroke, to succeed in bringing peace to the world. It is not clear, from this passage, how much violence Meng Zi regards as allowable in this "single bout of fury." (For clues about that see *Meng Zi* 4A14, 7B3, and 7B4, p. 151, below.) Meng Zi seems to be encouraging the king to develop the qualities of kingliness, which would bring him closer to being able to achieve what Wen and Wu (supposedly) did, without asking the king to give up his fondness for valor. Far from encouraging the use of the military, Meng Zi, rather cleverly, encourages the King to develop his fondness for valor in such a way that actual aggression on his part is made less likely.

1B6 Meng Zi addressed King Xuan of Qi: "Suppose that among Your Majesty's subjects there was one who entrusted his wife and children to a friend while he traveled to Chu, and when he returned found his wife and children cold and hungry. What should he do?"

The King said, "Be done with him."

Meng Zi said, "And if a warden is not able to manage his subordinates, what should be done?"

The King said, "Dismiss him."

Meng Zi said, "And if the whole state is not well ordered, what should be done?"

The King, looking left and right, spoke of other matters.

1B8 King Xuan of Qi inquired, saying, "Tang dispatched Jie [the tyrannical last ruler of the Xia dynasty], and King Wu sent an expedition against Zhòu [the profligate last ruler of the Shang dynasty]. Are there such cases?"

Meng Zi replied, "So the traditional teachings have it."

King Xuan asked, "Is it permissible for a subject to kill a ruler?"

Meng Zi explained, "One who injures *ren* (humanity) is called a 'villain.' One who injures conscientiousness (*yi*) is called a 'vicious scoundrel.' Vicious scoundrels and villains are called 'outcasts.' I have heard of the outcast Jie being put to death. But I have never heard of a ruler being killed."

Comment: Here Meng Zi makes an implicit appeal to *zheng ming* 正名, the proper use of terms. According to *zheng ming*, a ruler is someone who fulfills the responsibilities that go with that role. And thus, neither the tyrant Jie nor Zhòu were genuine rulers. Not fulfilling the responsibilities associated with genuine rulership, they were not due the corresponding benefits or immunities.

1B10 The people of Qi attacked (*fa* 伐) Yan and defeated it. King Xuan [of Qi] asked, "Some people advise me not to annex [Yan], others advise me to annex it. A state of 10,000 chariots defeating a state of 10,000 chariots in just 50 days is something beyond human strength. If I do not annex it, surely *tian* will bring down a calamity. What do you think about annexing it?"

Comment: By this time Yan has already been attacked and subdued by Qi. So this is not a question of whether or not to attack, but whether or not to keep possession of the captured territory.

Meng Zi replied, "If the common people of Yan would be pleased to have you annex it, then annex it. An example of someone of ancient times who did this is King Wu. If the common people of Yan would not be pleased to have you annex it, then don't annex it. An example of someone of ancient times who did this is King Wen. When a state of 10,000 chariots attacks a state of 10,000 chariots and the attacking army is welcomed with baskets and kettles of food and drink, how could it be otherwise [than that they are pleased]? [On the other hand, it is natural to] flee from floods and fire. If the people [treat your arrival] as though the water is deeper and the fire is hotter, you should simply turn round and leave."

1B11 The state of Qi attacked (*fa* 伐) Yan, and annexed it. Various lords were planning to help Yan. King Xuan [of Qi] said, "Many of the lords are plotting to attack me. What can be done about it?"

Meng Zi replied, "I have heard that from a territory of 70 *li* one can come to govern the whole civilized world. [The great King] Tang did this. But I have never heard of using a thousand *li* to overawe others. The *Documents* say, 'Tang's singular punitive expedition (*zheng* 征) began with Ge.' [From this] the world trusted (*xin* 信) him. When he marched (*zheng* 征) east, the western tribes felt aggrieved. When he marched south, the northern tribes felt aggrieved, saying, 'Why are we last?' The common people looked toward him as though in the midst of a great drought facing cloudy skies with a rainbow. Those returning to the city did not stop. Plowmen continued their work. [Tang] executed the ruler and comforted the common people, like the fall of a timely rain. The common people were delighted. The *Documents* say, 'We wait for our ruler. When he comes we are revived.'

"Now, the ruler of Yan was cruel to his people. When you, Your Majesty, set forth to march against (*zheng* 征) him, the common people believed they were being rescued from flood and fire, and so welcomed Your Majesty's troops with baskets of food and kettles of drink. How could it be acceptable to kill the older males, bind the younger ones, destroy their ancestral temples, and abscond with their valuables? The whole world certainly fears the strength of Qi. You have doubled your territory without putting *ren* governance into practice. This will galvanize the armies of the world [against you]. If Your Majesty quickly issues orders to return their old and young, stop [looting] their valuables, and, in consultation with the masses, establish a ruler and then leave them, then it is still possible that you may successfully stop [the attack]."

Dialogues with Duke Wen of Teng

1B13 Duke Wen of Teng inquired, saying, "Teng is a small state, pinched between [the powerful states of] Qi and Chu. Should I serve Qi or Chu?"

Meng Zi replied, "I am not able to offer a solution to this. However, if I were to venture one suggestion: Dig deeper moats. Build taller walls. If you defend it alongside the common people, such that they will risk their lives and not abandon you, then there is some chance."

1B14 Duke Wen of Teng asked, "I fear that the people of Qi will establish fortifications at Xue. What can be done?"

Meng Zi replied, "Formerly, King Tai lived in Bin, and the tribes of

Di encroached upon him. He moved to the foot of Mount Qi and dwelt there. It is not that he chose this, but that there was no alternative. If one is morally adept (*shan* 善), the children and grandchildren of later generations will surely have a [genuine] king. *Junzi* initiate courses of action that bequeath order to posterity, enabling continuity. Success depends on *tian* 天. What can you do about your situation? Simply strive to be morally adept (*shan* 善), that is all."

1B15 Duke Wen of Teng questioned Meng Zi, saying, "Teng is a small state. It has no way to escape being bled dry in the appeasement of large states. What can be done?"

Meng Zi replied, "Long ago, King Tai lived in Bin, and the tribes of Di encroached upon him. He made tribute of hides and silk, but that didn't work. He made tribute with dogs and horses, but that didn't work. He made tribute with pearls and jade, but that didn't work. So he gathered his elders and told them: 'What the people of Di want is my territory. I have heard: "*Junzi* do not use what is meant to nurture people to instead harm them." My friends, what trouble is there in lacking a ruler? I will leave here.' He left Bin, crossed over the Liang Mountains, founded a city at the foot of Mount Qi, and dwelt there. The people of Bin said, 'We cannot lose a person who has *ren* (humanity).' They followed him as though flocking to market.

"Others say, 'Generations have guarded it, it is not for me [to abandon it]. Even if it means my own death, I will not leave.' I ask you to choose between these two."

Comment: We find the same story narrated in the *Zhuang Zi* (see below, p. 368), but with a different significance.

Force and Moral Authority

2A3 Meng Zi said, "Those who use force as a substitute for *ren* (humanity) are hegemons. A hegemon will surely have a large state.

Comment: One would not try to dominate by force if one had only a small state.

"Those who use their influential virtue (*de* 德) and put *ren* (humanity) into practice are kingly. They do not have to wait until [their state] is large. [The great] Tang managed with only an area of 70 *li*, and King Wen had 100 *li*. When force is used to make people submit, it is not that they submit in their hearts, it is that their strength [to resist] is inadequate. But when influential virtue (*de* 德) is used to engender submission, the people are joyful in their hearts and submit sincerely, just as Confucius' seventy followers submitted to him. The *Odes* say, 'From the west, from the east, from the south, from the north. There was no thought of not submitting.' This expresses my meaning."

2B8 Shen Tong [a minister of Qi] asked in confidence, "Would it be permissible (*ke* 可) for a punitive attack (*fa* 伐) to be launched against Yan?"[13]

> *Comment:* Yan was in turmoil. The ruler of Yan, Zikuai, was tricked into offering to abdicate rule to his prime minister Zizhi, expecting Zizhi to decline the offer. That way Zikuai would be able to liken himself to the sage-king Yao, who relinquished power to Shun, while, in this case, not actually having to give up power. However, Zizhi accepted. Turmoil later resulted when Zikuai's son tried to regain power. (See also 1B10 and 1B11, pp. 147, 148, above.)

Meng Zi said. "It may be permissible (*ke* 可). Zikuai [the king of Yan] did not have the authority to give away Yan to another. And Zizhi [the prime minister] did not have the authority to receive Yan from Zikuai. Suppose there was an official that you favored, and, without telling the king, you privately gave him your salary and title. And, further, without a royal decree, he privately accepted these. Would that be acceptable (*ke* 可)? What is the difference between these cases?"

[Subsequently] the people of Qi attacked (*fa* 伐) Yan.

Someone asked [Meng Zi], "Did you ever advise Qi to launch a punitive attack on Yan?"

Meng Zi replied, "Never. Shen Tong had asked, 'Would it be permissible for a punitive attack to be launched against Yan?' I answered, 'It may be permissible.' [Qi] then went and attacked it. If he had asked, 'Who may launch an attack?' then I would have answered, 'An agent of *tian* 天 (the heavens) may do so.' Suppose someone asked about a murderer, saying, 'Is it permissible for this person to be executed?' I would reply, 'It is permissible.' If asked, 'Who may execute him?' then I would reply, 'If done by the chief officer, it is permissible to execute him.' Now, how could I have been encouraging [a state that is just as flawed as] Yan [namely Qi] to launch a punitive attack on Yan?"

---

13 Note that "*ke*" 可 means both possible and permissible, depending on the context. In this question it clearly means "permissible," but there may be some degree of ambiguity in Meng Zi's reply.

4A11 Meng Zi said, "The way (*dao* 道) is near, yet is sought in matters distant. Service is easy, yet sought in matters difficult. If people would have close relationships (*qin* 親) with their close relatives (*qin* 親), and treat their elders (*zhang* 長) as elders, the whole world would be at peace."

4A14 Meng Zi said, "When [Ran] Qiu served as a steward to the Ji clan, he was unable to reform their character (*de* 德), and he doubled the grain tax. Confucius commented, 'Qiu is no follower of mine. You, my young friends, have my permission to sound the drums and attack him.' Considering this, we see that Confucius would renounce anyone who enriched a ruler who does not put *ren* 仁 governance into practice. How much more would he renounce those who press for war? Waging war over disputed territory fills fields with the slain. Waging war for a city fills the city with the slain. This is called, 'causing the earth to consume human flesh.' It is a crime not recompensed by death. Thus, those who are good at war deserve the supreme punishment. Those who ally with the various lords deserve the next highest, followed by those who regulate lands to be toiled by others."

7B2 Meng Zi said, "During the Spring and Autumn period there were no honorable (*yi* 義) wars (*zhan* 戰). There were only some that were better than others. Punitive military expeditions (*zheng* 征) involve the superior striking (*fa* 伐) the inferior. Enemy states [of equal status] do not engage in punitive expeditions against each other."

> Comment: The Spring and Autumn period was from 771 to 476 BCE. Confucius (551–479 BCE) lived during the last part of this period. Meng Zi (372–289 BCE) lived in the Warring States period (475–221 BCE). Despite the difference in name, these periods were both characterized by de facto independent states vying for supremacy and survival.

7B3 Meng Zi said, "To trust the *Book of Documents* completely would be worse than not having it at all. I only accept two or three bits of the 'Wu Cheng' chapter. A person who has *ren* 仁 (humanity) has no enemies in the whole world. So when the most *ren* [King Wu] sent an expedition against the most inhumane (*bu ren*) [the tyrant Jie], how could it be that blood flowed so that it carried along shields?"[d]

7B4 Meng Zi said, "There are some who say, 'I excel at arranging battle arrays, and at warfare (*zhan* 戰).' This is a tremendous crime. A ruler of a state who is fond of *ren* 仁 (humanity) has no enemies (*di* 敵) in the world. When [King Tang] marched (*zheng* 征) south, the Di tribes of the north were resentful. When he marched east, the Yi tribes of the west were resentful, saying, 'Why does he put us last?' When King Wu defeated (*fa* 伐) the Yin, he did so with 300 chariots and 3,000 warriors. Yet the King announced, 'Fear not, and rest assured, the common people are not my enemy.' And the people bowed down as though they had collapsed. To punish militarily (*zheng* 征) means to set straight (*zheng* 正).[14] If each desires to set themselves straight, what need is there for war (*zhan* 戰)?"

> *Comment:* In addition to meaning 'enemy,' the character *di* 敵 also means 'a match; an equal.' So, the relevant line could be translated, "A ruler of a state who is fond of *ren* (humanity) is invincible." It seems plausible that Meng Zi intended both meanings, as these meanings reinforce and explain each other.

7B7   Meng Zi said, "I now have come to appreciate the gravity of killing someone's kin. If you kill someone's father, someone will likewise kill your father. If you kill someone's brother, someone will likewise kill your brother. So, though you did not kill them yourself, it is only a small distance between."

7B13   Meng Zi said, "There are cases in which an inhumane (*bu ren* 不仁) person obtained a state. But, there have been no cases in which an inhumane person has obtained the world."

> *Comment:* "The world" (*tian xia* 天下), literally all under the sky, refers to the known civilized world at the time (from the perspective of the early Chinese).

7B14   Meng Zi said, "The common people are most valuable. Altars for the gods of soil and grain come next. The ruler is of light value. So, win over the common people and one becomes emperor (*tian zi* 天子). Win over the emperor and one becomes a feudal lord. Win over a feudal lord and one becomes a great official. [...]"

> *Comment: Tian zi* 天子 is literally the son of *tian,* and suggests that one has earned the so-called "mandate of *tian*" (*tian ming* 天命) and thus has the authority to rule.

---

14   Cf. *Analects* 12.17 (p. 93).

SEQUENCE OF PASSAGES

Meng Zi's view of human nature
The sprouts of virtue
4B19, 6A6, 7A15, 4B12, 2A6, 4A27, 6A1, 6A2, 6A3, 6A7, 6A8, 6A10,
3A4, 3A5
Is *yi* internal or external?
6A4, 6A5
Meng Zi's ethical philosophy
Preserving and nourishing one's heart
2A2, 4B26, 7B31, 7B35, 4B28, 2A7, 7A1, 7A2, 7A3, 7B33, 7B16
What to do?
4A17, 3B1, 4B6, 4B8, 4B11, 7A9, 7A17, 7A33, 7A4, 7A37, 7A40
Critique of Yang Zi and Mo Zi
7A26, 3B9
Critique of "respectable villagers"
7B37
Meng Zi's political philosophy
Dialogues with King Hui of Liang
1A1, 1A4, 1A5, 1A6
Dialogues with King Xuan of Qi
1A7, 1B3, 1B6, 1B8, 1B10, 1B11
Dialogues with Duke Wen of Teng
1B13, 1B14, 1B15
Force and moral authority
2A3, 2B8, 4A11, 4A14, 7B2, 7B3, 7B4, 7B7, 7B13, 7B14

INDEX OF PASSAGES

6A1	117	7A3	129	7B4	151
6A2	117	7A4	132	7B7	152
6A3	118	7A9	131	7B13	152
6A4	123	7A15	115	7B14	152
6A5	124	7A17	132	7B16	129
6A6	114	7A26	133	7B31	127
6A7	119	7A33	132	7B33	129
6A8	120	7A37	132	7B35	127
6A10	121	7A40	133	7B37	134
7A1	128	7B2	151		
7A2	129	7B3	151		

ENDNOTES

[a] This statement by Confucius is the entirety of *Analects* 13.21, which is not repeated in our collection of *Analects* passages.

[b] See Bell 2008, Bai 2012, and Yan 2011.

[c] I have made precisely this argument in Hagen 2016a, "Would Early Confucians Really Support Humanitarian Interventions?"

[d] Regarding the interpretation of *chu* 杵 as "shields," I am following A. Charles Muller trans., *Mencius (Selections)*, last updated 2017, http://www.acmuller.net/con-dao/mencius.html.

6

Xun Zi

INTRODUCTION

Chronologically third of the three great Confucians of the classical period, Xun Zi (c. 325–c. 235 BCE) holds a place in the classical Chinese philosophical tradition similar to that held by Aristotle in classical Greek philosophy, having had the advantage of access to the ideas of his predecessors. Two of his students, Han Fei Zi (Chapter 12) and Li Si, became significant Legalists, leading some to view him as a proto-Legalist. However, though Xun Zi himself explicitly acknowledges some advantages of Legalism, he regarded it as far inferior to Confucianism.[1] Although Xun Zi himself became prominent, and his views remained influential for a time, his work fell out of favor when Meng Zi's view of the goodness of human nature became widely accepted.[2] Xun Zi's negative-sounding view of human nature may have led to his work being devalued on account of his supposed pessimism. Recently, however, there has been a renewed interest in Xun Zi's ideas.

The *Xun Zi* is generally believed to have been largely, though not entirely, written by Xun Zi himself. It is not only a much longer text than the *Analects* of Confucius and the *Meng Zi*, it is divided into more coherent chapters that contain more sustained arguments. Below, the most philosophically significant sections have been organized as follows:

"Encouraging Learning" (Chapter 1)

Xun Zi on motivation (Chapter 4 and §§22.5–22.6)

"Discussing the Military" (Chapter 15) and related passages

---

1 See the final comment in the chapter on *Han Fei Zi*, p. 435, and also *Xun Zi* 16.5, p. 177.

2 A comparison between the philosophies of Xun Zi and Meng Zi can be found in the Introduction to this book (pp. 21–23).

"A Discourse on *Tian*" (Chapter 17) and §§9.14, 9.16b, and 9.16c

"A Discourse on Ritual Propriety" (Chapter 19)

"Dissolving Beguilement" (Chapter 21)

"Proper Terminology" (Chapter 22)

"Natural Dispositions Are Detestable" (Chapter 23) and §9.16a

Introductions to the content are provided on a chapter-by-chapter basis.

"ENCOURAGING LEARNING," *QUAN XUE* 勸學 (CHAPTER 1)

Encouraging learning may seem uncontroversial (most people take the importance of learning for granted), but the emphasis on sustained effort and dogged determination displayed in Xun Zi's exhortations contrasts sharply with Meng Zi's notion of an unforced emergence of productive dispositions—captured most clearly in the image of a misguided farmer "helping" his crops grow by pulling on them (*Meng Zi* 2A2, p. 126).

Learning (*xue* 學) means more than book learning to Confucians. It involves developing character as much as becoming educated. It is hard work, but if one sticks to it, Xun Zi maintains, it is transformative. The *Shi Zi* is a text that was composed about the same time as the *Xun Zi*, and they share some characteristics. The first chapter of the *Shi Zi*, for example, is also entitled "Encouraging Learning." It begins as follows:

> Learning tirelessly is the means by which one orders oneself. Teaching without flagging is the means by which one brings order to others. [...] Learning is like sharpening. Even if you were to take the best metals of Kunwu and Zhufu, and have them cast into swords by the great blacksmiths Gan and Yue, if you do not sharpen them with a whetstone, they will neither pierce when you stab nor cut when you strike. However, if you first grind them on a grindstone and then further sharpen them with the yellow whetstone, they will pierce as though nothing stood in their way, and in striking they will cut straight through. From this, we see that the distance between applying the whetstone and not applying it is far indeed. Nowadays, everyone knows enough to sharpen their swords, yet they do not realize they should sharpen themselves. Learning is the whetstone for sharpening oneself.
>
> (*Shi Zi, Quan Xue*)[a]

Xun Zi's notion that quality in character is a product of hard work dovetails with his view of natural human dispositions, expressed in Chapter 23, "Natural Dispositions Are Detestable" (p. 218, below). Between petty persons and exemplary ones, deliberate human effort makes all the difference. Effort must be properly directed. And must occur within some structure. Traditional norms of ritual propriety (li 禮) play a critical role in providing the direction to, and structure for, this effort. But where did these norms come from? They are themselves products of the efforts and artifice of sages over long periods of time. And a transformed character is the most important of these products. So, Xun Zi's doctrines regarding learning with effort, following and appreciating ritualized norms, and the problematic nature of natural human dispositions, all come together to form a consistent philosophical dao 道—both a discourse and a path to improvement.

1.1ᵇ *Junzi* 君子 (exemplary persons) say: "Learning must never cease." Blue comes from the indigo plant, yet is bluer than indigo. Ice is made of water, yet is colder than water. Wood as straight as a plumb line may be bent into the shape of a wheel, with a curvature as true as a compass. Even if it is dried in the Sun, it will not return to its former straightness, because the bending process has made it like this. Thus, if wood is marked with a plumb line, it will become straight; if metal is put to a whetstone, it will become sharp; if *junzi* study broadly and examine themselves daily, their wisdom will become illuminating and their conduct will be without fault.

> *Comment:* The examples of ice, and of blueness bluer than the very source of blueness, show that it is possible to make something greater than it is found in its natural condition. So too, through deliberate transformative effort, human beings can be made better than they naturally are.

1.2 Thus, if one does not climb a high mountain, one will not appreciate the height of the heavens (*tian* 天). If one does not look down into a deep ravine, one will not appreciate the earth's thickness. If one does not listen to the words passed down from the former kings, one will not appreciate learning's breadth. Children of the Han, Yue, Yi, and Mo tribes make the same sounds when they are born, but when they are grown up they have different customs. Education has made them as they are. [...]

1.3 I once spent a full day thinking, but it was not as good as a mere moment of learning. I once stood on my toes and gazed into the distance, but it was nothing like the expansive view attained from climbing to lofty heights. Climb high and wave—it is not as though one's arms get longer, and yet one can be seen from afar. If one shouts downwind, it is not as though the sound travels faster, and yet one can be more easily heard. Avail yourself of a horse and chariot, and though you don't use your feet, you can travel a thousand miles. Avail yourself of a rowboat, and though you cannot swim, you can traverse rivers. *Junzi* are born no different from others, but they are adept at availing themselves of things [i.e., norms of ritual propriety and lessons of the sages].

> *Comment:* Sometimes Xun Zi is interpreted as believing that the sages, who are responsible for the development of rituals and culture, were specially endowed. But that does not seem to be the case. Xun Zi suggests that both *junzi* and sages (see §4.9, p. 163, below) are products of their own effort—guided by reliable norms, and exemplary models. But, if so, how did the process get started? The first sage would not have had a model to follow, nor established norms to train with. Since Xun Zi does not explicitly address this problem, I will simply suggest a plausible answer: It is misleading to talk of a "first sage." Where there have been human communities, there has been culture and ritual. Even the so-called barbarians of Confucius' day had culture enough to appreciate cultivated behavior (see *Analects* 13.19 and 15.6, pp. 83 and 84). So there is no "zero point" from which a full-fledged sage suddenly emerged. Rather, working with whatever cultural resources were available, individuals and communities gradually developed themselves and the norms that defined their culture. They were able to do this by virtue of the mind's ability to make judgments about what is appropriate and approvable, even when those judgments conflicted with the emotional desires that stem from *xing* 性, our natural dispositions (see *Xun Zi* 22.5a, p. 166). The most noteworthy exemplars were remembered and called "sages." There is no serious "bootstrap problem" here. Striving for improvement, a person sometimes hits on something productive and sensible, which is recognized and acknowledged as exemplary and becomes customary. The process becomes more systematic and reliable as norms of ritual propriety develop.

1.4 [...] The bitter fleabane, when growing among hemp, will grow straight without any support. And when white sand resides in black dye, it too becomes black.[c] A certain perfume is made from the root of an orchid. But if it is soaked in urine, the nobility will come nowhere near it, and the common people will not wear it. It's not that its qualities are not attractive. It's because of that in which it was soaked. Thus, *junzi* are sure to dwell in carefully chosen neighborhoods, and to travel and associate with aspirants (*shi* 士), thereby avoiding the crooked and unorthodox, and drawing near to the properly centered and upright (*zheng* 正).

1.5 There is surely some beginning from which each type of thing arises. The honor or disgrace that one experiences will surely be a reflection of one's character (*de* 德). Rotten meat produces maggots; fish left to spoil will produce worms. If one is lazy, slow, and neglects oneself, then disasters and calamities will ensue. [...] Where a target is placed, bows and arrows will arrive. Where forests are dense with trees, hatchets and axes will turn up. Where trees are shady, flocks of birds will roost. When vinegar is sour, gnats will gather. So too, there are words that court disaster, and actions that attract disgrace. *Junzi* are cautious about how they position themselves.

1.6 Accumulated soil makes a mountain, and wind and rain flourish as a result. Accumulated water makes an abyss, and flood dragons are born in it. Accumulated excellence (*shan* 善) makes compelling character (*de* 德), and in this way one obtains a spirit-like clarity as a matter of course, and the sagely mind is prepared. Thus, if one does not accumulate steps, one will lack the means by which to travel long distances. [...] Earthworms lack the benefit of claws and teeth, and the strength of muscle and bone, yet above they consume the dusty soil and below they drink of the yellow spring. This is due to concentrated attention. Crabs have eight legs and two pincers, yet were it not for holes made by snakes and eels they would have nowhere dependable to dwell. This is because they act on impulsive feelings. Without a deep enigmatic aspiration (*zhi* 志), there will be no clear bright insight. Without unappreciated groping effort, there will be no grand illustrious achievements. Those who [try to] travel two roads [at the same time] will not reach their destination. One who serves two lords will not please them. The eye cannot, when looking at two things, see them clearly. The ear cannot, when listening to two things, hear them well. [...]

Comment: The last part of the section translated above relates to the issue of whether or not Xun Zi thought of *dao* 道 as a singularly correct way. Just as, for practical reasons, it will not work for an individual to try to simultaneously "travel two roads," so too social harmony is best maintained when all members are on the same path. However, that does not mean that Xun Zi viewed the *dao* that he advocated as a metaphysically absolutist way. (Cf. *Xun Zi* 21.1, p. 201, below.)

1.8   Where does learning begin, and where does it end? I say: Regarding its method, it begins with reciting the classics and ends with studying ritual propriety (*li* 禮). Regarding what is appropriate and honorable (*yi* 義), it begins with becoming an aspirant (*shi* 士) and ends with becoming a sage (*sheng ren* 聖人). When one has accumulated one's strength for a long time, then one is ready to begin. Learning continues until death and only then stops. Thus, the method of learning has an end, but it is never honorable or appropriate (*yi* 義) to abandon it. To practice it is to be human; to abandon it is to be a beast. [...]

1.9   The learning of *junzi* enters through their ears, adheres to their hearts (*xin* 心), spreads to their four limbs, and is embodied in their actions. Every word, every subtle movement, may be taken as a model and pattern. The learning of petty people enters their ears and comes right out their mouths. The space between the mouth and the ears is but four inches. How could that suffice to make a six-foot person more admirable? [...]

1.10   In learning, nothing is as useful as drawing near to the proper people. Rituals (*li* 禮) and music may be taken as models but they do not offer explanations. [...]

1.12   Do not answer those whose questions are crude and insubstantial. Do not question those whose answers are crude and insubstantial. Do not listen to those whose explanations are crude and insubstantial. Do not engage in discriminating discourse with those of contentious spirit. If they have arrived where they are via the *dao*, only then engage them. If they have not, avoid them. Thus, if they respect ritual propriety (*li* 禮) only then can one speak meaningfully with them about the direction of the way. If their words are compliant only then can one speak meaningfully with them about the patterns of the way. If their demeanor is deferential, only then can one speak meaningfully with them about transmitting the way. [...]

Comment: Elsewhere Xun Zi says that *junzi* are cautious regarding ideas that spread through unofficial channels, but that they listen broadly to determine what has value and what does not.[d]

1.13 [...] If categories of moral relations do not come through [in one's actions], or if one has not integrated *ren* 仁 (humanity) and *yi* 義 (appropriateness), one is not worthy of being called "adept (*shan* 善) at learning." Learning is securing what one learns by integrating it. [...] Completely integrate one's learning, put it fully to use, and only then is one learned.

1.14 *Junzi* know that what is neither whole nor pure is not sufficient to be deemed beautiful or admirable (*mei* 美). Thus, by recitation and following regular patterns they habituate themselves to it [i.e., the beautiful/admirable^e]. By reflecting deeply they gain insight into it. By their own actions they dwell in it. They discard what is harmful and thereby manage and nurture it. They make their eyes unwilling to look at what is not thus [beautiful/admirable], and their ears unwilling to listen to what is not thus. They make their mouths unwilling to say what is not thus, and their heart–minds unwilling to consider what is not thus, until ultimately they fully cherish it. Their eyes cherish it more than the five colors, their ears cherish it more than the five sounds, their mouths cherish it more than the five flavors, and the heart–mind enjoys the benefits more than possessing the whole world. In this way, they cannot be prejudiced in their assessment of what is most beneficial; neither can they be moved by the masses. The whole world could not make them waver. Following this in life, following it until death, this is called "holding firmly to virtue (*de* 德)." Only when one is steadfast in character and integrity can one be resolute. When one is resolute, only then can one be responsive and adaptable. Such persons are called accomplished persons. The value of the heavens is seen to be its brightness; that of the earth is seen to be its breadth; what *junzi* value is their wholeness.

XUN ZI ON MOTIVATION—"HONOR AND DISGRACE" (CHAPTER 4) AND A DISCUSSION OF DESIRE FROM CHAPTER 22

Everyone desires to be honored. But, paradoxically, if one is not sufficiently modest when striving for honor, one will end up courting disgrace instead. Xun Zi recommends an indirect approach. Rather than striving to *be honored*, which in some degree depends on others, one is encouraged to strive to be honor*able*—by acting honorably. This has two benefits. First, fulfillment is securely in one's own control. Second, though one cannot control others, the most effective strategy to become honored by others in the long run is to become genuinely honorable.

Notice that there are two kinds of motivations involved here: natural desires which are shared by all people (to be honored), and desires, or *aspirations*, that are a product of character development, or self-cultivation. Xun Zi expresses this distinction explicitly in §18.9: "Cultivated in one's aspirational intent, rich in compelling conduct, luminous in knowledgeable consideration—this is honor that comes from within, and may be called 'appropriate honor.' Respected noble rank, rich in official salary, triumphant in the appearance of power, above as the Emperor or feudal lord, below as minister or functionary—this is honor that comes from without, and may be called 'circumstantial honor.'"

"Honor and Disgrace," *Rong Ru* 榮辱 (Chapter 4)

4.6 The great division between honor and disgrace, and a reliable (*chang* 常) predictor of safety and peril, and of benefit and harm, is as follows: Those who put honorable conduct (*yi* 義) first and profit (*li* 利) last will experience honor. Those who put profit first and honorable conduct last will experience disgrace. Those who are honored reliably end up achieving success. Those who are disgraced reliably end up being reduced to poverty. Those who achieve success reliably end up governing others. Those who are reduced to poverty reliably end up being governed by others. This is the great division between honor and disgrace.

4.8 In natural talent and disposition (*xing* 性), and in the capacity for knowledge, *junzi* 君子 (exemplary persons) and petty persons are as one. They are fond of honor, and detest disgrace; they are fond of profit and detest harm. In this *junzi* and petty persons are the same. But the way (*dao* 道) by which they strive to achieve things is different. Petty persons have a tendency to make boastful exaggerations, and yet they want others to trust them. [And so on.] [...] In the end, they will surely not get that of which they are fond, but will encounter what they detest.

Junzi are trustworthy, and also desire others to trust them. They exhibit wholehearted commitment (*zhong* 忠), and also desire others to hold them dear. They cultivate propriety, are meticulously well ordered, and also want others to regard them as good (*shan* 善). When they ponder something they readily come to understand. When they put something into practice it readily becomes settled. When they take hold of something, it is easy for them to stand by it. In the end, they are sure to get that of which they are fond and avoid that which they detest. [...]

Comment: Similarly, in §9.4, Xun Zi writes: "If a ruler of the people desires ease and stability, there is nothing like fair policies and loving the people. If he desires glory, there is nothing like exalting ritual propriety, and respecting aspirants. If he desires achievements and fame, there is nothing like esteeming the virtuous, and employing the able in government. These are the crucial points of a ruler. If these three points are properly dealt with, then all remaining matters will be properly dealt with."

Ren 仁 (humanity), conscientiousness (*yi* 義), virtue (*de* 德), and conducting oneself (*xing* 行) accordingly is characteristic of the style that reliably achieves security, even though the possibility of danger cannot be fully avoided. Crookedness, lack of discipline, assault, and thievery characterize the style that reliably engenders peril, even though the possibility of security is not fully eliminated. Thus, *junzi* lead (*dao* 道) according to what is reliable. Petty persons lead according to what is anomalous.

4.9 Generally speaking, people have commonalities and similarities. When hungry, they desire to eat; when cold, they desire warmth; and when weary, they desire rest. They are fond of what is advantageous, and loath what is harmful. This is how people are from birth; they need not wait to become so. In this, the sage Yu and the tyrant Jie were the same. The eye distinguishes white from black, beautiful from ugly. The ear distinguishes sounds and tones, clear and muddy. The mouth distinguishes sour, salty, sweet, and bitter. The nose distinguishes fragrances and perfumes from odors and stenches. The bones, body, and skin distinguish cold weather from warm, and illness from recovery. This is also something people have from birth, without waiting for it to be so. In this, Yu and Jie were the same.

Whether one is able to become a sage like Yao or Yu, or a tyrant like Jie or robber like Zhi, or a craftsperson or artisan, or a farmer or merchant, this resides solely in the accumulation of what one concentrates on and what one puts aside, and habits and customs.[f] This is also something people have from birth, without waiting for it to be so. In this, Yu and Jie were the same. If one becomes a Yao or a Yu, then one reliably (*chang* 常) will be settled and secure, and honored. If one becomes a Jie or Zhi, one is reliably in danger and will suffer disgrace. If one becomes a Yao or a Yu, then one is reliably content and at ease. If one becomes a craftsperson or artisan, or a farmer or merchant, then one will reliably undergo toil and trouble. Even so, [most] people strive for one and few for the other. Why is this? I say: They are uncultivated. The sages Yao and Yu were not born with [sagely] endowments. Those arose from alterations of their original [endowments], and were brought to completion through continuous acts of cultivation. It was only after exhaustive efforts that they were fully prepared.

4.10 People are born with the firm inner conditions of an inferior (*xiao* 小) person. If they lack a teacher and a model, they will see only personal profit (*li* 利). People are born with the firm dispositions of an inferior person, and in addition, owing to the disorder of the times, they acquire disorderly customs. In this way, the petty (*xiao* 小) replicate what is petty, and through disorder they acquire disorderliness. If a *junzi* does not achieve a position of influence, and therefrom oversee them, then there would be nowhere from which they could begin to make progress within themselves. Nowadays, people are governed by their appetites. How can they appreciate ritual and propriety (*li-yi* 禮義)? How can they appreciate yielding and deference? How can they appreciate integrity and a sense of shame, and what has been accumulated?

People munch and chomp their food, simply feasting until full [with no sense of quality]. If people lack teachers and models, their thoughts and feelings (*xin* 心) will be just like their appetites. Consider: If one had never tasted the meat of livestock, and rice and fine millet, but only beans, pulse leaves, husks, and chaff, then one would consider this sufficient. If one were then suddenly presented with portions of fine meats, rice, and millet, splendidly displayed, one would gaze at them with a look of horror and say: "What is this weird stuff?" But since the smell does not disturb the nose, the taste is sweet to the mouth, and consumption puts the body at ease, anyone [familiar with both] would abandon the original diet and take up the new one. [...]

> *Comment*: Following the Confucian way of ritual and propriety, yielding and deference, and acting with integrity and a sense of shame is like eating truly high-quality food. It provides a quality of satisfaction that cannot be achieved on the standard fare. Xun Zi suggests a "competent judge test" (reminiscent of J.S. Mill): What will someone who is acquainted with both choose? Xun Zi believes that if people try practicing ritual propriety they will become fond of it, and choose to pursue this way further, becoming "aspirants."

4.11 The emotional inclination (*qing* 情) of people is to desire to eat meat of livestock, desire to wear clothes decorated with embroidered patterns, desire to travel by horse and carriage, and desire extra valuables in order to save and amass wealth, so that even if lean years stretch out over generations one will not experience insufficiency. This is the emotional inclination of people.

Now, to survive, people know enough to raise chickens, dogs, and swine as well as cows and sheep. Yet they dare not dine on wine and meat. They have extra coins and cloth, and maintain granaries and cellars, yet they dare not wear fine silk. The frugal have supplies stored up in baskets and boxes, yet dare not travel by horse and carriage. Why is this? It is not that these things are not desired. It is because, deliberating extensively and taking the future into consideration, people fear that they may come to lack what they need to continue doing these things. As a result, they moderate expenses and resist desires. Restraining themselves, they store supplies in order to continue to have them. Is not such prudent concern for the long run and consideration of the future excellent? But those of shallow understanding, who give little attention to their livelihood, do not understand even this. They eat too extravagantly, and give no consideration to their future. They soon find themselves driven into poverty. For this reason they do not escape freezing and starving. They wind up emaciated in ditches grasping a beggar's gourd and a sack.

> *Comment:* While some fail to live prudently and end up in ditches, most people understand the importance of self-control. But they may not see the wider implications of this reasoning. The rather obvious observations about personal frugality are offered as an analogy for following *dao* in a larger sense, as expressed below.

This is true all the more of the way (*dao*) of the former kings, the guiding principles of *ren* (humanity) and honorable conduct (*yi*), and the distinctions expressed in the *Odes*, the books of *Documents*, *Rituals*, and *Music*. Those certainly contain the most important considerations in the world, which cause the populace to think hard, take the future into consideration, and safeguard future generations. [...]

> *Comment:* These passages reveal Xun Zi's philosophy to be based ultimately on enlightened self-interest, or a general and far-seeing prudence. It could be thought of as a kind of "strategic" prudence, compared to ordinary "tactical" prudence. It is an indirect (or second-order) type of prudence. For one is not advised simply to "be prudent," but rather to "follow the way," which is itself based on prudential considerations. In

addition, the payoff for following the way is complex. Not only are one's petty desires satisfied, but one develops new, more noble aspirations, which are also satisfied. And the process of realizing one's noble aspirations contributes to the general harmony of society.[8]

"Proper Terminology," *Zheng Ming* 正名 (Chapter 22), §§22.5–22.6 (A Discussion of Desire)

22.5a Generally speaking, those who contend that order depends on first getting rid of desires, having no way to guide desires, are distressed by their mere presence. Those who say that order depends on reducing the number of desires, having no way of moderating desires, are distressed that there are so many.[3]

"Having desires" and "lacking desires" are different categories (*lei* 類). They correspond to the living and the dead, not the ordered and the chaotic. As for having many desires or few desires—these are different categories having to do with the number of emotions, not with order and chaos. What is desired is not necessarily attainable (*ke de* 可得), but in striving for it one follows that to which one assents (*ke* 可). The fact that what is desired is not necessarily attainable is a natural condition;[4] the fact that in striving for it one follows that to which one assents is due to the mind (*xin* 心). When a particular natural desire is regulated according to multiple potential avenues of pursuit considered by the mind, the result is certainly difficult to classify as simply a natural condition.

> *Comment:* The word "*ke*" (可) can mean either "possible" or "admissible"—and to accept the admissibility of something is to assent to it. Above, '*ke de*' 可得 (attainable) seems to be contrasted with '*ke*,' which by itself is here understood as 'to assent.' However, as is often the case in somewhat ambiguous instances, the character may very well vaguely imply both meanings, to some degree. Below, I have sometimes chosen to use the word "viable" to retain this vagueness. For doing so maintains the richness of the text without unduly making its import murky or imprecise.
>
> While *xin* 心 generally means heart and mind, or the associated thoughts and feelings, in Xun Zi's usage it often seems more cognitive than emotional. Indeed, Xun Zi characterizes it as the means by which the emotions can be reined in. So, in many cases it is translated simply as "mind."

---

3 Cf. *Meng Zi* 7B35, p. 127, and *Lao Zi* 1 (p. 280), 3 (p. 316), 22 (p. 300), 37 (p. 318), and 64 (p. 320).

4 Literally, it is "something received from *tian*" (所受乎天).

What people desire most of all is life. What they detest most of all is death. Nevertheless, there are people whose engagement in life results in their death. It is not that they found life undesirable and wanted to die. Rather, life was not a viable option, but death was.[5] Thus, when people's desires go too far, and one does not act on them, it is the mind that stopped them. If what the mind considers viable is focused on patterns (*li* 理), then although desires are numerous, what harm is there to order? If one takes actions that go beyond what one desires, it is the mind that caused them. If what the mind considers viable disregards patterns (*li* 理), then although desires are few, how could chaos be avoided? Therefore, order and chaos reside in what the mind regards as viable, not what the emotions desire. If one does not seek it where it resides, but seeks it where it is not, although one may say, "I got it," one actually misses it.

22.5b Natural dispositions (*xing* 性) are the products of *tian* [i.e., they are natural conditions]. Emotions (*qing* 情) are the basic stuff of these natural dispositions. And desires are emotional responses. Regarding what is desired as attainable (*ke de* 可得) and pursuing it is something that emotions cannot avoid, though the route (*dao* 道) to that which one assents (*ke* 可) must come from intelligence (*zhi* 知). Thus, even for gatekeepers, desires cannot be eliminated, for they are the basic equipment of natural dispositions. And, even for the emperor, desires cannot be exhaustively fulfilled. However, although they cannot be exhaustively fulfilled, it is possible to move closer to fulfillment. And, although desires cannot be eliminated, their pursuit can be moderated. Although one cannot exhaustively satisfy one's desires, the pursuer may move closer to satisfaction. Although desires cannot be eliminated, and what is pursued is unattainable, those who reflect on this will desire to moderate their pursuits. When the way is advancing then desires will be nearly satisfied, and when in retreat, there will be moderation of pursuits. There is nothing in the world as good as this.

22.6a Generally speaking, everyone follows what is acceptable for them, and abandons what is not viable. There is no one who, knowing that there is nothing as good as knowing *dao*, does not follow it. Suppose a man desired to be in the south—he could not get enough of it—and who detested the north—he could not get too little of it. How could he depart from the south and head to the north on account of not being able to experience all of the south? Now, people cannot get too much of what they desire. And cannot get too little of what they detest. How could they depart from the

---

5 Cf. *Meng Zi* 6A10, p. 121, and the end of 1B15, p. 149.

path (*dao* 道) to the attainment of their desires and instead choose what they detest just because they can't exhaustively satisfy their desires? Thus, if one assents to the way and follows it, how could increasing desires cause disorder? If one does not assent to the way and departs from it, how could decreasing them bring about order?[h] Thus, the wise make assessments based on the way and that is all, while what is wished for in the treasured theories of the minor schools falls into decline.

22.6b Generally speaking, when people make choices, they never get only what they want. And when they dispose of something, they never get rid of only what they dislike. Thus, there are no actions that do not involve trade-offs. If the balance by which one weighs is not true, then the heavy side will rise and people will regard it as light, while the light side will fall and people will regard it as heavy. In this case, people will be deluded about what is heavy and what is light. If the balance is not true, then misfortunes will be judged according to what is desirable in them, and people will regard them as blessings, while blessings will be judged according to what is detestable in them, and people will regard them as misfortunes. This is the reason people are confused about blessings and misfortunes. *Dao* is the proper balance (*quan* 權) of the past and the present. Those who depart from *dao* and make choices from personal inclinations do not understand that on which fortune and misfortune depends.

> *Comment: Dao* can be thought of as a guiding discourse emphasizing ritualized norms of proper conduct. In the above passage, one is encouraged to follow these norms rather than personal inclinations because doing so will more reliably lead to satisfying results.

22.6c When a trader exchanges one for one, people say, "there is neither gain nor loss." If he exchanges one for two, people say, "there is no loss, but there is a gain." If he exchanges two for one, people say, "There is no gain, but there is a loss." Those who calculate take what is more. Those who plan follow what is acceptable. No one would exchange two for one since they understand the calculations involved. Proceeding according to the way is like exchanging one for two. How could there be a loss? Departing from the way and choosing from the inside [i.e., directly according to one's innate dispositions] is like exchanging two for one. How can there be a gain? The [fulfillment of] one's desires accumulated over a hundred years would be exchanged for the dubious [gratification] of a single instance. Anyone who does this does not understand the calculations involved.

22.6d Let us inquire more deeply into the matter, observing its concealed aspects and scrutinizing its difficulties. Of those who give light regard to the patterning (*li* 理) of their ambitions, all place value on external things. All those who value external things have inner anxiety. When their conduct departs from [established] patterns, they all face external dangers. And, facing external dangers, they all experience an inner dread. If one's mind is beset with anxiety and dread, though one's mouth may be full with fine meats, one will not appreciate the taste; though one's ears hear bells and drums, one will not appreciate the sound; though one's eyes behold fine embroidery, one will not appreciate its pattern; though provided with light warm clothes and a smooth grass mat, one will not appreciate their comforts.

Thus, facing the beauty of the myriad phenomena, one is unable to enjoy it. If one were to get some respite and enjoy it, one would not be able to leave [one's worries behind]. Thus, facing the beauty of the myriad phenomena, one is filled with anxiety; combining the benefits of the myriad things, one is overwhelmed by harm. This is a result of pursuing material things. Does it nurture life? Does it provide the nourishments for a long life span? Thus, if you wish to nurture your desires and indulge your emotions, then: wishing to nurture your natural tendencies (*xing* 性), you endanger your body; wishing to nurture your joy, you do violence to your mind (*xin* 心); seeking to nurture your fame, you disorder your conduct. Someone like this, although they may be made a feudal lord or named a ruler, they are no better off than common thieves. Although they may ride in carriages and wear ceremonial caps, they are no better off than those in straitened circumstances. This is what is called "making oneself a slave of material things."

22.6e If one's mind (*xin* 心) is tranquil and joyful, then even mediocre colors can nourish the eye, mediocre sounds can nourish the ear, course vegetables and thick vegetable soup can nourish the palate, clothes of coarse material and sandals of coarse silk can nurture the body. A tiny room with reed blinds and a straw mattress, together with a small table and a bamboo mat, can be used to nurture one's bodily form. Thus, though lacking the most beautiful things, one can nourish one's joy; and though lacking a position of authority or rank, one can nourish one's reputation. If, in addition, one were given the whole world, it would mean much for the world, but it would matter little to one's personal joy. All of this may be called "valuing oneself and making use of things."

22.6f Unsubstantiated theories, unprecedented conduct, and unheard-of schemes—*junzi* are wary of such things.

> *Comment:* This sentence has been dismissed as irrelevant in this context, and thus probably misplaced.ⁱ But a clear implication of this statement—that, likewise, one ought to be circumspect about unconventional terms—is a central theme of Chapter 22. Paraphrasing what was possibly a familiar saying with this implication does not seem an inappropriate way to cap the chapter. The statement also succinctly expresses Xun Zi's conservatism. But it does not express "realist" traditionalism, according to which the specific ways of the ancient sage-kings set unchangeable standards, a view sometimes attributed to Xun Zi. (For more on realist interpretations of Xun Zi, see Chapter 21, "Dissolving Beguilement," p. 200, below.)

"DISCUSSING THE MILITARY," *YI BING* 議兵 (CHAPTER 15), AND RELATED PASSAGES

A central question in "Discussing the Military" is whether successful military endeavors are a product of clever tactics and techniques, or whether such techniques are trivial compared to larger strategic issues that have ethical components. Xun Zi takes the latter view, namely, that the greatest strategic advantage comes from exercising *ren* 仁 (humanity), acting honorably (*yi* 義), following norms of ritual propriety (*li* 禮), and depending upon one's resultant influential character (*de* 德).

15.1a In the presence of King Xiaocheng of Zhao, the Lord of Linwu discussed the military with Xun Zi:

The king inquired, "May I ask about the essentials of the military?"

The Lord of Linwu responded, "Above, assure favorable climatic conditions; below, assure favorable geographic positions. Scrutinize the enemy's movements. Decamp last, but arrive first. These are the essential techniques of military deployment."

Xun Zi said, "This is not so. I, your humble servant, have heard that in the way (*dao* 道) of the ancients the fundamental issue in deploying the military for battle was, in general terms, unifying the people. If bow and arrow are not well coordinated, then even the great archer Yi would not be able to hit the bull's-eye. If a team of six horses were discordant, then even Zao Fu would be unable to reach distant places with them. If scholar-officials (*shi* 士) and the people are not committed to [their ruler] as if family, then even [the great kings] Tang or Wu would not have been assured victory. Thus, those adept at drawing the people close (*fu min* 附民) are adept at using the military. Thus, the essential point regarding the use of the military is drawing the people close, and that is all."

> *Comment:* "*Fu*" (附), in *fu min* 附民 ('drawing the people close'), has the sense of being or becoming near or attached to. But it also includes the sense of depending on, and agreeing to or submitting to, which may seem to suggest something like consent of the people as a requirement for successful warfare.

15.1b The Lord of Linwu responded, "This is not so. In the military, one treasures benefiting from tactical advantage, and conducts deceptive movements. Those adept at using the military move suddenly, covering great distances under cover of darkness, such that no one knows from where they have come. [The great generals] Sun Zi [author or *The Art of War*] and Wu Qi employed these tactics and were invincible. How could one need the support of the people?"

Xun Zi replied, "Not so. The *dao* to which I humbly refer involves the use of the military by persons who exemplify *ren* 仁 (humanity), which is the aspiration of [those who would become] kingly. What Lord Linwu treasures is scheming opportunism and benefiting from tactical advantages. Actions such as attacking for the purpose of taking by force, and deceptive movements, are the business of the feudal lords. A person of *ren*, in employing the military, does not permit (*ke* 可) deception.ʲ Those who can be deceived by others are careless and negligent, or are suffering clear distress. When the relations between ruler and ministers and between superiors and subordinates degenerate, then there is a divestment of influential character (*de* 德).

> *Comment:* The sentence literally refers to a moving away from *de*. *De* involves a potency, or power of influence, that has its root in the character of a person. And, the character of a person is not separable from the quality of his or her relationships. Thus the notion that deteriorating relationships results in diminished efficacy is implicit in the very concept of *de*.

"Thus, a [tyrant like] Jie will deceive another Jie. In such cases, cleverness or stupidity will determine their fortunes. But a Jie deceiving a [sage like] Yao is like throwing an egg against a rock, or stirring boiling water with one's finger, or entering water or fire—whereupon one will either be scorched or drowned. Thus, [under the rule of a] person with *ren* (humanity), superiors and subordinates, and the hundred generals are all unified in their thoughts and feelings (*xin* 心), and the three armies are coordinated in strength and effort (*li* 力). The ministers' relation to the ruler, and subordinates' relation to superiors, is like a son's service to his father, or a younger brother's service to his elder brother. It is like one's hands and arms protecting one's head and torso. Whether employing deception and then making a surprise attack, or first threatening and only then striking, the result will be the same. [...]"

> *Comment:* Let us connect Xun Zi's specific argument here to his more general arguments and positions. Notice, first of all, how Xun Zi appeals to the King's (presumed) desire to be kingly. All kings, he presumes, want wealth, power, and security. Indeed, that is our natural disposition, according to Xun Zi (see *Xun Zi*, Chapter 23, "Natural Dispositions Are Detestable," p. 218, below). And it was assumed that a "kingly" king, someone truly worthy of the title, would not only have a successful reign, but would unite the known civilized world. And what are the qualities of a true king? Do they not include, above all else, being *ren* 仁, that is, exhibiting humanity? In Xun Zi's more general theory, the way to achieve what we want is not to seek it directly, but rather to cultivate our character. He writes, for example, "*Ren* 仁 (humanity), conscientiousness (*yi* 義), virtue (*de* 德), and conducting oneself (*xing* 行) accordingly is characteristic of the style that reliably achieves security [...]" (*Xun Zi* 4.8). And this applies no less to military matters. Xun Zi explains, "If a ruler desires strength, security, peace, and joy, there is nothing better than turning back to the people. If one desires to make his subjects dedicated and to unify the people, there is nothing better than turning back to sound government" (*Xun Zi* 12.5). As for doing the opposite, Xun Zi states, "Piling up the conditions of danger, encroachment [of rival states], destruction, and annihilation, while seeking peace and joy, is a product of madness" (*Xun Zi* 12.5).

15.1f [Continuing the discussion with King Xiaocheng and the Lord of Linwu, who has become more agreeable, Xun Zi said:] "[...] With a [genuine] king (*wang* 王) there are punishments, but no battles. When cities are defended, he does not attack. Against a well-formed army, he does not strike. [On the contrary,] if superiors and subordinates [of a potential adversary] are pleased with each other, he congratulates them. [Further,] he does not butcher the inhabitants of an [annexed] city, does not conceal his forces, does not engage in mass arrests, and does not command military service for more than one season. Thus, those who have suffered chaotic rule delight in his governance. And those who are insecure under their current leadership long for his arrival." The Lord of Linwu indicated his approval.

15.2 Chen Xiao asked Xun Zi: "My teacher, in your discussions of the military, you consistently treat *ren* 仁 (humanity) and honorable conduct (*yi* 義) as fundamental. *Ren* 仁 refers to care for others, and honorable conduct involves according with practical coherence (*li* 理). So, explain again, what has this to do with the military? Ordinarily, to make use of the military is to create conflict in order to take something by force."

Xun Zi replied: "Your understanding is not correct. Those who have *ren* care for people. Thus, they hate it when others harm them. Honorable conduct involves according with practical coherence. Because they accord with practical coherence, they hate it when people create chaos. When they use the military, it is to stop violence and remove harm, not to create conflict in order to take by force. Thus, the use of the military by people who are *ren* [is as follows]: where present, it is miraculous (*shen* 神); where passing through, it is transformative. Just as with the fall of the seasonal rains, all are delighted. This is why [the great sage] Yao toppled Huan Dou, Shun toppled the rulers of the Miao, Yu toppled the Gonggong, Tong toppled the ruler of the Xia dynasty [the infamous tyrant Jie], King Wen toppled Chong, and King Wu toppled Zhòu [the last ruler of the Shang dynasty]. Of these four emperors and two kings, all conducted military activities throughout the civilized world with *ren* (humanity) and honorable conduct (*yi*). Those nearby loved their goodness. Those far off longed for their nobility (*yi*). Their armies did not bloody their swords, for both far and near willingly submitted. [...]

> *Comment:* It should be emphasized that this holds only if one's motives are truly pure, and one has accurately assessed the situation. If one merely uses the rhetoric of humanitarianism in the service of a petty hidden agenda, one can reasonably expect disaster. In this regard, consider the following comment, which Xun Zi makes elsewhere:
>
>> Seeing the desirable quality of something, one must sooner or later consider its detestable (*e* 惡) qualities. Seeing the beneficial aspects of something, one must sooner or later consider its harmful aspects. Weigh (*quan* 權) these aspects together, thoroughly gauge them, only then can one be confident whether the thing is desirable or detestable, whether to choose it or to reject it. This way, one will usually avoid falling into a great trap. Generally speaking, human tragedies are the result of skewed inclinations. Seeing the

desirable quality of something, one does not consider its detestable qualities. Seeing the beneficial aspects of something, one does not take into consideration its harmful aspects. If one acts in this way, one will surely encounter a pitfall, and suffer disgrace. This is the tragedy caused by skewed inclinations.

(Xun Zi 3.13)

These considerations are perhaps nowhere more important than when considering military interventions.

15.4 Norms of ritual propriety (*li* 禮) represent the highest culmination of distinctions conducive to governing well. They are the foundation of a strong state, express the way (*dao* 道) of awe-inspiring conduct, and serve as guidelines for achievement and fame. They are the means by which kings and dukes who follow them are able to acquire the whole civilized world (*tian xia* 天下). And those who do not follow them thereby bring ruin upon their Altars of Soil and Grain. Thus, solid armor and sharp weapons are not sufficient to be victorious. High walls and deep moats are not sufficient to be secure. Strict commands and numerous punishments are not sufficient to be awe-inspiring. If one follows the way (*dao* 道) [of ritual propriety], one will progress (*xing* 行). If one does not, one will collapse. [...]

15.6a Generally speaking, one who would unite people [by extending one's territory and bringing everyone under one's rule] has three options: using compelling virtuous character (*de* 德), using physical force (*li* 力), or using wealth.

If the people esteem one's fame and reputation, and admire (*mei* 美) the application of one's virtue (*de*), and desire to be one's subjects, then they would welcome one's entry with open gates and cleared roads. If one allows the common people to continue [their practices] and carry on living in the same place, and one leaves all the people in peace, they will abide by the laws and carry out one's commands, without anyone failing to be submissive. In this way, one's authority multiplies as one gains territory, and uniting the people [under one's rule] makes one's military strong. This is what comes of uniting people using virtue (*de*).

If the people do not esteem one's fame and reputation, and do not admire the application of one's influential character (*de*), but rather fear one's threats and are coerced under the forces one brings to bear, then the common people, although their thoughts and feelings (*xin* 心) are oppositional, will not dare to consider rebelling. In such a situation, weapons and armor will need to increase, and there are sure to be additional governing expenses. In this way, one's authority decreases more and more as one gains territory, and uniting the people [under one's rule] makes one's military weak. This is what comes of uniting people using physical force.

If the people do not esteem one's fame and reputation, and do not admire the application of one's influential character, but being poor they seek wealth, starving they seek food, then, with empty bellies and gaping mouths, they will come over to you in order to be fed. In such a situation, one will surely have to distribute rations, use one's stored grain to feed them, transfer one's wealth and goods to enrich them, and commit skilled and conscientious people to the maintenance of a bureaucracy to look after them. And then only after three years can the common people be trusted. In this way, one's authority decreases more and more as one gains territory, and uniting the people [under one's rule] makes one's country impoverished. This is what comes of uniting people using wealth.

Thus it is said, "One who uses virtue (*de*) to unite people will be kingly (*wang* 王). One who uses physical force (*li* 力) will be weakened. And one who uses wealth will be impoverished. In this the ancient and the present are as one."

Related Passages

9.7 Those who would use might: If city walls in other states are defended, and their people emerge to do battle, and I use my strength to defeat them, then there will surely be a great number of wounded among the common people of my adversaries. If so, they will surely detest me intensely. When other people detest me intensely, day by day they will grow more eager to fight with me. [In addition,] if city walls in other states are defended, and their people emerge to do battle, and I use my strength to defeat them, then there will surely be a great number of wounded among my own people. If there are a great number of wounded among my own people, then day by day they will grow less eager to fight for me. If others day by day grow more eager to fight with me, and my own people day by day grow less eager to fight for me, this is turning might into weakness. Territory is gained, but the people are lost. Exhaustive efforts are many, but achievements are few. Although [the territory] one defends increases, that with which one defends it decreases. This is how greatness is turned into ruin.

9.9 A [genuine] king (*wang* 王) is not like [a hegemon (*ba* 霸)]. His *ren* 仁 (humanity), integrity (*yi* 義), and majesty (*wei* 威) are the most marvelous in the whole world. His *ren* being the most marvelous in the world, there is no one in the world who does not feel a close affection for him. His integrity being the most marvelous in the world, there is no one in the world who does not esteem him. His majesty being the most marvelous in the world, there is no one in the world who would dare oppose him. By virtue of such majesty, he is unopposed. And by virtue of the *dao* of protecting and serving the people, he is victorious without battles, and gains [territory] without attacking, for the whole world submits without armor and weaponry being put to work. For one who knows the *dao* of kingliness: understanding these three strategies [using *ren*, integrity, and majesty], if he desires to be a [genuine] king, he will be one. [...]

> *Comment:* I've translated the character *wei* 威 as "majesty." But we would be wise to pause and consider this, for while Xun Zi is here using this term in a way that is surely intended to be taken positively, it has darker connotations that are relevant and should not be ignored in this context. In addition to meaning "majesty" and "dignity" (both of which we can imagine being supported by norms of ritual propriety), *wei* means "terrifying" and "to overawe," and we can easily see how those relate to no one daring to oppose such a king. I've chosen to use the more positive word "majesty" in the translation because Xun Zi's intent is to persuade his readers. But at the same time, we readers must be on our guard. Perhaps the two sides of this character tell us not so much what Xun Zi was thinking, but rather that, regardless of Xun Zi's intentions, personal charisma and intimidation are closely related, and the one can easily slide into the other. The striking example of Hitlerian fascism is hard to ignore.

10.5   When it comes to managing a myriad of changes, adjudicating[k] the myriad phenomena, nurturing (*yang*) the myriads of common people, and simultaneously governing the whole empire, people with humanity (*ren ren* 仁人) are the best (*shan* 善). Their wisdom and planning are sufficient to manage the changes; their humanity and generosity are sufficient to pacify the common people; and the resonance of their virtuous charisma (*de* 德) is sufficient to transform them. If such people are obtained, there will be order; if not, there will be chaos.

10.14   People who have *ren* 仁 (humanity) use their state not simply to hang onto what they have and no more, but to unify [all] people.

11.1a   One who uses the state to establish honorable conduct (*yi* 義) will be a [genuine] king (*wang* 王). One who uses it to establish trustworthiness (*xin* 信) will be a hegemon. And one who establishes scheming opportunism will be wiped out.

16.5 "The method of force should cease, and the method of *yi* (honorable conduct) should proceed." Why is this said? I say: it refers to the state of Qin. Qin's awesome military might rivals [that of the states ruled by the sage-kings] Tang and Wu, and its lands are as vast as those of the sages Shun and Yu. Yet it cannot conquer its own anxiety. Consumed by apprehension, Qin is in constant fear that the whole civilized world will unite to crush it. This is what it means to say, "The method of force should cease." [...] So what should Qin do? I say: It should moderate its military might, and stress civilian issues instead. It should then utilize *junzi* who are upstanding, honest, reliable, and whole to bring order to the civilized world. Availing themselves of this contribution to the state's governance, they should properly align right and wrong (*shi fei* 是非),[6] regulate the crooked and the straight, and put the capital, Xianyang, in order. Those who follow [the way] should be well placed. Those who do not should be punished only after their refusal. If this is done, then soldiers need no longer be sent beyond one's border, and yet decrees will be carried out throughout the civilized world. [...] In the case of our current age, the task of increasing territory is not as important as increasing trustworthiness.

18.2 King Tang and King Wu did not *seize* the world. They cultivated *dao* 道, and put honorable conduct (*yi* 義) into practice. They promoted the common benefit of the world, and eliminated the scourges, and so the whole world turned to them.

"A DISCOURSE ON *TIAN*," *TIAN LUN* 天倫 (CHAPTER 17), AND §§9.14, 9.16B, AND 9.16C

In the *Xun Zi*, the word "*tian*" (天) refers to the natural forces associated with the sky. In "A Discourse on *Tian*," Xun Zi argues against superstitious understandings of *tian*, and puts forward a view that may seem naturalistic. He uses the religious terms "auspicious" and "inauspicious," but shows how these need to be understood as the result of working with or against nature. Xun Zi sometimes uses "*tian*" 天 as shorthand for "*tian di*" 天地, 'the heavens and the earth,' and so the word "nature" can sometimes serve as a reasonable approximation.

---

6 For more on *shi fei* 是非, see *Xun Zi* 21.7b and 22.2a, pp. 207 and 210.

Xun Zi argues that there are limits to how much one should try to understand about the workings of *tian*. For this reason, Xun Zi has been blamed (unfairly) for China's slowness in adopting Western science. Xun Zi acknowledges that *tian* has the function of providing what is needed to make human flourishing possible. However, he stresses that what is most critical is to not overlook the role of human intelligence and effort in bringing to completion what *tian* has made possible. As Xun Zi writes elsewhere, "Nature (*tian di*) produces it, sages complete it" (*Xun Zi* 10.6 and 27.41). This expresses what Xun Zi describes as the "different roles of nature and humanity" (*Xun Zi* 17.1).

Notice how this attitude toward nature contrasts with Daoist attitudes. Daoists seek to ride the forces of nature like a benevolent wave, and they take natural propensities as indicative of strategies for living well. Xun Zi, on the other hand, suggests using our independent intelligence to harness what nature willy-nilly provides, and thereby making the most out of life. This does involve "going along" with nature (see *Xun Zi* 17.3a, p. 180, below), but in a different sense than the Daoists advocate. The way of the sages, he stresses, is not the way of *tian*, as he takes the Daoists, especially Zhuang Zi, to suggest; it is rather the way crafted by *junzi* (see 17.1, directly below). Just as Xun Zi views natural human dispositions as detestable and in need of reform (see Chapter 23, "Natural Dispositions Are Detestable," p. 218, below), so too the propensities of *tian* are not assumed to be automatically beneficial. On the contrary, Xun Zi suggests that we will have to combine intelligence and hard work to create a stable harmony. It is folly to simply depend on nature.

There is a sense in which "A Discourse on *Tian*" is *not* about *tian*. It is about the role of people, and how to create and maintain order, and reap the benefits thereof. Given the emphasis on following *tian* in Daoism, as well as Meng Zi's emphasis on naturally good human dispositions, perhaps Xun Zi felt the need to produce a treatment of *tian* that would clearly distinguish the role of humans from the role of *tian*.

(See Chapter 2, "Key Philosophical Terms," for more background on *tian*.)

17.1 Nature's course (*tian xing* 天行) has regularities, which do not exist for the sage Yao and then disappear for the tyrant Jie (cf. *Xun Zi* 23.4b, p. 227, below). Responding to them with orderly government is auspicious, while responding to them with chaos is inauspicious. If you strengthen the fundamentals and moderate expenditures, *tian* 天 (nature) cannot make you poor. If you are well nourished and act according to the seasons, then *tian* cannot make you ill. If you follow *dao* and do not go to excesses, *tian* cannot bring you to ruin.

Thus, neither flood nor drought can cause hunger or thirst, neither cold nor heat can cause illness, and unusual phenomena cannot cause misfortune. However, if one spends excessively while neglecting the fundamentals, then *tian* cannot bring prosperity. If one acts according to the unusual [rather than the normal] while fostering the trivial, then *tian* cannot keep [the state] safely intact. If, turning one's back on the way, one engages in rash and unreasonable conduct, then *tian* cannot bring good fortune. Thus, though struck with neither flood nor drought, there will be famine; though experiencing neither the slightest cold spell nor heat wave, there will be illness; though no unusual phenomena occur, there will be misfortune. Although subject to the same seasons as an orderly age, the calamities suffered will not be the same. One cannot blame *tian*, for its way (*dao* 道) is just as it is. Hence, those who are clear about the different roles of nature and humans (*tian ren zhi fen* 天人之分) can be called "the most competent people" (*zhi ren* 至人).

17.2a What is achieved without effort, or acquired without seeking, can be attributed to "the role of nature (*tian* 天)." This being so, truly excellent people (*qiren* 其人) do not ponder it even though it is profound, they do not apply their abilities to it even though it is vast, and they do not examine it even though it is exquisite. This is called "not competing for nature's job." The heavens (*tian*) have their seasons, the earth has its resources, and people have their government. This is called "being able to form a triad." One is surely deluded if, wishing to form such a triad, one abandons the means by which the triad is formed.[7]

> *Comment:* Xun Zi is using terminology from the *Zhuang Zi* here. For example, the supremely competent practice "undoing action" (*wu wei*), which, rather than meaning doing nothing, indicates skillful yielding and adapting to nature's ebbs and flows. Xun Zi suggests that the really competent person knows where to focus his or her efforts, that is, understands that nature and humans have different roles. According to Xun Zi, we should let nature be as it is, not seek to know its unknowable aspects, but rather work intelligently to create structures that allow people to effectively utilize its resources. In this sense, Xun Zi's competent person acts (*wei* 為), for not acting (*bu wei* 不為) is "nature's occupation," and people should not compete for that job. We have different responsibilities to attend to, namely, creating constructive artifice (*wei* 偽). This is

---

7 Cf. *Zhong Yong* 22, p. 243.

a theme in Xun Zi's Chapter 23, "Natural Dispositions Are Detestable,"
p. 218, below.

17.2b The constellations follow their circular paths, the Sun and Moon
shine in alternation, the four seasons supplant each other in turn, and
yin and *yang* perform great transformations. The wind and rain bestow
abundance. Each of the myriad creatures obtains conditions in harmony
(*he* 和) with what it needs to live; each obtains the nourishment by which
it achieves maturity. Its workings are invisible, yet its results are apparent. This is called "miraculous vitality" (*shen* 神). Everyone knows how
this is accomplished, but no one understands its intangible aspects. This
is called "*tian*'s work." Sages are exceptional in not seeking to know *tian*
(*zhi tian* 知天).

17.3a Nature's work is already established; its achievements are already
complete. It forms concrete provisions, and vitalizes life. The likes and
dislikes, the delights and aggravations, and the sorrows and joys contained therein are called "natural emotions" (*tian qing* 天情). Ears, eyes,
nose, mouth, and feeling, are all connected, yet they are not able to do
each other's work. They are called the "natural [sense] organs" (*tian guan*
天官). The mind resides in emptiness, thereby governing the five sense
organs, it is called the "natural ruler" (*tian jun* 天君). Resources that
are not of one's own kind but that nourish one's kind are called "natural
nourishments." Those who follow what is proper for their kind are said
to be happy, while those who go against this are called "hapless." This is
referred to as "nature's regulation" (*tian zheng* 天政).

To dim one's natural ruler, disorder one's natural sense organs, go
against nature's regulation, turn away from one's natural emotions, and
thereby forfeit nature's work—this may be called "extremely ominous."
Sages purify their natural ruler, attune their natural sense organs, make
preparations to attain their natural nourishment, conform to nature's
regulation, nurture their natural emotions, and thereby complete
nature's work.

> *Comment:* Notice that, despite Xun Zi's characterization of natural dis-
> positions (*xing* 性) as detestable (*e* 惡)—see Chapter 23, "Natural Dis-
> positions Are Detestable," p. 218, below—he here implies that there is *a
> sense in which* we are supposed to follow our nature.[8]

---

8 For a useful metaphor, see Ogyū Sorai's remark quoted near the end of the introduction to
the *Zhong Yong*, p. 237.

If this is the case, one knows what to do and what not to do. In this way, nature (*tian di* 天地) serves as an official, and the myriad things provide the labor. Their movements are channeled in an orderly manner, their nourishments are channeled as appropriate (*shi* 適), and living things are unharmed. This is called "knowing *tian* (*zhi tian* 知天)."

> *Comment:* Notice that 17.2b ended with the comment that sages do not try to know *tian*, whereas here, in 17.3a, Xun Zi seems to be approving of the idea of knowing *tian*. In the first instance (17.2b) Xun Zi is saying that one ought not to try to understand the intangible aspects of *tian*'s work, its dark secrets. Here (17.3a), however, Xun Zi is recharacterizing "knowing *tian*." He approves "knowing *tian*" only in his newly articulated sense. This is further clarified in the following section (17.3b).

17.3b Thus, great skill resides in what is not done;[9] great wisdom resides in what is not pondered. With regard to *tian* 天, the [wisdom and skill] to which one ought to aspire (*zhi* 志) goes no further than what is predictable in its observable phenomena. Regarding the earth, it ends with what can flourish according to its manifest suitability. Regarding the four seasons, it ends with what can be of service in their regular patterns. And, regarding *yin* and *yang*, it ends with what one can regulate in their observable harmonies. Officials oversee *tian*, and [the ruler] oversees the way (*dao* 道).

17.4 "Are order and chaos due to *tian*?" I say: The Sun, Moon, stars, and celestial points were the same for the sage Yu as for the tyrant Jie, yet Yu achieved order and Jie brought chaos. Order and chaos are not due to *tian*. "What of the seasons?" I say: Crops germinate, multiply, and grow in the spring and summer. They are harvested and stored in the fall and winter. This was also the same for Yu and Jie, yet Yu achieved order and Jie brought chaos. Order and chaos are not due to the seasons. "What about the earth?" I say: If there is fertile soil there will be growth, without it there will be death. This was also the same for Yu and Jie, yet Yu achieved order and Jie brought chaos. Order and chaos are not due to the earth. The *Odes* say, "*Tian* made high hills; the Great King cleared them. With that accomplished, King Wen made them bountiful." This expresses my meaning.

17.5 *Tian* does not suspend winter on account of people who loathe cold weather; the earth does not curtail its expansiveness on account of

---

9 Cf. Chapter 9, *Lao Zi*, p. 311.

people who detest great distance; and *junzi* (exemplary persons) do not discontinue moral conduct on account of the clamoring of petty people. *Tian* has a regular course, the earth has a constant measure, and *junzi* have a consistent deportment. *Junzi* proceed (*dao* 道) according to what is regular, while petty people reckon on what might be exploited. The *Odes* say: "Being without fault in the performance of ritual and propriety, why worry what others say?" This expresses my meaning.

> *Comment:* We can make an inference here about Xun Zi's ethical perspective. We understand that Xun Zi's goal is creating a stable harmony—where everyone can find fulfillment and largely have their desires satisfied. Thus, Xun Zi's ethical thinking seems to have a strong consequentialist component. However, he stresses that the best way to achieve what one desires is not by following one's spontaneous desires, but rather by following *dao* 道 (see §§22.6b–22.6c, p. 168, above), the path walked by *junzi* (§8.3, see the "Key Philosophical Terms" chapter: *dao*). And, in particular, the passage above (17.5) makes it clear that it is best to view things from a broad perspective, and to determine what kinds of behaviors (regularized as norms of ritual propriety) are most conducive to harmonious conditions—which will be most beneficial to everybody. These norms are attuned to the regularities of the human condition, including the regularities of nature. Xun Zi's view, then, bears some analogy to rule utilitarianism, in the following sense. It is best to follow a reliable path rather than seek advantage in what may seem like freak opportunities. Following the latter course, one may suppose, will often backfire with regard to its immediate aim, and will tend to undermine general harmony. For these reasons, "*Junzi* proceed according to what is regular."

17.6 For the king of Chu to have an entourage of 1,000 chariots does not indicate intelligence. For *junzi*, living in straitened circumstances does not indicate stupidity. This is due to the circumstances being what they are. On the other hand, aspiring to self-cultivation, manifesting much virtuous conduct, deliberating with clarity, and commemorating the past while living in the present—these things are up to us. Thus, *junzi* cherish what resides in themselves, not what resides in *tian* 天 [forces beyond their control]. Small-minded people disregard what resides in themselves, and cherish what resides in *tian*. Since *junzi* respect themselves, rather than cherishing the result of *tian*, they continually progress. Since small-minded people disregard what resides in themselves and admire what resides in *tian*, they continually regress. Thus, what accounts for the continual improvement of *junzi* and the continual worsening of the small-minded is one and the same thing. *Junzi* are separated from small-minded people by nothing but this.

17.7 Falling stars and crying trees terrify everyone in the country. They ask, "What does it all mean?" I say: These are nothing but variations in the natural world (*tian di* 天地), transformations of *yin* and *yang*, or something extremely rare. One may regard such things as strange, but one ought not to fear them. Solar and lunar eclipses, unseasonable weather, or the freak appearance of a strange star—there has been no age in which such things did not commonly occur. If rulers are clear-minded and their government stable, then even if all these phenomena occurred simultaneously, it would be of no harm. If rulers are benighted and their government reckless, then although not one of these things occurs, it will be of no advantage. The falling of stars and the crying of trees, these are variations in the natural world (*tian di*), transformations of *yin* and *yang*, or something extremely rare. One may regard such things as strange, but one ought not to fear them.

The most genuinely frightful things are [not natural anomalies, but rather] the ominous activity of people, such as tilling so roughly that crops are damaged, weeding and hoeing such that the whole crop is lost, or governing recklessly, leaving the people to die from neglect. When agriculture is poorly administered, and grain becomes so expensive that the people are starving, so that the roadsides are littered with corpses, this is an ominous phenomenon due to people. When government decrees are unclear and ill-timed, and misguided policies are promoted, so that fundamental affairs are not reasonably handled, these are ominous activities of people.

If laborers are put to work in the wrong season, then oxen and horses will interbreed, and the six domesticated animals will engage in monstrous behavior. If ritual and propriety are not promoted, inner and outer will not be distinguished. And, if men and women are promiscuous, father and son will doubt each other, rulers and subordinates will be at odds, and invasions and [internal] difficulties will occur simultaneously. These are ominous activities of people. Such ominous activities are the product of disorder. There is no peaceful state where these three blunders occur. The explanation is very near at hand, and the disaster is of tragic proportions.

One may regard [natural anomalies] as strange, but one ought not to fear them. A tradition says: "The *Documents* do not explain anomalous phenomena." Distinctions that serve no purpose, and observations on matters that are not pressing, should be disregarded and not mastered. But as for the appropriate relation between ruler and ministers, the close relations between father and son, and the respective roles of husband and wife, cut and polish them every day and do not give up.[1]

17.8 If one prays for rain and it rains, what does this mean? I say it means nothing. It is just like when one does not pray, yet it rains anyway. When the Sun or the Moon undergo eclipse, one tries to rescue it; faced with drought, one prays for rain; and, important matters are decided only after performing divination. It is not that one thinks one will get what one seeks through these means, they are to ornament the occasion. Thus, *junzi* regard them as ornaments, while the common people regard them as miraculous (*shen* 神). Regarding them as ornaments is auspicious, regarding them as miraculous is inauspicious.

17.9 In the heavens, there is nothing so illuminating (*ming* 明)[10] as the Sun (日) and the Moon (月). On the earth, there is nothing so clear and bright (*ming*) as water and fire. In things, there is nothing so brilliant (*ming*) as pearls and jade. In people, there is nothing so radiant (*ming*) as ritual and propriety (*li-yi*). If the Sun and the Moon were not high, their light would not shine with fiery awesomeness. If water and fire did not accumulate, their radiance and wetness would not be ubiquitous. If pearls and jade did not manifest themselves, kings and dukes would not regard them as treasures. If ritual and propriety are not applied in a state, its achievements and due fame will not be clearly apparent. Thus, the human condition (*ren zhi ming* 人之命) depends on nature (*tian*); the fortunes (*ming*) of the state depend on ritual propriety. The ruler who exalts ritual propriety and reveres virtuous people will be a [true] king. One who stresses law and has concern for the common people will be a hegemon. One who is fond of profit and is deceitful will be in danger. And, one who engages in schemes and intrigue, and commits subversive and devious acts, will be completely annihilated.

> *Comment:* The point of this passage is clear enough: Ritual propriety (which is a product of sages not the work of *tian*) is the key to kingly success. However, this interpretation of the comment about the *ming* of people (*ren zhi ming* 人之命—translated as "the human condition"), though not critical to understanding the point of the passage, is tentative. And an alternative is worth considering. The character *ming*, often

---

10   The character *ming* 明, repeated throughout this passage, is a pictograph of the Sun (日) and the Moon (月), symbolizing clarity and brightness.

translated "fate," and sometimes "life," as in one's fate to live or die, does not mean fate in a strict sense. Confucians were not fatalists. The future is not thought to be fixed or determinate. Rather, *ming* signifies something more like "the propensities of circumstances that condition events." Consider, for example, *Meng Zi* 7A2: "A person who understands *ming* does not stand beneath a wall that is poised to collapse." And thus the circumstances of people in general (*ren zhi ming*) is "the human condition." This interpretation fits well with the general point of the chapter—that *tian*'s role is to set the conditions, and the sage's role is to structure a way to secure harmony given these conditions. However, there is another very plausible interpretation, if *ren* is taken to mean not "people in general," but rather "a person," which contrasts nicely with larger matters of the state. In this case, *ren zhi ming* may mean something more like "personal circumstances" or "the life of a person." According to this interpretation, freak occurrences, which are out of one's control (an implication of being a product of *tian*), such as sickness, can be decisive with regard to an individual's life; but, as Xun Zi argues at the beginning of this chapter (p. 178), *tian* cannot ruin a well-run state. On this view, the point of the sentence is to make this contrast. However, Xun Zi also says that *tian* cannot make one sick. So, if we take it this way, Xun Zi seems to be inconsistent on this point. Then again, Xun Zi does say elsewhere, "Putting humanity (*ren*), honorable conduct (*yi*), and influential character (*de*) into practice is the method that *usually* achieves peace and safety" (4.8), though there is no guarantee. His real view of *tian*'s relation to an individual's health may be analogous. His claim about sickness at the beginning of the chapter may be read as hyperbole. In the end, it seems that both interpretations are plausible. And both can be regarded as consistent with, and even revealing of, Xun Zi's philosophy. One fits better with the theme of the chapter, the other does better contrasting two clauses in this passage.

17.10

Which is better, emphasizing *tian* and pondering it, or regulating things and livestock?

Which is better, following *tian* and singing its praises, or curbing its forces and utilizing them?

Which is better, observing the seasons and waiting for them, or responding to them and making use of them?

Which is better, relying on things and increasing them, or giving free rein to one's abilities and transforming them?

Which is better, contemplating things as if they were given, or patterning them so as not to miss their potential?

Which is more important, the source from which things are produced, or that by which they are completed?

Thus, if one neglects people and ponders *tian*, one will miss the
actual situation regarding the myriad things.

> *Comment:* As Xun Zi writes in §12.3, "Regarding the myriad things of
> *tian* and the earth, [*junzi*] do not devote themselves to explaining how
> these things are as they are, but rather are devoted to the skill of utilizing
> their resources." Similarly, in §23.3b, Xun Zi writes, "Those who are good
> at discussing *tian* must show the relevance to people."

17.11 If something did not change throughout the period of the hundred kings, this is enough to consider it a connecting thread of the way.
One should respond to the ups and downs of history with this thread.
If one applies patterns (*li* 理) to this thread, there will not be disorder.
But if one does not understand it, one will not know how to respond to
changing circumstances. The main principles of this thread have never
disappeared completely. Disorder is born of their divergence, order from
exhausting their details. Thus, as to the efficacy of the way, if [these
principles] are threaded together (*zhong* 中[11]), then [the way] can be followed; if they are scattered, one will be unable to govern; and if they are
hidden,[m] there will be great delusion.

   Those who ford rivers indicate the deep spots. If the indications are
not clear, people will fall in and get stuck. Those who bring order to the
common people indicate the way. If the indications are not clear, there
will be disorder. Norms of ritual propriety are the indicators. If ritual
propriety is rejected it will be a dark age, and in such an age there is
great upheaval. Thus, if the way is always clear, the outer and inner are
differently indicated, and there is regularity regarding what is concealed
and what is displayed, then the pitfalls that plague the common people
will be avoided.

> *Comment:* Notice that this metaphor does not imply that there is only
> one way to get across the river. Rather, the markers mark a known way
> across, with attention to avoiding known hazards. This is perhaps even
> clearer in a similar passage:
>
> > Those who ford rivers indicate the deep spots, allowing others to
> > avoid falling in. Those who bring order to the common people
> > indicate the sources of disorder, enabling others not to fall into

---

11   *Zhong* 中 (in the sense of "pierce") maintains the metaphor of a thread binding the way.

error. Rituals are the indicators. The former kings used rituals to indicate the sources of the world's disorder. To abandon ritual now is to remove the indicators. Thus, the common people are confused and misled, and fall into misfortune and disaster. That is why punishments are so numerous.

(*Xun Zi* 27.12)

17.12 The myriad things (*wan wu* 萬物)[12] make up one part of the way. One thing makes up one part of the myriad things. Foolish people, who make up just one part of one thing, yet believe themselves to know the way, lack [full] knowledge. [The Legalist] Shen Zi saw the value of what comes later [i.e., *fa* 法 (laws, models)], but failed to see the value of what comes first [i.e., *junzi*].[13] Lao Zi saw the value of yielding,[14] but failed to see the value of standing by one's words. Mo Zi saw the value of uniformity, but failed to see the value of the exceptional. And, Song Zi saw the value in reducing [consumption], but failed to see the value of increasing [productivity].

If one has what comes later [i.e., laws] but not what comes first [i.e., *junzi*], the masses have no gate to enter.[15] If there is yielding and no standing by one's words, then the noble and base will not be distinguished. If there is uniformity and no one is exceptional, then government decrees will not be carried out. If there is reduction [of consumption] but no increase [in productivity], then the masses will not transform [their ·character]. The *Book of Documents* says, "Do not do as you please. Follow the way of kings. Do not be adverse. Follow the road of kings." This expresses my point.

Comment: The point about laws—if there are no *junzi* the masses will not have a means to develop morally even if there are good laws—is expressed in more detail in *Xun Zi* 12.1:

There are rulers who produce chaos; there are no [naturally] chaotic states. There are persons who produce order; there are no formal models (*fa* 法) that can do so. The methods (*fa* 法) of the

---

12 The meaning range for the term "*wan wu*" 萬物 (the myriad phenomena–things–beings) can, at its most inclusive, include both all things and all processes ("the myriad phenomena"), or, it can suggest, on the less inclusive side, only animals ("the myriad critters").

13 This passage could also be read: "Shen Zi saw the value of following [the model/law] but did not see the value of leading." This amounts to the same thing. Cf. *Xun Zi* 21.4, p. 203. Similarly, a subsequent sentence could be read, "If there are followers [of the law], but no leaders, the masses have no gate to enter." Again, it amounts to the same thing.

14 See, for example, *Lao Zi* 36: "The supple and weak surpass the firm and strong."

15 Regarding what comes first (what is fundamental) and what comes later, see the "Canonic Core of the *Da Xue*" (in Chapter 3, p. 60).

archer Yi are not lost, yet such an archer does not appear generation after generation. The laws and norms (*fa* 法) of the sage-king Yu [of the Xia dynasty] still exist, yet the Xia could not continue its rule. Thus, *fa* cannot stand on its own; Categories (*lei*) cannot apply themselves. If there are good persons, then [the state] will survive. If there are no good persons then it will be lost. Laws and norms (*fa*) are the starting point of orderly government. *Junzi* are the wellspring of these laws and norms. Thus, if there are *junzi*, this is sufficient for a vast state, even if laws and norms are omitted. But if there are no *junzi*, then although a state may be equipped with laws and norms, it will misstep in the application of priorities, and its inability to cope with changing circumstances will suffice to result in chaos.

This idea is expressed again in *Xun Zi* 14.2:

> *Junzi* are vital for uniting *dao* with *fa* (law, model). They must not be neglected even for a short time. If they are acquired there will be order; if they are lost there will be chaos. If they are acquired there will be peace and security; if they are lost there will be danger. If they are acquired, [the state] will survive; if they are lost it will perish. Thus, there are cases in which there were good laws, and yet there was chaos. But I have never heard of a case, from ancient times to the present, of there being *junzi* and yet chaos. A tradition says, "Order is produced by *junzi*; chaos is produced by inferior people." This expresses my point.[16]

The point here is analogous to that expressed at the beginning of this chapter. That is, rather than being the work of *tian* (i.e., natural propensities associated with "the heavens"), it is the action of people that gives rise to fortune or misfortune. Similarly, laws by themselves cannot assure order; appropriate interpretation and implementation of those laws are also necessary.

From Chapter 9, *Wang Zhi* 王制, "Kingly Regulations," §§9.14, 9.16b, and 9.16c

9.14 By the Northern Sea there are galloping horses and yapping dogs; so the Central States acquire them and domesticate them. By the Southern Sea there are feathers and quills, tusks and hides, as well as copper

---

16 Cf. *Analects* 2.3, p. 94.

and cinnabar; so the Central States acquire them as resources. By the Eastern Sea there is purple dye, coarse cloth, fish, and salt; so the Central States acquire and use these for clothes and food. By the Western Sea there are skins, hides, and colored yak tails; so the Central States acquire and make use of them.

Thus, the people who live in marshland have enough timber. The mountain people have enough fish. Farmers neither carve or scrape, nor mold or smelt, and yet they are equipped sufficiently with tools. Craftspeople and merchants do not plough fields, yet they have sufficient beans and grain. And so, though the tiger and leopard may be fierce, the *junzi* nevertheless have them skinned and utilized. Everything that is covered by *tian* and supported by earth exhaustively fulfills its potential beauty, and achieves its full utility. Above, the worthy and good are thereby adorned. Below, the hundred families are thereby nurtured and experience peace and joy. Thus, this is called "the great marvel (*shen* 神)." The *Odes* say, "*Tian* made the high mountains. King Tai cultivated them. He completed the work. And King Wen enjoyed it." This expresses my meaning.

9.16b The regulations of sage-kings: In the season when grasses and trees flower, bloom, and grow large, axes are not to enter the mountain forests, so as not to cut short their lives, and cut off their growth. In the season when turtles, crocodiles, and fish are pregnant and laying their eggs, fishing nets and poisons are not to enter the marshes, so as not to cut short their lives, and cut off their growth. Ploughing in spring, weeding in summer, harvesting in fall, and storing in winter—these four are not to be neglected in their season. Thus, the five grains will not run out, and the hundred families will have surplus food. The seasonal prohibitions regarding ponds, lakes, rivers, and marshes are attentively observed. And so fish and turtles proliferate, and the hundred families have surplus supply. The seasonality of cutting down and of nurturing growth is not neglected. And so the mountain forests are not denuded, and the hundred families have surplus timber.

> *Comment:* Just as "A Discourse on *Tian*" was largely about the different roles for *tian* and for humans, emphasizing how humans bring to completion what *tian* has provided, this passage explains how sagely artifice, here emphasizing "regulations" and prohibitions involving the wise management of natural resources, enables both nature and humans to flourish.

9.16c The usefulness of sage-kings: They examine the heavens above, and establish [regulations] on the earth below. They fill in the space between the heavens and the earth, and add their contribution to the myriad things.

> *Comment:* Given the examples, examining *tian* may involve discerning the regularities of the seasons. Having done so, the sage then establishes a way of living that makes the most out of the natural conditions. Compare the last sentence with the notion that humans form a triad with *tian* and the earth, expressed in 17.2a, p. 179, above, as well as in 23.5a, p. 228, below (see also 19.6, p. 196).

"A DISCOURSE ON RITUAL PROPRIETY," *LI LUN* 禮論 (CHAPTER 19)

Confucius stressed the importance of *li* 禮 (ritual propriety) more than anything else, with the sole exception of the encompassing virtue of *ren* (humanity).[17] And *li* was the key to becoming *ren* 仁 (*Analects* 12.1). Meng Zi, however, though he did include *li* in his list of virtues—along with *yi* 義 (honorable conduct), *ren*, and *zhi* 智 (wisdom), he did not emphasize it. Indeed, given Meng Zi's view of natural dispositions and their development, it is not clear that *li* has a very important role to play.[18] Meng Zi did say, "Without ritual propriety (*li*) and honorable conduct (*yi*) there will be disorder between superiors and inferiors" (*Meng Zi* 7B12). But he did not go nearly as far as Xun Zi in insisting that *li* is of vital importance. In a chapter on self-cultivation, for example, Xun Zi writes, "People cannot survive without *li*. Endeavors will not succeed without *li*. Neither the state nor the home will be at peace without *li*" (*Xun Zi* 2.2).

In the present chapter, Xun Zi provides his account of the origin and function of *li*, including both how the development of character depends on *li*, and how *li* in turn depends on people with a developed character (see especially *Xun Zi* 19.6, p. 196). That is, there is a virtuous cycle in which ritual propriety, on the one hand, and sages, *junzi*, and aspirants, on the other, support and develop each other.

At the end of the chapter (especially from *Xun Zi* 19.7b, p. 197), Xun Zi explains the function of mourning rituals in particular, justifying the traditional periods of mourning. Mourning rituals are particularly important for Xun Zi because of the importance of dealing effectively

---

17   As a rough indication, in the *Analects* the character *li* 禮 occurs 75 times, *ren* 仁 occurs about 109 times, whereas *yi* 義 occurs only 24 times.

18   Xun Zi stresses this in his critique of Meng Zi in Chapter 23, "Natural Dispositions Are Detestable," 23.3a, p. 225.

with the beginning and ending of life, which are occasions, respectively, of great joy and great sorrow. Xun Zi writes, "Ritual propriety is cautious attentiveness in the management of life and death" (*Xun Zi* 19.4a). Mohists, on the other hand, find the lavish funerals and long mourning periods advocated by Confucians to be harmfully excessive. Xun Zi responds by suggesting that Mohists fail to take into account the *indirect* benefits of ritual propriety. (For Xun Zi's criticism of Mohism see *Xun Zi* 19.1d, 19.3, 19.8, pp. 192, 194, and 197, below, and 17.12 and 21.4, pp. 187 and 203.)

––––––––––

19.1a How did ritual propriety (*li* 禮) arise? I say: People are born with desires. If these desires are not fulfilled, [the object of desire] will surely be sought after. If this seeking has no measure or bounds, contention will be inevitable. If there is contention, then there will be chaos, and if there is chaos, there will be difficulty and impoverishment. The ancient kings detested this chaos. Thus they fashioned (*zhi* 制) ritual and propriety (*li-yi* 禮義), and thereby made divisions that nurture (*yang* 養) people's desires and provide for their satisfaction. They ensured that desires were not [so excessive] as to completely exhaust material goods, so that material goods would not be depleted by desires, but that the two—[material goods and desires]—were held in a lasting balance. This is how ritual propriety came about.

19.1b Ritual propriety is nurturing (*yang* 養). The meat of livestock, rice, fine millet, and the five flavors with their harmonious aromas, serve to nurture the mouth. Fragrant spices and sweet-smelling perfume serve to nurture the nose. Carved jade figures, engraved metal, embroidered robes, and decorative seals serve to nurture the eye. Drums and chimes, zithers and flutes, serve to nurture the ear. Homes, cushions, beds, and mats serve to nurture the body. Thus, ritual propriety is nurturing.

> *Comment:* It is not just that ritual propriety nurtures people in a way analogous to these other things. Rather, ritual propriety ensures these other nurturing material goods are sufficiently available to provide their nurturing qualities. So ritual propriety nurtures indirectly. More specifically, §19.1a tells us that ritual propriety was devised to make sure that desires and material goods remained in balance, with sufficient material goods to satisfy appropriately nurtured desires, while §19.1b reminds us how various material goods nurture us.

However, §19.1a also suggests that ritual propriety is not only instrumental in ensuring that desires are *satisfied*, but also that desires are themselves nurtured. But what does *that* mean? Here we have to speculate. The character translated "nurture," *yang* 養, has the following relevant senses: to rear, support, and enable to survive; to take good care of one's health; to educate; and, as a noun, provisions necessary for life. Perhaps the sense of "to educate" has prominence in this context. Desires remain even after self-cultivation through ritual propriety. But these desires have nevertheless undergone a kind of education, by repeatedly finding themselves adequately satisfied when ritualized norms are observed. This leads to an appreciation and fondness for these norms and the distinctions that they mark.

19.1c *Junzi*, having received their nurturance (*yang* 養) [made possible by ritual propriety], also cherish its distinctions. What are these distinctions? I say: The eminent and the lowly have an order of precedence according to their status. The young and the old have different responsibilities. Deficiency and abundance, triviality and seriousness, everything has a term that distinguishes its weight. [...]

19.1d Who understands that facing death when one's integrity is on the line is the way to nurture life? Who understands that incurring expenses in useful endeavors is the way to nurture wealth? Who understands that respectfulness, deference, and yielding is the way to nurture contentment? Who understands that ritual and propriety (*li-yi*), and refined patterns are the means to nurture one's feelings (*qing* 情)? [The answer is: Confucians do, and Mohists do not.]

Accordingly, those people who look only at how to stay alive will surely die. Those who only look to benefit [i.e., the Mohists] will surely incur harm. Those who seek ease in laziness, passivity, and cowardice will surely be endangered. Those who seek joy in emotional pleasures will surely be ruined. Thus, if people focus on ritual and propriety (*li-yi* 禮義), then they will achieve both [propriety and emotional satisfaction].[19] If they focus on emotional dispositions, then they will lose both. So, Confucians (*ru* 儒) will enable people to achieve both, and Mohists will cause them to lose both. This is the difference between Confucians and Mohists.

Comment: The first sentence of 19.1d does not seem to be a valid criticism of Mohism. But the second sentence refers clearly to the Mohist critique

---

19 The word "both" here most plausibly refers to *li-yi* and the satisfaction of our emotional desires, as Dubs suggests (1973, 215n8).

of Confucian ritual extravagance, especially extravagant funerals. Xun Zi argues that obsession with immediate material benefits blinds one to significant indirect benefits, some of which are also material, that accrue in time as a result of observing ritualized norms, even seemingly expensive ones (see *Xun Zi* 21.4, p. 203, below). This blindness, in the end, leads people who follow what they regard as a direct path to survival, ease, and joy to end up with the very opposite. Confucians understand this, Xun Zi maintains, and their emphasis on ritual propriety is based on the understanding of its indirect and long-term effects.

However, the characterization of Mohists here is problematic. As we have seen, the Mohists' concept of benefit was limited to basic necessities, and they were quite critical of any kind of material excess. The mutual accusation of hedonism between Ruists and Mohists is an oddity that is worthy of note.

19.2a Ritual propriety has three sources (*ben*本, root): Nature (*tian di* 天地) is the source of life, ancestors are the source of categories [i.e., clans], and rulers and exemplars are the sources of order. Without nature, how could there be life? Without ancestors, how could we emerge? Without rulers and exemplars, how could there be order? Were these three forsaken, there would be no contentment for humanity. Thus, ritual propriety serves the skies above and the earth below; it venerates ancestors, and exalts rulers and exemplars. These are the three sources of ritual propriety [...]

19.2c Generally, ritual propriety (*li*) commences with kindness,[n] culminates in refinement (*wen* 文), and concludes with delight and flourishing.

> *Comment:* This fits with assertions Xun Zi makes in other passages. For example, in §19.11 below, Xun Zi twice states that, "Memorial rituals accrue from mournful remembrance and the determination to commemorate." This suggests that at least some individual rituals have their origin in something like kindly feelings, which are not at first formalized. But when forms are adopted which give an outlet for these emotions, the results are satisfying and edifying to the actor and the observer alike.

Thus, the best is when natural emotions (*qing* 情) and refinements (*wen* 文) are both used to their fullest potential. The next best is when emotion and refinement each take precedence in turns. In the worst case, people revert merely to emotion, and thereby return to too much of one thing.

The earth and sky accord with each other [according to patterns of *li* (ritual propriety)]. The Sun and Moon thereby shine [in alternation], just as the four seasons proceed in order, and the stars traverse the sky. The rivers and streams flow [according to patterns of *li*], and the myriad things thereby flourish. Likes and dislikes are moderated [by *li*,] and pleasure and anger thereby suit the circumstances. [Through *li*] subordinates become deferential and superiors become insightful. The myriad transformations do not bring disorder. Deviating from *li* would bring sorrow. Has not ritual propriety reached great heights? Establish and exalt it, regard it as the most lofty, and nobody in the world can add to or subtract from it.

Comment: Notice the mystical tone Xun Zi takes in the above paragraph.

Root and branch adjust to each other; beginning and end respond to each other. Culture at its best enables [productive] distinctions; scrutinizing at its best enables explanations. Everywhere in the world, those who follow [norms of ritual propriety] are orderly; those who do not are in chaos. Those who follow them are secure; those who do not are in danger. Those who follow them live; those who do not perish. Petty people are not able to fathom this. [...]

19.3 It is in accordance with ritual propriety (*li* 禮) to regard material goods as having merely practical utility (*yong* 用), but to regard the distinction between eminent and humble as a matter of refinement (*wen* 文), and to regard issues of quantity as having merely practical utility, but to regard the contrast between flourishing and decline as truly important. When refined patterns (*wen li* 文理) multiply, and emotions (*qing* 情) and merely practical utility are reduced, this is the flourishing of *li*. But when refined patterns are reduced and emotions and merely practical utility intensify, this is the decline of *li*. When refined patterns and emotions and utility are made the inner and outer of each other—that is, the exterior expression and the inner content—and when they proceed in parallel yet as a mixed composite, this is the middle course of *li*. Thus, *junzi* at their highest bring forth its flourishing, at their lowest they get the most possible out of decline, and at the middle level they dwell in the middle. But whether they are walking slowly or galloping along, they never leave it. For it is their sacred world and palace. People who keep to this are *junzi* or aspirants (*shi* 士). Those who diverge from it are but ordinary people (*min* 民). And one who dwells in it, covering all directions and throughout the whole circumference, with every turn attaining the next sequence, this is a sage.

Comment: This is a critique of Mohism, as well as a corollary to Xun Zi's thesis that our natural emotional dispositions are detestable (*xing e*). "Practical utility," in this context, is concerning oneself with things that have merely direct practical usefulness. Xun Zi is concerned about these things too, but the way to address them is indirect, that is, by focusing on patterns of proper conduct. If one dwells in ritual propriety, other matters will take care of themselves.

Thus, generosity is the accumulation of ritual propriety; greatness is its expansiveness; elevation is its loftiness; brilliance is its exhaustive use. The *Odes* say: "Ritual ceremony, completely according to the standard; laughing and talking, completely appropriate." This expresses my meaning. [...]

Comment: According to the earliest extant commentary on the *Xun Zi*,[20] "By quoting this [Xun Zi] makes clear that, for the person who has *li*, every movement is fitting and appropriate." But what does that actually mean? Perhaps, rather than each movement according to some sort of script, each personalized assessment of the situation is expressed in exemplary conduct that is both within the bounds of proper norms and pleasantly effortless, as though "second nature" (cf. *Analects* 17.11, 12.1, pp. 76 and 81, and the additional passages cited in notes and comments there). Cf. *Xun Zi* 2.6: "Embody respect with a truly sincere heart. Practice *li-yi* (ritual and propriety) with the inner emotion of care for others. When traveling the world, although you may be surrounded by barbarian tribes, everyone will regard you with esteem."

19.5b Ritual propriety (*li* 禮) cuts off what is long and extends what is short; it decreases what is in excess and increases what is not enough. Making manifest refined forms of care and respect, it fosters and brings about the beauty of putting honorable conduct into practice. [...]

People certainly are born having in them the beginnings (*duan* 端; cf. *Meng Zi* 2A6) of both the emotions [of grief and delight in response to fortunate and unfortunate events]. If one trims them, extends them, broadens them, narrows them, increases them, decreases them, discriminates among them, gets the most out of them, hones them, and beautifies them, and if they span the root and the tip, the end and the beginning, and if everyone follows this thoroughly such that it is sufficient to be taken as a standard for ten thousand generations, then this is *li*. None but a *junzi* 君子 (exemplary person) who has undergone comprehensive cultivation can appreciate this.

---

20   This was written by Yang Liang in the early ninth century CE.

Comment: Xun Zi suggests that we should work hard to improve on our natural dispositions, to get the most out of the human condition. Ritual propriety provides the means by which we train and reform our emotional dispositions. (This connects to Xun Zi's view of natural dispositions, see *Xun Zi* 19.6, directly below.) Only *junzi* fully appreciate *li*, because they have personally experienced the value of following *li* and of undergoing the changes that such cultivation brings about.

19.6 Thus I say: Natural dispositions (*xing* 性) are the root and beginning, the unadorned raw material. *Wei* 偽 (artifice)[21] is the flourishing abundance of refined patterns. If there were no natural dispositions, then there would be nothing to which *wei* could add. If there were no *wei*, natural dispositions would not be able to beautify themselves. When natural dispositions and artifice come together, only then do sage-kings fulfill their name, and the achievement of unification of the world is accomplished in this. Thus I say: The heavens and the earth meet and the myriad things come to life. *Yin* and *yang* joining together, changes and transformations arise. Natural dispositions (*xing*) and artifice (*wei*) combine, and the world is ordered. *Tian* 天 can generate things but cannot articulate distinctions among them. Earth can support people but cannot order them. The myriad things of the whole world, and all living people, await sages—and only then are they apportioned. The *Odes* say: "They appease the hundred spirits (*shen* 神), and even the rivers and lofty mountains." This expresses my meaning. [...]

Comment: Notice that *xing* remains, but it is adorned with *wei*, which is added to it. This passage also expresses the notion of people forming a "triad" with *tian* (the heavens, that is, the forces associated with the sky) and *di* (the earth), which is expressed explicitly in §§17.2a and 23.5a, pp. 179 and 228. People complete what *tian* and *di* have made possible. As Xun Zi expresses it in §10.6: "Nature (*tian di*) produces it, sages complete it." And this completes a kind of circle. Here is how Xun Zi puts it in §9.15:

The heavens (*tian* 天) and the earth are the beginning of life. Ritual and propriety (*li-yi* 禮義) are the beginning of good government. *Junzi* are the beginning [i.e., the source] of ritual and propriety. Acting on them, stringing them together, increasingly emphasizing them, and bringing about a fondness for them is what first brings about *junzi*. Thus, the heavens and the earth produce *junzi*, and

---

21   For an explanation of *wei* 偽 see *Xun Zi* 22.1b, 23.1c, and 23:2a, pp. 209, 221, and 223.

junzi apply patterns (*li* 理) to the heavens and the earth. [...] If there were no *junzi*, the heavens and the earth would not be patterned.

Xun Zi believes that moral structure, which includes ritualized norms of proper conduct, is needed to shape people's character productively. However, those norms have their source in, and are continually adjusted by, *junzi* who have developed their own character through participation in the very system that they oversee. In other words, *junzi* are responsible for guiding the development of the very moral constructs that guided the development of their own character, a character that makes them qualified to do this. Another way Xun Zi expresses the mutual shaping of ritual propriety (*li*) and exemplary persons is as follows: "*Li* is that by which one's person is straightened (*zheng* 正). A teacher is the means by which *li* is straightened" (*Xun Zi* 2.11).

[Mourning Rituals]

19.7b Generally speaking, ritual propriety addresses birth by providing structured ornamentation to joy, and sees off the dead by providing structured ornamentation to grief. In sacrificial offerings it provides structured ornamentation to reverence, and in military marches it provides structured ornamentation to military might. This was the same for the hundred kings, and the ancient and present are united in this, though we do not know its origin. [...] The funeral rites are for nothing other than this: To illuminate what is appropriate in both death and life, and send off the dead with grief and reverence, finally to bury them. [...]

19.8 The depriving of the dead to give unto the living is called "Mohism." The depriving of the living to give unto the dead is called "delusion." The killing of the living to accompany the dead is called "murder." [On the other hand,] sending off the deceased in a way that represents the best of their life, assuring that from death to birth, from end to beginning, there is nothing that is not gauged so as to be fitting, and being fond of excellence (*shan* 善), this is the exemplary application of ritual propriety and consummate conduct (*li-yi* 禮義). Confucianism (*ru* 儒) is just this.

> *Comment:* Here is a succinct expression of the core of Confucianism, framed as a kind of middle way. Confucianism, on this view, is simply the well-intentioned striving to give appropriate form to judiciously balanced practices, wherein the symbolic meaning of actions, as well as their concrete consequences, are regarded as significant.

19.9a Why have a three-year mourning period? I say: It is a cultural pattern (*wen* 文) that was established according to natural feelings (*qing* 情), justified because it adorns society and provides a venue for distinguishing the intimate and the distant, as well as marking degrees of eminence or humbleness of station. And one must neither extend it nor truncate it. Thus it is said: "Unmatched, it is a method which has not altered." [...]

19.9c Shall we follow stupid, vulgar, wanton, and depraved people? If so, someone who dies in the morning will be forgotten by evening. If we follow this way, we would not even be as good as birds or beasts. How could such people associate with each other, form groups, and live together without chaos? Shall we [on the other hand] follow the cultivated and refined *junzi*? Then, finishing the twenty-fifth month [which marks the end] of the "three-year mourning" would be like a horse traversing a mere crack. If we proceeded in this way, mourning would have no end.

> *Comment:* Here Xun Zi may be being sarcastically critical of the practices of some of the more extreme Ruists.° Note that the so-called "three-year" mourning period is actually 25 months, that is, extending into the third year. In the West, years are counted as having been completed, so "three years" would mean 'three complete years' (or close enough). In China, however, years are counted from the beginning. A baby in its first year of life is said to be one year old. To say that the mourning period must be three years is to say that it must continue some time into the third year.

Thus, the former kings and sages settled the matter by establishing a middle course, fashioning a fixed term. Once it adequately achieves refined patterns, mourning should finally come to an end.

> *Comment:* Similarly, Xun Zi comments, "At the point when a change in emotion shows in one's countenance sufficient thereby to differentiate fortune from misfortune, and to clarify the distinction between the eminent and the humble, and the nearness or distance of relation, then the period [of mourning] comes to an end."[22]

So then, how is [the mourning period] to be apportioned? I say: Mourning for one's closest relative is to be cut off at one year. Why is this? I say: The world (*tian di* 天地) completes its changes, the four

---

22 This is from *Xun Zi* 19.5b, included here rather than above, because it addresses mourning rituals specifically.

seasons finish their cycle, and within the cosmos there is nothing that does not begin anew [at the end of a year]. Thus, the former kings set a limit using this as an analogy. Then why into the *third* year? I say: To add to its loftiness, they doubled it, and so added another year. What about periods of nine months or less? I say: To make sure that [these shorter mourning periods] do not reach the longer limits. Thus, the three-year period is regarded as [the most] lofty. The three-month and the five-month periods represent a reduction. And the one-year and nine-month periods are in between. Above, one finds an analogy in the heavens (*tian* 天). Below, one finds an analogy in the earth. In the middle one finds a guideline for people simply in that by which people can most reasonably live together in a harmonious (*he* 和) and unified community. Thus, the three-year mourning period is the height of cultural achievement in the way of people (*ren dao* 人道), and is referred to as the loftiest. In this the hundred kings were agreed, and it is a point on which antiquity and the present are as one.

19.11 Memorial rituals accrue from mournful remembrance and the determination to commemorate. No one can avoid being so stricken by emotion at some time that he or she winds up panting in despair. Thus, even when the people are happy and harmonious, faithful ministers and filial children may be so stricken. When this occurs, one feels a very great impulse to act. But if this is suppressed and pent up, those in whom the determination to commemorate accrues will be demoralized and discontented. And their ritualized management [of their feelings] will be defective and deficient. Thus, the former kings studied the matter, and established cultural patterns (*wen* 文), which achieved the utmost appropriateness in respecting those who are due respect (*zun zun* 尊尊), and showing familial love for one's loved ones (*qin qin* 親親).[23] This is why I say: Memorial rituals accrue from mournful remembrance and the determination to commemorate. They are the epitome of faithful commitment, care, and respect. They are the flourishing of ritualized norms and cultural forms. If it were not for sages, no one would be able to understand this. Sages know it clearly; aspirants and exemplars practice it with ease; officials regard it as their charge; and the common people become accustomed to it. *Junzi* regard it as a human way (*ren dao* 人道); the common people regard it as involving spirits. [...]

---

23 *Analects* 12.11 uses a similar construction: "Rulers rule (*jun jun* 君君); ministers minister (*chen chen* 臣臣); parents parent (*fu fu* 父父); and children likewise fulfill the roles proper to children (*zi zi* 子子)."

Comment: Here Xun Zi spells out an explicitly secular justification for mourning rituals which fits with his secular interpretation of *tian* 天 (expressed most explicitly in *Xun Zi* 17.1, p. 178; cf. also 17.8, p. 184, above).

"DISSOLVING BEGUILEMENT," *JIE BI* 解蔽 (CHAPTER 21)

The chapter title, *Jie Bi*, has been translated variously as "Dispelling Blindness" (Knoblock), "Dispelling Obsession" (Watson), "The Removal of Prejudices" (Dubs), and "Undoing Fixation" (Hutton). *Jie* means "to untie," and *bi* means blinders, such as worn by a horse to block its peripheral vision. So the idea is literally "untying the blinders." This is a metaphor for dissolving beguilement regarding *dao*. I translate this as "beguilement" to capture the sense of being led astray as a result of mental captivation.

Taken as a whole, "Dissolving Beguilement" seems to have been written to not only critique rival schools such as Mohism, Legalism, and Daoism but also to criticize rulers who fail to exercise good judgment. Of course, such judgment is thought to involve the acceptance of Xun Zi's own conception of the *dao*. And so Xun Zi is, practically speaking, encouraging rulers to employ Confucian advisers such as himself. However, good judgment is characterized as weighing all considerations as dispassionately as possible. Thus, Xun Zi is stressing the importance of thinking and acting intelligently, and wisely.

Some aspects of this chapter may seem to be about how to discern the *true* nature of reality. But notice that the idea of dissolving beguilement suggests a *via negativa* of sorts—saying what is *not*, rather than what *is*. This method allows for the possibility that there is not a pre-existing unambiguous truth to be discovered and articulated, or if there is, it is not Xun Zi's concern. Although Xun Zi does provide a way to achieve "clarity," to replace beguilement, it is an open question whether this should be understood as (1) clarity in one's discernment of the ultimate nature of reality (which implies metaphysical realism), or (2) clarity that leads to the stabilization of a productive set of distinctions which are nonetheless contingent products of unperturbed judgment, rather than pre-existing patterns. Some interpreters find support in this chapter for (1). The original text is consistent with both interpretations. In this translation, I endeavor to reveal the plausibility of (2), while not excluding the possibility of (1).

21.1 The downfall of most people is beguilement (*bi* 蔽) with one corner [of the way], while being in the dark regarding the greater coherence (*da li* 大理).[p] If this were mastered, there would be a revival of the classics. If there is doubt about two [conflicting views], then there will be confusion. There are not two ways in the world; a sage is never of two minds. Now, the feudal lords have different governments, and the Hundred Schools have different theories. Certainly some [of these ways] are to be affirmed, and others rejected; some [lands] are well governed, others are in chaos.

Comment: This passage has been the source of some controversy, especially the statement, "There are not two ways in the world." What does that mean? What *kind* of claim is it? Is it a metaphysical claim about the ultimate nature of reality? If so, should it be understood in connection with the "greater coherence"? Some scholars read this as a statement of metaphysical realism, that there is a single Great Pattern to the world[q]—and likewise to *dao*—a uniquely coherent holistic guiding discourse. Taking this passage by itself, this is surely one plausible interpretation. But it is not the only one. If some of the "different theories" of "the Hundred Schools" are to be affirmed, and if "some" lands, although different from each other, are well governed, then that suggests that there is *at least* some degree of variation that is tolerable. Further, the claim that there are not two ways in the world should probably be interpreted in light of the claims that come just before and just after it. Namely, if there is uncertainty there will be confusion, and the sage is not wavering or indecisive. This suggests that there are *practical* reasons (rather than metaphysical ones) for rejecting the idea that there can be two ways in the world: They cannot be made manifest in the world simultaneously, at least not fully or effectively. And this is precisely a point that Xun Zi makes more clearly elsewhere. He writes "The ruler is the most exalted in the state. The father is the most exalted in the family. Exalting one [results in] order; exalting two [results in] chaos. From ancient times to the present, there has never been a situation that was able to endure for very long with two exalted, each contending for respect" (14.7). And again, Xun Zi writes, "One who [tries to] travel two roads [at the same time] will not reach their destination. One who serves two lords will not please [them]. The eye cannot, when looking at two things, see them clearly. The ear cannot, when listening to two things, hear them well" (1.6). And later in this very chapter Xun Zi writes, "If one's thoughts and feelings (*xin* 心) branch off in two directions, there is no realization (*zhi* 知). [...] If the mind is divided, there will be doubts and confusion.

By making an appraisal upon examination, the myriad things can all be realized (*zhi* 知). And by making the most of what is given, one can attain a beautiful character. A category cannot be two things. Thus, the wise select one, and unify around it" (21.6a, not included below). Much in this last passage is unclear, and could be understood and translated in various ways. But the notion of selecting or choosing (*ze* 擇, choose, pick; differentiate) strongly suggests contingency stemming from someone's personal judgment. And the sentence about attaining a beautiful character almost seems out of place, unless we infer that the point being made throughout is unremittingly practical. If so, to realize (*zhi* 知) is not just to know intellectually, but to know in a way that can be put into practice—to be made real. These considerations should be kept in mind as one thinks about the rest of the chapter.

Rulers of chaotic states, and followers of confused schools of thought, without exception, sincerely strive to be upstanding and unbiased (*zheng* 正), and they believe that they are. While they hate to be misguided about the *dao*, others seduce them with what is congenial. Proud of their own merits, they only fear hearing of their flaws (*e* 惡). Viewing alternative methods by comparison to their own, they fear only hearing of the attractiveness (*mei* 美) of these other methods. For this reason, while departing from what supports order, they are unceasing in their self-affirmation. How could it be that they are not beguiled by one corner [of the way] and neglectful of precisely what should be sought after? If one's mind is not engaged, one will not see black and white in front of one's eye. Thunderous drums can sound at one's side and one will not hear them. Is this not the condition of those who are beguiled? Regarding people who follow the *dao* of virtue (*de* 德), the rulers of chaotic states reject them from above, and the followers of confused schools of thought reject them from below. How can this not be lamented?

21.2 What is the cause of beguilement? One may be beguiled by desires or aversions, by the beginnings or the ends, by what is distant or what is near, by what is broad or what is shallow, and by what is old or what is new. Whenever the myriad things are differentiated, each parsing will obscure (*bi* 蔽) others. This is the common downfall of the operations of the mind.

Rulers of the past who were beguiled include Jie of the Xia dynasty and Zhòu of the Yin dynasty. Jie, beguiled by [his concubine] Mo Xi and [his counselor] Si Guan, did not appreciate the value (*zhi* 知) of Guan Longfeng. As a result, his thoughts and feelings (*xin* 心) were confused and his conduct disorderly. [And Zhòu was beguiled with similar results.[24]] [...] Jie died on Mount Li, and Zhòu's head was hung on a red pennant. They could not foresee these events themselves, and there was no one who would remonstrate with them. These are the misfortunes of being obstructed by beguilements.

Successful Tang observed the case of Jie. Thus, he mastered his thoughts and feelings and cautiously regulated them. In this way he was able to employ the services of Yi Yin over a long period, and not lose the *dao* in his personal conduct. This is the reason he succeeded the last king of the Xia dynasty and received the Nine Possessions. [King Wen acted similarly, with similar results.[25]] Thus, [Tang's and Wen's] eyes were treated to the full array of colors, their ears entertained by every sound, and their mouths tasted the full array of flavors. They resided in well-provided palaces, and their name received the full complement of honorable titles. When alive, the whole world sang, and all within the four seas wept at their death. Now, this is called "the pinnacle of prosperity." The *Odes* say: "A male and female phoenix dance, their wings like shields, their sounds like flutes. There is a male phoenix, and a female, bringing joy to the emperor's heart." This expresses the blessings of not being beguiled. [...]

Comment: Section 21.3 (not included) tells additional stories that parallel those told in §21.2 above, making the same point.

21.4 The beguilement of the traveling advisers of former times is exemplified by representatives of the confused schools of thought. [1] Mo Zi was beguiled by utility (*yong* 用) and did not appreciate the significance (*zhi* 知) of refinement. [2] Master Song was beguiled by desires and did not understand (*zhi* 知) attainment. [3] Shen Dao [the proto-Legalist] was beguiled by law and did not appreciate the role of virtuous people (*xian* 賢). [4] Shen Buhai [the bureaucratic Legalist] was beguiled by influence and did not appreciate (*zhi* 知) wise advice (*zhi* 知). [5] Hui

---

24 Details omitted in the main text: "Zhòu, beguiled by [his concubine] Daji and [his counselor] Feilian, did not appreciate the value of Prince Qi of Wei. As a result, his thoughts and feelings were confused and his conduct disorderly. Thus, their entire body of ministers abandoned loyal devotion (*zhong* 忠) and instead served their own selfish interests. Resentful, the hundred clans rebuked them and refused to be employed. The able and virtuous retired or fled into hiding. This is how they lost the territory of the Nine Pastures, and weakened the country of their royal ancestral temple."

25 Details omitted in the main text: "King Wen took note of the fate of Zhòu of Yin, and thus took control of his thoughts and feelings and governed them cautiously. This way he was able to employ Lü Wang for a long time and not lose the way in his personal conduct. This is the reason he succeeded the last king of the Yin and received the Nine Pastures. None of the distant quarters failed to send their most rare treasures."

Zi [the logician] was beguiled by terminology (*ming* 名) and did not understand actual things (*shi* 實). And, [6] Zhuang Zi was beguiled by *tian* and did not appreciate the role of the human.

> *Comment:* Note that the schools of philosophy numbered (1) through (6) above are linked to the implications of these schools numbered (1) through (6) in the following paragraph.

Consequently, [1] considered merely in terms usefulness, *dao* is reduced to the pursuit of profit. [2] Considered merely in terms of desire, *dao* is reduced to the pursuit of satisfaction. [3] Considered merely in terms of law, *dao* is reduced to calculating. [4] Considered merely in terms of influence, *dao* is reduced to the gaining advantage. [5] Considered merely in terms of language, *dao* is reduced to discourse. [6] Considered merely in terms of *tian*, *dao* is reduced to going along with things.

Each of these various attempts address only one corner of the way. The *dao*, however, embodies regularities through all changes. Addressing one corner is not sufficient to raise it up. People with warped understanding perceive only one corner of the way, although they are not able to recognize this. Thus, assuming their one corner to be sufficient, they dress it up [as if it were the whole *dao*]. They thereby confuse themselves and mislead others. Superiors thereby beguile inferiors, and vice versa. These are the misfortunes of being beguiled and confounded.

Confucius [on the other hand] exhibited humanity (*ren* 仁) and wisdom (*zhi* 知), and moreover was not beguiled. His study of an eclectic variety of doctrines and arts is sufficient to rank him among the former kings. [Appropriating them into] a single school, he achieved an encompassing (*zhou* 周)[26] way. He promoted it, and put it to use, without being obsessed by old customs. Thus, he had transformative power (*de* 德) on par with the Duke of Zhou, and acquired fame equal to that of the three kings. These are the fortunes of not being obsessed or beguiled.

> *Comment:* The character *zhou* (周) occurs twice in the above passage, and while the second occurrence refers unambiguously to the Duke of Zhou (one of the founders of the Zhou dynasty), the first occurrence is ambiguous. Some interpret this passage to say that Confucius "taught the way of the Zhou" (Watson) or "grasped the way of the Zhou" (Hutton), as if Confucius was merely following a pre-established pattern.

---

26 For an example of drawing from various sources to formulate a particular set of standards, see *Xun Zi* 22.1a, p. 208.

However, the character *zhou* also has semantic meaning which fits the context. It means "careful, thorough; general, extend, spread all over, extending all over, pervade," or, as translated above, "encompassing." It may be being used as a pun, simultaneously alluding to the way of the founders of the Zhou dynasty, since it is immediately repeated in the latter sense.

Taken as a whole, especially considering the line about not being obsessed with old customs, this passage makes it clear that Confucianism does not support blind obedience to tradition.

21.5a Sages know the perils of ideology, and apprehend the misfortunes of being beguiled and confounded. Thus, they have no desires or aversions, no [presumption of] beginnings or ends, near or distant, sophisticated or superficial, or old or new. They simultaneously set out the myriad phenomena and impartially hang them in a balance. For this reason, the multifarious distinctions do not beguile (*bi*) each other and thereby throw their arrangement into chaos.

21.5b What do we call this balance? "*Dao.*" It is imperative for the mind to understand *dao*. [...]

21.5c Only after the mind understands (*zhi* 知) *dao* can it affirm *dao*. [...] Thus, what is essential to achieving order is to understand *dao*.

Comment: The character *zhi* 知 is often translated "to know" or "to understand." And this is sometimes adequate. But here we should be careful not to overintellectualize the word. It can mean something closer to "awareness" (as it does below). Sometimes I gloss it as "appreciate the significance"—to have a sense of something and be aware of its importance. Other times I render it "to realize," which gives it *more than* an intellectual aspect (rather than *less of* one). That is, the intellectual is but one component, the other is making the idea an actuality. This dual intellectual/practical-realization meaning of *zhi* has a parallel in the meaning of *zheng ming* (proper terminology)—which is about, on the one hand, making terminology constructive (which is an intellectual task), and on the other hand living up to the roles and responsibilities defined by such terminology.

21.5d How do people understand (*zhi*) *dao*? I say: With the mind (*xin* 心). How does the mind come to this understanding? The answer is:

emptiness, unity,[27] and stillness. The mind is never without something stored, and yet it has what I call emptiness. The mind never lacks multiplicity, and yet it has what I call unity. The mind is never without motion, and yet it has what I call stillness. People are born with awareness (*zhi* 知). With awareness comes aspiration. And one who aspires stores [things in one's mind]. Even so, there is what I call emptiness: *not using what is already stored up to disrupt what will be received* [i.e., open-mindedness]. The mind from birth has awareness[r] (*zhi* 知). Awareness (*zhi*) involves perceiving differences, of which one is aware simultaneously. Being simultaneously aware of differences is multiplicity [in awareness]. Even so, there is what I call unity: *not letting one perception interfere with another.* When one sleeps, the mind dreams; when one makes no effort, it wanders off on its own; when one puts it to work it concocts plans. Thus, the mind is never without motion. Even so, it has what I call stillness: *not letting dreams and fictions confuse one's understanding.* Now, those who are seeking *dao* but have not yet grasped it, I tell them: be empty, unified, and still. If one who seeks *dao* endeavors to be empty, it will be taken in. If one who seeks to serve *dao* endeavors to be focused, one may serve *dao* exhaustively. If one who seeks to ponder *dao* endeavors to be still, it may be scrutinized. To understand *dao* and scrutinize it, to realize (*zhi*) *dao* and put it into practice, this is to embody *dao*. Emptiness, unity, and stillness I call great clarity and insight.

21.5e [For people with such clarity and insight:] Of all the myriad things, nothing that has shape cannot be seen; nothing seen cannot be appraised; nothing appraised is given a faulty status. Such people sit in a room, and yet observe the four seas. They occupy the present, and yet evaluate the distant past. They keenly observe the myriad things, and understand (*zhi* 知) distinctive features (*qing* 情). They examine and compare [conditions leading to] order and disorder, plumbing their depths. They weave norms into the world (*tian di* 天地), tailoring functional roles for the myriad things. They fashion and carve out a grand coherence (*da li* 大理), [giving form to] the inner lining of the cosmos. So extensive, so expansive, who knows their limits? So broad-minded,

---

27 Although there are many passages in which Xun Zi uses this word, *yi* 壹, as a verb meaning "to unify," he also uses it, both as a noun and a verb, with the sense of focus, or unity of purpose: "The *junzi* focuses (壹) on instruction, the student focuses on learning, determined to accomplish" (*Xun Zi* 27.89). Here is another example: "There have been many who were fond of writing, but the name of Cang Jie alone is passed down, because of his unity of purpose (壹). [There are several other similar examples.] From ancient times until the present, there has never been anyone whose focus was divided (兩) and yet was able to become extremely proficient. Zeng Zi said, 'While considering whether he can kill a rat with a stick, how can he sing with me!'" (*Xun Zi* 21.7c). Cf. the comment to *Xun Zi* 21.1, p. 201, and *Xun Zi* 1.6, p. 159.

so boundless, who knows their virtue? Boiling and bubbling from one to another, who knows their form? Their brilliance (*ming* 明) forms a triad with the Sun (*ri* 日) and the Moon (*yue* 月). Their vastness fills up the Eight Poles. They deserve the name "Great Persons." How could such a person be beguiled? [...]

> *Comment:* Notice that the 'grand coherence' here is 'fashioned' (*zhi* 制) and carved out (*ge* 割). *Ge* means 'to sever with a knife.' The relevant meanings of "*zhi*" 制 include 'to make, institute, and establish,' with an underlying metaphor of 'to cut out clothes,' and thus 'to fashion' (*zhi* 製). In other contexts, Xun Zi writes that the sages "fashioned (*zhi* 制) ritual and propriety (*li-yi* 禮義)" (19.1a), and "fashioned the sounds of the Ya and the Song in order to guide [the people]" (20.1).

21.7b A person's mind is like a pan of water. If you place the pan properly and don't move it, then the mud will settle to the bottom, and it will be so clear and bright on the top that one can see one's beard and eyebrows, and inspect the patterns on one's skin. But if a gentle breeze passes over it, the mud will move at the bottom, and the clarity and brightness will be disturbed at the top, such that one will be unable to see even large shapes properly. The mind is also like this. If you guide it with patterns (*li* 理), support it with clarity, and let nothing destabilize it, this will suffice for it to establish right and wrong (*ding shi fei* 定是非), and resolve (*jue* 決) doubts and suspicions. But if one is distracted by minor issues, then the propriety of one's overt behavior will be altered, and one's mind will be internally askew, and thus inadequate for the resolution (*jue* 決) of even general patterns.

> *Comment:* First, *shi fei* can mean "is and is not" as well as "right and wrong." And *ding*, "establish," has the sense of deciding, defining, and stabilizing. Similarly, *jue* means to resolve, in the sense of decide, as in a court decision. It involves making a judgment. More literally, it means getting rid of obstructions (remember that that is precisely the theme of this chapter), and more specifically dredging a channel. A realist interpretation downplays the contingency implicit in the meanings of *ding* and *jue*, and emphasizes the stability they also suggest. This view is suggested to the modern Western reader by what may seem to be an allusion to a correspondence between what is seen in the pan and *Reality*. It is not altogether clear, however, that Xun Zi meant to imply this. It is certainly true that Xun Zi is concerned about order and stability. But is the stability he seeks something that he views as a product of the

judicious, though contingent and underdetermined, decisions of someone who is calm and objective? Or is the presumed possibility of stability an indication that Xun Zi thinks of this as a problem with a single
solution—where the answer is already determined—rather than calling
for contingent *resolution*?

"PROPER TERMINOLOGY," *ZHENG MING* 正名 (CHAPTER 22), §§22.1A–22.4C

Note: For §§22.5–22.6, see the section included in, "*Xun Zi* on Motivation," p. 166, above.

On the surface, this chapter seems to be about the philosophy of language. But it is just as much about ethics and social philosophy. Recall
that Confucius said, in *Analects* 13.3, that the first thing he would do, if
entrusted with the governance of a state, is to make names proper (*zheng
ming* 正名). Likewise, Xun Zi writes, "[S]pecifying, naming, making distinctions, and explaining [...] are the beginning of the kingly enterprise"
(*Xun Zi* 22.3f).

   Xun Zi stresses the importance of establishing clear and sensible
agreed-upon terms of all kinds in order to avoid confusion, and the
social chaos that can result from it. He is also concerned more specifically with terms that have implications for our moral reasoning, terms
such as "*xing*" 性 (natural dispositions), "*qing*" 情 (emotions), and "*wei*"
偽 (artifice). (*Xing* and *wei*, in particular, are discussed in more detail in
Chapter 23, "Natural Dispositions Are Detestable," p. 218, below)

––––––––––

22.1a Regarding the established terms (*cheng ming* 成名) of the later
kings: penal terms came from the Shang dynasty, terms of nobility came
from the Zhou dynasty, and cultural terms came from the *Rituals*. The
miscellaneous terms attached to the myriad phenomena came from the
social practices of the various kingdoms of the Xia dynasty. Remote villages with differing customs rely on them to communicate.

Comment: Notice that, on Xun Zi's view, there is not a single basis for
terms. Rather, there are several different ways in which terms have
become legitimately grounded. These 'established terms' are, it seems,
contingent products of history. And thus they are neither rationally
privileged nor *ultimately* grounded, though they do have an adequate
grounding in tradition to function as standards.

22.1b Miscellaneous terms regarding what resides in people are as follows: The means by which life is as it is—this is called "*xing* 性" (natural disposition). *Xing* coordinates the natural living process, with the subtle conjoining of sensation and response. That which requires no work, but is naturally so of itself—this is called "*xing* 性." The likes and dislikes, delights and aggravations, and the sorrows and joys that are part of *xing* are called "emotions" (*qing* 情). When the mind (*xin* 心) makes choices, given these emotions, this is called 'deliberation.' When the mind is able to act on its deliberations, this is called '*wei*' 偽 (artifice, i.e., deliberate human activity). After deliberations have been accumulated and abilities have been trained, so that there is an achievement—this is [also] called '*wei*' 偽 (artifice, i.e., the products of deliberate activity).

> *Comment*: "*Wei*" 偽 is a technical term for Xun Zi. It is a tricky one because he gives two different definitions of it. It means both deliberate human activity and the products there of, such as norms of ritual propriety. Another significant product of deliberate activity is the character of the individuals who 'deliberately' train and habituate themselves in accordance with these norms. So, "*wei*" sometimes has the sense of 'acquired character.' (For more on this, see *Xun Zi* 23.1c, p. 221, below.)

Acting for the sake of the proper (*zheng* 正) and beneficial (*li* 利) is called 'work' (*shi* 事); acting for the sake of the proper and honorable (*yi* 義) is called 'proper conduct' (*xing* 行). What resides in people whereby they have knowledge (*zhi* 知) is called 'understanding' (*zhi* 知). The part of our understanding responsible for coherence (*he* 合) is called 'intelligence' (*zhi* 智). The means in people by which they are enabled is called 'ability' (*neng* 能). The part of ability responsible for coherence (*he* 合) is also called 'ability.' When natural disposition (*xing* 性) is injured, this is called 'illness.' The conditions one encounters are called 'the circumstances of one's life' (*ming* 命). These are the various terms regarding what resides in people. They are the terms established by the later kings.

22.1c Thus, when a [true] king institutes (*zhi* 制) terms, firmly establishing them and distinguishing objects (*shi* 實), putting *dao* into practice and conveying his intentions, he cautiously guides the people and unifies them. Thus, hair-splitting expressions and creating terms without proper authority throws proper terms (*zheng ming* 正名) into disarray, causing the common people to be confused and uncertain, and ordinary people to be argumentative and quarrelsome. This is called a "great corruption." It is as blameworthy as falsifying tallies or measurements. None of [a true king's] people would dare jumble proper terms on account of strange expressions.[28] Thus, the common people will be acquiescent. When they are acquiescent they are easy to employ. When they are easy to employ there will be achievements. None of his people would dare jumble proper terms on account of strange expressions. Thus, there would be unity with the way and the model, which would be cautiously abided by. In this way he would have a lasting legacy. Such a legacy and achievements are the epitome of good government, they are the successes that come from being cautious in securing agreed upon terms.

> *Comment:* Notice Xun Zi's appeal to good consequences as a standard of evaluation. However, here what is largely responsible for the good consequences is not the *brilliance or rationality* of the attunement of language, but rather the fact that there is *agreement* on terms.

22.2a   Now, the sage-kings are no more, the preservation of terms is lax, strange expressions have arisen, and terms (*ming* 名) and their objects (*shi* 實) are in disorder. When the contours of "this" and "not this" (*shifei* 是非, which include value distinctions) are not clear, even officials who uphold the law and the Confucians (*ru* 儒) who recite and enumerate it are confused.

> *Comment:* Cf. *Xun Zi* 18.9: "Ordinarily, discussions must first establish ample standards of correctness (*zheng* 正) and only then is one able to assent [to a conclusion]. If there are no such standards, then 'what is' and 'what is not' (and value distinctions) are not differentiated, and arguments and controversies will not be resolved. Thus it is said: 'The great and lofty of the world, the boundaries of "this" and "not this" (and value distinctions), what gives rise to differentiating duties and naming forms, this is kingly government.' Therefore, ordinarily, when discussions turn to specifying, assigning names (*ming* 命), and saying 'this is' and 'this is not' (including making value distinctions), people should take the sage-kings as their teachers."

If [true] kings were to arise, they would certainly go along with old terms and create (*zuo* 作) new ones. That being the case, [1] the reason for having terms, [2] tracing the origins of sameness and difference, and [3] the pivotal and essential points of instituting terms must be scrutinized.

---

28   Xun Zi is presumably referring here to the "strange expressions" that he addresses below. See §22.3, p. 214.

Comment: Notice that, despite his emphasis on maintaining tradition, Xun Zi does suggest it would be legitimate for a true king to create new terms.

[(1) "The Reason for Having Terms"]

22.2b When different appearances pass through the mind and are mutually compared, they are understood as different things. When terms and actual things (*shi* 實) are obscure and muddled, then noble and base are not clear, and similar and different are not distinguished. In this way there will surely be disasters resulting from misunderstood intentions, and there will surely be misfortune caused by exhaustion and waste. Therefore the wise make distinctions and institute (*zhi* 制) terms, using them to identify objects. In this way noble and base are made clear, and things that are similar are distinguished from those that are different. When the noble and base are clear, and the similar and the different are differentiated, there will be no disasters resulting from misunderstood intentions, and there will be no misfortune caused by exhaustion or waste. These are the reasons for having terms.

Comment: While the word "*zhi*" 制 can have the sense 'to institute,' as it seems to here, it should be remembered that the underlying metaphor is 'to cut out clothes,' thus 'to tailor,' as mentioned above (p. 207). Etymologically it is the same as *zhi* 製, 'to fashion, invent, compose.' This suggests some degree of conventionality is probably assumed.

[(2) "Tracing the Origins of Sameness and Difference"]

22.2c So, then, how do we trace the origins of similarity and difference? I say, we trace them to our natural senses (*tian guan* 天官). For all [creatures] of the same type, having the same conditions, the perceptions of their natural faculties are the same. When things are compared side by side, resemblances are perceived the same everywhere. This provides the means by which agreed-upon terms (*ming* 名) are stipulated in relation to one another.

Comment: Notice that "terms" (*ming* 名) here seems to mean something like 'concepts.'[8] In reading the following several paragraphs notice when "term" (*ming*) seems to mean 'label' and when it seems to mean something more like 'concept,' the idea to which the label refers.

22.2d Shapes and forms, as well as colors and patterns, are differentiated by the eye. Various sounds, such as clear and muddy, tuning and timbre, and unusual sounds, are differentiated by the ear. The sweet and the bitter, salty and bland, spicy and sour, as well as unusual flavors, are differentiated by the mouth. Fragrances and unpleasant smells, such as the aroma of herbs and the stench of urine, putrid odors and the smell of rotting wood, as well as unusual smells, are differentiated by the nose. Illness and recuperation, cold and heat, smooth and rough, and light and heavy are differentiated by the body. Pleasure and grief,[t] delight and anger, sorrow and joy, as well as love, hate, and desire, are differentiated by the mind (*xin* 心).

22.2e In the mind there is evidential knowledge. As far as evidential knowledge goes, tracing it to the ears, it is possible to know sounds; tracing it to the eyes, it is possible to know images. In this way, evidential knowledge must wait for the senses to register a type (*lei* 類), only after which can there be such knowledge. If the five senses register something but don't understand it, or if the mind examines it but has no explanation, naturally everyone would call this "not knowing." This is how we trace the origins of similarity and difference.

[(3) "The Pivotal and Essential Points of Instituting Terms"]

22.2f After [perceiving things], name (*ming* 命) them accordingly: treat the similar (*tong* 同) as similar, and the different as different. If a single term suffices to express the meaning, then a single term is used. If it does not suffice, then a combination may be used. If there is both a single term and a combination, so long as there are no conflicts, there is no harm in having both. We understand different things through different terms. Thus, different objects all have different terms, which cannot cause confusion. Likewise, similar (*tong* 同) objects are all given the same (*tong* 同) term. Although the things of the world are many, there are times when we want to refer to them all. Thus, we call them 'things.' "Thing" is the broadest general term. We extend generalizations so long as there are more generalizations to be made, and stop only after we reach the point where there is nothing more general. There are times when we wish to indicate something specific. Hence, we speak of 'birds and beasts.' "Birds and beasts" is a broad distinguishing term. We extend our distinctions so long as there are more distinctions to be made, and stop only when we reach a point where there are no more distinctions to be made.

Comment: Note that this paragraph immediately follows a discussion of 'evidential knowledge' based on sense experience. Note also that assigning a name/term (*ming* 名) involves commanding (*ming* 命). Xun Zi indicates that linguistic divisions form a hierarchy of generality (*gong* 共) and specificity (*bie* 别), with "thing" as the most general term.

22.2g Terms have no intrinsic appropriateness (*gu yi* 固宜). They are agreed by decree (*ming* 命). Conventions that are settled to the point of becoming customary are called "fitting." If something differs from the convention then it is said to be "not fitting." Terms do not have intrinsic actual objects (*gu shi* 固實). Their actual object is agreed by decree (*ming* 命). If the conventions are settled to the point of becoming customary, the term may be called the object's name (*ming* 名).

Comment: Elsewhere Xun Zi writes, "Among the myriad things, different concrete things have similar appearances. There is no [intrinsic] appropriateness, but there is a use for people. This refers to the 'art of discriminating regular patterns'ᵘ (*shu* 數)" (*Xun Zi* 10.1).

Terms (*ming* 名) do have intrinsic aptness (*shan* 善). Terms which are straightforward and simple, and do not conflict, are called 'apt terms.'

Comment: The potential 'aptness' and 'usefulness' of ('proper') terms suggest, on the one hand, that there are standards by which terms are judged. They are not radically conventional. But, on the other hand, aptness and usefulness fit comfortably into a 'many good answer,' pluralist, worldview. (However, Xun Zi is not a *political* pluralist, he thinks that multiple competing *dao*s will lead to chaos.)

22.2h We can differentiate between things that are similar in appearance but occupy different locations and those that are different in appearance but occupy the same location. Those that are similar in appearance but occupy different locations, although they can be matched together, they are referred to as 'two objects.' If an object's form changes, becoming different but without turning into something distinct, this is referred to as 'transformation.' When something transforms without becoming something distinct, it is called 'a single object.' This is the process by which one assesses actual things and determines their quantity. These are the pivotal and essential points in instituting terminology. The establishment of terms by the later kings must be scrutinized.

[Unorthodox Expressions]

22.3a "Receiving an insult is not humiliating." "Sages do not care for themselves." "Killing a robber is not killing a person." These statements mislead by using terms to confuse terms. If one checks these statements with the reason for having terms, and observes their consequences, one will be able to put an end to them.

> *Comment:* Because of the conceptual relationship between receiving an insult and being humiliated, denying that receiving an insult is humiliating is like claiming a bachelor is married. To do so is "using terms to confuse terms." The "reason for having terms" is to convey intentions clearly (see §22.2b, above). Thus, these expressions are to be rejected because they introduce confusion and paradox into the understanding of terms.

22.3b "Mountains and abysses are flat." "Emotions and desires are few." "Hay-fed animals do not contribute to culinary pleasures, and great bells do not contribute to joyful music." These statements mislead by using objects (*shi* 實) to confuse terms. If one checks these statements with that which we rely on to determine similarity and difference [i.e., the senses], and observes whether they can be reconciled, one will be able to put an end to them.

> *Comment:* These "unorthodox expressions" involve factual inaccuracies. Thus, they are using (false claims about) actual things in the world to confuse or distort the meaning of the terms involved. One determines their falsity empirically.

22.3c "The flying arrow does not pass the pillar."ᵛ "Having oxen and horses is not having horses."ʷ These statements mislead by using terms to [cause] confusion [about] actual things. If one checks these statements with agreed upon terms, by showing that what they accept conflicts with what they reject, one will be able to put an end to them.

> *Comment:* These sorts of paradoxical expressions are typical of Hui Zi and the Linguistic school (or 'school of names'). Considering only the *terms* involved, "having oxen and horses" is not the same as "having horses." But in *actuality*, one who has both oxen and horses does have horses. And so, this is a case of using terms to cause confusion about what actually is the case. In the last line, "what they accept" refers to the

first part of each paradox, namely, that the arrow is flying, and that one has oxen and horses. And, "what they reject" refers to what is denied in the second part of each paradox, namely, that the arrow passes the pillar, and that one has horses. One can't reasonably accept one (e.g., having oxen and horses) and reject the other (having horses).

22.3d Generally, depraved doctrines and unorthodox expressions that diverge from standard discourse (*dao*) and are presumptuously created can all be categorized into these three types of confusion. Thus, enlightened rulers, understanding these distinctions, do not participate in such arguments.

22.3e The common people are easily unified with the way (*dao* 道), but cannot be provided with reasons. Thus, enlightened rulers presided over them from a position of influence (*shi* 勢), guided them with the way (*dao*), instructed them with mandates, regulated them with pronouncements, and deterred them with punishments. And so the common people were transformed to [follow] the way (*dao*) as though inspired by spirits.

> *Comment:* This passage articulates a set of ideas that will be emphasized and pushed to extremes by the Legalist philosopher Han Fei Zi, who was a student of Xun Zi. Perhaps the most troubling feature of Xun Zi's philosophy is his distrust in people's ability to reason and make their own judgments. Correlated with this is his assumption that, without a commonality of purpose and acceptance of shared norms, chaos would be inevitable. These two assumptions serve as a basis for his political paternalism. Still, Xun Zi's political philosophy was at least theoretically meritocratic. In §9.1 Xun Zi writes, "Although one may be a descendent of commoners, if one accumulates culture and learning, is upright in personal conduct, and is able to devotedly apply oneself to the observance of ritual propriety and honorable conduct, such a person should be brought up to the status of chief minister or high official." Practically, however, rising from the bottom would have been difficult indeed.

What use was there for the art of dialectics? But now the sage-kings are no more. The world is in chaos. And treacherous speech has arisen. "*Junzi*" lack the skills with which to direct the people, and lack punishment to deter them. And so we have the practice of persuading with dialectics.

[Exemplary Use of Terms and Distinctions]

22.3f When things and events (*shi* 實) are not understood [by the people], assign a name (*ming* 命) [to clarify them]. When this naming is not understood, specify. When specifications are not understood, explain. When explanations are not understood, make incisive distinctions (*bian* 辨). Thus, specifying, naming, making distinctions, and explaining are important language patterns (*wen* 文) of practical use (*yong* 用), and they are the beginning of the kingly enterprise. Making actual things or events understood when the term (*ming* 名) is heard is the practical use of terms. Accumulating and completing cultural patterns is the beauty of terms. Achieving both practical use and beauty is called "knowing words" (*zhi ming* 知名).

> *Comment:* Note that "knowing" is here defined in terms of practical and aesthetic accomplishment, rather than merely a cognitive one. Similarly, Xun Zi elsewhere writes, "Completely integrate one's learning, put it fully to use, and only then is one learned" (*Xun Zi* 1.13).

Terms (*ming* 名) are that by which different[x] objects (*shi* 實) are specified. A phrase unites the terms for various objects so as to state a single meaning. Distinctions and explanations, by being consistent regarding terms and objects, illustrate the *dao* of movement and stillness. Specifying and naming (*ming* 命) are the practical uses of distinctions and explanations. With distinctions and explanations the mind imagines *dao*. The mind is the craftsperson and manager of *dao* 道. And *dao* consists of the norms and patterns of governing well.

> *Comment:* Notice that Xun Zi suggests that the mind is not only responsible for originally crafting *dao*, but also for managing its development. There is a consistency in Xun Zi's treatment of *dao*, in the above paragraph, and his treatment of language, which is the subject of this chapter, and also his treatment of *tian* (natural forces) and *xing* (natural dispositions), which are the subjects of Chapters 17 and 23 respectively. In all cases, Xun Zi takes a managerial approach. Just as *xing* and *tian*, our inner dispositions and the natural environment, are both natural conditions that must be intelligently shaped and managed, so too *dao*, and the terms in which it is articulated and understood, must be well constructed and yet continually overseen.

[When] one's mind is in accord with *dao*, explanations accord with the mind, and phrases accord with explanations, then there is proper naming and specification, and characteristics and circumstances are understood. Distinctions differentiate without going too far [i.e., splitting hairs]. Categories are extended [by analogy] without inconsistency. Listening accords with refined patterns (*wen* 文). And distinctions are made with exhaustive reasoning. Taking the proper way (*dao* 道) and differentiating it from what is corrupt, is like stretching a cord to oppose crooked and straight. For this reason improper (*xie* 邪) explanations are not able to cause disorder, and the Hundred Schools have nowhere to flee.

Comment: Sometimes glossed as "evil," *xie* 邪 is the opposite of *zheng* 正, and means "crooked, awry, askew" or "heretical, irregular," and by extension "improper, illegitimate" and even "wicked or depraved." Perhaps most tellingly, in Chinese medicine it indicates unhealthy influences that cause disease—just as ill-conceived distinctions can lead to moral and social degradation.

22.4a The sage has a clarity resulting from listening to all sides, and yet displays no impulsiveness or arrogance. He has a breadth that covers all aspects, and yet shows no sign of self-congratulation. If such a person's teachings are put in practice, the world will be set straight (*zheng* 正). If they are not put in practice, he expounds the way and does not^y retire into obscurity. The distinctions and teachings of the sages are of this nature. An Ode says: "Dignified and majestic, like a jade scepter or a jade mace. Admirable in reputation; admirable in vision; joyful and filial *junzi* (exemplary persons) serve as the guide rope for the whole empire." This expresses my meaning.

22.4b [*Junzi* and aspirants are distinguished by the following characteristics:] the moderating influence of expressions of deference, the patterned yielding of old and young, avoiding mention of taboos, and not introducing strange expressions. They explain with thoughts and feelings (*xin* 心) of *ren* 仁 (humanity), listen with a mind to learn, and make distinctions with a sense of public spiritedness. They are not swayed by the criticism or praise of the masses. They do not charm the ears and eyes of those who observe them. They do not present gifts for influential power. And, they do not capitalize on what is said at court. Thus, they can dwell in the way without having second thoughts. They express disapproval, but are not contentious. They provide benefits, but do not simply go along with the course of things. They value public uprightness and despise petty quarreling. These are what distinguish the speech of aspirants (*shi* 士) and *junzi*. An Ode says: "Through the long night without end, always thinking of self-respect, I do not neglect the greatness of antiquity, and do not overstep in ritual and propriety. What do I care what other people say?" This expresses my meaning.

22.4c *Junzi*'s words are lucid yet subtle, unassuming yet apt, varied yet unified. They use proper terminology and suitable expressions in order to make their intended meanings clear. Their terms and expressions are the messengers of their intended meanings. When they are sufficient for mutual communication they leave it at that. To go further has pernicious consequences. Thus, when terms are sufficient to indicate actual things, and expressions are sufficient to set forth conditions, they leave it at that. Going beyond this is called 'labored speech.' This is what *junzi* reject, and what fools pick up and make a personal treasure. Thus, the words of a fool are ill-considered and unrefined, contentious and impertinent, rambling and inconsistent. They employ enticing terms, and bewildering expressions, but there is no depth to their meaning. They exhaust every pretext yet attain nothing. They toil in vain. They are corrupt and remain anonymous. [In contrast], the words of the wise are easy to understand when considered, acting on them fosters security, and holding fast to them facilitates one in taking one's stand. In the end, they will surely attain what they cherish, and will not encounter what they detest in it. The foolish are just the opposite of this. An Ode says: "Were you a ghost or a water imp, you could not be seen. But since you have facial features, I can see you are someone who will stop at nothing. I have composed this fine song, by which I show how extremely capricious you are." This expresses my meaning.

> *Comment:* Here the topic changes, and for the remainder of the chapter Xun Zi discusses desires. Those sections (22.5–22.6) can be found the chapter entitled "Xun Zi on Motivation," p. 166, above.

"NATURAL DISPOSITIONS ARE DETESTABLE," *XING E* 性惡 (CHAPTER 23), AND §9.16A

The slogan that forms the title of this chapter expresses the idea for which Xun Zi is most famous, or infamous. But negative language does not necessarily express a thoroughly negative idea. And in this case, Xun

Zi is certainly not a pessimist regarding human potential. Indeed, he is explicit in his confidence that even ordinary people have the potential to develop themselves into sages (*Xun Zi* 23.5b). It is just that, in Xun Zi's view, there is a right way and a wrong way to understand how this transformation can take place. Specifically, Xun Zi criticizes Meng Zi for expressing the view that human dispositions are naturally good. The reason Xun Zi adamantly rejects the view of a fellow Confucian with a dramatic slogan—"Natural dispositions are detestable!"—is that he thinks Meng Zi's view is not only wrong, but also dangerous. He explains that if Meng Zi were right, then there would be really no point in talking about ritual propriety, and the sages would not really have made a significant contribution. For if we could count on moral development to take place naturally, then we wouldn't need sages or their norms of ritual propriety. Yet to turn our backs on the sages, in Xun Zi's view, would be a disastrous mistake.

The slogan *"xing e"* is sometimes translated "Human nature is evil." However, this is misleading. First of all, the word "evil" suggests malevolence, intentionally causing harm and suffering, doing wrong for the sake of doing wrong, or, at least, it suggests incorrigibly bad character. And yet none of these meanings come close to Xun Zi's intent. The relevant word, *"e"* (惡), means 'ugly,' 'crude,' and thus 'detestable'—it is the opposite of *"mei"* (美), 'beautiful,' 'admirable.' Our innate dispositions are detestable because they lead us to the horrors of chaos, but certainly not because we *want* that to happen. It is just that we are basically selfish, and that if we don't use intelligence and effort to reform our character we unwittingly invite disaster.

One may also question whether or not "human nature" is an appropriate translation of *"xing"* (性), as it implies that our problematic emotional desires constitute an unchanging essence, a quality that makes humans human. But it is not our natural dispositions that define us as human (*ren* 人). Rather, it is our sense of what is appropriate and right; this is expressed in §9.16a, included at the end of this chapter (p. 231). Further, Xun Zi maintains that sages and *junzi* "transform *xing*" (*Xun Zi* 23.2a and 23.4a). This either means that they transform *xing* itself, or that they transform their character from one based on natural dispositions (*xing*) to one based on artifice (*wei* 偽). Either way, *xing* does not define humans.

Still, Xun Zi suggests that ordinary people cannot be expected to rid themselves of basic natural desires. After all, Xun Zi writes, "'Having desires' and 'lacking desires' [...] correspond to the living and the dead, not the ordered and the chaotic" (*Xun Zi* 22.5a). Even *junzi* (if not sages[29]) presumably continue to desire food when hungry, and desire security, and honor as well. Xun Zi is explicit about their desire for profit: "[*Junzi*] desire profit, but will not do what is wrong" (*Xun Zi* 3.2; see also 4.8, p. 162, above). For, "The *junzi*'s talent is using public-spirited integrity (*gong yi* 公義) to triumph over personal desires" (*Xun Zi* 2.14). Xun Zi also writes, "The various classes of people have a point in common—what they seek is similar. But their paths (*dao*) are different. Their [basic] desires are the same. But their understanding is different" (*Xun Zi* 10.1). So, moral improvement, for Xun Zi, is not primarily about getting rid of desires. Rather, it involves learning how to intelligently satisfy them, or overpower them, as appropriate. Xun Zi writes, "Although the sages Yao and Shun were not able to rid the common people of their desire for profit, they were nevertheless able to make sure their desire for profit did not overcome their fondness for what is honorable" (*Xun Zi* 27.62). One overpowers and triumphs over desires not by the sheer force of will, but by becoming fond of ritual and honorable conduct. We fully realize our genuine human potential by accumulating a new set of altruistic motivations that overpower our petty desires. This chapter is about the need to do that, and how to do it.

23.1a Human natural dispositions (*xing* 性) are detestable (*e* 惡); our goodness is a product of artifice (*wei* 偽). From birth, human dispositions include a fondness for profit. If this is pursued, quarrels and contentions will grow, and deference and yielding will perish. We also possess, from the time of birth, feelings of jealousy and hatred. If we indulge these, then injury and theft will increase, and faithful service (*zhong* 忠) and trustworthiness (*xin* 信) will pass into oblivion. We are also born with the desires of the ears and eyes—a fondness for sounds and colors. If we chase after these, licentiousness and debauchery will proliferate, and ritual propriety, honorable conduct, and refined patterns (*li-yi wen li* 禮義文理) will die out.

That being the case, if people follow their natural dispositions and go along with their emotions, then quarrels and contention will be inevitable. The combination of a culture of criminality with chaotic social

---

29   Regarding sages, Xun Zi writes, "Desiring food when hungry, warmth when cold, and rest when weary; being fond of profit and detesting harm—these are qualities people have from birth. One does not have to wait to become like this. In this, even the sage Yu and the tyrant Jie are alike" (*Xun Zi* 5.4). It may be that sages are endowed with the same natural dispositions as everyone else, but transform them, or that they retain those dispositions even after transforming their overall character.

patterns will result in savagery. Thus, there must first be a transformation of a teacher and a model, and a path of ritual and propriety. Only then would deference and yielding emerge. Forming these into a refined pattern would bring order. From these considerations, it is clear that natural human dispositions are detestable (*xing e* 性惡), and our goodness is a product of artifice.

> Comment: As will become clear, Xun Zi thinks that we can transform our character into something admirable. Our innate human dispositions—natural emotional desires—do not have to govern our behavior. With intelligently directed effort we can make ourselves good. When Xun Zi repeats his slogan "*xing e*," we must understand "*xing*" to mean something like 'natural human dispositions,' those that we are born with but which do *not* define us, and by which we are *not* condemned to be ruled.

23.1b Thus, bent wood must first be put to a straightening board, steamed, and pressed before it will become straight. Dull metal must first be ground and whet before it will become sharp. Now, people's natural dispositions are detestable. They must have a teacher and a model before they can become upright. They must become accomplished in ritual and propriety before they can be well ordered. If people have no teacher or model, then they will be inclined to wrongdoing,[z] rather than being upright. If they lack ritual and propriety, they will be rebellious and disorderly, rather than well governed. In ancient times, the sages regarded human dispositions as detestable, as inclined to wrongdoing, not upright, rebellious, disorderly, and not well governed. It is for this reason that they initiated ritual and propriety, and formulated methods and standards, thereby to straighten and adorn people's emotional dispositions, and make them upright. By training, they transformed people's emotional dispositions and guided them, and everyone began to move towards order, and to cohere with *dao* 道. Nowadays, people who are transformed by teachers and models, accumulate culture and learning, and are guided (*dao* 道) by ritual and propriety become *junzi* (exemplary persons). Those who indulge their dispositions and emotions, are self-satisfied and reckless, and go against ritual and propriety—they become inferior people. From these considerations, it is clear that natural dispositions are detestable, and our goodness is a product of artifice.

23.1c Meng Zi says, "People's learning is a function of the goodness of their natural dispositions (*xing* 性)." I say: This is not so. It reveals a failure to achieve an understanding of the natural dispositions of human beings, and obliviousness to the distinction between *xing* (natural dispositions) and *wei* 偽 (artifice). Natural dispositions (*xing*) are products of *tian*. They cannot be learned nor acquired through work. Ritual and propriety (*li-yi*) are products of sages. They are what people become capable of through learning; they are what people can accomplish through work. Human qualities that cannot be acquired through learning or through work are called "*xing*" ('natural dispositions'). Those that can be acquired through learning or through work are called "*wei*" ('artifice,' 'acquired character'). This is the distinction between *xing* and *wei*.

> *Comment*: The word "*wei*" (偽) is a combination of *ren* 人 (human) and *wei* 為 (to do, to become). "*Wei*" is clearly a technical term for Xun Zi, but one that seems to evolve as the chapter progresses. In its earlier occurrences it seems to mean artifice in the sense of intelligently directed human activity and effort. Later, it takes on the meaning of artifice in the sense of something intelligently made by humans (*ren wei* 人為), such as ritual propriety, as well as a "made human"—or "acquired character," as John Knoblock has aptly rendered it. (Cf. *Xun Zi* 22.1b, p. 209, above.)

23.1d Now, natural dispositions (*xing* 性) include that which makes the eye able to see, and the ear able to hear. The ability to see clearly involves no deviation from [the nature of] the eye, and the ability to hear acutely involves no deviation from [the nature of] the ear. Obviously, clearness of eye and keenness of ear cannot be learned. Meng Zi said that human dispositions are good, but that in time everyone loses their natural dispositions. I say: these claims are mistaken. Suppose people's nature (*xing*) is such that after birth we deviate from our basic and primordial endowments such that we inevitably lose and forfeit them. From these considerations, then, clearly, natural human dispositions are detestable. If natural dispositions were good (*xing shan*), people would not deviate from their basic nature, but would beautify it. We would not depart from our natural endowments, but would reap their advantages. For, [according to the view that human nature is good,] the relation of rudimentary endowments to beauty and the relation of goodness to the intentions of the mind is thought to be analogous to the ability to see clearly not deviating from [the nature of] the eye, and the ability to hear acutely not deviating from [the nature of] the ear. Thus it is said, "[natural dispositions are like] the clarity of eyesight and acuity of hearing."

> *Comment*: This may be a bit confusing. But perhaps it is clearer if we look at it this way: The nature of the eye is to see clearly. And this can neither

be learned nor does it change. The nature of the human mind should be analogous, namely, not learnable and not discardable. However, according to Meng Zi's view, although natural dispositions are good, most people lose this goodness. So, according to this reasoning, Meng Zi's view cannot be right. It is nevertheless possible, Xun Zi maintains, for people to become good, even if they retain their petty desires. This is not because of naturally good tendencies, and so it does not happen as a mere matter of natural development. Rather, as the following passage explains, beautifying oneself requires intelligently directed effort—effort against one's natural dispositions.

23.1e Now, human dispositions are such that: when hungry we desire to be full; when cold we desire warmth; and when weary we desire rest. These are the emotional dispositions of human beings. Now, when people are hungry, for those who dare not to eat before their elders, there are conditions under which they yield. When weary, they dare not seek rest, for they must relieve others. The son yields to the father, the younger brother yields to the older. The son relieves the father, and the younger brother relieves the older. With regard to these two behaviors, everyone *goes against* their natural dispositions, and does what is contrary to emotion. In this manner, the ways of filial sons are [embodied in] the refined patterns of ritual and propriety. Thus, if one follows one's emotional nature, then there will be no yielding or deference. Yielding and deference go against emotional dispositions. From these considerations, it is clear that natural dispositions are detestable, and our goodness is a product of artifice.

23.2a Someone may ask, "If natural human dispositions are detestable, where do ritual propriety and honorable conduct come from?" I would reply that ritual and propriety are produced by the artifice (*wei* 偽) of sages. They are not products of people's natural dispositions. The potter makes a vessel using a clay mold. If this is so, then the vessel is generated (*sheng* 生) by the artifice of the potter, not by natural human dispositions. The carpenter carves wood to make a vessel. If this is so, then the vessel is generated by the artifice of the carpenter, not by natural human dispositions. The sage accumulates thoughts and deliberations, and develops artifice through repeated practice, thereby generating ritual propriety and appropriateness (*li-yi* 禮義), and gives rise to laws and standards. If this is so, then likewise *li-yi*, and laws and standards, are generated by the artifice of sages, not by natural human dispositions.

The eyes are fond of colors, the ears are fond of sounds, the mouth is fond of flavors, and the mind is fond of profit. Bones, body, and skin are fond of sensual delights and leisure. These are all products of human emotional dispositions (*qing xing* 情性). These feelings occur naturally (*ziran* 自然). No work is required before they are produced. Feelings that cannot occur naturally, but require work to become as they are—these are called "*wei* 偽" (artifice). These considerations show that what natural dispositions produce and what artifice produces are not the same.

Thus, the sages, transforming their natural dispositions (*hua xing* 化性), gave rise to *wei* 偽 (artifice), which in turn produced ritual and propriety, and which led to the systemization of methods and norms. In this way, ritual and propriety, and methods and norms, are what sages produce. Thus, what the sages have in common with the masses, and what is in no way different from the masses, is their dispositions (*xing* 性). They differ from and exceed the masses in their *wei* 偽 (artifice). Human emotional dispositions include fondness of profit and desire for gain. Suppose material possessions are to be divided among brothers who follow their emotional dispositions—namely, fondness of profit and desire for gain. In such a case, the brothers would squabble. But, if transformed according to the refined patterns of ritual and propriety, they would offer these possessions to their fellow citizens. Thus, following emotional dispositions leads brothers into contention, whereas transformation according to ritual and propriety leads to deference to one's fellow citizens.

23.2b Generally speaking, people desire to become good because their natural dispositions are detestable. Those of mean temperament wish they were magnanimous; the ugly (*e* 惡) wish they were beautiful (*mei* 美); the cramped wish for spaciousness; the poor wish for abundance; and the lowly wish for nobility. If there is something lacking on the inside, it must be sought from without. Thus, the wealthy do not wish for valuables, and the nobility do not wish for influence. If it is possessed internally then one need not reach for it externally. Looked at in this way, people desire to become good because their natural dispositions are detestable.

Now, human dispositions are originally devoid of ritual and propriety. Thus, through vigorous learning, people seek to possess them. Natural human dispositions do not [automatically lead to] the understanding of ritual and propriety. Hence, it is through thinking and reflecting that people seek to understand them. That being the case, in the condition in which they are born, people lack ritual and propriety, and they do not understand them. If people lack ritual and propriety there will be chaos; if they do not understand them there will be delusion. In the condition in which people are born, delusion and chaos reside within. From these considerations, it is clear that natural human dispositions are detestable, and our goodness is a product of artifice.

23.3a Meng Zi says, "Natural human dispositions are good." I say: This is not so. What has always been called "good" (*shan* 善) is what is upstanding, patterned, peaceful, and orderly. What is called "detestable" (*e*) is prejudicial, precarious, rebellious, and chaotic. This is the distinction between good and detestable. Can it be sincerely believed that human dispositions are intrinsically upstanding, patterned, peaceful, and orderly? If so, then of what use are the sage-kings? Of what use is ritual and propriety? Even if there are sage-kings, and ritual and propriety, how could they add to something upstanding, patterned, peaceful, and orderly? But this is not how things are. Human dispositions are detestable. Thus, in olden times, sages considered human dispositions to be detestable—considered them prejudicial, precarious, and not upright; rebellious, chaotic, and not orderly. Thus, on that account, they established rulers on high with influence to oversee the people. And they elucidated ritual and propriety in order to transform them. They gave rise to models of propriety, thereby to order them, and heavy punishments to indicate what was prohibited. They enabled everyone in the world to exhibit orderly conduct, and accord with what was good. This is the order of the sage-kings and the transformation of ritual and propriety (*li-yi zhi hua* 禮義之化).

> *Comment:* Here Xun Zi insists on definitions for terms that differ from Meng Zi's understanding and usage. Meng Zi meant that within natural human dispositions there is an *impulse toward goodness*. He never suggested that people were naturally *fully* upstanding, peaceful, and orderly. Xun Zi's position is that our natural dispositions, on the contrary, incline us to wrongdoing, and following them gets us into trouble.

Now, as a test, suppose that we were to rid ourselves of the authority of rulers, and that there was no transformation of ritual and propriety. Suppose we do away with the order provided by models of uprightness, and that there was nothing prohibited with punishments. On this basis, let us see how the people of the world get along with each other. In this case, the strong would harm the weak, robbing them. The many would attack the few, causing mayhem. Rebellion, chaos, and mutual annihilation of the whole world would quickly ensue. From these considerations, it is clear that natural human dispositions are detestable, and our goodness is a product of artifice.

Comment: Xun Zi never admits that there could be some sense in which Meng Zi is right. But *we* need not be so strident. Here is a more conciliatory way of appreciating Xun Zi's point: Even if Meng Zi is right in thinking there is a natural impulse toward goodness. Focusing on the goodness, and sloganeering "human dispositions are good," misleads people into disregarding the need for a system to improve our character. For, if we really want to become admirable, it is going to require intelligently directed effort. It doesn't just happen spontaneously. Assuming it will happen spontaneously leads to disaster.

23.3b Those who are good at discussing antiquity must show its applicability to the present. Those who are good at discussing *tian* (nature) must show the relevance to people (*ren* 人). Theories are valued for coherent distinctions and conformity to experience. Sitting, one discusses it. Rising, one is able to establish it. Extending it, one is able to carry it out and put it into practice (*xing* 行). Now, Meng Zi says, "Human dispositions are good." This is both incoherent and fails to conform to experience. Sitting, one may discuss it, but rising, one is unable to establish it. And extending it, one is unable to carry it out and put it into practice. How could it not be a colossal mistake? If human dispositions are good then we may cast aside the sage-kings, and put an end to ritual propriety and conscientiousness (*li-yi* 禮義). But if our natural dispositions are detestable, then, along with the sage-kings, we place value in *li-yi*.

Straightening boards were produced because of bent wood. The carpenter's marking line came about due to lack of straightness. Likewise, the establishment of rulers on high, and of clear rituals and norms of propriety was because natural dispositions are detestable. From these considerations, it is clear that natural human dispositions are detestable, and our goodness is a product of artifice.

23.3c Straight wood does not wait for a straightening board to be strait; its disposition is straight. Bent wood must be put to a straightening board, steamed, and pressed before it becomes straight, because its disposition is not straight. Now, people's natural dispositions are detestable, and must wait for the order of sage-kings, and the transformation of ritual and propriety, before they can all exhibit orderly conduct, and accord with goodness. From these considerations, it is clear that natural human dispositions are detestable, and our goodness is a product of artifice.

23.4a A questioner may say: "Ritual and propriety, and the accumulation of acquired characteristics (*wei* 偽), are due to human dispositions, that is why sages could produce these things." I respond: This is not so. Potters produce earthenware utensils from clay. So how could the utensil be a product of the potter's disposition? The carpenter carves wood to produce an implement. So how could the implement and wood be the natural disposition of the carpenter? The sages' relation to ritual and propriety is like the potter producing pottery. So how could it be that ritual and propriety, and the accumulation of acquired character (*wei*), are inherent in natural human dispositions? The natural dispositions of ordinary people are the same as those of the sage-kings Yao and Shun, and of the tyrant Jie and Robber Zhi; *junzi* and inferior persons likewise share the same natural dispositions. Now, how could ritual and propriety, and the accumulation of acquired character, be considered natural human dispositions? So why then do we value the sage-kings Yao and Yu? Why do we value *junzi*? Because the sages Yao and Yu, and *junzi*, are able to transform their natural dispositions (*hua xing* 化性) and are able to give rise to acquired character (*wei*), and in turn produce ritual and propriety. Thus the ritual and propriety of the sages and their accumulation of acquired character is like a potter producing pottery. From these considerations, how could it be that ritual and propriety, and the accumulation of acquired character (*wei*), come from natural human dispositions? What is despised about the tyrant Jie, Robber Zhi, and inferior people is that they follow their natural dispositions, and go along with their emotional nature; they are self-satisfied and reckless; they act out of greed for profit; and they are quarrelsome and contentious. Thus, it is clear that natural human dispositions are detestable, and our goodness is a product of artifice.

23.4b *Tian* 天 did not show favoritism toward Zeng, Qian, or filial Yi while withholding it from the masses. And yet, these three alone were profoundly filial in actuality, and unequivocally regarded as such. Why is that? It is because they made the most out of ritual and propriety. *Tian* did not favor the people of Qi and Lu to the exclusion of Qin. And yet, among the people of Qin, the appropriateness of relations between father and son and the distinctions between husband and wife are inferior in filiality, respectfulness, reverence, and culture to the people of Qi and Lu. Why is that? It is because the people of Qin follow their natural emotional dispositions, they are self-satisfied and reckless, and they are remiss with respect to ritual and propriety. How could it be due to differences in their natural dispositions?

> *Comment:* When we look around, we see that some people are more admirable than others. And even some communities are better behaved

than others. Can that be because some people—and even some whole communities—are born with better dispositions than others? Xun Zi doesn't think so. The explanation must be, he reasons, that some people *do* something different with their natural endowments (cf. *Analects* 17.2, p. 105). Some follow their natural selfish dispositions; others reform themselves by following norms of propriety.

23.5a What does it mean to say, "An ordinary person can become a Yu." I answer: Yu became the sage that he was through his practice of *ren* 仁 (humanity) and honorable conduct (*yi* 義), by following a model (*fa* 法), and by being upstanding (*zheng* 正). Thus, *ren, yi, fa*, and *zheng* have a pattern (*li* 理) that is understandable and enabling. Everybody, even an ordinary person, understands (*zhi* 知) the basic substance of *ren, yi, fa*, and *zheng* and has the wherewithal (*neng* 能) to develop these abilities. Thus, it is clear that an ordinary person can (*ke* 可) become a Yu.

Now, what if *ren, yi, fa*, and *zheng* lacked a pattern that was understandable and enabling? Then, even Yu would not have understood them, and would not have been able to develop those qualities. Does the ordinary person originally lack the wherewithal to understand them, and lack the capacity to develop them? If so, then the ordinary person would neither be able to understand the appropriate relation between father and son at home, nor be able to understand uprightness among rulers and ministers abroad. But this is not so. All ordinary people can do this. So, it is clear that the requisite wherewithal to know, and capacity to develop, does reside in ordinary people. Now, the ordinary person's wherewithal to know, and capacity to develop, has its root in being able to understand the patterns of *ren* and *yi*. Since people have the capacity to develop, it is clear that they can become a Yu. Now, if ordinary people devoted themselves to the arts of learning, focused their minds on a single aspiration, pondered deeply and observed thoroughly for a long time, and accumulated goodness without rest, then they would break through to an extraordinary (*shen* 神) clarity (*ming* 明), and form a triad with *tian* and the earth. Thus, sages represent the highest culmination of what can accrue in people.

23.5b Someone said, "Sages are the highest culmination of what can be accrued. Even so, not everyone can accomplish this. What do you say to that?" I say: They have the potential but cannot be made to fulfill it. Thus, an inferior person can become a *junzi*, yet is not willing to become one. And, a *junzi* can become an inferior person, but is not willing to become one. Among inferior people and *junzi*, there has never been one that *could* not exchange places with the other. Even so, they *do* not change places. They can do it, but cannot be made to do it.

[Further,] while an ordinary person has the *potential* (*ke* 可)ᵃᵃ to become a Yu, it is not necessarily the case that an ordinary person has the *ability* (*neng* 能) to become a Yu. Although one does not have the *ability* to become a Yu, that does not diminish one's *potential* for becoming a Yu. Feet have the potential to traverse the whole world, nevertheless there has not yet been anyone able to actually do it. A carpenter, a farmer, or a merchant, have never lacked the potential to do each other's work, and yet there has never been one who was able to do the work of the others. From these considerations we see that when one has the potential to do something, one does not necessarily have the ability to do it. Although not being able to do it, that does not diminish one's potential to do it. That being so, the difference between *ability* and *potential* is far indeed; they clearly cannot be used interchangeably.

> *Comment:* Similarly, people generally have the potential to become virtuoso pianists—or at least attain a reasonable level of proficiency. But most people lack the ability to play the piano at all. It is not due to lack of potential; they have simply not trained themselves. Through ritual propriety, and the observance of exemplary models, people can train themselves to be admirable, even to the extent of the sage Yu.

23.6a Yao asked Shun: "What do you think of human emotions?" Shun answered: "Human emotions are extremely repulsive. Why do you ask about them? When a man has a wife and child, his filial feelings toward his parents decline. When one acquires what one desires, one's commitments (*xin* 信) to one's friends diminish. When one attains rank and nobility, one's efforts on behalf of one's lord decrease. Oh, human emotions! Human emotions! So very repulsive, why ask about them?" Only for the virtuous (*xian* 賢) is this not so.

> *Comment:* The word *xian* 賢 (virtuous) implies having integrity, respectability, and excellence. But as a verb it also has the meaning "to work hard." So, it is possible that Xun Zi uses this word to emphasize the point that it is *effort* rather than some natural quality that makes the difference between ordinary people, who exhibit the traits that Shun here bemoans, and exceptional people.

23.8 The Fanruo and Jushu were the finest bows of antiquity. But if not for the pressing frame, they could not have attained the proper shape by themselves. The Zong and Que [among several others] were the finest swords of antiquity. Even so, had they not been put to the whetstone they would not have been able to become sharp; without human effort (*ren li* 人力) they would not have been able to cut anything. The horses Hualiu, Qiji, Xianli, and Lu'er were the finest horses of antiquity. Even so, they at first had to be reined in with a bit and bridle, and then urged on with a whip. Finally, when one adds the skillful driving of Zao Fu, only then could they traverse a thousand *li* in one day.

Even if one has dispositions and qualities that are admirable, and a mind of discriminating understanding, one must first seek out and serve a worthy teacher, and choose worthy friends to associate with. If one finds and serves a worthy teacher, one can hear of the ways of the great Yao, Shun, Yu, and Tang. If one finds good friends to associate with, then one can witness faithful service (*zhong* 忠), living up to one's words (*xin* 信), respect, and deference being put into practice. In their moral character (*shen* 身) they will make daily progress with respect to *ren* 仁 (humanity) and honorable conduct (*yi* 義) without even realizing it, for it is proximity[bb] that makes it so. On the other hand, if they dwell with the morally inept (*bushan* 不善), then they will hear of deceit, slander, cheating, and fakery, and will witness debasement, wanton depravity, and corruption in action. Without even noticing, they will be doing terrible violence to their moral character (*shen* 身), for it is proximity that makes it so. A tradition says: "Not knowing someone, observe their friends; not knowing a ruler, observe his attendants." It just rubs off on you. It just rubs off on you.[cc]

From Chapter 9, *Wang Zhi* 王制 ("Kingly Regulations"), §9.16a

In the passage below, Xun Zi classifies the varieties of things into several categories, and identifies the distinctive characteristic of each: non-living things, plants, animals, and humans. At the lowest level are non-living things; these are all constituted of *qi*, material energy. Note that in this cosmology, what we might call 'matter' is conceived of as a kind of energy. Then come plants, which are characterized by life in addition to *qi*; above them are animals, which have *qi*, life, and conscious awareness. At the highest level are humans, with the distinguishing characteristic of possessing ethical ideals, *yi*, in addition to all the rest. Thus, while Xun Zi emphasized selfishness as a problematic human disposition, he also recognized positive human qualities. Using *yi*, people are able to flourish in harmonious communities.

9.16a Water and fire possess *qi* (氣 vital energy) but not life. Grasses and trees have life, but no awareness. The birds and the beasts have awareness, but lack *yi* 義 (a sense of what is right and appropriate). Humans have *qi*, life, and awareness, and moreover have *yi*, and thus are the most precious in the world. They are not as strong as oxen, and not as fast as horses. So how is it that they make use of oxen and horses? I say: People are able to form communities (*qun* 群), while the others cannot. How can people form communities? I say: By division (*fen* 分) [of roles]. How are we able to put social divisions into practice? I say: it is because of *yi* 義. When *yi* is used in making social divisions, there is harmony (*he* 和); with harmony, there is cohesiveness (*yi* 一); with cohesiveness, force increases; with increased force, there is strength; and when strong, people will get the better of animals. And so they are able to live in palaces and houses. Thus, the ordering [of affairs in accordance with] the four seasons, regulating the myriad things, and concurrently benefiting the whole world is due to nothing other than this: the success in establishing divisions based on *yi*.

Thus, humans cannot survive without community. If communities are not divided [by roles] there will be strife. If there is strife, there will be chaos. If chaos, there will be defection. If defection, there will be weakness. If weak, humans will not be able to get the better of animals, and so will not live in palaces and houses. This is why it is said, "One must not abandon ritual and propriety (*li-yi* 禮義) for even a moment."

The ability to serve one's parents is called "filiality." The ability to serve one's elder brother is called "fraternity." The ability to serve one's superior is called "compliance." The ability to serve those below is called "rulership." A ruler excels at organizing community. If the way of organizing community is suitable, then the myriad things all receive what is fitting. The six domestic animals all grow to maturity, and members of all classes of living things will live out their full life span. Thus, if nurtured and provided the time to grow, the six domestic animals will breed. If harvested and planted seasonally, the grasses and trees will flourish. If government decrees are timely, then the hundred families will be unified, and the worthy and good will comply.

ENDNOTES

ᵃ From the "Encouraging Learning" (*Quan Xue*) chapter of the *Shi Zi* (see Sellman 2001, 62–63, for more context).

ᵇ John Knoblock's section numbers have been adopted for ease of reference and comparison.

[c] This sentence is not found in extant editions of the *Xun Zi*, but has been preserved, in connection with the previous sentence, in a quotation regarded as reliable. See Knoblock 1988–94, vol. 1, 268n19, and Lau and Chen 1996, 1n14.

[d] *Xun Zi* 14.1, not included in this anthology.

[e] The text just says "it" (*zhi*). What this "it" refers to is not entirely clear. If it refers to something mentioned previously in the passage, as opposed to some general concept like "the way," then *mei* (beautiful/admirable) seems the most likely candidate. The notion that the *junzi*'s "eyes cherish it more than the five colors," and so on, supports the contention that "it" refers to an aesthetic category. Yang Liang suggests it means "learning." But this does not seem well supported.

[f] Reading 執 as 勢, and 錯 as 措.

[g] See Hagen 2011.

[h] Reversing *yi* 損 and *sun* 益.

[i] Duyvendak 1924, 253, Knoblock 1988–94, vol. 3, 345.

[j] On the one hand, this sentence could, and probably does, suggest that true kings do not regard such activities as acceptable (one meaning of *ke* 可 is approvable or acceptable). This interpretation fits with the context leading up to this sentence. On the other hand, the context immediately following this sentence strongly suggests a different, though not incompatible, interpretation: The person of *ren* (humanity) is not capable of being deceived (*ke* also means possible, or capable). The translation here is intended to maintain the ambiguity, allowing both interpretations, which may be simultaneously implied.

[k] Reading *cai* 材 as *cai* 裁, following Knoblock and Yang Liang. The meaning of *cai* 裁 comes from the idea of cutting cloth. It is made up of *zai* (to cut) and *yi* 衣 (clothing). It has derivative senses of "to regulate," "to moderate," and "to decide."

[l] In these two paragraphs, there are significant discrepancies between editions. I have followed the ICS (Institute of Chinese Studies) concordance (Lau and Chen 1996). See Knoblock 1988–94, vol. 3, for an extensive reconstruction of the passage.

[m] Reading *te* 慝 as *ni* 匿 "hidden," which is judged to make more sense given the metaphor involved.

[n] The primary meanings of the character translated as "kindness" (稅) do not make much sense here. So, it is generally assumed to stand in for some similar character. Some interpreters read it as 脫 (become disconnected, cut the meat off the bones). This is plausible, since Xun Zi does advocate refraining from following one's petty desires spontaneously—cutting oneself off from certain activities. It is read here as 悅 (a character which also appears at the end of the sentence, in the phrase 悅校), and is interpreted, in the first instance, in the sense of *he yue* 和悅 (kindness).

o This is suggested by Knoblock 1988–94, vol. 3, 321n122.

p Brook Ziporyn, who uses the phrase "Greatest Coherence," offers a radical understanding of '*li*' as 'coherence' in an effort to dissolve the realism/constructivism debate. See Ziporyn 2012, 213–14.

q See, for example, Stalnaker 2004.

r Context strongly suggests that here *zhi* 知 indicates something like awareness.

s See Hagen 2007, 61–69 and 156 for *ming* as "concept."

t Reading 故 as 苦.

u See Hagen 2007, 34n65 and 75n54, and also Knoblock 1988–94, vol. 2, 301n1.

v The text seems to be corrupt at this point, and I have followed Knoblock's reading. The basic idea is that, in archery, the arrow is shot while standing between pillars. So, the sentence expresses a conflict between a "flying arrow" and one that goes nowhere. See Knoblock 1988–94, vol. 3, 339–41nn54–55, for more details, and alternative possibilities.

w Some scholars assume this to be corruption of "a white horse is not a horse," but it seems unnecessary to assume this part is corrupt.

x Reading *lei* 累 as *yi* 異.

y In some editions the "not" (*bu* 不) does not occur, suggesting that, though one should continue to expound the way in such a situation, one does so having retired into obscurity. It is hard to judge which version is correct since the tradition is ambivalent about what to do when one's wise advise is not followed.

z I am borrowing the phrase "incline to wrongdoing" from Yan Xuetong. The phrase *pian xian* 偏險 literally means slanted toward danger, and thus in this context suggests being dangerously disposed. It is wrongdoing that brings danger, and it is the dangerous nature of certain activities—their tendency to result in calamity—that makes them wrong. Thus, "inclined to wrongdoing" is an apt gloss that contrasts nicely with being upright.

aa Kim-Chong Chong characterizes *ke* as "(having the) capacity." I've used the word "potential" because it better communicates the intended distinction between *ke* and *neng*. See Chong 2003 for more on this distinction.

bb Reading *mi* 靡 as *mo* 摩, which most basically means "rubbing together," but also has the derived senses of proximity. The phrase is repeated below, and the character appears again in the last sentence, which John Knoblock translates: "It is the environment that is critical!" Burton Watson renders it similarly. I have tried to maintain the rubbing metaphor in this instance, but the intended import is the same.

cc This is a complete translation of the chapter with the exception of two sections, 23.6b and 23.7, which are of marginal relevance.

7

Zhong Yong 中庸: "Excellence in the Ordinary"

INTRODUCTION

The *Zhong Yong* is a text traditionally attributed to Zisi, who was Confucius' grandson and the reputed teacher of Meng Zi (Mencius). But it is probably of somewhat later origin. Like the *Da Xue*, the *Zhong Yong* is a chapter in the *Book of Rites* (*Li Ji*), and was selected, along with the *Da Xue*, the *Analects*, and the *Meng Zi*, by the Neo-Confucian philosopher Zhu Xi as one of the "Four Books," which served for centuries as content for civil service exams. Zhu Xi viewed the *Da Xue* as an introduction to Confucianism, while he regarded the *Zhong Yong* as a more advanced text to be studied after the *Analects* and the *Meng Zi* (the *Xun Zi* being regarded as heterodox).

The title, *Zhong Yong* 中庸, is enigmatic, and translations vary considerably. It is most commonly known in English as the "Doctrine of the Mean," as it was famously translated by James Legge in 1861. However, even Legge was apparently unsatisfied with that rendering, and later retranslated it as the "State of Equilibrium and Harmony." Other translations include, "centrality and commonality" (Tu 1976), "Focusing the Familiar" (Ames and Hall 2001), and "Maintaining Perfect Balance" (Gardner 2007). The phrase "*zhong yong*" may be understood quite literally as hitting the mark (*zhong* 中) in common practices (*yong* 庸). To hit the mark is to achieve excellence. And so the phrase *zhong yong* is here translated as "excellence in the ordinary."

Interpretations of the central theme in the *Zhong Yong* also vary. According to Chenyang Li, "the *Zhongyong*'s central theme is the ideal of grand harmony in the universe and how human beings can participate in and promote such an ideal" (C. Li 2004, 173). Put that way, it seems that there are two sides, a cosmological side (the ideal of grand harmony) and a practical side (how people promote it). Ni Peimin suggests that it is the latter aspect that is paramount. He writes, the "fundamental aim [of the *Zhong Yong*] is not to *describe* what or how the world *is*; it is rather to *instruct* people *how* to live their lives" (Ni 2004, 190). Both of these comments were made in response to Roger Ames and David Hall's 2001 translation and interpretation, in which they write that the central message is "to encourage the ongoing productive confluence of 'the way of *tian* 天道' and 'the way of human beings 人道' through human virtuosity" (Ames and Hall 2001, 27). On this view, there is no fixed "ideal of grand harmony" postulated. Rather, the world is an opportunity for a productive mutually influencing interaction between humans and their natural conditions.[1] And the emphasis is on where people have the most leverage: striving for excellence in ordinary circumstances.

While the importance of, and the difficulty of, truly achieving excellence in the ordinary is certainly a significant theme in the *Zhong Yong*, perhaps the most philosophically interesting aspect of the text is its treatment of the concept "*cheng*" 誠. Although it has a primary sense of 'truly' or 'sincerely,' in this text "*cheng*" appears to be a technical term. I've translated it "authenticity," but that is a placeholder for a concept that must be understood by carefully attending to the contexts in which it is used. In any case, it is portrayed as a fundamental component of a truly successful life. For a person to be authentic (*cheng*) is to fully express one's *ren* 仁 (humanity), wisdom (*zhi* 知), and potency of character (*de* 德) (see *Zhong Yong* 20, 25, 32, pp. 241, 244, 245).

One may wonder whether the *Zhong Yong* is more in line with the philosophy of Meng Zi or that of Xun Zi. This is not easy to resolve. Perhaps it succeeds, at least to a significant degree, in conforming to both. On the one hand, it may seem that, with its emphasis on authenticity, the *Zhong Yong* adopts a Mengzian position regarding human nature. Namely, human nature is good, and so by developing our true nature—becoming authentic—we realize *ren* 仁, our humanity expressed through empathetic effort. On the other hand, somewhat surprisingly, it is Xun Zi who uses the character *cheng* in much the way it is used in the *Zhong Yong*. And there are also other connections between the *Zhong Yong* and the *Xun Zi*, such as the notion that *tian* (the heavens), *di* (the earth), and

---

1   Hall and Ames explicitly state that, according their view of the *Zhong Yong*, "*tian* is very much influenced by human beings" (Ames and Hall 2001, 27).

ren (people) form a "triad" (*Zhong Yong* 22, p. 243; *Xun Zi* 17.2a, and 23.5a, pp. 179 and 228; see also 19.6, and 21.5e, pp. 196 and 206). Further, while it is easy to see how authenticity fits nicely into a Mengzian view in which natural human sprouts of goodness develop into full-fledged virtues, it is still possible to view it from a Xunzian perspective. From this perspective, people bring to fruition a profound wisdom and compelling character through deliberately directed effort and self-training. A thoroughly reformed nature, despite being in some sense artificial, may still be regarded as "authentic" since it is a fulfillment of a genuine and noble human potential. Excellence is a product of human intelligence and effort in the context of the world (*tian di*) and one's innate dispositions (*xing*).

To help understand how the text can be both Xunzian and Mengzian at the same time, it may be useful to reflect upon a metaphor offered by Ogyū Sorai, a Tokugawa-period Confucian scholar who was himself strongly influenced by Xun Zi. Sorai explains:

> Zisi wrote the book [the *Zhong Yong*] in order to extend our Confucianism, and to say that the former kings made this way in conformity to human nature. He did not say that this *dao* exists naturally in the world, and he did not say that conforming to the natural tendencies of human nature does not [involve] the creation of something artificial. It is like felling trees to make a palace. Although one builds the palace in accordance with the nature of the trees, how could the palace be the tree's nature?[a]

As Sorai says, the *Zhong Yong* extends Confucianism. In addition to its contribution to the concepts of excellence in the ordinary and authenticity, it also further develops more familiar concepts such as *dao*, and *de* (potency of character).The important philosophical concepts are discussed in the following sections:

zhong yong 中庸 (excellence in the ordinary): 2, 3, 11, cf. 13

zhong 中 (centrality, hitting the mark): 1, 2, 6, 10, 20

cheng 誠 (authenticity): 16, 20, 21, 22, 23, 25, 32

dao 道 (the way; forge a way): 1, 13, 15, 20, 25, 27

de 德 (potency of character): 13, 16, 20, 25, 27, 32

tian 天 (the heavens, sometimes left untranslated): 1, 20, 32

xing 性 (natural dispositions): 1, 21, 22, 25, 27

1 What *tian* endows (*tian ming* 天命) [in people] is called *xing* 性 (natural disposition). Leading natural disposition is called *dao* 道 (guidance). Elaborating *dao* is called edifying (*jiao*教). It is not acceptable to diverge from *dao* even for a short while. If it were acceptable to diverge from it, it would not be *dao*. And so, *junzi* 君子 (exemplary persons) are on guard and cautious [even] when they are not being observed. They are apprehensive and careful [even] when no one is listening. For nothing is so conspicuous as the hidden. Nothing is so obvious as the subtle and mysterious. Thus, *junzi* are cautious in their solitude.[2]

When delight and anger, and sorrow and joy, have not yet manifested, this is called *zhong* 中 (being centered). When they manifest such that they are all on target (*zhong* 中[3]) and well regulated (*jie* 節), this is called being in harmony (*he* 和). Hitting the center (*zhong* 中) is the great foundation of the whole civilized world (*tian xia* 天下). Harmony (*he* 和) is the spreading of the way (*da dao* 達道) throughout world. Bringing forth a centered harmony (*zhong he* 中和): therein one takes one's place in the world, and therein the myriad creatures are nourished.

2 Confucius said, "*Junzi* achieve excellence in the ordinary (*zhong yong* 中庸). Petty persons do the opposite. *Junzi* are able to achieve excellence in the ordinary because they are at all times centered (*zhong* 中). Petty persons do the contrary because, being petty persons, there is nothing from which they prudently abstain."

3 The Master said, "Excellence in the ordinary (*zhong yong*) is of the highest importance! But the common people rarely can maintain it for long."

4 The Master said, "I know why the *dao* is not followed: the wise go too far, and the simple-minded don't go far enough. I know why the way is not clear: those who are worthy exceed it, while those who are not fail to reach it. Everyone drinks and eats, but few know [discriminating] taste."

> *Comment:* This passage shows us that excellence in the ordinary is found in hitting the balance between two extremes, or finding the 'mean.' Further on, the *Zhong Yong* says, "In archery there is a similarity with being a *junzi*: when the arrow misses the target, you must go back and look for [the reason] in yourself." The metaphor of 'hitting the target' may also

---

2 Cf. *Da Xue* 6, p. 63, and *Analects* 2.10, p. 92.
3 Cf. *Meng Zi* 7B37, p. 134, in which "strike the center (*zhong* 中) of the way [...]" is contrasted with being either rash or overly scrupulous.

lie at the root of the etymology of the term "*zhong*" (中), the box representing the target, and the vertical line the arrow passing through the center. Hitting the target requires poise and precision: one can neither fall short, nor go too far. Similarly, in cultivating any virtue, there are not one, but two, ways in which we may go wrong: we may either fall short of the quality we wish to cultivate, or we may go too far. In *Analects* 8.2, Confucius points out that we can have too much of a good thing: too much caution "results in timidity," and too much bravery "leads to chaos." In *Analects* 11.22, Confucius explains that Ranyou is too hesitant while Zilu is too eager, so he encourages Ranyou and restrains Zilu. This is comparable with Aristotle's doctrine of the mean (hence, the traditional translation of "中庸").

6 The Master said, "Great indeed was the wisdom of Shun! He was inquisitive and examined the doctrines of those who were close to him, screening out the bad and accentuating the good. Grasping two extremes, he applied the mean (*zhong* 中) [in governing] the common people. It is precisely for this that he is Shun!"

> *Comment:* The ability to discriminate where the optimal balance lies between two extremes is a subtle skill that most people lack. But Shun was able to sense it and use it to govern the people.

10 Zilu asked about strength. The Master said, "The strength of the southerners, the strength of the northerners, or your own strength? Educating with generosity and gentleness, and not taking action against those who lack the way, is the strength of the southerners. *Junzi* live by this. Being armed for battle, without revulsion against dying, is the strength of the northerners. The strong live by this.

Therefore, *junzi* foster harmony (*he* 和), but do not merely go along with the current. Such is their strength and poise. They stand by the mean (*zhong* 中), without leaning. Such is their strength and poise. When the *dao* prevails in their state, they do not vary from when they were blocked from it. Such is their strength and poise. When *dao* does not prevail in their state, they do not vary even if it means death. Such is their strength and poise."

> *Comment:* Southerners and northerners excel at different kinds of strength. The strength of the southerners lies in gentleness and forgiveness. The strength of the northerners, on the other hand, is tough and fearless. While gentleness and forgiveness are good, the *junzi* should ideally rest in a stable

balance between these two extremes, not too gentle, and not too tough. They should maintain their balance and composure throughout all circumstances, without falling too far to one side or the other.

11 The Master said, "Later generations will have stories of hermits and their eccentric conduct; I do not do this kind of thing. Then there are *junzi* who follow the way in their conduct, yet give up halfway; I am not able to stop. And then there are *junzi* who are grounded in excellence in the ordinary (*zhong yong* 中庸). Withdrawing from the world, they go unnoticed but have no regrets. Only sages are able to do this."

> *Comment:* The first kind of hermit's eccentricity results in some notoriety, but is without substance. The person who withdraws from the world but practices excellence in the ordinary is different. When the way does not prevail, it is wise to go back to one's family and contribute to bringing order back to the world in the inconspicuous ways that the situation will allow. (See *Zhong Yong* 27, p. 244, below; *Da Xue*, Canonic Core, p. 60; and *Analects* 5.2, 5.21, 8.13, 18.8, pp. 102–04.)

13 The Master said, "*Dao* is not far from people. If a person's enactment of *dao* were far from people, it could not be regarded as *dao*.[4]

> *Comment:* One way to appreciate the intuitive plausibility of this claim is to look at it this way: *Dao*, for Confucians is *ren dao*, that is, the *dao* of people. How could the *dao* of people not be close at hand for people?

"The *Odes* say, 'Hewing an axe handle. Hewing [while holding] an axe handle. The model is close at hand.' [Taking *dao* to be far away] is like holding an axe handle thereby to hew an axe handle, glancing to the side to see it, and yet regarding it as far away. Thus, *junzi* use [their own] humanity (*ren* 人) to bring order to others (*ren* 人). They reform them and nothing more. Wholeheartedly committed (*zhong* 忠) with empathetic consideration (*shu* 恕), one does not deviate far from *dao* 道.[5] Do not impose on others what you would not wish imposed upon you.[6]

"The *dao* of *junzi* has four [parts], and I have not been able to fulfill a single one of them. I was not able to serve my father with what I expect from a son. I was not able to serve my lord with what I expect from a minister. I was not able to serve my seniors with what I expect from my juniors. And I was not able to first carry out toward friends and colleagues what I expect of them."

---

4 Cf. *Analects* 7.30, p. 85.
5 Cf. *Analects* 4.15, p. 82.
6 Cf. *Analects* 15.24, p. 83.

In ordinary situations (*yong* 庸), [*junzi*] conduct themselves with influential character (*de* 德), and attend carefully to their own words. Where there is insufficiency, they dare not slacken their efforts; where there is excess, they dare not use it all. In what they say, they are mindful of their own conduct. In conduct, they are mindful of what they have said. How could *junzi* fail to make a wholehearted effort in such matters?

15 The *dao* of *junzi* is like traveling a great distance; one must proceed from what is near. It is like ascending a great height; one must proceed from what is relatively low. The *Odes* say, "Wife and children united in fondness, like the playing of lutes and harps; elder and younger brother entirely in tune with each other, like the joy of being steeped in music; fitting to your house and home, enjoy (*le* 樂) your wife and children." The Master commented, "Won't such a father and mother receive ready compliance!"[7]

> *Comment:* Starting from what is near at hand, the Ode suggests, is start-ing from natural, familial love. Presumably, the reference to a "great distance" suggests that this familial love is not the end. Rather, as Meng Zi argues, these feelings must be extended, cultivated, and enlarged. Notice that the theme of musical enjoyment carries through the Ode to the end, even in the last line, the character "*le*" 樂 means 'music' as well as 'joy' (pronounced "*yue*" when meaning music).

16 The Master said, "How vigorous are the ghosts and spirits in their potency (*de* 德)! Looked for, but not seen. Listened for, but not heard. They are vital to things, but cannot leave a trace. They compel the people of the whole world, donned in their most luxurious attire, to make sacrificial offerings to their ancestors. Then from above and all around they rush like a flood! The *Odes* say, 'The intentions of the spirits cannot be fathomed, still less can they be dismissed.' The manifestation of the subtle and mysterious (cf. *Zhong Yong* 1) is like the inability to conceal authenticity (*cheng* 誠)."

20 Duke Ai [of Lu, Confucius' home state,] asked about governance (*zheng* 政). The Master said, "The governance of [the great] kings Wen and Wu is described on wood and bamboo documents. If such people are present, their governance will be upheld. When these people are gone, (proper) governance comes to an end.[8] The way with regard to people (*ren dao* 人道) is diligent governance, [just as] the way with regard to the earth is diligent planting. As for governance, it is the shaft of a reed.[b]

---

7 Cf. *Meng Zi* 4A11, p. 151.
8 Cf. *Xun Zi* 17.12, p. 187, and accompanying comment.

Thus, governing depends on people. Win over people with character (*shen* 身). Cultivate character with *dao* 道. Cultivate *dao* with *ren* 仁 (humanity). *Ren* 仁 is being [authentically] human (*ren* 人).[9] Intimacy (*qin* 親) among close relatives (*qin* 親) is of great importance.[10] And appropriateness (*yi* 義) is what is fitting (*yi* 宜). [In this] deference to the worthy (*xian* 賢) is of great importance. Norms of ritual propriety stem from the extent of intimacy among close relatives, and the degree of deference to be shown to the worthy. [...]c

Thus, *junzi* cannot but cultivate their character (*shen*). Considering the cultivation of their character, they cannot but serve their close relatives. Considering the service of their close relatives, they cannot but understand and appreciate (*zhi* 知) others. Considering their appreciation of others, they cannot but understand and appreciate *tian* 天. There are five prominent ways in the world. And there are three ways of putting them into practice. The five prominent ways in the world are said [to regard]: (1) ruler and minister, (2) father and child, (3) husband and wife, (4) elder and younger brother, and (5) the relations among friends and colleagues. Wisdom (*zhi* 知), *ren* 仁 (humanity), and courage are the three prominent virtues (*de* 德) in the world. These are the means by which [the five *dao*] are put into practice. Some people are born with wisdom; some gain it through study; and others do so through life's struggles. But their understanding is the same. Some put it into practice with ease, some are motivated by the benefits (*li* 利), and some diligently force themselves. But their achievement of success is one and the same.

The Master said, "Being fond of learning is close to wisdom (*zhi* 知). Making an effort in one's conduct is close to *ren* 仁 (humanity). Having a sense of shame is close to courage. If one understands these three things, one will know how to cultivate one's character. If one knows how to cultivate one's character, one will know how to manage others. If one knows how to manage others, one will know how to manage the world, the state, and one's family." [...]

[Naturally] being authentic (*cheng* 誠) is the way of *tian* (*tian zhi dao* 天之道). Acquiring authenticity is the way of people (*ren zhi dao* 人之道). Being authentic [naturally] involves hitting the mark (*zhong* 中) effortlessly, and achieving without deliberating. Those who hit the mark of *dao* with ease are sages. Those who acquire authenticity choose moral efficacy (*shan* 善) and cling to it. [...]

---

9   Cf. *Meng Zi* 7B16, p. 129.
10   Cf. *Meng Zi* 4A11, p. 151.

Comment: Although there are passages in the *Xun Zi* (§§3.9a–3.9c, not included in this anthology) that are reminiscent of this discussion of authenticity (*cheng* 誠), one difference is that Xun Zi seems to take sages to be just like everyone else, except that they actually did the work required to transform themselves. In contrast, the *Zhong Yong* seems to treat sages as naturally gifted. This conclusion is reinforced by the passage below.

21 Insight (*ming* 明) stemming from authenticity (*cheng* 誠) is attributed to natural disposition (*xing* 性). Authenticity stemming from insight is attributed to instruction. Authenticity assures insight, and vice versa.

Comment: The character for "*ming*" (明) consists of radicals that represent the Sun (日) and Moon (月), and indicates clearness and brightness. It suggests both the inner light of insightfulness and outwardly shining brightly, like the Sun and the Moon. Here it is suggested that insightfulness can be a natural gift, but insight can also be acquired through instruction. One might infer that the natural brilliance of the sages assures that *others* will achieve their own authenticity, and consequently their own insight, allowing for a self-supporting cycle of continuous personal and societal fulfillment, radiating outward and into the future. This is more explicit in the following passage.

22 Only the world's most authentic (*cheng* 誠) are able to exhaust the potential of their natural dispositions (*jin qi xing* 盡其性). Being able to exhaust the potential of their own natural dispositions, they are able to exhaust the potential of others. Being able to do this, they are able to exhaust the potential of the natural tendencies of things (*wu zhi xing* 物之性). They are thus able to assist in the transformative nurturing provided by the heavens (*tian* 天) and the earth. Being able to do this, they can thereby take their place as members of a triad with the heavens and earth.

Comment: The most authentic persons form a 'triad' with the heavens (*tian*) and the earth by bringing to completion what is made possible by natural conditions (see *Xun Zi* 17.2a, 23.5a, and 19.6, pp. 179, 228, and 196).

23 The next best is to thoroughly develop one aspect [of one's genuine potential]. This aspect can be authentic (*cheng* 誠). If it is authentic, it will take form. If it takes form, it will be evident. If it is evident, it will shine. If it shines, it will influence. If it is influential, it will cause change. If it causes change, it will be transformative. Only the world's most authentic are able to be transformative.

25 Authenticity (*cheng* 誠) is self-actualization (*zi cheng* 自成), and *dao* is self-guidance (*zidao* 自道). Authenticity is the beginning and end of things (*wu* 物). Without authenticity, there is nothing. This is why a *junzi's* becoming authentic is what is valued. Authenticity is not only realizing (*cheng* 成) oneself, it is that by which one accomplishes (*cheng* 成) other things. Realizing oneself involves *ren* 仁 (exhibiting humanity). Accomplishing other things involves wisdom (*zhi* 知). Potency of character (*de* 德) [rooted in] natural disposition (*xing* 性) merges the inward and outward *dao*s. It accounts for fittingness of time and place.

> *Comment:* The inward *dao* is the self-guided process of self-actualization, becoming truly *ren*. The outward *dao* is accomplishing things. Presumably this includes bringing out authenticity in others.

27 Great indeed is the *dao* of the sages: a vast reservoir gushing forth to nourish all things—mountain peaks reaching into the heavens. Vast indeed is its greatness! Ritual ceremonies numbering 300, and rules of etiquette numbering 3,000—only after such great people appeared were these put into practice. Thus it is said, "Without the utmost potency of character (*de* 德), the utmost *dao* will not solidify."

Thus, *junzi* honor the natural dispositions of virtuous potency (*de xing* 德性) [in the sages] as they forged the way (*dao* 道) of inquiry and learning. They extend broadly and expansively, and exhaust the subtle and minute. Achieving the pinnacle of brilliance, they forge a *dao* of excellence in the ordinary. Those who rekindle the old with an understanding of the new[11] exalt ritual propriety (*li* 禮) with earnestness and profundity.

> *Comment:* To proceed on the way (*dao* 道) is to authentically (*cheng* 誠) harmonize (*he* 和) one's present conditions, while being attentive to enduring propensities and dispositions (*tian* 天, *xing* 性), starting from what is most proximate (see *Zhong Yong* 13, 15, pp. 240, 241), to achieve a productive equilibrium. What is most proximate, ultimately, is one's own person. So, cultivating one's own character is a clear priority. The next most proximate is one's immediate family, so productive familial relations are likewise emphasized. In order to cultivate oneself, nurture familial relations, and be in a productive relation to one's ancestors, Confucians emphasize attentiveness to ritual propriety (*li* 禮).

---

11   This phrase also occurs in *Analects* 2.11, p. 72.

For this reason, they are not arrogant when in a superior position, and are not contrary as subordinates. When the *dao* obtains in a state, their words enable them to thrive. When the *dao* does not obtain in a state, their silence enables them to endure. The *Odes* say, "With insight and wisdom one protects one's person (*shen* 身)." This captures the meaning.

32 Only the world's most authentic (*cheng* 誠) are able to weave the threads of the great warp and weft that governs the civilized world (*tian xia* 天下[12]), to establish its most important fundamentals, and to understand the transformative nurturance of the natural world. How could there be anything on which they must depend? They are earnest in their *ren* 仁, deep as an unfathomable abyss, and vast as the heavens (*tian* 天). If not those of firm, insightful, and sagely knowledge, they who manifest a celestial (*tian* 天) potency of character (*de* 德), then who can understand it?

> *Comment:* Compare Xun Zi's remark: "[People of great insight] weave norms into the world (*tian di* 天地), tailoring functional roles for the myriad things. They fashion and carve out great patterns (*da li* 大理), [giving form to] the inner lining of the cosmos" (*Xun Zi* 21.5e, p. 206).

ENDNOTES

[a] Ogyū Sorai, *Bendō* 4. See Najita 1998, 6–7, for comparison.

[b] The phrase here is enigmatic, and interpretations vary wildly. So, I have stuck with a literal interpretation of the text that does make some sense. But given the controversy, and thus the tentativeness of the translation, I refrain from teasing out any philosophical implications. Ames and Hall point out that it has been suggested that this is part of an interpolated commentary (2001, 125n53).

[c] Omitting a sentence that seems out of place. See Ames and Hall 2001, 125n57.

---

12 Whereas *tian di* 天地 (the heavens and the earth) indicates the natural world, *tian xia* 天下 (all under the sky) includes the people living in it. It refers, in other words, to the known civilized world from the perspective of the early Chinese peoples.

PART II

Mo Jia: The School of Mo (Mohism)

8

Mo Zi

INTRODUCTION

The Mohists were an extraordinary phenomenon. They were a guild of carpenters who participated in the philosophical debate over the way to social flourishing. They were a brotherhood of warriors, respected for their might and military strategy, and yet also articulated pacifist arguments against warfare. They were empirically minded, even developing a theory of optics, and yet also believed in the existence of ghosts and spirits. And they embodied this curious mix of apparently inconsistent characteristics with effortless ease.

They were straightforward common-sense thinkers who had little patience with the aesthetic flourishes of Ruist cultivation, and articulated a more systematic and utilitarian philosophy in response. Their social *dao* is grounded in a justification of the origins of social structures: a mythical reconstruction of an antagonistic primal state that necessitated a universal, hierarchical power structure to be imposed from above. The resulting state has three major goals if it is to flourish: population, wealth, and order. They are most celebrated for their principle of *jian'ai* (兼愛) "impartial concern," which they believed to be the only policy that can guarantee a harmonious society.

The Mohists appear to be the first school to be concerned with specifying modes of epistemic justification, that is, the acceptable ways in which knowledge claims may be justified. They identify three principles: collate historical evidence ("examination"), identify observational evidence ("tracing to the source"), and experiment to identify whether a policy has positive or negative effects ("application"). This last need not always be actual experiment, since a well-reasoned thought experiment may sometimes be enough to identify the negative or positive consequences of a policy or course of action.

I begin the translation with the Mohist formulation of their epistemological criteria. The rest of the translation is divided into two main sections, the "Philosophical System" and "Rhetorical Criticisms of Ruism." The first provides the core doctrines of the Mohist political system, which I have translated in the following order to make clearer the theoretical development of the ideas:

"Conforming with Superiors" presents a social origins story that aims to justify hierarchical social structures and a universalist system of value;

"Intentions of *Tian*" attempts to provide a semi-naturalistic account of the origins of this system of value in the functioning of the Cosmos itself;

"Promoting the Worthy" shows practically how one might be able to achieve these idealistic goals, by identifying and promoting those who have the greatest worth and ability, once such a state has been established;

"Impartial Concern" provides a second principle for achieving these goals: it argues against the Ruist ethic of graded concern, where one is ethically obligated to put one's own family above those of others; the Mohists argue that all people must be treated with equal concern, and that we can achieve this by expanding the boundaries of our self-identification;

"Against Aggression" follows this principle of impartial concern, and argues that aggressive warfare is the greatest wrong; the Mohists present themselves as champions of the oppressed and of the underdog.

The second half of this translation presents the Mohists' rhetorical criticisms of Ruism. Like the critiques of the Ruists made by the Utopian Daoists in the *Zhuang Zi* (in Chapter 11), they are entertaining to read, but appear to be based on misrepresentations of actual Ruist values.

PHILOSOPHICAL SYSTEM

Excerpt from Book 9, Chapter 37

Master Mo said, "In propounding any doctrine, one cannot but first establish a standard. To profess it before establishing a standard is like establishing the time of day on a revolving potter's wheel. I think that even though there is a distinction between sunrise and sunset one would never in the end be able to establish it. Thus, doctrines have three criteria (*fa* 法). What are they? Examination; tracing to the source; and application.

"How do you examine it? *Examine the deeds of the former sage-kings.*

"How do you trace it to the source? *Investigate the circumstances of the eyes and ears of the people.*

"How do you use it? *Set it out in the administration of the great families of the state and of the ordinary people and observe it.*

"These are the three *fa*."

> *Comment:* Three epistemological criteria are appealed to in order to justify any doctrine. The first is *historical* precedent: provide evidence that it worked in the past. The second is *empirical* experience: examine the observational evidence of the people. The third is *experimental* testing: try it out and see if it works, either in reality or in a thought experiment. All of these are pragmatist in spirit, as they all appeal to evidence that the doctrine will work in practice.

"Conforming with Superiors" (Book 3, Chapter 11)

Master Mo said, "In ancient times, when people were first born and did not yet have any form of government, there was a saying: 'People differ regarding their ideal sense of what is right (*yi* 義).' So, one person had one ideal (*yi* 義), two people had two, ten had ten: the more numerous the people, the more numerous their (conflicting) ideals. So people affirmed (*shi* 是) their own *yi*, and by doing so refuted (*fei* 非) those of others. Thus, when interacting they opposed (*fei* 非) one another. Within the home, resentments and hatreds arose between father and child, elder and younger; and once separated they were unable to reconcile harmoniously. Ordinary people throughout the world used water, fire, and poisons to harm one another, and wouldn't help one another out if they had strength to spare. In fact, they would even prefer surplus goods to rot rather than share them. The way of virtue was hidden, not shared between them. The chaos in the world was beastly.

> *Comment:* Note Mo Zi's use of "*yi*" here in a more general sense: a sense of what counts as a virtuous ideal or right behavior. They assume that such ideals will vary from person to person. This appears to be grounded in a presupposition that people are first and foremost self-interested. The Mohists clearly assume that social differences will stand in conflict, if not prevented from doing so. The only way to prevent such conflict would

then be to impose a single system of rightness universally. In what follows they develop a systematic argument showing the means by which such a system must be identified and universalized.

It could be clearly discerned that the reason for the turmoil of the world was that there were neither governments nor leaders. So, they chose the most worthy (*xian* 賢) and capable in the world, and established them as emperor. But because the emperor's strength was insufficient, they also chose the (next) most worthy and capable in the world and established them as the three dukes. Once the emperor and the three dukes were set up, since the world was so broad and vast, the distinctions between right (*shi* 是) and wrong (*fei* 非) and between benefit and harm regarding the people of distant states and foreign lands could not be clearly discerned. Thus, they delineated the many states, and set up the feudal lords and rulers of the states. Once the feudal lords and rulers were established, since their strength was insufficient they then chose the most worthy and capable in each state, and set them up as the governing leaders.

> *Comment:* 'Worthiness' and 'ability' here refer to practical qualities that can be discerned independently of any ethical system. "Worthiness," *xian* 賢, here refers literally to one's worth or value: you count as 'worthy' if you have proven your worth to a ruler who has specific goals. In Confucian contexts, it means 'ethically virtuous,' but here remains ambiguous between the two senses.

When the governing leaders were all set up, the emperor issued a government order to the people of the world saying, "Whatever you hear, good and bad, is to be reported to your superiors. What the superiors affirm (*shi* 是) everyone must affirm; what they reject (*fei* 非) everyone must reject. When superiors are at fault you must gently remonstrate with them regarding the rules; when inferiors are good one must draw them close and recommend them. When one conforms with the superior, and does not ally oneself with those below, this is to be rewarded by the superiors and praised by those below.

"Suppose one hears what is good but does not report it to one's superiors, does not affirm what the superiors affirm or reject what they reject; suppose when superiors are at fault one does not gently remonstrate, or when those below are good one does not draw them close and recommend them; suppose one allies oneself with those below and cannot bring oneself to conform with one's superior. This is to be punished by the superior and condemned by those below."

This is how the superiors understand reward and punishment, making clear investigations to ensure that their judgments are reliable.

Now, the villagers with greatest humanity became the leaders of the villages. They issued a government order to the people of their villages saying, "Whatever you hear, good and bad, is to be reported to your district leader. What the district leader affirms everyone must affirm. What the district leader rejects everyone must reject. Abandon your own bad doctrines and learn from the district leader's good doctrines; abandon your own bad practices and learn from the district leader's good practices. Then, how could there be turmoil in the villages?" When we examine the reason for order in the district, what do we find? Just that the district leaders were able to assimilate (*tong* 同) the *yi* (sense of rightness) of the district, and so the district was orderly.

Now, the district leaders were the people of the districts with greatest humanity. They issued a government order to the people of the districts saying, "Whatever you hear, good and bad, is to be reported to the lord of the state. What the lord of the state affirms everyone must affirm. What the lord of the state rejects everyone must reject. Abandon your own bad doctrines and learn from the lord of the state's good doctrines; abandon your own bad practices and learn from the lord of the state's good practices. Then, how could there be turmoil in the state?" When we examine the reason for order in the state, what do we find? Just that the lords of the state were able to assimilate the *yi* of the state, and so the state was orderly.

Now, the lords of the state were the people in the state with greatest humanity. They issued a government order to the people of the district saying, "Whatever you hear, good and bad, is to be reported to the emperor. What the emperor affirms everyone must affirm. What the emperor rejects everyone must reject. Abandon your own bad doctrines and learn from the emperor's good doctrines; abandon your own bad practices and learn from the emperor's good practices. Then, how could there be turmoil in the world?" When we examine the reason for order in the world, what do we find? Just that the emperor was able to assimilate the *yi* of the world, and so the world was orderly.

If the ordinary people of the world conform (*tong* 同) with the emperor but not with *Tian*, then calamities will not be avoided. Heavy winds and bitter rains will accumulate endlessly. This is how *Tian* would punish the people who do not conform with it.

Comment: Since difference is equated with social chaos, social harmony is equated with conformity and sameness (*tong* 同). The means to achieve social harmony must therefore be a system of unification by assimilation. (Contrast this with *Analects* 13.23, p. 78.) Notice the role of *tian* here. On the one hand, it is spoken of as having 'intentions' (*zhi* 志), and 'punishing' the people, and so it can easily be interpreted in a supernatural sense. But the justifications given in "The Intentions of *Tian*," translated immediately below, appeal to the natural consequences of misunderstanding the nature of the Cosmos itself: if our behavior does not conform with the laws of the natural world, we will inevitably court natural disaster. If this is right, then it would seem that the Mohists were also beginning to move away from a personal or 'divine' understanding of *tian* towards a more naturalistic one.

"The Intentions of *Tian*" (Book 7, Chapter 26)

In this chapter, Mo Zi attempts to identify what is valued by *tian*, the intentionality (*zhi* 志) implicit in the natural workings of the Cosmos. What brings flourishing and what brings disaster are traced to the natural order of things. Value is thereby understood as an intrinsic part of the natural world: 'intended' as it were in the very nature of things. While the language of 'intentions' might give the impression that *tian* has explicit intentions, the actual justification given appeals more to implicit values in the natural ordering of the world itself. The text retains a stubborn ambivalence between natural and divine interpretations of '*tian*.'

Master Mo said, "Nowadays, the lords and officials in the world understand petty things but not the great. How do we know this? We know it from their conduct in the household. If in conduct at home you commit an offense against the head of the household, you may still be able to flee to a neighboring household. But relatives and siblings coming to know of this will all admonish you saying, 'You must be watchful! You must be vigilant! How can it be acceptable to commit an offense against the head of your household in your conduct at home?'

"But it is not only in one's conduct at home, it is also so in one's conduct in the state. If in conduct in the state you commit an offense against the ruler of the state, you may still be able to flee to a neighboring state. But relatives and siblings coming to know of this will all admonish you saying, 'You must be watchful! You must be vigilant! How can it be acceptable to commit an offense against the ruler of the state while conducting yourself in the state?'

"The admonishment is this serious when there is a place to flee and hide. How much more so when there is no place to flee! The admonishment must surely be even more serious! There is a saying about this, 'In broad daylight! You commit an offense! How will you be able to escape this?' There is no place to escape it! Even in the deserted hidden corners of the forests and valleys, *Tian* will certainly have a clear view of you. And yet, when it comes to *Tian*, the lords and officials in the world suddenly don't know how to admonish one another. This is how we know that the lords and officials in the world understand petty things but not the great.

> Comment: Those who commit the most extensive atrocities in the empire become tyrants and warlords, and yet are praised for their achievements. While there may be no imperial power above the warlords to admonish and punish them, their atrocities are nevertheless clear as daylight.

So, what is it that *Tian* desires and what does it detest? *Tian* desires what is right (*yi* 義) and detests what is not right. So, if we lead the ordinary people of the world to follow ideal conduct (*yi* 義), then we do what *Tian* desires. If we do what *Tian* desires, then *Tian* does what we desire. So, what do we desire and what do we detest? We desire wealth and fortune, and detest disaster and malicious havoc. If we do not do what *Tian* desires, but instead do what *Tian* does not desire, then in leading the ordinary people of the world they will follow their affairs into havoc and disaster."

"But, how do we know that *Tian* desires what is right and detests what is not right?" He said, "When the world is right there is life; when it lacks rightness there is death; when there is right there is wealth; when it lacks rightness there is poverty; when it is right there is order; when it lacks rightness there is turmoil. Therefore, *Tian* wants us to live, and detests that we should die, wants us to be wealthy and detests that we should be poor, wants there to be order and detests that there should be calamity. This is how we know that *Tian* desires what is right and detests what is not right.

> Comment: The reference at the end of the preceding paragraph to the heavens responding to human misbehavior with havoc and disaster is ambiguous: it may be interpreted literally as punishment from an overseeing spirit. But the fuller discussion here suggests a more naturalistic interpretation. If we behave ethically we flourish because we enable natural life to flourish; but to behave unethically is to cause destruction,

disorder, and social chaos. This is because there are natural values inherent in the very functioning of the world; they can be identified as those that promote life, flourishing, and order.

"Moreover, rightness is orderly government. One cannot order the superior by governing from below; one must order those below by governing from above. Therefore, the peasants exhaust their efforts in following their affairs. They do not overstep themselves in order to govern, but are governed by the officials. The officials exhaust their efforts in following their affairs. They do not overstep themselves in order to govern, but are governed by generals and great leaders. The generals and great leaders exhaust their efforts in following their affairs. They do not overstep themselves in order to govern, but are governed by the three dukes and feudal lords. The three dukes and feudal lords exhaust their efforts in tending to affairs of state. They do not overstep themselves in order to govern, but are governed by the emperor.

"The emperor does not overstep himself in order to govern, but is governed by *Tian*. The officials and lords of the world clearly understand that the emperor governs the three dukes, feudal lords, officials, and peasants; but the ordinary people of the world do not clearly understand that it is *Tian* that governs the emperor." [...]

Comment: The very nature of orderly government itself dictates a hierarchy of power, imposed top–down, as we saw above. This order of power ultimately arises from the Cosmic forces of the world itself. The emperor cannot choose any structures and values but must choose those that by their very nature will promote flourishing. (On a more 'religious' reading, these are the values favored by the Heavens.)

To accord with the intentions of *Tian* is to practice rightness (*yi*) when governing. To turn against the intentions of *Tian* is to use force when governing. So, how do we go about practicing rightness when governing? Master Mo said, "One resides in a large state without attacking smaller states; one resides in a large household without usurping smaller households; those with power do not oppress those who are weak; the rich do not demean the poor; the sharp-witted do not cheat the gullible. This will certainly benefit *Tian* above, the spirits in the middle, and the people below: there is nothing that it will not benefit. Thus, one will be held up with the honorable title, 'Sage-King.'

"Those who govern with force are different: in their doctrines they reject all this, in their actions they oppose it, racing off in the opposite direction. Residing in a large state they attack smaller states; those who reside in large households usurp smaller households; those with power oppress the weak; the rich demean the poor; the sharp-witted cheat the gullible. This brings no benefit to *Tian* above, to the spirits in the middle, or to the people below. These bring no benefit anywhere. Thus, they are branded with the ugly title of 'Despots.'"

> *Comment:* This passage contains a negative account of rightness: a list of actions that one does *not* do. Rightness is the absence of force, aggression, and oppression. When there is difference of power (whether of size, wealth, or intelligence), if one wields that power to attack, usurp, oppress, and cheat, then one does not act rightly. Wrongness consists in oppression and exploitation of those with less power. Sage-kings do not engage in such despotic activity. When one refrains from such actions, the result is universal benefit.

Thus, Master Mo said, "Having the intentions of *Tian* can be compared with a wheelwright's having a compass, or a carpenter's having a square edge. When wheelwrights and carpenters have compasses and squares, they are able to set the measures for the squares and circles in the world. Those that match are affirmed; those that do not are rejected." [...]

Excerpt from End of Book 7, Chapter 27

Thus to Mo Zi, *Tian* is no different from compasses to a wheelwright or a square edge to a carpenter. A wheelwright grasps a compass to measure what is circular and what is not circular in the world saying, "What matches my compass is circular, what does not match is not circular. In this way, I am able to know what is circular and what is not." What is the reason for this? Because the standard (*fa* 法) on which a circle is modeled is clear. A carpenter, too, grasps a square edge to measure what is square in the world and what is not, saying, "What matches my square edge is square, and what does not is not square. Thus am I able to know what is square and what is not." What is the reason for this? Because the standard to which a square is modeled is clear.

Thus, Mo Zi has the intentions of *Tian* to use to measure the government of the kings, dukes, and great leaders above, and to measure the cultural teachings and doctrines of the many people in the world below. Observing their actions, if they follow the intentions of *Tian* they are called actions with excellent intention; if they go against the intentions of the Cosmos, they are called actions with bad intention. Observing their doctrines and sayings, if they follow the intentions of *Tian*, they are called excellent doctrines; if they go against the intentions of *Tian* they are called bad doctrines. Observing their government, if it accords with the intentions of *Tian* it is called excellent government; if it goes against the intentions of *Tian* it is called bad government. If we hold onto this as a model, establish this as a standard, we can use it to measure the humanity or inhumanity of the kings, dukes, and great leaders of the world as though distinguishing black from white.

Thus, Mo Zi said, "Now if the kings, dukes, great leaders, officials, and lords in the world desire to lead with the *dao* and benefit the people efficaciously, they must examine the root of humanity and rightness. The intentions of *Tian* *must* be followed, because the intentions of *Tian* constitute the standard of rightness."

"Promoting the Worthy" (Book 2, Chapter 8)

Master Mo said, "In ancient times, the kings, dukes, and great lords in governing desired wealth for the nation, a numerous population, and orderly government. But they gained poverty rather than wealth, population decline rather than growth, and disorder rather than order. So why did they gain what they detested and not what they desired?"

Master Mo said, "It is because in governing the nation, the kings, dukes, and great lords do not promote the worthy and employ the capable. Thus, when there are many worthy and excellent officers in a state, the nation is richly ordered; when there are few worthy and excellent officers, the nation is poorly ordered. Thus, the task of the great officials lies solely in increasing the number of worthy people."

How do you increase the number of worthy people? Master Mo said, "It's the same as if you wanted to increase the number of excellent archers and charioteers: you would have to enrich, honor, respect, and praise them. Then you'd be able to increase the number of excellent archers and charioteers in the state. It is even more so with worthy officers: rich in virtuous action, discriminating in their words and discussions, broad in the arts (of the way), they are the nation's riches, and (may be called) the attendants of the ceremonial altars. They must be enriched, honored, respected, and praised if you are to succeed in increasing the number of virtuous officers in the state."

Now, in ancient times, when the wise kings governed, they said, "Do not enrich those lacking in virtue (*bu yi*); do not honor them, do not consider them to be kin, do not draw near to them." So, when the rich and honored in the state heard of this, they retreated and deliberated saying, "Until now, we have relied on our wealth and honor. But now, the superiors promote virtue (*yi*) and do not pass up the poor. From now on, we *must* act according to our highest ideals (*yi*)." When those who were closely related heard it, they also retreated and deliberated saying, "Until now, we have relied on our kinship. But now our superiors promote virtue and would not pass up those who are not related. From now on, we must be virtuous." When those who were near (to the ruler) heard this, they also retreated and planned saying, "Until now, we have relied on our proximity (to the ruler). But now our superiors promote virtue and will not overlook those who are distant. From now on, we cannot but be virtuous."

When those who were distant heard it, they also retreated and deliberated saying, "At first we thought our distance was an obstacle. But now our superiors promote virtue and do not pass up those who are distant. From now on, we cannot but be virtuous." This reached the ministers in the suburbs and the distant outlying reaches, the younger generations of the court, the population of the state, and the peasants from all regions. Hearing about it, they all competed with each other to be virtuous. Why? Because what the superiors charged their subordinates with was but one thing, and what the subordinates served their superiors with was but one art.

An analogy: A rich man has a deep palace with a high wall, cautiously completed, with but one doorway carved out. A thief who enters may be locked in, and when sought for will have no escape. Why? Because the superior has grasped the essential.

Thus in ancient times, when the wise kings governed they ranked people by order of virtuosity (*de*) and promoted the worthy. Whether farmer or worker, if they had ability they were promoted, given higher status, granted a weighty salary, entrusted with responsibilities, and given their own authority to command. They said, "If status is not high, the people will not be respectful; if the salary is not generous, the people will have no faith in them; if their command is not authoritative, the people will not fear them." They conferred these three on the worthy, not as a favor, but because they wanted their affairs to be successful. So, then, they ranked by virtue, assigned duties according to office, bestowed rewards according to effort, and distributed salary by measuring achievements. In this way, no officials were always honored, and no people remained always in poverty. If they had ability they were promoted, if not they were dismissed. They promoted public-mindedness and virtue, and they avoided private scheming and enmity. This is the meaning of their doctrines. [...]

Excerpt from Book 2, Chapter 9

Master Mo said, "Nowadays, the kings, dukes, and great lords when ruling the people, presiding over the ceremonies, ordering the states and clans, desire to cultivate preservation without loss. Should they not attend to promoting the worthy as the root of good government? How do we know this is the root of good government? When the honored and wise govern the unintelligent and lowly, there is order; but when the unintelligent and lowly govern the honored and wise, there is turmoil. This is how we know that promoting the worthy is the root of governing. Thus in ancient times, the wise kings greatly valued promoting the worthy and appointing the capable. They were not partisan towards fathers and brothers; were not partial to the honored and wealthy; and showed no bias towards those who were good-looking. The worthy were lifted and raised, enriched and honored, and made officials and leaders. The unworthy were restrained and removed, impoverished and debased, and made servants and laborers. Thus, the people all strove for the rewards, wary of the punishments, and competed with each other to be virtuous. Thus, the worthy increased in number while the unworthy decreased. This is what it is to progress in virtue. [...]"

"Impartial Concern" (Book 4, Chapter 16)

Master Mo said, "The task of a person with humanity must be to serve to increase benefit to the world and eliminate the harms." If so, then which are the greatest harms in the world nowadays? He said, "If great states attack small states, great families disturb small families, the strong plunder the weak, the majority oppress the minority, the crafty swindle the simpletons, the rich demean the poor, these are harms to the world. Also, rulers who are not magnanimous, ministers who are not loyally devoted, fathers who are not fatherly, and children who are not filial, these are harms to the world. In addition, base people who wield weapons and poisons, water and fire, to plunder one another, these are harms to the world."

> *Comments:* As with 'rightness' above, 'benefit' here is not defined positively but by contrasting it with 'harm.' And 'harm' is explained through examples of aggression, oppression, and cheating.

Let us try to root out the origin of the multitude of harms. From where do they arise? Do they arise from loving and benefiting others? We must surely say not. We must say that they arise from hating and robbing from others. Should we call hating and robbing people 'impartiality,' or 'partiality' (*bie* 別)? We must call it 'partiality.' It is dealing with people partially that really produces the great harms in the world. Thus, Mo Zi said, "Partiality is wrong (*fei* 非)."

Master Mo said, "If you criticize a person, you must give something in exchange. To criticize something but give nothing in exchange, is like using water to stoke a fire. There will be nothing acceptable in one's explanation." So, Mo Zi said, "Exchange partiality for impartiality (*jian* 兼)."

> *Comment:* The term "*jian*" (兼) is sometimes translated "universal," but its use here is more specific: it means applying to all inclusively and equitably. All people, no matter their power, wealth, station, or intelligence, must be treated fairly and impartially. The family relationships favored by the Ruists should have no place when caring for other people. "*Jian*" contrasts with "*bie*" (別), which literally means "difference," but the guiding metaphor is 'splitting into differences' or factions. It implies making preferential distinctions. The difference between "*bie*" and "*jian*" is the difference between 'partiality' and 'impartiality.' Recall that the Mohists already equate difference with antagonism between individuals; here it is equated with difference between factions.

All right, but then how might we exchange partiality for impartiality? Suppose we were to consider other people's countries (*guo* 國) as though they were our own; then who would uphold their own country by attacking that of another? It is because we would act on behalf of the other (*bi* 彼) as we would do for ourselves (*ji* 己). If we consider the cities of others as our own, then who would uphold their own city in order to demolish another's? It is because we would act on behalf of the other as we act for ourselves. If we consider other people's families as our own, then who would uphold their own family by destroying the families of others? It is because we would act on behalf of the other as we act for ourselves. Thus, states and cities would not mutually attack or uproot each other, and clans would not destroy or plunder one another. Would this be a harm to the world, or a benefit? Of course, we must say that it would be a benefit.

> *Comment:* "To act on behalf of others as we act for ourselves." This represents a version of the Golden Rule. The Mohists are arguing that if all antagonism is caused by self-interest, then the solution is to treat the other as ourselves. This is a form of expanding the boundaries of selfhood. When we diminish the boundaries between self and other,

the well-being of others is indistinguishable from our own. The result of this way of thinking is called 'mutuality' (*xiang* 相) in what follows.

Thus, when we try to trace the root of the many benefits to what produces them, what do we find that they arise from? From hating and robbing people? Of course, we must say that this is not so; we must say that it is from caring about (*ai* 愛) and benefiting people. Assigning a name to caring about and benefiting the people of the world, should we call it 'partiality' or 'impartiality'? Of course, we must call it 'impartiality.' Thus, if we treat each other with impartiality, it really does result in benefit to the world! Therefore, Master Mo says "Impartiality is to be affirmed."

> *Comment: "Ai"* 愛 has a basic sense of 'love,' but in this more objective context, it means 'concern,' or 'caring concern,' but without any trace of sentimentality. The Mohists had a great sense of duty and fairness, but took great care not to be emotional about it.

We previously said, "The task of a person with humanity must be to serve to increase benefit to the world and eliminate the harms." Now we have traced the origins of the great benefits to the world to impartiality, and of the great harms to the world to partiality. Thus, Master Mo said, "To reject partiality and affirm impartiality is what emerges from such a method (*fang* 方)."

Now, if we want to adopt a policy to correctly seek to benefit the world, we should take impartiality as correct. In this way, those who are intelligent and clear sighted will see and hear with mutuality (*xiang*). Those with strong arms and legs will move and govern with mutuality. Those who have the way will instruct and admonish with mutuality. In this way, those who are elderly and without wives or children can trust that they will be nourished in order to live a long life. The young and orphaned, though they are without parents, will have the resources to be clothed and grow strong. Now, if taking impartiality as correct is so beneficial, I cannot understand the reason that the officials of the world can hear of impartiality and yet reject it.

And yet, the scholars of the world reject the doctrine of impartial concern, as though it is not yet settled, saying, "Although it may be excellent, how could it be put into practice?" Master Mo said, "If it could not be put into practice, even I would reject it. But how could there be anything that was excellent that could not be put into practice? Well, let us closely examine two cases. Suppose there are two scholars, one of whom upholds a doctrine of partiality, the other a doctrine of impartiality. The partial scholar says, 'How could I take my friend to be myself, my friend's parents and close relatives as my own?' This is how they look at their friends: when hungry they will not feed them; when cold they will not clothe them; when ill they will not nurse them back to health; and when dead they will not bury them. This is what the words and actions of the partial scholar are like.

"The words of the impartial scholar are not like this, nor are their actions. They say, 'I have heard that the noble scholars in the world will certainly treat their friends as their own person, and their friends' parents and close relatives as their own. Only then can they be the noblest scholars in the world.' This is how they look at their friends: when hungry they feed them; when cold they clothe them; when ill they nurse them back to health; when dead they bury them." This is what the words and actions of the impartial scholar are like.

These two scholars have contradictory doctrines and opposing practices. Let's suppose that they are trustworthy in words, so that they fulfill them in their actions: their words and deeds match like a tally, with no doctrine left unpracticed [i.e., they take these attitudes to the logical conclusion in practice]. So, let us make an inquiry. Imagine now a broad field, where people are armoring up for battle; they have no way of knowing who will live and who will die. And again, imagine a lord assigned for duty far away in the territories of Ba, Yue, Qi, or Jing, with no way of knowing whether he will ever return. Don't we know that they will entrust the care of their parents and support of their wives and children to the impartial person? Or will they entrust them to the partial person? I think there are no foolish husbands and wives in the world. Even if they themselves reject impartiality, they will certainly entrust their families to the impartial person. They may argue against impartiality, and yet they will choose impartiality. So what they say about impartiality is worthless. I cannot understand the reason why all the scholars in the world hear about impartiality and yet reject it.

And yet the scholars of the world do reject impartiality, as though it is not yet settled, saying, "This idea might be used to select an ordinary official, but cannot be used to select a ruler." Let us examine these two closer still. Suppose there are two rulers, one a proponent of impartiality, the other of partiality. So the partial ruler will say, "How could I treat my thousands of subjects as my own self (*shen* 身, 'person')? This would be too contrary (*fei* 非) to the circumstances of the world. A human life on earth is fleeting: like a chariot rushing across a crevice." Looking upon their subjects this way, they will not feed them when hungry, clothe them when cold, take care of them when sick, or bury them when they die. The words and actions of the partial ruler will be like this. Not so with the impartial ruler's words and actions. They will say, "I hear that the enlightened rulers of the world will surely place their subjects before their own persons, in order to be [truly] enlightened." Looking upon their subjects this way, when hungry they feed them, when cold they clothe them, when sick they look after them, and when they die they bury them. The words and actions of the impartial ruler are like this.

These two rulers reject each other's words and oppose each other in practice. Let's suppose that they are trustworthy in words, so that they fulfill them in their actions: their words and deeds match like a tally, with no doctrine left unpracticed. So, let us make an inquiry. Suppose the crops are blighted and the people are laboring, freezing, and starving; the dead rolled into ditches and gullies are already a multitude. Don't we know which of these two rulers we should choose to follow? I think that in such a situation no man or woman in the world is a fool: even if they reject impartiality, they will certainly follow the impartial ruler. In their doctrines they reject impartiality, but in their practical choices they adopt it. Their words and deeds oppose each other. I cannot understand the reason why all the scholars in the world hear about impartiality and yet reject it.

And yet the scholars of the world do reject impartiality, as though it is still not yet settled, saying, "Impartiality may indeed be humane and right. But, how can it be acted on? Its impossibility is like lifting Mount Tai and crossing the Yangzi and the Yellow Rivers. So, even though I am completely willing to be impartial, how could it possibly be done?" Master Mo replied, "From ancient times until the present, no person who has ever lived has been able to lift Mount Tai and cross the Yangzi and Yellow Rivers. But now, as for impartial mutual concern, and exchanging mutual benefit, the former sages and the six kings themselves practice it." How do we know that they practiced it? Master Mo said, "I wasn't born at their time, did not personally hear their words or see their visages. It is from the writings on bamboo and silk, the engravings on metal and stone, inscriptions on ceremonial utensils, that they are passed down to later generations for their descendants to learn about."

[...] And yet the scholars of the world reject impartiality, as though it is not yet settled, saying "Isn't it harmful to filiality not to be devoted to the benefit of one's *own* parents?" Master Mo said, "Let us try to trace the reasoning behind a filial child's actions towards their parents. I wonder if they wouldn't also desire others to care for and benefit their parents. Or would they want them to loathe and destroy them? From my theory we can see that they would want them to care for and benefit their parents. So, what should we do first to attain this? Should my first duty be to care for and benefit others' parents, so that they care for and benefit mine in return? Or should I begin by reviling their parents? Surely, I must first follow my duty by caring for and benefiting them for them to repay me with the same. So in exchanges between filial children, don't they attain their goals by caring for and benefiting the parents of others? Or are all the filial children in the whole world so stupid that they are incapable of doing what is correct?" [...]

Perhaps they think that it is too difficult to put into practice? But there are more difficult things that have been done. In the past, King Ling of Jing was fond of small waists. During his reign, the officers of Jing had no more than one meal a day; they couldn't get up without firm support or walk without leaning on a wall. Restricting one's diet is difficult to do, but people did it because King Ling took pleasure in it. In less than a generation the people were transformed because they sought to conform with their superiors.

In the past, Gou Jian, the King of Yue, was fond of bravery. For three years he trained his officers and ministers, but wasn't sure how well he knew them. So he set fire to his ships and then sounded the drums to advance. The officers trampled one another in their advance and countless numbers leapt into the fire and water to their deaths. Even when the drums ceased, they did not retreat. The officers of Yue were certainly petrified, and self-immolation is a difficult thing to do, but they did it because the King of Yue took pleasure in it. In less than a generation the people were transformed because they sought to conform with their superiors.

In the past, Duke Wen of Jin was fond of sackcloth clothing. During his reign, the officers of Jin had audiences with the Duke and walked through the courts wearing simple robes, sheep's hide, hats of plain silk, and straw sandals. Wearing sackcloth clothing is a difficult thing to do, and yet people did it because Lord Wen took pleasure in it. In less than a generation the people were transformed because they sought to conform with their superiors.

Now restricting diet, self-immolation, and wearing sackcloth for clothing are the most difficult things in the world to do, and yet people did them because their superiors took pleasure in them. In less than a generation the people were transformed because they sought to conform with their superiors.

Now impartial concern and mutual benefit are immeasurably beneficial and easy to practice. So, I believe it's simply that no superior takes delight in them. If a superior were to take delight in them, encourage them with rewards and praise, discourage them with punishments, I think people would move towards impartial concern and exchanging mutual benefit just as fire moves upwards and water moves downwards. Nothing in the world could stop them.

Thus impartiality is the way of the sage-kings, the means by which the kings, dukes, and great leaders achieved peace, and was sufficient to ensure that the many people were clothed and fed. The ruler can do no better than to look closely at impartiality and strive to practice it. As a person the ruler will be benevolent (*hui* 惠), the minister will be loyal, a father will be fatherly, children will be filial, elder brothers will be good friends, and younger brothers will be fraternal. Thus, if the ruler desires nothing more than benevolent rulers, loyal ministers, fatherly fathers, filial children, friendly elders, fraternal younger brothers, impartiality *must* be practiced. This is the way of the sage-kings and the greatest benefit to the people.

"Against Aggression" (Book 5, Chapter 17)

Now, suppose there was a person who entered someone else's orchard and pilfered their peaches and plums. Everyone who heard about it would condemn it. He would be punished by a superior governor who caught him. Why is this? Because he diminishes others to benefit himself. As for seizing the dogs, boars, chickens, and suckling pigs of others, this is more 'unright' (*bu yi* 不義) than entering an orchard to steal another's peaches and plums. Why is this? Because the harm to others is much greater. [...] [This formula is repeated for stealing horses and cows.] As for killing an innocent person, stealing their clothes and taking their weapons, its 'unrightness' is greater than entering a farm and taking a person's horses and cows. Why is this? Because the harm to others is much greater: the greater the harm to others, the greater the inhumanity, the more serious the crime. Thus, the rulers (*junzi*) in the world all know enough to condemn this and call it 'unright.' But at its greatest, attacking another state, they do not know enough to condemn it, but instead praise it and call it 'right.' How can you call this understanding the difference between right and not right? [...]

Now, suppose there were someone who saw a little black and called it 'black,' but when seeing a lot of black called it 'white.' Then we would say that this person did not understand the distinction between black and white. We would say that one who tastes a little bitter and calls it 'bitter' but tastes a lot of bitter and calls it 'sweet' does not understand the distinction between bitter and sweet. Now, to know enough to condemn a smaller wrong, but not to condemn the greater wrong of attacking another state, and on the contrary to praise it and call it right: can this be called knowing the distinction between right and not right? This is how we know that the rulers in the world are confused about the distinction between right and not right.

Excerpt from Book 5, Chapter 19

Have we not observed states that are fond of aggressive expeditions? Suppose they were to raise an army. They would need several thousands of lords and peasants, tens of thousands of foot soldiers, before they could set out. It could take several years; at the quickest several months. Those above would have no spare time to tend to the affairs of government; the officials (*shi* 士) would have no time to order their administration; farmers would have no time to sow and reap; women would have no time to spin and weave. In this way the families of the state would lose their soldiers, and the ordinary people would exchange their duties [for inappropriate tasks]. Moreover, the chariots and horses would become worn out. Of the tents and hangings, army supplies, and shields and weapons, if only one-fifth were retained, this would still be a bounty. Besides, they would also get lost along the road; and the road would be so long that provisions would not last; when the food and drink does not last, the laborers would be starving, cold, frozen, sick, and would writhe dying in the ditches along the roadside. There could be no victory. This is of no benefit to the people, but a great harm to the entire world. Yet, kings, dukes, and great leaders enjoy doing this: they enjoy robbing and plundering the people of the world. How perverse! [...]

Now, those who are fond of aggressive expeditions, pretty up their words saying, "It is not that we find our treasures, servants, and land to be insufficient. It is that we wish to establish a worldly reputation for doing what is right, and attract the feudal lords with our virtuous potency." Mo Zi said, "If you want to establish a worldly reputation for doing what is right and attract the feudal lords with your virtuous potency, then just stand and wait, and the whole world will submit to you. This is because the world has been suffering aggressive attacks for so long (like gentlefolk who have been treated like horses)."[1] Now, if there were one who could be trusted to benefit the feudal lords of the world,

---

1 The analogy is very brief and somewhat odd. It is sometimes translated, "like a child who has been playing horses."

they would be sympathetically concerned about the unjust (*bu yi* 不義) actions of the great states. When large states attacked small states, they would join in defense; if the defensive walls of the small state were not intact, they would make sure they were fixed; if they were lacking textiles and grains, they would supply them; if their resources and provisions were insufficient, they would share their own. If the large states were treated in this way, the rulers of the small states would be pleased.

Others may toil, and yet one can strengthen one's own army while remaining at ease: if one is generous and kind, replacing anxiety with leisure, then the people will surely move [into your jurisdiction to serve you]. Give up aggressive attacks, and govern your own state, and the successes will multiply. If we then measure our military expenditures in competition with the deathly wastage of the feudal lords, we would certainly gain and end up in a position of relative profit. If we oversee with correctness, make ourselves known for doing what is right, we must serve our people with generosity, trust our armies, and extend this practice to the armies of the feudal lords; then in the entire world we will have no enemies, and will be endlessly invincible. This is the benefit to the world, and yet kings, dukes, and great leaders don't know how to put it to use. This is what it is not to know the greatest service of benefit to the world.

Thus, Mo Zi said, "Nowadays, the heart's desire of the kings, dukes, great leaders, officials, and lords is to raise the benefit to the world and eliminate its harms. But if they multiply their aggressive attacks, this is really of the greatest harm to the world. If they desire humanity and rightness and seek to become high officers, if they wish to accord with the *dao* of the sage-kings and desire to benefit the ordinary people of the states, then they cannot but consider carefully this theory of condemning aggressive warfare."

RHETORICAL CRITICISMS OF RUISM

"Against *Ming* (Fatalism)" (Book 9, Chapter 35)

Master Mo said, "In ancient times, kings, dukes, and great leaders in governing the houses of the state desired that they be wealthy, populous, and well ordered. However, they gained not wealth but poverty, not increase in population but decline, not order but disorder, thus fundamentally losing what they desired and obtaining what they despised." Why is this? Mo Zi said, "It is because there are many among the people who put into practice a doctrine of fatalism (*ming* 命).

Comment: The term 'ming' 命 (circumstance) here is clearly being used in the sense of 'fate.' The Mohists here are criticizing a doctrine that there are no circumstances in life that we have any power over. Regardless of what we do, the chips will fall where they will.

"Those who practice fatalism say, 'If wealth is *ming* (fated) then you will be wealthy; if poverty is *ming* then you will be poor [. . .] [This formula is repeated replacing 'wealth' with 'population,' 'order,' and 'long life']. No matter how vigorously you exert yourself, you cannot improve your *ming*.' Above, they persuaded the kings, rulers, and great leaders of this; below they used it to discourage the people from performing their tasks. Thus, those who practiced a doctrine of fatalism were lacking in humanity (*bu ren*). So this doctrine that they upheld must be clearly analyzed."

But how do we go about making a clear analysis? Mo Zi said, "We must establish standards. To teach a doctrine that has no standard is like trying to establish the time of day or night on a revolving potter's wheel. The distinction between right and wrong, benefit and harm, will not be clearly understood. Thus doctrines must have three criteria."

What are the three criteria? Mo Zi said, "The root, the source, and the application. In what is it rooted? It is rooted above in the practices of the ancient sage-kings. Where does its source lie? Its source lies below in the confirmations of the eyes and ears of the people. How is it applied? It is set out in administration, observing the benefit to the ordinary people. These are the three criteria." [. . .]

The fatalists say, "Reward or punishment from a superior is a matter of *ming*, not of worth or misconduct." Thus, at home they show neither parental nor filial love to their families; abroad they show no levels of deference to the townsfolk. Whether at leisure, in their actions, or in relations between the sexes, they show neither measure, moderation, nor appropriate distinctions. Thus, in governing a treasury they would steal from it, in protecting a city they would be treacherous, they would neither die for a ruler nor accompany them into exile. This is what superiors punish and the ordinary people reject. But the fatalists say, "Punishment and reward from a superior is a matter of *ming*, not of personal worth or misconduct!" Therefore, as lords they have no sense of duty, as ministers no sense of commitment, as fathers no parental affection, as children no filiality, and regarding seniority they are neither meritorious nor deferential. The insistence on putting this into practice is where this exceptionally vile doctrine comes from. It is a way of cruelty.

"Against the Ruists" (Book 9, Chapter 39)

They (the Ruists) also insist on *ming*, and explain their doctrine, "Long life and short, poverty and wealth, safety and danger, order and turmoil, are certainly the decree (*ming* 命) of *Tian*; they can be neither diminished nor improved. Impoverishment and success, reward and punishment, good luck and otherwise have their extremes, but human understanding and effort are able to do nothing about them. When the clerical officers believe this they will be negligent in the apportioning of their responsibilities; when the ordinary people believe it, they will be negligent in carrying out affairs. Without order there is turmoil; when agricultural duties are delayed there is insufficiency; insufficiency is the root of disorderly rule. That the Ruists take this as the teaching of the way is to rob the people under the Heavens." [...]

> *Comment:* The Mohists attribute this doctrine to the 'Ruists,' who are usually understood to be the Confucians. The Confucians, however, do not emphasize a doctrine of 'fatalism' of this sort. We do find such a doctrine in Chapter 6 of the Daoist text, the *Lie Zi*, where it appears to be an offshoot of a line of Daoist thought. We see in the following that their criticisms of Ruism do not really apply to the sorts of Confucianism promoted by Confucius, Meng Zi, and Xun Zi. This could, however, also indicate that the term "Ru" had not yet fully come to denote exclusively the doctrines of the followers of Confucius.

The Ruists say, "The *junzi* must follow ancient dress and doctrines in order to be *ren* (仁)." We answer, "What are called ancient doctrines and dress were all once new. When the ancients adopted them, were they not *junzi*? If not, then we must adopt the dress and doctrines of those who were not *junzi* in order to be *ren*!"

They also say, "The *junzi* is compliant and does not innovate."[2] We answer, "In ancient times, Yi invented the bow, Yu invented armor, and Xi Zhong invented the chariot (wheel), and Qiao Chui invented the boat. If so, then are modern tanners, armorers, and carpenters all *junzi*, and Yi, Yu, Xi Zhong, and Qiao Chui all petty people? But what they comply with must have been innovated. So, what they follow is the way of the petty person!"

---

2 See *Analects* 7.1, p. 71.

"Moderation in Expenditures" (Book 6, Chapter 20)

When a sage governs a state, the state can proliferate; when expanded to governing the world, the world itself can proliferate. Their proliferation is not a matter of annexing foreign territory. If one relinquishes the wasteful expenditures of the great families of the state, this is enough for it to proliferate. When sage-kings govern, they issue orders to increase duties and put the resources of the people to use, but without anything that is not of practical use. Thus, in using resources they were not wasteful, and the potency and ability (*de* 德) of the people were not exhausted. Rather, there was great increase in benefit.

Why do we make clothes and furs? In the winter, to protect against the cold; in the summer, to protect against the heat. In the *dao* of manufacturing clothing, it should increase warmth in the winter and coolness in the summer. Luxurious embellishments should not be added, but rejected.

Why do we make palaces and dwellings? In the winter, to protect against the wind and cold; in the summer, to protect against the heat and rain, and to provide fortifications against robbers and thieves. Luxurious embellishments should not be added, but rejected.

Why do we make helmets, shields, and weapons? To protect against bandits, robbers, and thieves. Where there are bandits, robbers, and thieves, if you have helmets, shields, and weapons, you will prevail; if not, you will not prevail. This is why the sages invented helmets, shields, and weapons. In making helmets, weapons, and shields, they should be made light and sharp, sturdy, and hard to break. Luxurious embellishments should not be added, but rejected.

What is the function of boats and carts? Carts are for traveling on land; boats are for traveling through rivers and valleys, to reach the four corners of the world to transport their benefits. In the way of making boats and carts, they should be made light and beneficial. Luxurious embellishments should not be added, but rejected.

In making all these nothing is added that is not functional. Thereby, in using resources there will be no waste, and the potency and ability of the people will not be exhausted. Rather, there will be great increase in benefit.

"Against Musical Delights" (Book 8, Chapter 32)

"*Yue*" or "*le*" 樂 means both 'music' and 'joy.' As the opening paragraph makes clear, the word is being used in its most immediate sense of the delightful sounds of lush music, but is intended to stand for all sensory delights. The Mohists were known for their simple utilitarian values and approach to life. Their ideal of wealth was sufficiency for all people: no one should be in want. In this chapter, they attempt to demonstrate that extravagant state ceremonies for the pleasure of the ruling elite are not only useless in dealing with the needs of the people; such extravagance also imposes heavy burdens on ordinary people that make it impossible for them to attend to life's necessities, and thereby damage the well-being of the people and of the state. The writer tries to convince the reader that Mo Zi has nothing against pleasure as such, but is only critical of its uselessness. But from the social disutility of extravagant state ceremonies, Mo Zi repeatedly seems to want to draw the more sweeping conclusion that all pleasure and merrymaking is wrong.

Such 'merrymaking' will turn out to be a critique of the supposed extravagance of Ruist ceremony. However, it seems clear that such sensory excess was in fact inconsistent with Confucian values. Moreover, even if it were true that Confucian ceremonies were in practice wasteful and extravagant, this by itself would at best only entail that their practice was inconsistent with their ideals; it would not by itself constitute a successful critique of the ideals themselves.

Master Mo said, "The task of humane people must be to serve to seek to inspire benefit to the world and to eliminate the harms in the world. In considering what to model for the world they will practice it if it benefits people, and will stop when it does not. The measure of the humane person in acting on behalf of the world is not what the eyes find beautiful, or what the ears delight in, what the mouth savors, or what the body finds easeful. When these deprive the people of their resources, their food and clothing, a person with humanity will not practice them." Thus, in criticizing delights (*yue* 樂), it is not that Mo Zi does not consider the sounds of bells and drums, zithers and flutes to be delightful (*le* 樂), or the sights of carvings and ornaments to be beautiful, or the flavors of succulent meats to be delicious, or resting in lofty apartments, sumptuous pavilions, and secluded retreats to be easeful. Although the body knows what it finds comfortable, the mouth what is sweet, the eyes what is beautiful, and the ears what is delightful, still when we examine them against the ancient texts we find that they do not match up to the deeds of the sage-kings, and when we test them out in the world below we find that they do not benefit the people. This is why Master Mo says that acting for delights is wrong.[3]

> Comment: Two of the three epistemological criteria are appealed to here: the authority of the ancient sages, and advance consideration of the consequences that would evidently follow if the policies were to be put into practice.

Suppose now that the kings, dukes, and great leaders have not constructed musical instruments; if they were to do so in the service of the state, they couldn't just extract them from the water or dig them out of the dirt. Rather, they would have to impose heavy taxes on the masses of people just to create the sounds of bells and drums, zithers and flutes. The ancient sage-kings did indeed impose heavy taxes on the masses of people to make boats and carts. When they were completed the people asked, "How may we use them?" They replied, "Boats are used on the water and carts on the land so that the rulers (*junzi*) may rest their feet in them and the common people (*xiao ren* 小人) may rest their arms and shoulders." So the masses of people offered up their wealth in taxes and found no cause to grumble. Why is this? Because the benefit would be returned to the ordinary people (*min* 民). So, if the benefit of musical instruments could be returned to the ordinary people in the same way, even I would not dare to criticize.

The people have three worries: that when hungry they will not obtain food, when cold they will not obtain clothing, and when exhausted they will have no rest. These are the three great worries of the people. All right then, let's sound the great bells for them! Beat the drums! Pluck the zithers! Blow the flutes! Raise the sticks and batons! Will this enable them to obtain resources for food and clothing? I really don't think so!

But never mind that. Suppose a great state is attacking a small state, the great clans are uprooting the small clans, the strong are taking advantage of the weak, the majority is oppressing the minorities, the clever are deceiving the naive, the high-born are treating the lowly with arrogance, robbers and thieves are arising everywhere and cannot be stopped. All right, now let's bang the big bells, hit the drums, pluck the

---

3   To compare Confucius' perspective on leisure and enjoyment see *Analects* 7.6 and 16.5, p. 79.

zithers, blow the flutes, and raise the sticks and batons! Will the world's turmoil be restored to order? I really don't think so.

So, Mo Zi says, "If you impose heavy taxes on the masses of people to make great bells, drums, zithers, and flutes, it will be of no use in increasing the benefit to the world and eliminating harm." This is why Master Mo says that acting for delights is wrong. [...]

Now, humans are surely different from birds, beasts, and bugs. The latter adapt their feathers and furs as clothing, their hooves and claws as shoes, and the rains and grasses as their food. Thus, the males of the species are freed from the need to plow and till, the females have no need to weave and sew. They already possess the resources of food and clothing. But humans are different from this. They must rely on their efforts in order to survive. If they don't then they won't survive. If the rulers (*junzi*) do not diligently attend to government, then governing will fall into disorder; if the humble people do not diligently carry out their tasks, then resources will be insufficient....

Thus, Master Mo said, "Now, the rulers of the world desire to increase benefit to the world and eliminate harms; they have no choice but to put an end to the making of objects of delight." [...]

Comment: Mo Zi goes on to apply the same critique to state funerals. They are wasteful, and not only do not bring benefit, but in taxing the people to excess, prevent the state from growing resources and population, and lead to social turmoil. They thus prevent achieving the three goals for any ruler of a state (i.e., population, resources, and order).

PART III

Dao Jia: The School of Dao (Daoism)

9

Lao Zi

The *Lao Zi*, also popularly known as the *Dao De Jing*, is one of the most well-known texts of Chinese philosophy. It is a brief anthology of philosophical verse arising from a distinctive perspective. It expresses an understanding of humanity, action, and governing, that has its roots in a nature-oriented cosmology.[1] It thus recommends a dual-aspect way: simultaneously cosmological and political. Hans-Georg Moeller calls this a 'metapolitics' in contrast with the Greek tendency toward metaphysics. The cosmology has 'mystical' or 'spiritual' tendencies, expresses a profound reverence for the mysteries of existence, and is rooted in a phenomenological awareness of the productive potency of the Cosmos. From this cosmology, it develops two diametrically opposed political philosophies: a small-scale Utopianism, quasi-anarchist in spirit, and a large-scale Imperialism grounded in a quasi-libertarian philosophy of non-interference. Both appear to grow from the same cosmological insights regarding the non-deliberate functioning of natural phenomena.

There are two important traditional recensions: one edited by the scholar Wang Bi, the other traditionally attributed to a monk, under the name 'He Shang Gong.' Recent excavations have also unearthed two early versions of the text: the Ma Wang Dui silk manuscripts, and the Guo Dian bamboo strips.

The text appears to be the repository of an ancient oral tradition of meditation, reflection, and practice with the goals of cultivating life processes, worldly flourishing, and wisdom. Its philosophical style is poetic and holistic. Concepts are not analyzed through distinctions and definitions;

---

1   For the purpose of comparative philosophy, a 'metaphysics' is a theory of the ultimate nature of reality that presupposes a distinction between an ultimate, or transcendent, reality and the empirical world as we experience it; a 'cosmology' is an account of the basic nature of the world that does not presuppose such a distinction. A metaphysics is therefore 'dualistic,' while a cosmology is 'holistic.'

instead, our understanding of phenomena is deepened by juxtaposing images, metaphors, and concepts, and exploiting their mutual resonances.[2] Such poetic philosophizing tends to be vague, open, and suggestive, and rich with significances that need to be uncovered by the reader. But much of the meaning that might have been more accessible within its own earlier context remains tacit and unexplained.

Since it attempts to describe the most fundamental aspects of the Cosmos, ordinary language, which developed for practical empirical purposes, inevitably falls short. Attempts to talk about what lies at the limits of the natural world end up in paradoxes (or 'antinomies' as the eighteenth-century German idealist Kant called them, in another context). The text is thus dispersed throughout with paradoxical language: they sometimes blur the boundaries between apparent opposites, or attempt to show how one side of an apparent dichotomy results from its partner. As Chapter 78 says, "Upright words seem to go back on themselves."

The text is divided into numbered 'chapters,' which are not necessarily single thematic units, but are often themselves holistic juxtapositions of shorter stanzas. Accordingly, D.C. Lau divides the traditional chapters into smaller numbered subsections. Within each chapter, there is no closer connection between these thematic subsections than there is in the text overall. For example, Chapter 5 has a verse on ethics, one on metaphysics, and one on discipline. Why this is the case is not clear. One possibility is that such groups are structured as 'holographic' fragments that mimic the holistic structure of the text as a whole; or it may be mere historical accident that they are grouped as they are.

Concepts and themes recur and interweave between passages throughout the collection, though not always necessarily in a mutually consistent way. It is possible that they form a single complex philosophy requiring oral elaboration to explain the subtleties and resolve the apparent inconsistencies. But it is also possible, and perhaps more likely, that these variations represent different philosophical possibilities or strands of thought. For the purpose of interpreting philosophical content, one need not assume a necessary unity of any particular traditional grouping.

Indeed, the holistic fragmented structure of the text is something of an obstacle for the novice reader. In order to alleviate some of this difficulty, I have arranged this translation thematically, adopting the subdivisions suggested by D.C. Lau, for the most part. I have translated repeated passages only once, in the relevant thematic section. The reader

---

2 Moeller (2006) discusses the 'hyperlinked' connections scattered throughout the text, and Wagner emphasizes the conceptual content that is conveyed through interlocking parallel grammatical structures.

who has been introduced to the ideas of the text in this way will then be prepared to engage in a much richer way with the text in its traditional arrangement.

I have adopted the following overall thematic order: I begin with the passages that discuss the ontology and cosmology of the *Lao Zi*: its account of the origination of things and the nature of the Cosmos. Then come passages that describe the meditative practices that bring our understanding and lives into harmony with these natural productive forces. In the next two sections, the *dao* of the Cosmos is compared with the *dao* of humans. In the last section, these ideas are used to derive two contrasting political theories of Daoist rulership: one anarchist, the other imperialist in spirit.

Classical Chinese also expresses meaning through structured patterns, where the reader is invited to make contrasts and comparisons. Sometimes, commentaries are appended to passages; or related ideas may be interpolated. None of these levels of meaning are explicitly marked, but are intuitively evident only to someone familiar with the feel and style of the original text in the original language. Because these are integral to the linguistic formulation of the philosophical ideas, I have represented them structurally through the use of parentheses, indentations, spacing, and other techniques. And since their significance is not explicit in the original text, I invite readers to formulate their own interpretations.

Note: Chapter numbers are written at the top of each selection; the numerals on the left refer to Lau's subdivisions, which I refer to as 'paragraphs.'

ONTOLOGY AND COSMOLOGY

The first chapter of the *Lao Zi* is probably one of the most famous passages of all of Chinese philosophy, and for good reason. It is a beautifully constructed verse that employs many of the major concepts and metaphors of the cosmology and phenomenology of the *Lao Zi*. As such it serves as a miniature representation of the text as a whole. Its central concern is the process of origination of all the varieties of things, and in reflecting on this it begins to shape a converse notion of an originating power, prior to things, and prior to language.

Ostensibly, its reflections are 'ontological,' that is, they are concerned with the production of existing things. But its meditative mood and reference to 'language' and 'desires' also suggest 'phenomenological' reflections: how a 'variety' of 'things' emerges in our awareness. Naming is implicated in the differentiation of phenomena, while the undifferentiated and mysterious unknown that precedes them remains nameless. Acquisitive desires then objectify phenomena into desirable and undesirable things and thereby obscure our ability to sense the deep and wondrous mystery.

Ontology

Chapter 1

1

Dao can guide,
   but not as any ordinary (*chang* 常) *dao*,
Names (*ming* 名) can name,
   but not as ordinary names.

2

Nameless:
   the beginning (*shi* 始) of the world,
Naming:
   the mother (*mu* 母) of the varieties of things.

3

Constantly (*chang*) undoing (*wu*) desires (*yu* 欲),
   one observes the wondrous subtlety (*miao* 妙),
Constantly having desires,
   one observes [only] the outer borders.

   These two emerge simultaneously, but differ in name.
   Together, they form a mysterious depth (*xuan* 玄):
   Deeper and yet deeper still:
   The gateway (*men* 門) for the many wondrous subtleties.

Comment: Here, the parallel structure reveals complementary pairs: on the one hand, the deep, mysterious source (*shi* 始) that is prior to linguistic categories and evaluations; on the other, the superficial, linguistic differentiation (*ming* 名) that gives birth to the variety of worldly phenomena, as objects of desire and acquisition.

   It is easy to presuppose a dualism or dichotomy between two realms: one worldly and one transcendent. And this is certainly one way in which the text has been read. But, a more holistic reading of the text suggests a subtler interpretation of this pairing: it hints, not at two distinct realms, but at contrasting sides of a single process of emergence of the myriad phenomena.

The depth, *xuan* 玄, is profound, dark, mysterious, inky black, like the clear night sky—a source from which all the teeming varieties of natural phenomena emerge. It is thought of as giving birth to them, like a maternal creature: this sense of the endless fertile productivity of the natural world is expressed metaphorically several times in the *Lao Zi* as a maternal creature. In Chapter 6, it appears as a '*pin*,' which could also have a more specific sense of a maternal bird. In Chapter 10 (in the section "Phenomenology, Meditation, and Spiritual Cultivation," p. 294, below), the term '*ci*' (雌) is used, which is also ambiguous between a female animal in general and a maternal bird. If this sense is intended, it is noteworthy that a bird gives birth by laying eggs. If so, the text indirectly invokes the indeterminate and primordial fertility of an egg.

Chapter 6

17

The valley spirits are undying
    this is the deep and mysteriously (*xuan* 玄) maternal (*pin* 牝).

The gateway of the deep and mysterious mother
    is the root (*gen* 根) of the Cosmos,

A gossamer stretched so fine, it barely exists
    and yet functions without exhaustion.

Comment: In the *Lao Zi*, the prevailing metaphors through which the 'origination' of things is understood are biological. Emerging into existence is understood as a form of birth, and the productivity of nature is understood through the metaphor of a 'genetrix,' a maternal creature, *pin*. But no sooner is this animal metaphor raised than it is equated with the botanical metaphor of a root (*gen* 根), perhaps the finest network of extensive fibers that extend deep throughout the earth, and that have inexhaustible productivity.

Chapter 4

11

The way gushes forth from emptiness (*chong* 沖) and in use is ever
                              unfinished
Like an abyss, it seems to be the Ancestor (*zong* 宗) of all things. [...]

13

So deep: it seems barely to be present,
We do not know whose progeny:
  it seems prior to the divine Emperor (*Di* 帝).

Comment: This mother, as the source of all things stretching to the distant past, is thereby the deepest, most ancestral (*zong* 宗) source of all things. The term "*chong*" (沖) evokes a gushing and surging, but also has a sense of 'emptiness.' Two other words are used to evoke depth in this chapter: first "*yuan*" 淵, 'a dark abyss,' and then "*zhan*" 湛, 'a crystal pool.'

(Paragraph 12 is in the section, "*Tian Dao*: The Way of the Cosmos," p. 301, below.)

Chapter 14

32

Looked at, it does not appear,
—it is called 'elusive'
Listened for, it is unheard,
—it is called 'rarefied'
Grasped, but unattained,
—it is called 'subtle.'

These three are indiscernible
And so blur into a continuity (*yi* 一).

33

Above, it is *not* bright,
Below, it is *not* dark, ...
Endlessly *un*nameable,
it returns again to *no*-thing.

This is called the formless form,
the appearance of no-thing:
This is called 'vague' and 'obscure.'

Greeting it you will not see its beginning.
Following it you will not see its end.

34

    Manage the ancient way
        to control what exists today.
    The ability to understand the ancient beginning
        is called the thread of *dao*.

Comment: The most primordial source of all worldly phenomena could not itself be a worldly phenomenon: it would not itself have visible, auditory, or tactile qualities. And as it could not be one of the many things, it would not be discernible as having any determinate shape or form. The attempt to perceive or describe it would only result in endless negation: not bright, not dark, not red, not blue, not large, not small. As such it eludes the crude terminology of empirical contrasts: no such terms could meaningfully apply. Notice the paradox of even attempting to say this: to talk about it at all seems to require reifying 'it' as some kind of linguistic 'object.' But ultimately what we are attempting to understand has no determinate form and is, after all, no thing.

For this reason, I translate "*yi*" — as 'a continuity.' 'One' would imply delineation in a way that is explicitly rejected here. 'Continuity,' on the other hand, expresses an idea of wholeness that is not defined through boundaries.

The last line (par. 34) is not only 'mystical,' but is also relevant to practical endeavors: managing and controlling are forms of governing. A non-linguistic understanding of the originative potency of natural processes is of direct relevance to successful action in the present. This sort of idea undergirds the political applications of the spiritual practices that we shall see in the last section below ("*Wu Wei*: Politics, Utopianism, and Empire").

Chapter 21

48

    The capacity of the potency of emptiness
        follows only the way.

49

    The way as a 'thing':
        is obscure and vague.

Vague and obscure!
    Within, there are phenomena.
Obscure and vague!
    Within, there are things.
Secluded and dark!
    Within, there is something seminal.
The seminal is utterly genuine;
    within, there is reliability.

Comment: Even when we attempt to reify it, to treat it as a thing, 'the Way' will inevitably remain indeterminate. We vaguely sense a presence, though we cannot articulate it without misrepresenting it. It remains uncontainable, and thereby appears vague and indeterminate. But this ineliminable vagueness does not diminish either its genuineness or its potency.

Chapter 25

56

Some thing
forms in confusion,
produced before the world
Still!
Empty!
Singularly upright
and unswerving
Revolving
Without slacking.

It could be the mother of the world.

We do not know how to name it,
but label it *"the way."*
Forced to name it,
we call it 'vast and expansive' (*da* 大).

'Vast and expansive' means it passes away.

'Passing away' means it recedes into the distance.
'Receding' means it
returns (*fan* 反).

57

Thus, *dao* is vast (*da* 大),
The Cosmos is vast,
The earth is vast,
Kingship is also vast.
Within the realm there are four vastnesses,
    and kingship resides among them.

58

Humans are guided (*fa* 法) by the earth,
The earth is guided by the heavens,
The heavens are guided by *dao*,
dao is guided by itself (*ziran* 自然).

Comment: If I might paraphrase Chapter 21, p. 283, above, deep within the words of par. 56 one can discern an image. I have taken the liberty of hinting at this image through the visual form of the passage. The metaphor implied is that of a vortex, the still center of revolutions of 'ontogenesis' (the production of things). It spreads outward, extends everywhere, vast expansive, never swerving from its central balance, or in its constancy (see *chang* in Chapter 2, "Key Philosophical Terms"). Cosmic *dao* revolves by itself and for this there is no further explanation. Compare Chapter 40 (at the end of this section, p. 290, below) for a discussion of "*fan*" 反 'returning.'

The metaphor is of fundamental philosophical significance. It emphasizes the priority of a center, not that of a foundation. Foundationalism brings with it presuppositions of building blocks and orders or layers of construction: priorities and hierarchies are fixed in this way of thinking. The metaphor of the center is associated instead with coherentist philosophies that emphasize the interdependence of things in their mutual origination.

Paragraph 58 states explicitly that for humans to flourish we must follow the patterns of the natural processes of the earth and the Cosmos. We must treat them as a model (*fa* 法) and allow ourselves to be guided by them. We will see the connections between the human, the political, and the Cosmic developed in the section, "*Ren Dao*: The Way of Humans," below.

Cosmology

Chapter 39

85

Those that, from ancient times, achieved integration (*yi* 一):
  The heavens achieving integration, thereby became clear.
  The earth achieving integration, thereby became solidified.
  Spirits achieving integration, thereby became perspicacious.
  Valleys achieving integration, thereby became full.
  All things achieving integration, thereby came to life.

  Lords and kings achieving integration,
    thereby became pillars of integrity for the people of the world.

At the extremes:
Without the means to become clear,
    the heavens I fear would split apart.
Without the means to solidify,
    the earth I fear would crumble away.
Without the means to become numinous,
    the spirits I fear would expire.
Without the means to become full,
    the valley I fear would be exhausted.
Without the means to live,
    the many things I fear would be destroyed.

Lacking the means of being honored,
    the feudal lords and kings I fear would fall.

Comment: "*Yi*" (一) 'one,' here refers to integration, the process of coming together, holding together; the natural processes of ontogenesis of 'things.' Full maturity of integration is observed as thinghood; its counterpart is disintegration. The mutual distinguishing of opposites is a form of integration: as one thing comes together in a particular way, it becomes distinguished from what it is not. Processes of integration are productive processes, and take different forms for different kinds of things: clearing, solidification, becoming aware. Longevity results from processes that sustain integration.

A word of caution: it might seem that "*yi*" must be equivalent to the Western metaphysical concept of 'the One,' but there is no unambiguous textual articulation of this concept. Therefore, in the absence of a clear contextual or historical justification for this reading, it is wiser to avoid simply presupposing and imposing this philosophical interpretation. Indeed, by avoiding the presupposition, we are able to discover a distinctively Chinese alternative cosmology.

At the end of each stanza an application of the natural principle is made to the rulers of the various states, perhaps even an empire.

Chapter 42

93

The way produces one (*yi* 一),
one produces two (*er* 二),
two produces three (*san* 三),
three produces the varieties of phenomena.

94

All things shoulder *yin* and embrace *yang*,
Flooding the energies to make them harmonious.

Comment: Here we have a cosmology describing the production of multiplicity from an undifferentiated whole. Again, we should caution against imposing easy misinterpretations. We should refrain from simply assuming that the numerals, 'one,' 'two,' and 'three' name numbers as abstract entities, as in the Pythagorean and Platonic metaphysical traditions. A richer interpretation may draw from other significances: 'one' may connote unity, integration, wholeness, continuity, undifferentiation. 'Two' may connote a splitting path, or division and distinction into complementary and contrasting pairs; it is glossed by later interpreters as referring to *yin* and *yang*, which are mentioned in the next verse. 'Three' is sometimes interpreted as referring to the triad *tian, di, ren*: the heavens, the earth, and the human. In any case, we have an overall development of multiplicity out of wholeness, which itself emerges from a primordially undifferentiated *dao*.

(Paragraphs 95 and 96, which have a political focus, are translated on p. 324, below.)

Chapter 51

114

The way (*dao*) produces them;
Potency (*de*) nurtures them.

Things form them;
    Propensities (*shi* 勢) complete them.
Thus, all things venerate the way and value (*gui* 貴) potency.

That the way is venerated and potency valued
    is not commanded by Circumstance,
    but is always spontaneous (*ziran* 自然).

115

Thus, the way produces them,
    potency nurtures them,
    grows them and rears them,
    completes them and brings them to maturity:
        raises them, and overturns (*fu* 覆) them.

116

Producing without possessing (*buyou* 不有),
Acting without dependence,
Rearing without leading,
This is the potency of *xuan* (mysterious depth).

Comment: While the *Lao Zi* is critical of the cultivation of artificial Confucian virtues, it does not reject evaluation altogether. We see here that it is precisely the productive and nurturing way and potency of the Cosmos that are valued (*gui* 貴) and honored. These values arise naturally (*ziran* 自然), and are not artificially constructed in a human, social system. While the artificial values of the Ruists are rejected elsewhere, we are told here that it is *dao* and *de* that emerge as natural values.

    These are the stages in the emergence, development, and maturation of worldly phenomena. Although there is no specific, determinate 'thing' that is actively responsible, the text uses the terms "*dao*" and "*de*" as though reifying them. In this way, the language of the text inevitably becomes paradoxical.

    "Propensity" (*shi*) is a complex term, drawn from military strategy; it refers to the changing array of potentials in a developing terrain. In par. 116, the potency that nurtures the variety of things does not assert its own presence, but remains hidden in the mysterious depths (*xuan*). The implication is that if we want to flourish naturally, then we must also rear without leading, nurture by remaining hidden in the depths. The term '*fu*' in par. 115 can mean to overturn and overthrow, but it can also mean to cover and protect. Translators and commentators usually take it in the latter sense. But the word itself, 'overturn,' cries out to overturn its own meaning. It also contains the radical "*fu*" (復) as a component, which means 'to return,' often used in the *Lao Zi* in the sense of cycling and returning to the source (similar in meaning to '*fan*' 反).

Moreover, though the natural world produces everything, it possesses nothing: there is no applicability for the artificial concept of "property." We find a similar statement in Chapter 2, immediately below.

Chapter 2

7

The myriad things thereby arise and are not abandoned:
Producing without possessing,
Acting on behalf of them, but without dependence;
When achievements are brought to completion they do not dwell in
them.
It is only because they do not dwell in them
That they do not cast them aside.

Chapter 11

27

Thirty spokes combine in one hub: in the absence (*wu* 無) lies the
function (*yong* 用) of the wheel.
Mold clay to make a utensil: in the absence lies the function of the
utensil.
Chisel doors and windows to make a room: in the absence lies the
function of the room.

Thus, the gain (*li* 利) lies in what is there (*you* 有); the function in
what is not there (*wu*).

Comment: Wu (無) "absence" has both cosmological and pragmatic significance. The capacity of a tool to function requires space for movement. We tend to pay attention to what is present, to the stuff that fills space, to value it as a possession. But functioning requires movement, and movement requires free space: without empty space our possessions are of no use. In a way, this is the mirror image of Parmenides' metaphysical argument that Being must be full (altogether without absence) and therefore can manifest no movement at all.

Chapter 40

88

> The way moves by Returning (*fan* 反).
> The way functions through Weakness.

89

> The many things in the world are produced from presence (*you*).
> Presence is produced from absence (*wu*).

Comment: This way of understanding absence as that from which presence emerges contrasts dramatically with Parmenides' concept of non-Being, which not only cannot produce Being, but is itself logically impossible. In further contrast with Parmenides' Being, the way is not still, but moves. And it does so, not by moving forward, but by constantly returning. Strength and progress are *yang* phenomena: bright, rising, and energetic, constantly moving forward. But the continuous progress of natural phenomena is predicated on continuous return: things return to nothing, presence returns to absence, which is thereby able to remain a productive source of things.

The philosophical commentator, Wang Bi (226–49 CE), finds this absence to be an ultimate source; but par. 5 of Chapter 2 (in "*Tian Dao:* The Way of the Cosmos," p. 300, below) says that presence and absence produce each other. Are these two passages mutually complementary or at odds? If complementary, one may solve the paradox by taking Chapter 40 to emphasize the *central* status of *wu*, while Chapter 2 emphasizes the mutuality of *you* and *wu*. The centrality of *wu* is not inconsistent with the mutuality of the pair. Center and periphery may be logically mutually complementary and determining, but in natural terms, the center of an originating force (gravity or magnetism, for example) plays a more significant functional role.

Like absence, weakness is ordinarily disvalued. But, again, without yielding there is no possibility of movement. This is applied as a general model to be imitated in all realms of human engagement, but has its most direct application as a model for governing. Positions of power are conventionally conceived of as means of control that require strength. The Daoist inversion of this ideal is that of a position of nurturing that relinquishes control and requires softness, weakness, and yielding in order to guide creatures to fulfill their natural potential.

The image of returning (*fan* 反) as the movement of the way is central to understanding the philosophy of the *Lao Zi*. It appears in several places in different forms: as doubling back (*fu* 复), or as returning home (*gui* 歸). Thus, it involves repeated cycles of return, turning back over a distance covered, but with the lower phase of the cycle functioning as a central locus of departure and return.

PHENOMENOLOGY, MEDITATION, AND SPIRITUAL CULTIVATION

Western philosophers typically use logical reasoning in their attempts to understand how things come into existence. But Daoist philosophy is not simply confined to ontological speculation and political theorizing. An integral part of Daoist practice is phenomenological observation: careful inward concentration, reflection, and 'description.' This sort of reflective awareness of our own arising (the coming into presence of our awareness at each moment), and of how we understand the arising of 'things' in our awareness, provides a source of evidence which it would not be reasonable to simply dismiss out of hand. Such reflection seems to reveal our living conscious presence as a central productive source. Rephrasing phenomenologically: reflecting deeply on our awareness of our presence in the world reveals an awareness of 'being-central,' 'being-productive,' and 'being-originary.'

Chapter 52

117

The world had a beginning,
    which we take to be 'mother' of the world:
Understand the mother
    to understand her offspring;
Understanding her offspring,
    return to sustain (*shou* 守) the mother.
And the course of one's life will be unhampered.

118

Block the openings,
Close the doors:
And to the end of your life there will be no toil.

But open the holes,
And assist with worldly affairs (*shi* 事):
    Then to the end of your life you will be beyond help.

119

Seeing the minute is called 'clarity' (*ming* 明),
Holding fast (*shou* 守) to weakness is called 'strength':
Using the light, return once again to the clarity,
there will be no loss or bodily danger.
This is called constancy of practice.

Comment: The *Lao Zi* advocates meditative practices that are understood
as nurturing, sustaining (*shou*), or cultivating this productive center, and
thereby thought to promote health and longevity. In the *Zhuang Zi*, we
find words that suggest a similar practice: "*bao*" 保, "*quan*" 全, and "*yang*"
養, 'protecting,' 'maintaining whole,' and 'nurturing' (respectively).

'Blocking the openings' is a metaphor for maintaining one's wholeness against encroachments from the outside. In this verse, cultivation of
these inner life conditions is incompatible with involvement with worldly
affairs. Keep clear of interference with worldly service; attend only to
preserving and nourishing one's life. This philosophy of renouncing
political service for life cultivation resurfaces in the Utopian critiques
of Ruism in the *Zhuang Zi* text, especially in the passages that A.C. Graham attributes to Yang Zhu.

Chapter 50

113

In emerging into life and returning to death:
one third are the attendants of life,
one third are the attendants of death,
one third are human life moving towards the place of death.

Why is this? Because of the over-abundance of life producing life.

I have heard of those who excel at conserving life:
when walking abroad, they do not encounter tigers and rhinos,
entering a battle, they are not subjected to weapons;
rhinos have no place to thrust their horns,
tigers have no place to set in their claws,
weapons have no place to find room for their blades.

Why is this? Because there is no place of death.

Comment: While death is the inevitable end of life, there are places in
life where death is possible but avoidable. In part, weaknesses arise when

one 'assists with affairs' (see Chapter 52, immediately above), that is, gets involved in worldly politics. Preserving life, keeping it full, is a matter of filling in those weaknesses. If one is able to do this successfully, one may encounter dangers with minimal risks, and live out one's fullest lifespan.

The 'over-abundance of life producing life' may possibly be referring to the greediness for a luxuriant life of the elite classes.

Chapter 76

182

In life, humans are soft and weak,
In death, hard and strong.

In life, the varieties of flora and fauna are soft and fragile,
In death they are withered and dry.

Thus, hardness and strength are the attendants of death;
Softness and weakness are the attendants of life.

183

For this reason, when an army is strong there is no victory;
When a tree is strong, it will be axed.

Thus, the hard and big reside below;
Softness and weakness reside above.

Comment: In par. 183, it is the roots and trunk that are 'hard and big,' the sprouts and leaves that are 'soft and weak.'

Chapter 10

24

In managing your spirits and keeping them integrated (*yi* 一),
    can you keep them from scattering?
In concentrating your *qi* to the utmost softness,
    can you be like an infant?
In cleansing the profound (*xuan* 玄) mirror,
    can you remain unblemished?

In caring for the people and governing the state,
    can you refrain from active control?

In opening and closing the gateway of nature,
  can you be the maternal creature (*ci* 雌)?
With clear insight extending in all directions,
  can you refrain from cleverness?

Comment: In this verse, in contrast with the one just above (Chapter 76, par. 183), the practice of life cultivation is associated, not with refraining from politics altogether, but with governing a state by minimal interference. This political application of spiritual practice anticipates the Mystical Imperialism passages of the *Zhuang Zi*. (See "*Ren Dao:* The Way of Humans," below, and Chapter 11 of this book.)

Spirits (*po* 魄) are understood in the plural; they may be held together, as when we are awake and attentive; or they may be scattered, as manifested in our fragmented dream experiences. A concentrated attention exemplifies the ideal of integration.

Chapter 16

37

Extend attenuation (*xu* 虛) to its limit;
Sustain stillness (*jing* 靜) to the utmost.

> All things arouse one another,
>   and so we observe their return.
> Things teeming and swarming,
>   each returns again to its root.

Returning to the root is called 'stillness':
this is called 'returning' (*fu* 復) to 'Circumstance' (*ming* 命).
Returning to Circumstance is called 'constant regularity' (*chang* 常).
Understanding constant regularity is called 'insight' (*ming* 明).
Not understanding the constant regularities gives reckless rise to
                                                    danger.

38

To understand constant regularity is to be capacious;
To be capacious is to be impartial;
To be impartial is to be kingly;
To be kingly is to be Cosmic (*tian* 天);
To be *tian* is to follow the way;
To follow the way is to endure.
To the end of one's life one will be unendangered.

Comment: Daoist meditation involves a practice of phenomenological 'attenuation' (*xu* 虛): a meditative process of emptying out the heart–mind of distractions, creating conditions that minimize external perceptions, and emotional disturbances. One thereby attains and sustains a tranquility (*jing* 靜) of spirit that allows the most subtle processes that lie hidden at the core to become manifest to one's awareness. As we shall see, both emptiness and stillness are appealed to elsewhere in the *Lao Zi* as conditions of enlightened rule, and are adopted by the mystically oriented Imperialists (or Syncretists) in the *Zhuang Zi*. "Tian" (天) here is used as a 'stative' (or adjectival) verb. It appeals to the Cosmic insofar as it is vast, expansive, and all-encompassing. Here, spiritual practice in tune with the Cosmic is presented as a condition of virtuous rulership, insofar as it cultivates all-encompassing concern for the realm.[a]

Chapter 47

106

> Without leaving one's door,
>   understand the whole world;
> Without glancing out the window,
>   the way of the Cosmos will manifest (*jian* 見).
> The further one goes
> The less one knows.

107

> Thus, the wise understand without traveling,
> Are clear though it may not appear,
> Succeed without controlling.

Comment: Insofar as these meditative phenomenological practices reveal our own innermost conditions of productive presence, they also reveal the innermost conditions of the productivity of the Cosmos itself. One can understand the deepest aspects of the furthest reaches of the Cosmos simply by observing them within oneself.

TIAN DAO: THE WAY OF THE COSMOS

We have seen in Chapter 51, p. 288, above, that the way and potency of the natural world are naturally valued. The *Lao Zi* constantly seeks to draw parallels and apply lessons drawn from the natural workings of the Cosmos, to enable us to live well and flourish harmoniously within it. But the attempt to describe what is ultimate and all-encompassing, the attempt to pursue the Cosmic to its limits, either leads to paradoxes or requires us to turn back. The way of the Cosmos is therefore a way of reversal, as we read in Chapter 40 (p. 290, above; and in Chapter 78, in "*Wu Wei*: Politics, Utopianism, and Empire," p. 325, below, we read: "upright words seem to turn back on themselves").

In a different context, the German philosopher, Immanuel Kant, referred to paradoxes derived in this way as 'antinomies.' The *Lao Zi* simply asserts the paradoxes without attempting to make the reasons explicit. The Daoist attitude to such contradictions is that since they are inevitable, they are not to be avoided, but on the contrary we must reflect on them in order to appreciate the paradoxical nature of the *dao*. But neither the reflection nor the appreciation of the paradoxes need involve explicit reconstruction of the logical reasons.

Speaking poetically, we might say that the Cosmos succeeds at everything, yet it does not have to try. It doesn't speak; it doesn't command; it doesn't worry; it doesn't plan; it doesn't control. And yet it contains everything, loses nothing, and everything comes to completion. The practical consequence for those who cultivate the way of *tian* is that they must attempt to embody these paradoxical qualities in their behavior: enable things to flourish without taking control, planning, or commanding; they must lead without being a leader.

Chapter 73

179

The way of the Cosmos:
    excels in victory, but without contending,
    excels in responding, but without speaking,
    excels in attracting, without beckoning,
    excels in planning, without extensive deliberation.

179a

The net of the Cosmos is the merest gossamer, stretching vast and yet
leaking nothing.

Chapter 7

18

The heavens are lasting, and the earth is enduring.
The reason why heaven and earth are able to last and endure

Is that they do not produce themselves.
(This is why they are able to last and endure.)

19

Thus, the wise:
    make themselves followers,
        and yet find themselves ahead;
    Exclude themselves,
        and yet find themselves sustained.

19a

Isn't this because they are without self-interest (*wu si* 無私)?
This is why they are able to fulfill their own interests.

Comments: That is, the sky and the earth should not be thought of as separately self-creating and self-sustaining; rather each is formed through its contrast and differentiation from the other. Another way of interpreting this is to say that the Cosmos does not simply bring itself into existence, but is manifested in the very process of producing and nurturing the many things.

Confucius is also critical of self-interest as a motive for action, especially when it distracts one from doing what is right (*yi*). While Confucius affirms rightness as the justified motive for action, the *Lao Zi* promotes minimizing self-concern (*wu si*) as a fundamental condition of wisdom.

Superficially, the rhetoric of 19a is not quite consistent with the ideal of altruism. Excluding self-interest seems to be justified in terms of achieving self-interest. This is usually the kind of argument given by an individualist, not by a critic of individualism. On a deeper level, however, the same rhetoric may be interpreted as stating that one is fulfilled *by* cultivating others, even though one does not do so for this purpose.

Another way of putting this is to say that one leads by following. This is not just an underhand way to gain the upper hand, whereby one follows, but only in order to really take the lead. Rather, it is a paradoxical insistence that the only genuine leadership must itself be a kind of following. This may be interpreted either as a form of democratic rule, or as a form of nurturing guidance.

Chapter 41

90

> When the highest aspirants (*shi* 士) hear of the way,
>> they work hard to put it into practice.
> When mediocre aspirants hear of the way,
>> they maintain some of it, and they lose some;
> When the lowest aspirants hear of the way,
>> they laugh at it:
> If they didn't laugh, it wouldn't be good enough to be the way.

91

> Thus, there are the established sayings:
>> "The bright way seems dark"
>> "The way forward seems to retreat"
>> "The smooth way seems knotty"
>> "Lofty potency is like a valley"
>> "The greatest purity seems sullied"
>> "Widespread potency seems insufficient"
>> "Cultivated potency seems pilfered"
>> "Genuine (*zhen* 真) stuff (*zhi* 質) seems uncontained"
>
>> "The greatest (*da* 大) square has no corners"
>> "The greatest instrument is late to be completed"
>> "The greatest sound can scarcely be heard"
>> "The greatest image has no form."

92

> The way is hidden and has no name.
> Only the way excels at bestowing and fulfilling.

Comment: The aspirants (*shi* 士) were a social class of people aspiring to become soldiers or officials, or to cultivate Confucian nobility. In paragraph 90, above, this significance is overturned: the highest *shi* is not the social 'climber,' but the Daoist aspirant who seeks to reverse course and cultivate the paradoxical qualities of the natural world.

From an everyday point of view, pursuing a way of life from a Cosmic perspective seems utterly ridiculous. Alternatively put, what we overlook and devalue from an everyday perspective, either because we consider it to be beneath us (undeveloped natural phenomena), or irrelevant (the

Cosmos), is recognized to be the key to genuine flourishing from a Daoist perspective.

This arises in part because that which is greatest (*da* 大) in degree of vastness is no longer subject to the same contrasts that allow relative determinations to arise. Only small and finite squares can have corners. If one extends a square endlessly, all its edges effectively become equally distant. The greatest instrument will take the longest time to complete: effectively it can never be completed.

Chapter 45

101

The greatest completeness seems lacking:
    used but never worn out.
The greatest fullness seems to gush from emptiness:
    its use is inexhaustible.

The greatest straightness seems crooked;
The greatest skill seems awkward;
The greatest argument seems tongue-tied.

102

Being energetic prevails in the cold;
Stillness prevails in the heat.

103

Clear and still:
    become the axis (*zheng* 正) of the empire (*tian xia*).

Comment: It is worth noting here that the terminology in par. 103 ("clear," "still," "empire") anticipates the Mystical Imperialism of the later chapters of the *Zhuang Zi* anthology (in Chapter 11, p. 407).

Chapter 2

4

The whole world knows that the beautiful is beautiful:
    this is already ugly.
All know that the good is good;
    this is already not good.

5

Thus, something and nothing engender each other (*xiang* 相)
Difficult and easy complete each other
Long and short contrast with each other
High and low incline towards each other
Sound and voice harmonize with each other
Front and back follow each other.

Comment: Xiang (相) "mutuality" is the relationship between contrasts—in contrast with 'opposites.' Opposites oppose or negate each
other; contrasts each enable the other to stand out. Contrasts are mutually dependent: mutually producing, completing, and even transforming. Qualities are thus understood as coming in pairs that harmonize
with one another; hence the inclusion of the otherwise surprising pair
of "sound and voice."

Chapter 22

50

It is in being bent that one is whole;
In being crooked, one is straight.
In being hollow, one is full;
In being worn out that one is new.

To lessen is to gain;
While profusion is confusion.

50a

Thus, the wise person embraces integration (*yi* 一),
    And becomes a model for the world.

50b

It is in not showing oneself,
    that one will shine (*ming* 明);
Not affirming oneself,
    one will be illustrious;
Not pulling oneself up,
    one will have success;
Not promoting oneself,
    one will endure.

50c

It is only because they are not combative,
That none in the world can combat them.

50d

When the ancients said "Bent, one is whole"
How could these be empty words?
Trust completely and return to them.

Comment: In par. 50, contrasting pairs are juxtaposed. Superficially, these might refer to cyclical processes of mutual transformation: neither crookedness nor straightness, hollowness nor fullness remains permanently, but each eventually gives way to some degree to the other. But it also suggests an order of dependence. The first five are *yin* qualities: being bent, crooked, hollow, worn, and lessening. These are presented as necessary conditions for the positive *yang* qualities. In the last, increase is presented as the condition for confusion. This seems to be a pragmatic paradox: we generally pursue wholeness, fullness, and gain, and despise emptiness, crookedness, and loss. But the pursuit of increase is unsustainable: you must be hollow if you want to be full; you must lessen if you want genuine gain. You must be self-effacing if you want to be illustrious. Embracing integration in 50a contextually seems to refer to the functional integration of opposites, with the understanding that pursuing the *yin* quality results in the *yang* quality. The pragmatic significance of integration is slightly different from that of par. 85 in Chapter 39, p. 286, above.

Self-effacement and non-aggression may also become a model for the ruler of an empire: one gains the empire by letting go of it.

Chapter 4

12

Subduing the sharpness
Releasing the profusion
Diffusing the brightness
    Blending with dust.

Comment: This names several types of natural *yin* processes of return that are recommended by the *Lao Zi*. They also name phenomenological (or meditative) processes of shifting attention from the focus to the periphery, relaxing the tensions, decreasing the contrast to allow one to merge with the background context.

Chapter 27

60

Excellence (*shan* 善) in traveling
    follows no ruts and leaves no tracks.
Excellence in speaking
    is flawless and blameless.
Excellence in planning
    makes no use of procedures and stratagems.
Excellence in sealing tight
    uses no locks, yet the seal cannot be opened.
Excellence in tying
    uses no knots, yet it cannot be loosened.

61

In this way, the wise always excel in giving relief to the people
    and thus abandon no one;
always excel in rescuing creatures
    and abandon none.
This is called inheriting insight (*ming* 明).

62

Those who excel at being human are the model for those who do not;
Those who do not excel at being human are the material for those
                            who do.
If you do not honor the model, or care for the material,
Though you may be clever, you will be greatly lost and confused.

This is called essential subtlety.

Comment: This chapter appeals to an evaluative term "*shan*," which has the senses of 'good,' 'beautiful,' 'fortunate,' and 'excellent.' In this passage, it clearly refers to excelling in several types of activity, and identifies characteristics of excellence that run counter to what one might ordinarily expect (with the exception of excellence in speaking). It is significant though, that while it is an evaluative term, it does not always have ethical application: an excellent knot is not an ethically virtuous one! Nevertheless, par. 61 implies that positively ethical consequences follow from applying these modes of excellence when engaging with people and creatures.

We have seen in Chapter 47 above (at the end of "Phenomenology, Meditation, and Spiritual Cultivation," p. 295) that the most extensive understanding does not require traveling, and we know that the Cosmos does not speak or plan. If one does not travel, speak, or plan, then one will leave no tracks, say nothing blameworthy, and make no use of procedures. This is certainly one level of meaning of the text. But other significances can be drawn out by treating the sentences as riddles, exercises in lateral thinking that open up our imaginations: what kind of sealing or tying could use no locks or knots, and yet be infallible? Still other significances can be constructed by treating them as paradoxes: how might one travel without traveling, teach without speaking, or plan without procedures? Lastly, one can recognize that the negative term "*wu*" (無) tends not be used as an absolute negation in Daoist texts, but rather as a modifier to indicate a form of pragmatically optimal minimization. Ordinary traveling follows the paths set by others, and is modified by the traveler. But to wander spontaneously one pays little attention to well-worn tracks, and to meander harmoniously *with* one's environment one makes a minimal impact. It seems that the last line of par. 62 is referring to the paradoxical subtleties of par. 60.

The first part of par. 62 has a notably Confucian sensibility: raw material is crafted into an excellent form by following a model example.

Chapter 81

194

Trustworthy words are not beautiful
 Beautiful words are not trustworthy;
Those who excel do not argue
 Those who argue are not excellent;
Those who know are not broad
 Those who are broad do not know.

195

The wise do not hoard,
Since they take acting for others as having more themselves,
So they take giving to others as having still more themselves.

196

The way of the Cosmos is to benefit and not harm;
The way of the wise ruler is to act without contending.

Comment: Paragraph 194 expresses a suspicion, not necessarily of language as a whole, but of beautiful rhetoric and of disputation. This is in contrast with par. 56, which makes the more radical claim more typically associated with Daoist thought, "Those who know do not speak; those who speak do not know."

The attitude towards fancy language here is comparable with that of the Mohists. But it creates a problem. Unlike the *Mo Zi*, the *Lao Zi* itself is appreciated for its poetic beauty. While the text does not criticize itself explicitly, it would appear to undermine itself in a kind of 'performative paradox.' By embodying linguistic beauty in the statement that linguistic beauty is not to be trusted, it implies that this very statement is not to be trusted. But while this constitutes an amusing performance, it isn't really an insurmountable philosophical problem. If the text is not deliberately undermining itself, then the linguistic beauty that is criticized would have to be of another kind. The reference to disputation and being knowledgeable suggests that it is the words of those with political aspirations who are being critiqued. In dramatic contrast with the florid rhetoric of the political persuaders, the linguistic beauty of the *Lao Zi* lies in a bleak and honest simplicity.

Paragraph 196 is puzzling. In what sense is it true that the way of the Cosmos is to benefit and not harm? Don't we see both in the natural world? Is this a denial that anything that happens naturally should be thought of as a harm? But to the extent that is true, it also follows that nothing that promotes flourishing should be thought of as benefiting. It also seems inconsistent with Chapter 5, translated next, which tells us that the Cosmos exhibits no humane concern for anything at all.

Chapter 5

14

The Cosmos is not humane (*ren* 仁):
It treats all things as straw dogs.
The wise are not humane:
They treat the ordinary people as straw dogs.

Comment: The moral of this verse is deeply problematic from an ethical standpoint. It raises an issue that is a problem for any philosophy that promotes a cosmic perspective, since value seems to arise only from the perspective of particular creatures: human value arises from within the human perspective. From a cosmic perspective, the difference between humanity and inhumanity vanishes. *Ren*, humanity, is a human addition to nature; the Cosmos itself has no special place for human interests. In fact, nothing in the world is favored over anything else: everything is equally valuable or valueless. As a description of the objective indifference of the Cosmos to human concerns, this is not in itself problematic. The problem arises because the wise ruler is supposed to adopt the Cosmic perspective: *the wise ruler must therefore also treat all people and all things as equally valueless.* It is unclear how this unsettling statement is to be reconciled with par. 196 that we just read immediately above.

"Straw dogs" is usually taken to refer to effigies used during ceremonies and then discarded as useless.

Chapter 15

35

The ancients who excelled as *shi* (土) were:

> Intricate and subtle,
> Profound and penetrating
> deep and incomprehensible.

Simply incomprehensible, but I shall struggle to portray their character:

> Hesitant!
>   — as though wading through a winter stream,
> Apprehensive!
>   — as though fearing neighbors on all sides,
> Solemn!
>   — as though standing on ceremony,
> Loose!
>   — like ice as it begins to melt free,
> Guileless!
>   — like natural simplicity,
> Open!
>   — like a valley,
> Hazy!
>   — as though turbid.

36

> Who can be turbid,
> > and by stilling slowly become clear?
> Who can be settled,
> > and by moving slowly become alive?

> One who preserves this way, does not desire to keep filling.
> Only by being unfilled, can one be worn down and return to
> > > completion.

Comment: The term "*shi*" (士) is complex. It refers to a scholar in training, one committed to a discipline of learning in order to aspire to a higher position, either in the military, the intelligentsia, or in government. Here it used to refer to a person, perhaps a soldier, considered to have cultivated excellence from a Daoist perspective. This verse reads like a riddle, filled with images and metaphors that are hard to fathom. Given that they are 'simply incomprehensible,' explanatory commentary seems altogether inappropriate.

Chapter 8

20

> The highest excellence (*shan* 善) is like water.
> Water excels in benefiting (*li* 利) all things, and is not combative.
> It resides in the places that most people disdain
> And so is close to the way.

21

> In dwelling, find excellence in the earth;
> With the heart–mind, find excellence in (bottomless) depth;
> In giving, find excellence in humanity (*ren* 仁);
> In speaking, find excellence in trust (*xin* 信);
> In governing (*zheng* 正), find excellence in regulation (*zhi* 治);
> In service (*shi* 事), find excellence in ability (*neng* 能);
> In movement, find excellence in timeliness (*shi* 時).

22

> Only without combat can there be no blame.

Comment: In par. 20, we find an explicit account of the value of excellence as exemplified in the natural benefits of low-lying water. The highest excellence is to benefit (*li* 利) everything in the way that water benefits all living things. There is a sort of naturalizing of value here: we should benefit all things by imitating the beneficence of water. We then observe under what conditions water enables things to flourish, and seek to embody and exemplify those. Overturning what one might expect, value should be sought for in the places we usually regard as being beneath our contempt. As we shall see in the next section, the Daoist ruler, imitating the lowly beneficence of water, also embodies self-deprecation.

Of course, water is not always beneficial: floods have the capacity to harm living things. Indeed, Chapter 78 (p. 325, below, in "*Wu Wei*: Politics, Utopianism, and Empire") points out the strength of water in destroying the strongest and hardest of things. But the point here is that the highest excellence is to be found in imitating the beneficial properties of water for living things.

Paragraph 21 is not particularly Daoist in spirit. Several of the examples of excellence—humanity, trustworthiness, governing, ability, and timeliness—are much more representative of both Confucian and Mohist political values.

REN DAO: THE WAY OF HUMANS

Even though humans are an integral part of the natural world, there is an aspect of the human way that seems to have distanced itself from the more fundamental modes of natural functioning. The *Lao Zi* diagnoses this displacement as having its origin in several human capacities: cognition (*zhi* 知), language (*yan* 言), evaluation (*gui* 貴), desire (*yu* 欲), active doing (*wei* 為), and acquisition (*de* 得). These processes interact to construct an increasingly artificial environment in which we are immersed, and which we value more than our unconstructed natural environment. According to the *Lao Zi* these processes result in artificial objects, and desires for these artifices, that are completely out of alignment with the natural processes from which they are constructed. We divide, describe, evaluate, and desire things according to artificial criteria that have no grounding in the natural workings of the Cosmos. This 'human' way stimulates artificial dissatisfactions and results in conflict and contention, as it fuels our acquisitive desires. But the most surprising and controversial claim of the *Lao Zi* is that ethical values, as articulated especially by the Ruists—humanity (*ren* 仁), rightness (*yi* 義),

and propriety (*li* 禮)—are themselves artificial constructs that stimulate acquisitive desires and lead to conflict and contention. As a solution to the problems of the Warring States they are simply counterproductive.

Chapter 77

184

The way of the Cosmos is like a stretching bow:

> It restrains the higher,
>> And raises the lower.
> It reduces the excessive,
>> And repairs the insufficient.
>
> The way of the Cosmos takes from excess
>> and repairs insufficiency.

The way of humans is not like this:

> It takes from the insufficient
> And serves it to those with excess.

Who is able to take the excess and offer it to the whole world?
> Only one who has the way.

185

Thus, the wise:
> act but without being presumptuous,
> and succeed in their undertakings without dwelling on them.
It is that they do not desire to display their 'worthiness.'

Comment: While the human way (*ren dao*) distinguishes the honorable from lowly, the way of the Cosmos (*tian dao*) equalizes them. Only one who has the way could have enough detachment to serve the whole empire with the same kind of impartiality.

Heraclitus uses the metaphor of a stretched bow, but with a very different significance: tension and antagonism are necessary to keep the world energized. In fact, a tensed weapon seems to be an odd choice of metaphor, itself in tension with other Daoist ideals.

The *Lao Zi* accounts for unequal distribution of resources as a result of human action, not of natural processes. The human way is to exacerbate inequality. People distinguish between the honorable and the humble, and reward the honorable while confiscating from the humble. From a Cosmic point of view such social distinctions vanish as mere products of human artifice. The wise ruler who rules according to natural principles would ensure that resources are available to benefit everyone equally. This is not necessarily a redistribution of 'property,' as the Daoist rejects the very notion of 'ownership' of resources as an unnatural imposition, as we saw in Chapter 51 in our discussion of the "Cosmology" of the *Lao Zi*, p. 288, above.

This is reminiscent of the Mohist ideal of impartial concern, but the Mohist idea is still a deliberate attempt to impose equality or impartiality within an artificially constructed system.

Chapter 18

42

When the way of vastness (*da dao*) is discarded:
    there are humanity and rightness (*ren yi*),
When cleverness and intelligence emerge,
    there is great artifice (*wei* 偽).

When the six family relationships are out of harmony:
    there is filiality and parental virtue,
When the state is dimmed with turmoil,
    there are loyal (*zhong* 忠) ministers.

Comment: The artifices of humanity, rightness, cleverness, and intelligence are forged when people stop trusting the way of the Cosmos. When natural relationships break down, artificial virtues arise to disturb the state. While the Confucian philosopher Xun Zi would agree that these virtues are products of artifice, *wei* 偽, the author of the *Lao Zi* passage here is intending it in a pejorative sense, implying that since they are not natural they lack genuineness, and so are false and hypocritical.

Here we see one reason why the *Lao Zi* is suspicious of deliberation: calculating and scheming can result in shrewd and crafty manipulation. Intelligence and cleverness are associated with artifice, both as deliberate human purposive construction, and as artful trickery. Like the Mohists, the author of this text is also critical of the clever and crafty who use their wits to exploit those who cannot see through their ploys. The accusation of hypocrisy is echoed in Zhuangzian philosophy, and in the Utopian strand of Daoist thought in the *Zhuang Zi*. In their rejection of clever manipulation, the Daoists are like the Mohists; they disagree, however, on what causes it and how to remove it.

With the juxtaposition of Confucian virtues and cleverness, the *Lao Zi* implies that artificial virtues are means of deceit. But this line of critique fails to take into account the Confucian emphasis on sincerity. Confucius is also critical of cleverness, as we are reminded by Meng Zi in 7B37 (p. 134).

Desire

Chapter 46

104

> When the world has the way,
> > wandering steeds manure the soil,
> When the world lacks the way,
> > war horses are raised in the outskirts.

105

> There is no greater misfortune than dissatisfaction,
> No greater fault than the desire (*yu* 欲) to acquire (*de* 得).

> So understand that enough is enough,
> > and it will always be enough.

Comment: Compare the Utopian idealist chapter, "Horses' Hooves," in the *Zhuang Zi* (in Chapter 11, below).

Chapter 12

28

> The five colors are blinding to people's eyes;
> The five tones deafen their ears;
> The five flavors sizzle their palates.

> Hunting and chasing drive the human heart wild;
> Goods hard to acquire (*de* 得) impede people's conduct.

29

For this reason, the wise act for the belly, not for the eye.
Therefore, reject that and select this.

Comment: Sensory profusion and confusion—the many colors, sounds, and tastes, the excesses of embroidered silks, musical ceremonies, courtly cuisine—overstimulate our desires, and ultimately deaden our senses. But the use of the number 'five' also connotes artificial systems of classification. The divisions, associations, and evaluations of artificial conceptual systems set up systems of desire whereby some, on account of their rarity, are considered more precious and more desirable. They thereby prevent us from fully appreciating all the varieties of things in their natural unsystematized state. The wise ruler therefore acts to satisfy the people's natural needs, and does not attend to their desires for excess.

The references of "that" (or "the former") and "this" (or "the latter") in the last line have no agreed upon reference and are open to interpretation.

Chapter 9

23

Clutching and filling to the brim,
    don't compare with stopping when enough.
Hammer it sharp,
    it cannot be preserved (*bao*) for long;
Fill the halls with gold and jade,
    and no one can protect (*shou*) them.

When proud of wealth and honor,
    you court disaster;
When a task is successful,
    name and reputation follow.

But the way (*dao*) of Nature (*tian*) is to step aside.

Comment: Flourishing from a Cosmic perspective is the inverse of social success. Applying the paradoxes of the way of nature leads to a minimalist philosophy: less is more. The *yang* qualities of excess, acquisition, and self-assertion have disastrous consequences; we may crave success and fame, but these also set us up for a painful fall. More importantly, self-assertion and self-promotion are fundamentally wrong-headed: they are out of sync with the self-effacing ways of nature. The productive forces of nature promote and nurture their offspring while remaining themselves in the shadows. It is such *yin* qualities that should provide the model for humans to emulate.

The language of preserving (*bao* 保) and protecting (*shou* 守) echoes the spiritual practice of sustaining the natural ancestral tendencies that are the wellspring of our life processes that we saw in the section above, "Phenomenology, Meditation, and Spiritual Cultivation."

Against Exploitation

Chapter 75

181

The people are hungry
    because those above consume too much in levies:
    that's why they're hungry.
The people are hard to govern
    because those above actively control:
    that's why they're hard to govern.
The people don't care about dying
    because those above are too greedy for life:
    that's why they don't care about dying.

Only those who do not act in order to live
    are more worthy than those who value life.

Comment: This chapter identifies three conditions that contribute to social unrest. The first is when those in power use it to extract wealth from the people. Interestingly, it does not reject the imposition of levies altogether, but only excess that results in impoverishing the people to the point of hunger. The second is attempting to control (*you wei* 有為) or micromanage the people. This at first sounds like a laissez-faire sort of libertarianism, but as we have seen above the *Lao Zi* recommends not simply refraining from interfering, but a more maternal form of nurturing: creating spaces of possibility that allow the people to grow. We shall read more about the converse concept, "*wu wei*" (無為), below. The third condition is when those above act to promote the richness of their lives at the expense of the people. Under such conditions, the people will be less likely to value their own lives.

Against War

Chapter 31

71

Fine weapons are instruments of misfortune, what creatures detest.
Thus, one who has the way does not abide them.
When the nobles are in residence, they honor the left;
   when they take up arms, they honor the right.

Weapons are instruments of misfortune, not the instruments of a
                                                            noble.
They are used only when unavoidable:
   at most, they are used without the taste for it.

Victory is not beautiful.
Those who consider it beautiful delight in the massacre of people.
Those who delight in the massacre of people
   cannot be allowed to achieve their intentions in the world.

Fortunate affairs are valued on the left;
   disastrous affairs are valued on the right.
The adjutant general resides on the left;
   the commanding general resides on the right.

That is to say, they abide by the rites of mourning:
When multitudes of people are slaughtered,
   they weep for them, grieving and lamenting.
When victorious in war, they abide by the rites of *mourning*.

Comment: A profoundly moving and passionate anti-war poem. War
may sometimes be necessary, but it is never a beautiful thing. Even victory in war is not a cause for celebration, but a cause for grief.

WU WEI: POLITICS, UTOPIANISM, AND EMPIRE

The *Lao Zi* advocates that we should retreat from this artificially constructed world that fuels and is in turn fueled by our desires, and turn
inwards to reflect on the natural processes of the Cosmos in order to
learn how it is able to flourish. We then selectively apply these lessons
to undo our human activity and return to the way of the Cosmos. In
the section, "*Tian Dao*: The Way of the Cosmos," above, we investigated
the *Lao Zi*'s account of how the Cosmos functions. Simply put: without

cognition, language, desire, or manipulation. And we saw hints of how the wise person will attempt to adopt these modes of behavior. Now we shall see how these modes of non-deliberate 'action' are to be applied to guiding human interaction in social settings, both simple, small societies and large-scale empires.

Utopianism

To apply what we learn from the Cosmos we must imitate its non-human perspective. The Cosmos does not control or speak, so we should act without deliberate control, and without the oversimplification of clear laws and rules. The *yang* qualities that humans favor and desire should yield to the *yin* qualities that are no less valuable in the natural world. Indeed, from the human perspective the relation of the Cosmic to the human appears to be that of *yin* to *yang*. The Cosmos is deep, profound, productive, mysterious, unfathomable, the surrounding empty space that is the condition of the possibility of the temporary brightness of human understanding, deliberating, acting, and desiring. According to one strand of Daoist thinking we should abandon the complexities of a socially constructed existence, especially those promoted by socially oriented thinkers such as the Ruists and the Mohists, and return to a simple, natural way of life. This is expressed through the concept of *pu* 樸, "unrefined simplicity" (sometimes translated as "the uncarved block"). Politically, this results in an extreme Utopian democratic ideal: self-rule, self-governance, no interference from an authority. (*Ziding* 自定: self-determination; *zihua* 自化: self-transformation; *zizheng* 自政: self-governing; *ziran* 自然: being spontaneously from one's natural self.)

Chapter 80

193

A small state (*guo* 國) with few people:
    Even if it were to have a variety of implements (*qi* 器),
        they would not use them;
    Even if they were concerned about dying,
        they would not migrate to distant places.
    Although they may have boats and carts,
        they would have no place to ride them to;
    And though they may have armor and weapons,
        they would have no occasion to display them.

Make the people return (*fu* 復) to using knotted ropes,
    enjoy their food,
    appreciate their clothes,
    rest contented in their homes,
    and take pleasure in everyday things.

Neighboring states may be seen in the distance,
Their chickens and dogs would hear each others' cries.
But their residents would grow old and die
Without ever encountering one another.

Comment: This is an account of a human social group (*guo* 國, 'state')
at its simplest and most unrefined (*su* 俗). Though the term for 'state' is
used, what is described is no bigger than a small village. People live simply and naturally, minimizing the use of technological implements (*qi*
器) even if they were present in abundance. The language connotes military implements, though the criticism throughout the verse is against
all technology. The presence of such tools implies not an original state
of human relations, but a rejection of the need for sophisticated conve-
niences, and a return (*fu* 復) to a simpler form of social life. Note that
technology is not abandoned altogether: they use clothes and knotted
ropes, but it is deliberately maintained at a basic level of development.

Chapter 19

43

Eradicate wisdom (*sheng* 聖), abandon cleverness:
    And the people will benefit a hundred times over.
Eradicate humanity (*ren*), abandon appropriateness (*yi*):
    And the people will return (*fu* 復) to filiality (*xiao* 孝) and parental
                          affection (*ci* 慈).
Eradicate trickery, abandon profit:
    And there will be no robbers or thieves.

These three take culture (*wen* 文) as insufficient.
So something must be added:

Manifest plainness,
Embrace simplicity (*pu* 樸),
Lessen selfishness,
Diminish desires.

Comment: Here, the Confucian cultural values of humanity and appropriateness are not only associated with shrewdness, deception, and theft, they are explicitly listed as conditions that circumvent feelings of affection between parents and children. (But, note that this is in contrast to Chapter 18 (p. 309), where *xiao* and *ci* are listed as artificial Confucian virtues. Also in this chapter 'wisdom' (*sheng*) is taken in a negative sense and associated with shrewdness and deception.) The solution to the problems of a life of artifice is a return to natural artlessness.

Chapter 3

8

> Do not promote the worthy (*xian* 賢)
> > and the people will not become contentious;
> Do not value (*gui* 貴) rare goods
> > and the people will not become thieves.
>
> When the desirable does not appear, the heart will not be disturbed.

9

> Thus, in the regulation (*zhi* 治) of the wise:
> > They empty the heart–mind (of desires),
> > > but fill the belly,
> > Weaken the aspirations,
> > > but strengthen the bones.
>
> So the people remain innocent and without acquisitive desires,
> And the 'clever' do not dare to interfere.

10

> Act without artifice (*wu wei* 無為), and there will be no misrule.

Chapter 2

6

> Thus, the wise ruler (*sheng ren* 聖人)
> > deals with affairs (*shi* 事) without active control (*wu wei* 無為),
> > and practices a teaching without speaking (*buyan* 不言).

Comment: Chapter 3 categorically rejects the Mohist and Ruist ideal of rule by promoting the worthy (*xian* 賢) to positions of power. The Ruists and Mohists believe that a harmonious society can be achieved simply by promoting those who have proved themselves to be worthy. But the Utopian strand of thought in the *Lao Zi* sees the root cause of disharmony as the artificial creation of desirable goods through the act of promotion itself. Value of any kind incites desire and contention.

This, of course, does not mean that we should promote the unworthy to positions of power. That would simply be to perpetuate competitive systems of power. Rather, the wise would not allow artifice and its attendant desires to arise; instead they attenuate or weaken the distractions of the heart–mind, its artificial desires and aspirations, and tend instead to the natural needs (metonymically speaking, the belly and the bones) of the people. Thus, the regulation (*zhi* 治) of the wise is not a hierarchical system of control, not a 'government' as such, but rather ordering by healing (*zhi* 治) and nurturing the needs of the people. The *sheng ren* is not a lord, a ruler, or an emperor, but a wise caregiver.

The Cosmos does not act linguistically (*buyan*) and does not take active control (*wu wei*). Nature does not grant honorable titles, or issue instructions. Nor does Nature deliberately manage things: things emerge, arise, and flourish by themselves. But we have seen that the potency of Nature lies in its nurturing role. So, while nurturing does not take active control, it does not sit idly by either. One nurtures by watching over one's wards, leaving open the conditions that enable them to explore, grow, and flourish. The Daoist ruler should seek to emulate the sort of wordless teaching and functioning that is exemplified by the processes of the natural world.

Transition from Utopianism to Imperialism

The notion of *wu wei* plays a central role in Daoist philosophy. The attempt to take it seriously as a mode of action, especially as a mode of action of a wise person who is in charge of others, results in more directly political applications. As the idea is developed, it will eventually become a tool that has a theoretical role even in the government of an empire. The following passages exemplify this more explicitly political application of *wu wei* as a criterion of rulership that allows the people to flourish, but do not necessarily represent a full-blown theory of imperial rule.

———————

Chapter 37

81

The way doesn't 'do' anything (*wu wei*),
   and yet nothing remains undone.
If lords and kings could abide by this,
   all things would transform by themselves (*zihua* 自化).
Should desires arise as they transform,
   we would subdue them with the simplicity (*pu* 樸) of namelessness.
When subdued by the simplicity of namelessness (*wu ming* 無名),
   they will lessen their desires (*yu* 欲).
Dispassionate and tranquil,
   the empire will settle itself (*ziding* 自定).

Comment: We see in these lines the possibility of applying the utopian model of non-interference to states large enough to have lords and kings, perhaps even an empire. They might be able to achieve a quasi-anarchist harmony if they give up ruling, and instead become wise caregivers, allowing the people to transform themselves and settle themselves. 'Self-transformation' and 'self-settling' here imply processes of mutual adjustment that maximize harmony by yielding to one another.

Ordinarily, through processes of socialization we learn to classify phenomena and events, evaluate them as better or worse, and in doing so we stimulate our desires. The human way is to name (*ming* 名) and evaluate and thereby to provoke acquisitive desires (*yu* 欲). We then act deliberately and create constructions that satisfy our ever-insatiable desires. Repeated convolutions of this process result in increasingly complex, highly structured, social and political environments. The role of the wise lords and kings approved by the *Lao Zi* would be to reverse this process: from complexity to simplicity. Rather than inculcating classifications of things that stimulate our desires, they encourage a return to appreciating things as they are, without layers of social approval and disapproval. When nothing is more precious than anything else, there is nothing to desire. The natural way is to dissolve all boundaries and hierarchies—returning to the simplicity (*pu* 樸) of namelessness (*wu ming* 無名)—and thereby subdue acquisitive desire, and spontaneously return to a state of tranquil harmony.

The next two chapters make it clear that *wu wei*, 'not doing anything,' cannot be interpreted too simplistically. They provide more detail in understanding the complexities of 'acting without acting' or 'refraining from manipulation.' Paragraphs 149 and 150 in Chapter 63, and 152 and

153 in Chapter 64, draw our attention to how the large-scale is constituted from the small-scale, and to the stability and instability of circumstances, respectively. They also draw attention to how being responsive to conditions at the subtlest levels can have consequences that extend effortlessly throughout the whole.

Chapter 63

148

> Act without 'acting' (*wu wei*);
> Serve without 'service';
> Savor the tasteless.
>
> Magnify the small; give more to the few.
>
> Repay grievances with *de* (potency 德).

149

> Plan for difficulty while it is easy.
> Enact the large-scale through the minutiae.
>
> The difficult affairs in the world
>   surely arise from the easy;
> The large-scale affairs in the world
>   surely arise from the minutiae.

150

> It is because the wise do not in the end enact the large-scale
> That they are able to achieve it.

151

> Taking one's promises lightly surely diminishes trust.
> With more ease there will surely be more difficulty.
> For this reason, the wise seem to find things difficult
>   and so in the end encounter no difficulty.

Comment: Everything has a composition, is constituted by lower-scale constituents. The large-scale is composed of its small-scale constituents; the many of the few. The grandest and most complex affairs are composed of minuscule events. Paragraphs 149 and 150 point out that it is easier to pay attention to what is directly in front of you than to try to control a large system: but if one understands how the large system is constructed out of its constituents, then one begins to understand how one might affect the large-scale indirectly, by paying attention simply to what is present at hand. This interpretation of *wu wei* will become the central principle for the Syncretist strand of Daoist thought, whereby one is able to preside over a vast empire without involvement or interference in its workings, as we see in the following section ("Mystical Imperialism," below).

Chapter 64

152

> What is stable is easy to uphold:
> It is easier to plan before the signs begin.
> The brittle is easy to fracture;
> The fine is easy to disperse.
>
> Enact it through what has not yet (*wei* 未) arisen;
> Order it before disorder arises.

153

> A tree one fathom around grows from a flimsy sapling.
> A tower of nine terraces arises by accumulating dirt,
> A journey of a thousand leagues begins with a footfall.

154

> One who actively takes over will ruin it;
> One who grasps and manipulates it will lose it.
> For this reason, the wise ruler
> > refrains from active control (*wu wei*), and so ruins nothing;
> > refrains from manipulation, and so loses nothing.

155

> When the people pursue their affairs,
> > they often ruin them just before the point of completion;
> So, be as cautious at the end as at the beginning;
> > then tasks will not be ruined.

156

Thus, wise rulers
desiring not to desire,
   do not value goods hard to obtain;
They learn to unlearn,
   and go back (*fu* 復) to the place that everyone else has left behind.
They thereby enable the varieties of things to be themselves (*ziran*
自然),
  and do not dare to control them.

Comment: The first two paragraphs of this chapter distinguish types of dispositional qualities: circumstances may have stable or unstable dispositions. These are indicated through the use of the temporal negation, *wei* (未) 'not yet.' It refers to the 'presence' of potential qualities before they have begun to manifest. One need not be concerned about stable dispositions: they are easy to maintain. The problem arises with unstable, or even explosive, situations, those that have a trigger point. A brittle object, for example, has a degree of strength and stability, and it will be able to withstand a gradual increase in pressure without buckling—but only up to a certain point. Above that point, the structure will suddenly fracture. Socially speaking, a particular community may have an inner structure that makes it brittle in a similar way: there will be a limit to its tolerance of stress; above that point it will erupt into disorder.

In a more extreme situation, extreme fragmentation can result in extreme instability: dust, for example, can remain settled only so long as there is no movement of air. It cannot withstand much pressure before it will be disturbed: even a gentle breeze can cause it to disperse. Applying this socially, a community that lacks cohesiveness will be easy to undermine. These sorts of negative dispositions, dispositions towards disorder, should be understood and prepared for before they are manifested. It is understanding the trigger points that allows for minimal interference. Note that minimal interference is not inconsistent with concentrated attention: to refrain from interfering does not mean that one is paying no attention. On the contrary, attentive nurturing awareness that anticipates the tendency to disorder, and makes gentle adjustments in advance as appropriate, is indispensable for avoiding disorder.

The focus on the small-scale may seem utopian in spirit at first, but the *wu wei* ideal is articulated precisely to be applied to the running of a large-scale state. The 'ruler' of an anarchist confederation must refrain from interfering with its small-scale constituents, or they risk destroying the state. Large-scale events and achievements are the results of accumulated small-scale phenomena. If one deals with the small-scale, the large-scale phenomena will result automatically with no further effort.

Mystical Imperialism

The lessons learnt from nature are eventually applied to politics in a counter-intuitive way. The Utopian strain of Daoism understandably wants to promote 'degrowth' and return to a simpler, more natural way of life. But the Imperialist strand of Daoist thought applies the same principles in a paradoxical way to develop an organic orchestration of a large-scale empire. The Ruists and Mohists also promote grass-roots social structures that begin with the family and extend outwards. The Mohists have an explicit set of laws and values applied locally, but because they are all identical, the result is uniformity throughout the whole empire. The Ruists have no explicit set of laws, though they do have an intuitively understood set of virtues; they begin with self-cultivation, which spreads throughout society of its own accord. The Imperialist Daoist has only *wu wei*, non-interference, which allows harmony to spread of its own accord. But in order to succeed, the ruler must have no desire to gain an empire. Such acquisitive desire guarantees failure, given Daoist principles and values.

Chapter 28

63

Understand the male, but sustain the female:
    Be the ravine of the Empire.

As the ravine of the Empire,
    the potency of constant regularity (*chang de* 常德) will not leave
                                            you,
    and you will return again (*fu gui* 復歸) to the state of the infant.

Understand the white, but sustain the black:
    Be a model to the Empire.

As model to the Empire,
    the potency of constant regularity will not be excessive,
    and you will return to the limitless (*wu ji* 無極).

Understand the glory, but sustain the disgrace:
    Be a valley to the Empire.

As a valley to the Empire,
>the potency of constant regularity will be sufficient,
>and you will return to uncontrived simplicity (*pu* 樸).

64

Those whose uncontrived simplicity has been dispersed become
>utensils.
The wise person puts them to use as officials and leaders.

65

Thus, great governing does not cut apart.

Comment: The understanding of complementary pairs is applied to the role of the rulers at the center of a large empire. We should know and understand the *yang* (bright) qualities, but preserve and nurture the *yin* qualities in the shadows. To do so is to embody the function of the valley to which all waters flow, and to return to a natural and uncontrived simplicity.

The potency of the Ruists is a form of political charisma that enables the exemplary person to rule by example, embodying virtues that effortlessly influence the people. In this passage the potency is understood in a more primordial sense, as an internal source of potential. This potential arises from the undifferentiated potential of the Cosmos itself in its indeterminate, 'limitless' state (*wu ji* 無極). The cosmological concept of the 'limitless' will appear in the various strands of the *Zhuang Zi* as the 'inexhaustible' (*wu qiong* 無窮).

Chapter 66

159

Rivers and oceans are able to be the Kings of the valleys because they excel in being beneath them.
>This is why they are able to be Kings of the valleys.

160

So the wise rulers
>desiring to be above people
>>must demean themselves with their words,
>desiring to be ahead of people
>>they must place themselves personally behind.

161

> In this way, the wise rulers
>> may reside above
>>> but will not weigh the people down,
>> may reside in front,
>>> but will not harm people.

> Thus, the Empire will delight in and encourage them and will not be
> oppressed by them.

162

> It is because they do not contend
>> that none in the Empire contend with them.

Chapter 42

95

> What people hate is to be:
>> 'orphaned,'
>> 'widowed,'
>> or 'destitute.'
> Yet Kings and Dukes take these as their titles!

96

> Thus, some things diminish and thereby increase,
> Others increase and thereby diminish.

Comment: The ruler who attempts to mimic the role of the Cosmos is taking on an unenviable task. As parent to all the people, the ruler has no parent. As a single ruler, they have no partner. And as provider to all the people, they have no one to ensure that they themselves are provided for. At best they have to be parent, partner, and provider to themselves. But this is a lonely role to play.

Chapter 48

108

> Acting for learning one increases daily;
> Acting for the way one decreases daily.

Decreasing and decreasing,
Until one acts no more.
Without acting, nothing is not done.

109

Attain the Empire by always refraining from its business,
Interfering with its business will not enable you to attain the Empire.

Comment: The way of humans is to increase, and the Ruist way is devoted
to learning. The way of the Cosmos, in contrast, becomes a way of reversal, decreasing deliberate action, and decreasing learning. This is not an
anti-intellectualism, but a dismantling of traditionally inculcated modes
of understanding. This undoing, or unlearning, allows us to become
open to the processes of the natural world, and acquire modes of action
that may not be representable using conventional concepts.

Chapter 78

186

Nothing in the world is gentler (*rou* 柔) and weaker than water,
And yet when attacking the hard and strong nothing can defeat it;
this is because there is nothing it changes (*yi* 易) into.

187

That the weak overcomes the strong,
And the soft overcomes the hard,
Everyone can understand, but no one can put it into practice.

188

Thus, the wise rulers say:

It is at the 'Pillar of the Temple of Agriculture'
where the dregs of the states collect;
It is the 'Ruler of the Empire'
who takes on the misfortunes of the states.

189

Upright words seem to go back (*fan* 反) on themselves.

Comment: Following the way of nature results in paradoxical modes of action: one achieves more by acting less, becomes stronger by cultivating softness, and achieves the highest status or rulership by demeaning oneself. These Daoist paradoxes go back on themselves (*fan* 反), and thereby might appear at first glance not to say anything at all.

Incidentally, the concept of the way of gentleness will give rise to the 'soft' style of martial arts. "Judo" is the Japanese pronunciation of "*rou dao*" and means 'the gentle way' or 'the way of weakness.'

The strength of water lies in the fact that it is already broken down. A rock when broken down is exchanged for sand. But when water is broken down, it remains water.

Chapter 38

82

> The potency of the superior (*shang de* 上德) is not potent;
>   this is why it has potency.
> The potency of the subordinate (*xia de* 下德) does not lose potency;
>   and so it lacks potency.
>
> The potency of the superior minimizes active control (*wu wei* 無為),
>   and has no means by which to act (*wei* 為).
> The potency of the subordinate controls them,
>   and has the means by which to control them.
>
> The humanity (*ren* 仁) of the superior actively controls them,
>   but has no means by which to act;
> The rightness (*yi* 義) of the superior actively controls them,
>   and has the means by which to act.
> The propriety (*li* 禮) of the superior controls them,
> But when none respond, it rolls up its sleeves and pushes them around.

Comment: The language of this passage resonates closely with the Mystical Imperialism described in the later strands of the *Zhuang Zi*. It seems to encapsulate part of a theory of imperial rule distinguishing the roles of the superior and subordinates. It is clearly far from complete as it stands. We can glean from it that potency (*de*) is the non-interfering role of the superior, while humanity, rightness, and propriety are lesser means of control that must be delegated to subordinates.

The traditional reading of this passage takes "*shang de*" (上德) and "*xia de*" (下德) to be referring to higher and lower forms of potency, which is a perfectly acceptable reading. But in doing so it misses the striking parallels with the Mystical Imperialist strand of the *Zhuang Zi*. I nevertheless translate the complete chapter below (repeating par. 82) with this alternative reading:

Chapter 38

82

The highest potency is not potent
   This is why it has potency
The lowest potency does not lose its potency
   And so it lacks potency.

The highest potency minimizes active control
   And has no means by which to act.
The lowest potency controls them,
   And has the means by which to control them.

Highest humanity actively controls them
   But has no means by which to act.
Highest rightness actively controls them,
   And has the means by which to act.
Highest propriety actively controls them,
   But when none respond, it rolls up its sleeves and pushes them
                            around.

83

Thus, when the way is lost, there is potency
When potency is lost, there is humanity
When humanity is lost, there is rightness
When rightness is lost, there is propriety.

84

As for propriety,
   it is a flimsy form of loyalty and trust
   And the beginning of social disorder.
And as for understanding (*qian shi* 前識),
It is the fancy manifestation of a way
And the beginning of stupidity.

84a

Thus, the great leader abides in the firm
  And does not reside in the flimsy
Abides in the fruitful result,
  And not in the flowery promises.

84b

Rejects that and chooses this.

Comment: The reference to 'understanding' (*qian shi* 前識) in par. 84 is mysterious. The term literally means "foreknowledge," but I follow a line of commentators who take it to refer indirectly to "*zhi*" (智), the Confucian virtue of 'wisdom' and understanding. This interpretation has the advantage of following the traditional sequence of virtues: *ren*, *yi*, *li*, and *zhi*, and it parallels the remarks on propriety at the beginning of the same paragraph.

ENDNOTE

[a] D.C. Lau moves the last line of 37 to the beginning of 38. I do not follow his emendation.

10

Zhuang Zi I: Zhuangzian Philosophy

INTRODUCTION

Person

Master Zhuang has generally been taken to be a real person, but in recent years a few scholars[1] have become skeptical of the historical authenticity of the character, because of the insufficiency of independent evidence. He is thought of as a cheerful and brilliant sage who lived free of social ties and ambitions. In the text, he is portrayed as scrawny and sallow, wearing sackcloth and shoes tied with string. He resides in a small alley, weaving sandals for a living. And yet, despite his lowly circumstances he is often courted by kings and princes who recognize his capacities and seek to employ him in a position of power. Like the Utopian primitivists we will meet in the next chapter, he always refuses office, preferring a life of poverty and obscurity for the freedom that it affords.

According to traditional dating (369–298 BCE), Zhuang Zi would have been an almost exact contemporary of the Ruist thinker Meng Zi (Mencius), though there is no clear evidence of philosophical interaction between them. The philosopher and statesman, Hui Shi, or Hui Zi (380–305 BCE), is represented as a close friend of Zhuang Zi, though unconvinced by his philosophical musings. There appears to have been a friendly rivalry between the broad- and mythic-minded Zhuang Zi and the politically motivated Hui Zi, who is critiqued in the text as a small-minded paradox-monger.

---

1 See articles by David McCraw and Esther Klein.

Text

The *Zhuang Zi* anthology is ranked among the greatest of literary and philosophical masterpieces that China has produced. Its style is complex—mythical, poetic, narrative, humorous, indirect, and polysemic. Though it has been traditionally attributed to a single author, the passages derive from different strands of Daoist thought, some of which can be dated to the Han dynasty.

The received edition of the text is the result of the editing and arrangement of the Jin dynasty thinker and commentator Guo Xiang (d. 312 CE). He reduced what was then a work in 52 chapters to the current edition of 33 chapters, excising material that he considered to be spurious. Guo Xiang's edition is divided into three collections, known as the *Inner Chapters* (1 to 7), the *Outer Chapters* (8 to 22), and the *Miscellaneous Chapters* (23 to 33). The *Inner Chapters* are generally considered to be the work of Zhuang Zi himself, though the evidence for this attribution is unclear. Guo Xiang's commentary provides an interpretation that has been one of the most influential over the subsequent centuries. The versions of Daoist philosophy expressed in the *Zhuang Zi* anthology were highly influential in the reception, interpretation, and transformation of Buddhist philosophies in China.

Several types of Daoist thought can be discerned in the anthology. A distinctive strand can be found in the *Inner Chapters* and developments (and variations) of it can be found throughout the majority of the rest of the text. These developments and variations have been attributed to a 'school' of followers. Since they are closely related, and since we have no decisive way to distinguish which of the variants are earlier and which are later (except for a very small number of passages), I refer to them collectively as a school of 'Zhuangzian' philosophy.

Another distinctive strand is that of the Utopian Daoists, who were also influenced directly by the anarchistic tendencies of the *Lao Zi*. A third strand of Daoist philosophy is that of the Imperialist Daoists, who sought to synthesize the competing philosophies into a single *dao* of mystical rulership of an Empire. These last two strands, the Utopian and the Imperialist, are translated in the next chapter.

Overview

The overall orientation of the 'Zhuangzian' strand of philosophy is existential in spirit, concerned with the contingencies of life and the inevitability of death. It espouses a holistic philosophy of life, encouraging disengagement from the artificialities of socialization, in order to live a simple and natural, but skillful and flourishing life, in authentic acceptance of our mortality.

To achieve this state, we must engage in a psychophysical cultivation of our 'ancestral' tendencies, the biological and spiritual potentialities that lie deep within us. This involves also cultivating our embodied sensitivity to natural processes as we develop extraordinary levels of skillful and wordless responsiveness to circumstances. We will then live in tune with the natural world, live the fullest and healthiest life possible, in deepest tranquility, unperturbed by the never-ending dramas of life and death.

The world of the *Zhuang Zi* is one of constant cyclical transformation (*hua* 化): it appears to presuppose a kind of process philosophy, according to which change is ontologically primary, and substances or enduring things are merely extended phases of relative stability in the development of those processes. Nature is constituted of continuous seasonal (*shi* 时) cycles of transformation, growth, and disintegration. And human life is also an endless stream of contrasting experiences, emotions, and outcomes: happiness and sadness, anger and joy, success and failure, living and dying. From a human perspective, we judge some circumstances to be preferable to others, we take the dramas of social life with the utmost seriousness, and so the shifting and precarious conditions become a source of anxiety and grief, of ill health and even early death. But if one can cultivate an expansive attitude from the all-inclusive perspective of the Cosmos, able to accept all transformations with equanimity, one can live a long and healthy life in tune with the natural world. Zhuang Zi calls this the contrast between the petty (*xiao* 小) and the vast (*da* 大). From such a perspective the distinctions and values by which we ordinarily judge things, and over which we argue with such conviction, lose their hold. From a cosmic perspective the distinction between what is beautiful and what is ugly is a mere artifice, as is that between the noble and the mean, right and wrong, and even that between life and death. From the perspective of the whole, one sees that the 'grindstone' of nature (*tian ni* 天倪) blends such 'opposites' into a continuous process of transformation. Zhuang Zi describes a life lived from such a perspective as 'genuinely human' (*zhen ren* 真人). It is a life of minimal artifice (*wu wei* 無為), at home in a vast and indifferent cosmos.

From such a lofty distance, the sage observes critically, and with a somewhat skeptical eye, a multiplicity of competing perspectives that divide and evaluate the world in different ways. These internal drives propel different strands of Daoist thought in different directions, and lead interpreters and translators to emphasize different epistemologies.

First, we have the greatest appreciation for the grandest perspective of the Cosmos; second is an appreciation for the multiplicity of perspectives, and third, a refusal to choose between them. Epistemologically, the second approach tends towards various forms of pluralism: contextualism, perspectivism, and at its most extreme, radical relativism. The third approach leads to various forms of skepticism, according to which we should refrain from making any judgments at all. The first approach acknowledges a Cosmic way or ways, and recommends that a flourishing life will be in tune with the Cosmos.

From our ordinary perspective of social utility, the life of such a sage appears utterly useless and perhaps even dangerous. Indeed, how can a person who recognizes no distinction between benefit and harm, and who has no anxiety in the face of death even be regarded as fully human? The use of such a useless mode of being, according to Zhuang Zi, is that it promotes health and natural longevity to their fullest possible extent.

———————

In the following translation I arrange the passages by dominant theme, starting with the broad philosophical overview and setting each theme in the context of the previous one.

VASTNESS AND WANDERING BEYOND

The "Wandering Beyond" chapter of the *Zhuang Zi* explores two related themes: an appreciation of the value of cosmic vastness (*da* 大), and wandering beyond limitations as a means to cultivate vastness. The title of the first chapter of the *Zhuang Zi* has also been translated as "Free and Easy Wandering" and "Going Rambling without a Destination." Both of these reflect the sense of the Daoist who has retreated from the dangers of social life in order to live a healthy, joyful, and peaceful natural life. But this expression also implies going beyond the boundaries of familiarity. We ordinarily dwell within the limited realm of our social roles, expectations, and values. But Zhuang Zi dismisses the values that arise from this perspective as petty (*xiao* 小). It is only by freeing our imaginations to reconceive ourselves, and our worlds, that we may begin to understand the deeper tendencies of the Cosmic transformations. As we identify with the vast perspective of the Cosmos, we rise to a height from which formerly important distinctions lose what appeared to be their crucial significance.

From Chapter 1, *Xiao Yao You*, "Wandering Beyond"

1.1 In the northern darkness there is a fish: its name is "Kun."[2] Kun's size is so vast (*da* 大), we don't know how many thousands of miles it is. It transforms (*hua* 化) into a bird, named Phoeng,[3] whose wingspan is countless thousands of miles across. It gets aroused and flies off, its wings like clouds draped across the sky. As the oceans writhe, this bird begins to migrate towards the southern abyss. The southern abyss is the deep of the Cosmos.

Xie, from the state of Qi, documented extraordinary phenomena. He said, "When Phoeng journeys to the southern abyss, it beats the water for 3,000 miles, whirling and winding, rising, and then up 90,000 miles, because it will be gone for an interval of six months."

Wild horses! Clouds of dust![4]

Living creatures blow each other around with their breath.

(The deep azure of the sky (*tian*), is this an actual color? Or is it rather that its distance never reaches a limit? Then, looking down, it would be just the same.)[5]

If water is not collected deep enough it lacks the strength to support a great boat. Overturn a cup of water into a hollow in the floor, and a mustard seed will become a boat. But if you placed the cup there it would stick: this is because the water is too shallow and the 'boat' is too big. If the wind is not collected deep enough it would lack the strength to support great wings. Thus, only 90,000 miles up with the air currents below does it break through the winds. With the deep dark cosmos on its back, nothing can stop it short, and now it sets its course for the south.[6]

Comment: Guo Xiang (the Jin dynasty scholar and commentator who edited and rearranged the text) has a relativistic interpretation that became influential among Zhuang Zi interpreters. He comments that the reason that Phoeng has to fly so high is that its wings are too big.

---

2 Kun: The word also means 'fish roe' and so while evoking the sense of a primordial birth, it also creates a cognitive dissonance regarding the size of this creature.

3 Phoeng (Peng): With this neologism I try to incorporate the Tang dynasty commentator Lu Deming's suggestion that *Peng* is a phoenix (*feng* 鳳).

4 Translations usually overinterpret these powerful images. I prefer to leave this segment as literal as possible, since the text simply gives us the images and does not interpret them.

5 Some statements that have the feel of parenthetic remarks are placed in parentheses.

6 These passages have the feel of explanatory commentary. This is a common technique of early Chinese writing. Though the early texts make no physical differentiation, I have expressed this change in voice with italics throughout my translation.

The vast and the small each have their own distinctive spheres, and their own limitations. So neither should be considered better than the other; everything is equal in value.

Now, while Zhuang Zi is clearly discussing limiting conditions, it is not clear that his intention is to equalize the great and the small in this way. While it is true that the vast loses sight of distinctions noticed by the petty, it does not follow that they are thereby equalized, as Guo Xiang suggests. On the contrary, the mood of the whole chapter is to draw our attention to the greater value of a perspective that we ordinarily dismiss as pointless and irrelevant, far from human concerns. Indeed, the very next passage *explicitly* devalues the perspective of the petty in comparison with the vast: "petty understanding cannot match vast understanding." For the vast still embraces the petty in virtue of its very vastness. The petty, precisely in virtue of its limitations, is not able to reciprocate.

Moreover, Zhuang Zi will soon explicitly compare the Ruists with the petty creatures. This critique of Ruism continues throughout several of the strands of the *Zhuang Zi* anthology, and on its face appears to be inconsistent with the claim that this passage espouses an *all-inclusive* relativism. We will, however, find an articulation of a possible radical relativism when we reach the "Autumn Floods" chapter, further below.

The cicada and the scholar-pigeon laugh at it, saying "When we decide to rise up and fly, we dart to the elm and sappanwood trees, but sometimes we don't make it and simply rein ourselves back to the ground. What is it with this '90,000 miles to the south'!"

If you go off to the countryside you return after three meals with your belly still full. If you travel hundreds of miles you spend your nights pounding grain. If you travel thousands of miles, you must collect grain for three months. How could those two little birds understand this? Petty understanding cannot match vast understanding.

And the short-lived cannot compare with the long-lived. How do we know that this is so? The morning mushroom does not know dusk or dawn. The summer cicada does not know spring or fall. These are the short-lived. South of Chu there are the ming ling (spirits of the abyss) whose spring [i.e., youth] lasts 500 years, and whose autumn [i.e., age] lasts 500 years. In ancient times there was the great Chun, whose spring lasted 8,000 years, and whose fall lasted 8,000 years. But nowadays Peng Zu[7] is renowned for his longevity, and ordinary people measure their lives against his. Isn't this pathetic?

---

7   Peng Zu is a mythical figure said to have lived for several hundred years.

Comment: Again Guo Xiang here takes the ridicule of the little creatures at face value: everything has its own nature. Phoeng cannot take itself to be better than the little birds. The moral, according to this reading, would be that the Daoists cannot take themselves to be better than the Ruists. But the consequence of this would be that the Cosmic perspective of the Daoists and the social worries of the Ruists would have equal value. The inconsistency surely makes this interpretation implausible. Indeed, in context, the rhetorical force of the story is to expose the limitations and blindness of the petty creatures. (Compare this with Chapter 41 of the *Lao Zi*, "When the lowest officials hear of the way, they laugh at it; if they didn't laugh, it wouldn't be good enough to be the way.")

This is what Tang asked of Ji.[8] In the desolate north there is a dark ocean, the Lake of *Tian*. In it there is a fish several thousands of miles wide, and no one knows how long. Its name is Kun. In it there is a bird, whose name is Phoeng. Its back is like Mount Tai, its wings like clouds draped across the sky. It rides on the ram's horn whirlwind and rises 90,000 miles, breaks through the cloudy vapors, with the deep dark Cosmos behind its back. Then it heads south towards the southern abyss. The marsh quail laughs at it saying, "Where is *that* thing going! I leap and hop and rise no more than several yards before I drop, fluttering and hovering amidst the grasses. This indeed is the height of flying. Where is *that* thing going!" This is the dispute (*bian* 辯) between the vast (*da*) and the petty (*xiao*).

Comment: Here, the dispute between the vast and the petty represents the dispute between the Cosmically oriented 'Daoists' (though this is not a term they used for themselves) and the humanistic and socially oriented philosophers such as the Ruists and the Mohists.

Now, those whose understanding is apt for one position in office, whose conduct is suitable for one village, whose political efficacy (*de*) measures up to that of one ruler, and whose capacity manifests in one state, view themselves in just the same way. Yet Master Song Rong[9] would calmly smile at them. If the whole world praised him, it wouldn't encourage him; if the whole world rejected him, it wouldn't discourage

---

8   Chapter 5 of the *Lie Zi* is called "The Questions of Tang." There, Tang asks Ji about the vast (*da*), and the minuscule *xiao*—what is vaster than the vastest, what is more minute than the minuscule? The questions attempt to articulate a concern with the infinite and the infinitesimal. But there is no passage about Kun and Phoeng.

9   Song Zi, also called Song Qing: a somewhat stoic-minded scholar who was not motivated by either praise or blame.

him. He determined the difference between the inner and the outer; he distinguished the limits of honor and disgrace. That is all. He wasn't bothered by worldly things. Nevertheless, there was still something that hadn't yet taken root.

Now Lie Zi traveled by harnessing the winds: so cool and fine! He didn't return for fifteen days! Master Song Rong may have remained unbothered while spreading good fortune, and Lie Zi may have avoided walking, but there was still something they depended on (*dai*). If, however, they were to mount the axis of the Cosmos, and harness the changes of the six energies (*qi*) in order to wander through the inexhaustible, what then would there be to depend on?

So, it is said: "The person of consummate humanity (zhi ren 至人) *has no self* (ji 己); *the person of insightful spirit* (shen ren 神人) *has no accomplishment; the sage* (sheng ren 聖人) *has no name."*

> Comment: This passage represents the activities of those with political ambitions (including the Ruists), as seen from the lofty perspective of the Daoists. Below, in the human realm, they struggle for public recognition and social success, and have no inkling that in the grander scheme of things these goals have little value.
>
> 'The axis of the Cosmos' (*tian di zhi zheng* 天地之正) is a metaphor comparable with 'the axis of the way' (*dao shu* 道樞) that appears in the *Qi Wu Lun*, Chapter 2 of the *Inner Chapters* (p. 386, below). If all natural cyclical processes have a center of revolutions or oscillations, then perhaps the Cosmos as a whole can be thought of as having a unifying axis of its own. The claim seems to be that if one identifies with, and aligns oneself with, the center of the natural transformations of the Cosmos, then one will no longer be dependent on the alternating conditions of a confined life. "*Dai*" (待) means "depend on, wait on, wait for." One waits upon a partner, a double, or a ruler, a superior. In the context of Zhuangzian philosophy, it appears to refer to that on which one depends, some object or condition that allows one to be so. In the *Xun Zi* what one does not have to wait for is what one already is naturally.
>
> The last line mentions three types of ideal: the *zhi ren* (至人), the 'utmost' human, or person of consummate humanity; the *shen ren* (神人), the 'spirit' person, or person of insightful spirit; and the *sheng ren* (聖人), the sage, or wise person. These (in addition to the *zhen ren* (真人) which we will encounter later) should not be thought of as necessarily different kinds of people, but rather as exemplars of ideal Daoist qualities. It is also, I think, a mistake to try to order them as though they name distinct types of people, or hierarchies of rank (both of which are

completely inconsistent with the spirit of Zhuangzian Daoist thought). This would be like assuming that an honest person and a just person were two different kinds of people and that one has to be better than the other!

To have utmost humanity is to live in harmony with, and complete acceptance of, the transformations of the Cosmos. To have insightful spirit (*shen*) is to have a deep understanding of, and sensitivity to, the tendencies of transformation. The sage is simply a person who is profoundly wise, but the term is not always used positively in the *Zhuang Zi*: sometimes it is equated with the wisdom of the Ruist sages, and sometimes with the shrewdness of the unscrupulous.

Self, accomplishment, name (or renown) are goals of those who are interested in worldly pursuits. The Daoist ideals involve rejecting such 'petty' goals.

1.2 Yao, ceding the empire to Xu You, said, "If the Sun and Moon have come up and we don't extinguish the torches, isn't this just being excessively difficult about the light? If the seasonal rains have fallen, and we continue to water the fields, isn't this wasting excess labor on irrigation? Now you have your position [on the outside] and the empire is in order, and yet I [who am on the throne] feel like your mere body double. I find my role to be lacking, and request to pass on the empire to you."

Xu You replied, "But you have ordered the empire, and so the empire is already ordered. If I were to take over for you, would it be for the reputation? But the reputation is just a visitor after the real achievement. Am I to be a mere visitor?

"When a wren nests in a deep forest, it takes up no more than a single branch. When a vole drinks from a river, it takes no more than a bellyful. Go back, sir! I have no use for the empire. Even if a cook were to fail to run an orderly kitchen, a spirit medium wouldn't leap over the sacrificial vessels to take over his job."

Comment: Yao, the first sage-emperor of mythical antiquity, here represents the active pursuit of worldly government through cultivation of social virtues. Xu You, a recluse, represents the dismissive attitude of the Zhuangzian Daoists towards control of worldly affairs. And yet we also find here the seed of the Syncretist idea that a society, and even the whole empire, can be harmonious only when one subordinates rulership to cultivation of potency.

Guo Xiang takes the analogies of the forest creatures to imply that nothing must overstep its place in the social order. But Yao has already recognized that it is Xu You's potency that is responsible for the order of the empire, comparing him with the light of the Sun and Moon, and dismissing his own talents as no better than a torch fire. Earlier, the small birds with limited vision were compared to the Ruists, or those with social pretensions. (Following this analogy, I would suggest, in contrast with Guo Xiang's interpretation, that it is Yao and his empire that are being represented by the wren, the vole, and their miniature nesting places.)

1.3 Jian Wu asked a question of Lian Shu saying, "I heard the doctrines of Jie Yu:[10] vast (*da*) and entirely off the mark, off they went and never came back! I was astonished by them, endless (*wu ji* 無極) as the Milky Way, grand (*da*) and strange, not even coming close to the human condition (*ren qing* 人情[11])." Lian Shu replied, "What on earth did he say?"

"'In the distant Gu Ye mountains live the *shen ren* (神人 'marvelous' people). Their flesh and skin are like ice and snow; they are gentle and graceful as maidens. They eat no grains, but inhale the wind and drink the dew. They ride the cloudy *qi*, harness the flying dragons, and wander (*you* 遊) beyond the four seas. When they concentrate their spirit they protect creatures from disease, and make the yearly grain ripe for harvest.' I think this is crazy and will not believe a word of it."

"Of course," said Lian Shu, "the blind have no way to get anything from observing patterns and ornaments; the deaf have no means to get anything from the sound of bells and drums. How can it be only the body that has blindness and deafness? The understanding has them too. These doctrines are pregnant with meaning. These people, their potency (*de*), they are about to become co-embodied with all things. As a world in conflict clamors out, who would wear themselves out for its sake, and take on the affairs of the empire? These people! Nothing can harm them. A great flood could reach the heavens, but they would not drown. An intense heat wave might melt metal and stone and scorch the land and hills, but they would not burn. Yao or Shun[12] could be molded from their dust and chaff! Who would be willing to take on [worldly] things as their business?"

> *Comment:* Wandering beyond the four seas implies going beyond the realms of ordinary human and social concern. This metaphor also represents reaching the innermost recesses of the human spirit (which perhaps

---

10 The madman of Chu. He appears also in *Analects* 18.5 (not in this anthology). He is a recluse who ridicules Confucius for his attempts to 'save the world.'

11 *Ren qing*—human circumstances, human feelings, including human relations.

12 The mythical sage emperors of old, who have never been surpassed in virtue, and who devoted themselves to bringing the world to order and harmony.

coincide with the outermost reaches of the Cosmos) through intensive meditative cultivation.

The traditional significance of dragons includes: transformation, power, energy, flexibility, and shape-shifting; they are considered to be potent, pliant beings who have the power to protect people. Here, they seem to represent the potent forces of nature. The essential point of the passage is that there is a realm of concern that goes beyond the troubles of the social order.

Note that the *shen ren* are initially described as having marvelous abilities, but are subsequently described in terms that evoke the 'stoic' tranquility of the *zhen ren*, the genuinely human, which we will encounter in Chapter 6 (pp. 353–54). Though the grammar is ambiguous, the rhetoric implies that although such people are at one with nature and promote health and well-being, they would never enter political office to attempt to bring harmony to a world in disorder.

A person from the state of Song did business in ceremonial headwear, and sent it (south) to the state of Yue. But the people of Yue shaved their heads and tattooed their bodies, and had no use for them.

Yao governed the people of the empire and reigned peacefully over all within the four seas. He went for an audience with the four masters of the distant Gu Ye mountains. But at the southern banks of the Fen River he fell into a daze and lost his empire there.

Comment: The people and place names seem to function 'metonymically' here: they stand in for the cultural values of the people and places they are associated with. Song is a state in the central plains, the refuge of the descendants of the displaced Shang royalty; here it represents the traditional culture admired by the Ruists, as does the sage emperor, Yao. Yue is a state in the south, dismissively treated by the inhabitants of the central plains as 'barbaric.' If Song represents the 'high' culture of the Ruists, then here Yue represents those who have 'no use' for such culture. The same seems to be true of the significance of the Fen River, a tributary of the Yellow River in the central plains (in modern-day Shanxi province). Yao has thus probably returned from his visit to the mythical Gu Ye mountains when he loses himself and his empire in this way.

1.4 Hui Zi said to Zhuang Zi, "The king of Wei [aka King Hui of Liang] presented me with seeds of a huge (*da*) gourd. I planted them, and they grew into fruit that weighed five stone! If filled with liquids, they weren't strong enough to support themselves. If cut into ladles, they were too shallow to contain anything. They were indeed extraordinarily big, but I thought they were useless, so I smashed them." Zhuang Zi replied, "You, sir, are certainly inept at making use of the vast.

"In Song, there were people who excelled at making a cream for chapped hands. For generation after generation they remained in the silk-bleaching business. A traveler heard about their hand cream, and offered to buy the formula for a 100 pieces of gold. They gathered the clan together and considered the proposition, saying: 'For generations we've been bleaching silk, but have barely made a few pieces of gold. Now, in one day we can sell the technique for a hundred! Let's give it to him.'

"The traveler took it, and persuaded the king of Wu to use it. The state of Yue was causing trouble, and so the king of Wu deployed him as a general. In the winter he engaged in a naval battle with the people of Yue, and soundly defeated them. Their territory was divided, and he was enfeoffed.

"Its emollient capacity was the same: but one used it to gain a territory, while the others did not escape bleaching silk. So, the use to which they put it was different.

"Now, you had gourds that weighed five stone. Why didn't you consider making them into giant floats, and drift over rivers and lakes? Instead you worry about their being too shallow to contain anything. This is because your mind is still overgrown."

Comment: The association of vastness with uselessness (*wu yong* 無用) continues in this and the following passage. Now, a soaring imagination from the perspective of the Cosmos may be wild and wonderful, but it is extremely impractical and seems altogether useless from the perspective of our daily concerns, as Hui Zi implies. But Zhuang Zi chides him for failing to recognize the value of the vast, because his mind is 'overgrown,' that is, filled with ingrained preconceptions that block creative freedom and expansive insight. A creative and spontaneous engagement with the world around us requires that we empty our minds of such preconceptions. In the same way, in §1.3 above, Lian Shu expresses disappointment in Jian Wu; his inability to appreciate the usefulness of the vast is a kind of blindness of the spirit.

The useless does have a kind of use, but not the kind of use that manifests on the ordinary level of practical affairs. Its 'use' lies in the cultivation and nurturing of the *shen* (spirit, or insightful capacity), in protecting the ancestral, and preserving one's life, so that one can last out one's natural years to the fullest and flourish, even if the simplicity of such a natural life seems unsuccessful and unappealing from a worldly point of view.

The allegory of the traveler, however, does not seem entirely in keeping with the spirit of Daoist philosophy. He appears to be praised for gaining riches and territory by succeeding in battle, but none of these worldly values would mean anything to a Daoist. These are precisely the kinds of uses that are criticized by the Zhuangzian Daoists. For this reason, I use italics to suggest a voice of interpolated commentary.

1.5 Hui Zi said to Zhuang Zi, "I have a huge (*da*) tree. People say it's a chu tree.[13] Its giant trunk is gnarly and swollen, and can't be made to match a plumb line. Its smaller branches are knotted and twisted, and can't be made to match compasses and square. It stands by the roadside, and no carpenter pays any attention to it. Now, your teachings too are vast and useless, and so everyone rejects them."

Zhuang Zi replied, "Haven't you seen a wildcat or weasel? It bends and crouches low, and lies in wait for passers-by. It leaps and pounces in all directions, avoiding neither heights nor depths—but then it falls right into a trap, and dies in a net. Now, the yak is vast, as clouds draped across the sky—vast indeed! But it cannot catch a mouse.

"Now, you have a huge tree, and worry that it's useless. Why don't you plant it in a village of nothing at all, an empty wilderness, dilly-dally 'doing nothing' (*wu wei*) by its side, 'wandering beyond' while sleeping beneath it. Its life won't be chopped short by the carpenter's axe; nothing will harm it; if there is no place to make use of it, where can it come to grief?"

Comment: The plumb line, compasses, and square are tools used by carpenters to impose a straightforward uniformity on nature, to tame its excesses. They are instruments used in transforming natural materials into artificial tools. The Mohists make practical use of these carpenters' instruments, and in their philosophy apply them as metaphors to explain how to bring order to language, and to society. The same metaphors will also be used by Xun Zi as a measure of proper conduct. Zhuang Zi here attempts to undermine this sensibility with a radical re-evaluation of what is valuable from a less humanistic perspective.

In the *Lao Zi*, *wu wei* (無為 literally, "doing nothing") is a laissez faire means of ordering a state. In the *Zhuang Zi* it has an entirely apolitical significance. Success should not be measured in terms of social achievement. Rather, one should flourish harmoniously with nature, far from the machinations of political power. *Wu wei* involves undermining (*wu* 無) the artifices (為 *wei*) of linguistic construction, social conventions,

---

13   Latin *Ailanthus altissima*—'tree of heaven,' a tree that grows tall very quickly.

and moral judgments. From a conventional perspective, a person who finds value communing spontaneously with nature, and taking delight in the Cosmos, appears utterly useless.

Superficially, Zhuang Zi seems to be criticizing the yak for being vast and useless. But this is inconsistent with the general tenor of Zhuangzian philosophy, which praises the vast and the use of the useless. If we reverse the order of presentation of the two creatures, however, the significance of the analogy becomes clear: the vast creature may be useless for catching worthless vermin, but the wildcat and the weasel risk cutting short their natural years precisely because of their usefulness.

Notice that 'wandering beyond' is here associated with sleep, and later will be associated with dreaming. In sleep one wanders beyond the ordinary boundaries that define the world of everyday consciousness. In dreams one lives new, unheard of possibilities. (In other passages in the anthology, dreaming has a different significance: life is a mere dream, while death is an awakening.)

PHILOSOPHY OF VASTNESS AS DEVELOPED IN THE *OUTER CHAPTERS*

Chapter 17 of the *Zhuang Zi*, known as the "Autumn Floods," develops the philosophy of vastness, and explores several possible significances of cultivating an ever-expanding perspective: spatial, temporal, doctrinal, pragmatic, and ethical. It is in this chapter that we find an *explicit* attempt to equalize the vast and the minute, and thereby to deny the superiority of the vast. (Many interpreters take these passages as justifying Guo Xiang's reading of Chapter 1 of the *Inner Chapters* as a form of radical relativism.) Since the larger and the smaller are here equalized, it is no longer appropriate to translate the term "*xiao*" 小 as 'petty.'

I have divided the chapter into eight passages. The first seven (a to g) take up several questions about the nature of vastness and the consequences of iterating the process of expanding one's perspective: (a) encountering the vast; (b) no absolute standards; (c) the indivisible and the unencompassable; (d) application to relative measure and value; (e) context-dependence of function and value; (f) consequences for action; and (g) the paradox of valuing (*gui* 貴) *dao*. The last passage (h) explicitly addresses the significance of the distinction between the Cosmic (*tian* 天) and the human (*ren* 人). The reader should not presuppose that the answers given to each question necessarily combine to form a single consistent theory. Indeed, some passages espouse a pragmatic contextualism, while others argue for more radical forms of relativism.

From Chapter 17, "Autumn Floods"

(a)

The time of the autumn floods had arrived! And streams by the hundreds gushed out into the Yellow River. The current was so vast that from one bank to the other you wouldn't be able to distinguish a cow from a horse. The Lord of the River was delighted at this, and so pleased with himself that he took all the beauty of the entire world to lie within himself.

He flowed along, moving east, until he finally arrived at the Northern Ocean. But as he looked eastwards, he could see no end to the waters! At this, Lord River began to reel, turning in all directions; then, gazing out toward Ruo, the Northern Ocean, he sighed and said, "There's a popular saying: 'I've heard about the way a hundred times, and yet continue to believe that nothing compares to me.' That was me. I had heard those who belittled the learning of Confucius and trivialized the virtuous behavior of Bo Yi,[14] but I didn't believe them. Now I set eyes upon your inexhaustibility. If I had not arrived at your gate, it would have been disastrous. I would have been ridiculed relentlessly by the school of the way of Vastness."

Ruo the Northern Ocean said, "You can't discuss the ocean with a frog in a well, because it's stuck in its hole. You can't talk about ice with a summer insect, because it's limited by its season. And you can't discuss the way with bent-over scholars (*shi* 士), because they are tied down by their doctrines. But, only now that you have emerged from the cliffs and banks and gaze into the vast ocean, do you understand how pathetic you are. So now I can discuss the natural ordering (*li* 理) of Vastness with you.

"Of all the waters in the whole world, none are vaster than me, the ocean. All the rivers return to me, and yet no one knows when I could ever be filled. I drain away at the center, and yet no one knows when I could ever be emptied. Neither spring nor autumn alters me; neither flood nor drought has any impact on my awareness. I surpass immeasurably the currents of the Yellow and Yangzi Rivers. And yet I have never taken myself to be much on account of this. I was formed by the Cosmos and received my *qi* (energy) from *yin* and *yang*. My presence in the world is like a pebble or sapling on a great mountain. How could I take myself to be much when I remain aware of my paltriness?

---

14 Bo Yi and his brother Shu Qi were known for their commitment to virtuous behavior. They remonstrated with King Wu, and preferred to starve themselves to death, rather than engage in what they perceived to be an unethical battle. The Utopian Daoists sometimes use them as examples of the dangers of ethical high-mindedness.

"When you assess the four seas against the Cosmos in which they lie, don't they seem like a puddle in a vast marsh? When you reckon the extent of the Central States within the fours seas, doesn't it seem like a mere grain in a vast silo?

"We number things by the 'tens of thousands,' but humans constitute only one of them. Even in the nine regions where *humans* throng, where the harvest grains are produced, and boats and carts pass through, humans take their place as only one among them. Compared with the myriads of things, don't they seem like a wisp of down on the body of a horse? [...]"

> *Comment (encountering the vast):* We fully come to terms with our own limitations only when we are confronted with something vaster. This process can be repeated indefinitely.
>
> Here, the Northern Ocean uses the term "*li*" (理) to refer to the recursively embedded relationship between the larger and the smaller, where what seems at first large becomes a minor detail in a larger context. This 'fractal' type patterning continues indefinitely, each stage of magnification (or order of magnitude) making the previous stage seem petty in comparison.

(b)

Lord River replied, "If that is so, then if I took the Cosmos as vast and a wisp of down as small, would that be acceptable (*ke* 可)?"

Northern Ocean said, "No! Regarding 'things': their measure is inexhaustible (*wu qiong* 無窮), their seasons continue endlessly, their proportions have no constancy (*chang* 常), their ends and beginnings no fixed reason (*wu gu* 無故). For this reason (*gu* 故), when great (*da*) understanding observes the near and the distant, it does not take the small to be little or the vast to be much, because it understands that measure is inexhaustible; when appraising past and present, it does not brood over what is far gone, or yearn for what is close at hand, because it understands that the seasons will continue endlessly; when examining the processes of filling and emptying, it is not happy to gain or worried about loss, because it understands that proportions have no constancy; when illuminating the open path ahead, it does not delight in living or consider dying a misfortune, because it understands that ends and beginnings cannot be held onto.

"In reckoning what humans know, it does not compare what we do not know. The time during which we live does not compare with the time before living. So, to attempt to use the utterly minute to exhaust the realm of the utterly vast is muddled and deluded, and cannot succeed. Looking at it this way, how could we know whether a wisp of down is enough to determine the limit of the utterly minute, or whether the Cosmos is enough to determine the realm of the utterly vast?"

> *Comment (no absolute standards)*: Great (*da*) understanding is understanding from the perspectives of the Vast (*da*): not confined to any particular position, but ever expanding. In this way, nothing ever retains its prior value: what at any time appears to be the greatest will always diminish and will eventually become minuscule. In this passage, the term "*chang*" does appear to be used in the sense of 'constancy': looking down from above, nothing endures forever; all the events of life, from birth to death, and everything in between, form a relentless stream of change.
>
> In evaluating philosophical disputes, the question asked is not whether claims are 'true' or 'false,' but whether they are acceptable (*ke* 可) or unacceptable (*bu ke* 不可). This appears to be true across philosophical schools, and even in non-philosophical contexts, and suggests that even when ultimate questions are at stake, the presupposition is not necessarily that of a thoroughgoing realism. That is, the question is not whether the Cosmos is vast *in itself*, but whether it can be taken to be the vastest in terms of *our understanding*. Again, at the end of this passage, the rhetorical question is phrased epistemologically: how could we *know whether* the Cosmos is the ultimately vast?

(c)

Lord River said, "The debaters of the world all say, 'The finest essence (*zhi jing* 至精) has no apparent form; the utterly vast cannot be encompassed.' Is this a trustworthy account of the conditions of things?"

Northern Ocean replied, "If we look at the vast from the perspective of the minute, it cannot be taken in its entirety; if we look at the minute from the perspective of the vast, it doesn't appear clearly. The finest essence is the small at its most subtle; the expansive is the vast at its grandest. Thus, the difference is contextual and lies in the relative circumstances (*shi* 勢).

"Now, fineness and coarseness are limited to what has form. But the formless is what number cannot subdivide, and the unencompassable is what number cannot exhaust. The coarseness of things can be discussed with language (*yan* 言), and the fineness of things can be reached with thoughts (*yi* 意). But what language cannot discuss and what thoughts cannot reach for scrutiny is what is not limited to the fine and the coarse."

Comment (the indivisible and the unencompassable): The empirical world, the world of form, can be characterized in terms of relative 'fineness' and 'coarseness,' which are observable. They remain within the realm of linguistic discussion and are thinkable. At the (infinite) extremes, the fine ('microscopic') becomes formless, and the coarse ('macroscopic') becomes as unencompassable, and in this sense cannot be reached by language and thought. The finest essence (*zhi jing* 至精) is the unattainable limiting condition: the end point of the result of diminishing if it ever could be achieved. But the infinitesimally small effectively has no finite form. Since only what has form can be subdivided, the formless cannot be subdivided. This is directly contrary to the Greek concept of the atom, according to which the smallest physical form must be indivisible. Here, the claim is that anything that has form must be divisible; the only indivisible would be that which has nothing to divide.

"*Shi*" 勢 is a term that refers to the shifting array of potentials that make up a terrain. In texts on military strategy it is often translated as 'strategic advantage'; François Jullien's rendition of the term as 'propensity' has been influential. In this passage, it is used to refer to the context-dependence that arises as conditions transform perspectivally; so I have rendered it here as 'relative circumstances.'

(d)

Lord River asked, "How far can we extend things, inwardly and outwardly, to the limiting points (*ni* 倪) of value (*gui* 貴) and inferiority (*jian* 賤), or the limiting points of the small and the vast?"

Northern Ocean replied, "Looking at them from the perspective of the way, nothing is noble (*gui* 貴) or inferior. While looking at them from the perspective of things, they each consider themselves noble and the other inferior. But from the point of view of custom, neither value nor inferiority lies within oneself.

"Observing their discrepancies, if you consider something big because it is relatively big, then of all the varieties of things, not one is not big; and if you consider something small because it is relatively small, then nothing is not small. But when you understand that the Cosmos is a mere grain, and that a wisp of down is a mountain, then you have seen the measure of difference!

"Observing their achievements, if you consider something to be present (*you* 有) because of what is present, then nothing is not present; and if you consider it to be lacking (*wu* 無) because of what it lacks, then nothing is not lacking. But when you understand that east and west are counterparts to each other that cannot mutually be lacking, then you can determine the portions of achievement.

"Observing their preferences, if you take something to be right (*ran* 然; literally, 'so') because of where it is right, then nothing is not right; if you take it as wrong (*fei* 非) because of where it is wrong, then everything is wrong. But, if you understand that Yao and Jie took themselves to be right while taking each other to be wrong, then you will see how to grasp their preferences."

> *Comment (application to relative measure and value):* Lord River pushes the question of the limiting points (*ni* 倪) of the greater and the lesser, regarding both size (*da xiao* 大小), and value (*gui* 貴 high value, nobility; *jian* 賤 low value, inferiority, baseness). The Northern Ocean explicitly draws a radically relativistic conclusion from the discussion of the relativity of the vast and the petty. At each point of value everything below will be considered inferior. But from the perspective of the whole (if it could ever be attained) everything is superior to something (everything below it) and inferior to something else (everything above it). The conclusion is drawn that from the ultimate perspective there can be no such thing as superiority and inferiority, as everything would have both qualities. It is only when you can know how to attribute either quality that you truly understand the measure of value (which seems to be that it has no ultimate value).

(e)

"[...] A battering ram may be used to breach a city wall, but it cannot be used to plug up a cavity. This is because they are specialized (*shu* 殊) tools. Qiji and Hualiu were steeds who could gallop a thousand miles in a single day, but they couldn't catch a mouse the way a cat or fox does. This is because of their specific (*shu* 殊) skills. At night, an owl can pincer a flea and scrutinize a wisp of down, but in broad daylight with eyes wide open it couldn't see a hill or mountain. This is because of its specific natural tendencies.

"Thus, if you say, 'Why not follow right (*shi* 是) and eliminate wrong? Follow orderly government and eliminate disorder?' This is to have failed to understand the natural make-up (*li* 理) of the Cosmos, or the conditions (*qing* 情) of the variety of things. It would be like following the sky and eliminating the earth, or following *yin* and eliminating *yang*. It is clear that this is not feasible. So, to insist on talking this way is either foolish or deceptive [...]"

Comment (context-dependence of function and value): The function and value of things depends upon context and purpose. Functions and abilities are specific (*shu* 殊) to the types of things: everything is capable of something, and for that very reason not capable of other things. The specific conditions that enable a capability are also conditions that prevent other abilities. From this sort of relativity, a skeptical conclusion is drawn about right and wrong, order and disorder. It is impossible to eradicate disorder: what appears orderly to us now will appear disorderly in a different context or from a different perspective, and vice versa. This sort of skepticism is often found in postmodern critiques of the concept of 'progress.' But while it may be true that perfect order is unattainable, it doesn't follow that no progress can be made. A society in which racial injustice has been overcome, for example, may not be perfect: it may have countless other problems evident from other contexts, some of them even resulting from having taken steps to overcome the injustice. But this does not mean that the eradication of racial injustice itself is not an improvement.

(f)

Lord River asked, "If that is so, then what should I do, and what should I not do? In the end, should I accept or decline, follow my inclinations or renounce them?"

Northern Ocean replied, "From the perspective of the way, how could there be honorable and inferior? [...] How could there be less or more? [...]

> Stern! Like the ruler of a state, whose favors are impartial;
> Generous! Like the earth god at a sacrifice, whose blessings are
> > impartial;
> Vast! Like the inexhaustibility of all directions, with no bounded
> > regions.

If you embrace all things, which will you take under your wing? This is to be without a direction. If all things are smoothed out, which would be shorter or longer?

"The way is without end or beginning, and yet things have their living and dying, though they are never sure they will reach fulfillment; they continuously alternate between emptying and filling, taking no stand in any particular form. The years cannot be held up, the seasons cannot be paused: dissipating, growing, filling, and emptying, they end and then begin again. This is the crux of how we talk about the significance of vastness, and how the varieties of things fit together (*li* 理). Creatures live as though rushing and galloping: there is no action in which they are not altering, no moment in which they are not changing. What should you do? What should you not do? Surely you will transform by yourself!"

Comment (consequences for action): The consequence of such a radically relativistic view for practical action is that it makes no difference one way or the other: nothing is more honorable or less, and nothing is more inferior or less, because there is no objective measure of 'more' and 'less.' Everything is to be equally embraced. Something will inevitably happen, and we should not worry about whether it is for the better or the worse, because the evaluative distinctions have no ultimate value. This is an explicit statement that all value judgments should be abandoned.

The last paragraph presents a process cosmology, in which it is stated that there is no moment in which things are not altering and changing. So, even if one doesn't act, something will inevitably happen.

(g)

Lord River asked, "If that is so, then *why value (gui 貴) the way at all?*"

Northern Ocean replied, "To understand the way one must thoroughly understand *li* (理). To have profound understanding of *li* one must be clear about balances of power. If one is clear about balances of power one will not harm oneself with 'things.'

"Those with the greatest potency: fire cannot burn them, water cannot drown them; the midwinter cold and midsummer heat cannot harm them; wild beasts cannot do them injury. This does not mean that they make light of these things; it means that they scrutinize safety and danger, but remain tranquil whether in good fortune or bad, and are cautious about where they tend towards or away from. This is why nothing can harm them.

"Hence it is said, '*Tian* lies within, the human extends outward; potency lies in *tian*. Understand both cosmic and human processes (*xing* 行); root yourself in the Cosmos, establish your place through potency. Advancing or retreating, shrinking or stretching, return to the essential in order to discuss the extremes.'"

Comment (paradox of valuing dao): Lord River correctly notices the logical problem regarding any philosophical view that promotes adopting no values. To promote such a view is to consider it to be of value, and so to adopt that view we would have to be persuaded that it is more valuable than not adopting it, or at least that it is not less valuable than not adopting it. If we are not persuaded that it has any value, then we would not have any motive to adopt it. If the way is to renounce all evaluations, then that leaves us with no reason to value the way at all. Isn't valuing the way (of not valuing) inconsistent?

Northern Ocean's response attempts to resolve the problem by eliminating the notion of 'valuing' from the discussion altogether: we need only to understand everything as it actually is. If we do so, then we will understand the conditions of things and will be able to keep ourselves free from harm. The implication of this type of answer is that this does not really amount to 'valuing' the way; it is simply a matter of understanding it as it is. We are to refrain from imposing artificial values on natural conditions and instead allow them to teach us their own circumstances. While this is a strong response, it is not clear whether it really succeeds in being free from all evaluative concepts altogether. After all, it presupposes that we ought to avoid harm, that there is such a thing as the way the world functions (*xing* 行), and that we ought to learn to understand these processes.

(h)

Lord River asked, "What do you mean by '*tian*'? What do you mean by 'human' (*ren* 人)?"

Northern Ocean replied, "That cows and horses have four legs: this is *tian*. Tethering a horse's head and piercing an ox's snout: this is *ren*. Thus, it is said, 'Do not use the human to destroy *tian*; do not use deliberation to destroy the life into which you have been called by the Cosmos; do not gain by dying for the sake of reputation. Be cautious and preserve it: do not lose it! This is called returning (*fan* 反) to the genuine (*zhen* 真)."

> *Comment (explanation of the Cosmic and the human):* Note that the explanations of *tian* and *ren* are not definitions. Rather, they attempt to give paradigm cases that exemplify the relevant characteristics. From the contrast between the two paradigms we are to infer further ranges of significance and application of these two terms. The contrast is between what occurs naturally and what happens as a result of human transformation of the natural. It is by reflecting and meditating more deeply on the conditions of such human transformations that we deepen our understanding of the philosophical significance of the contrast.

[...] Gongsun Long said to Prince Mou of Wei, "When I was young I studied the way of the former kings. As I grew older I became clear about the practice of humanity and appropriateness; I merged the same and the different, while separating the hard from the white. What is so I made to be not so, what was acceptable to be unacceptable. I confounded the understanding of the philosophers of the various schools, and exhausted the arguments of all the speakers. I thought I had reached the epitome of far-reaching understanding. But now, I hear the doctrines of Master Zhuang and I am adrift in their strangeness. I can't tell if it is my arguments or my understanding that fall short of his. Now, there's no way I'd open my beak. I dare ask, what is your explanation of this?"

Prince Mou leaned on his portable scholar's desk and sighed deeply, looked up to the sky and smiled, saying, "Haven't you heard about the frog in the well? It said to the turtle of the Eastern Ocean, 'I am so happy! I leap onto the railing of the well, and I stop to rest where a brick is missing from the wall. When I enter the water, it touches my armpits and supports my chin, and when I fall in the mud it buries my feet all the way up to the arches. The mosquito larvae, crabs, and tadpoles in my surroundings are no match for me. To take possession of the water of a gulley and to pounce and grab all the joy of a well: this is as good as it gets! Why don't you come in some time to take a look?' But before the turtle of the Eastern Ocean put in its left foot, its right knee got stuck. At that, it backed out hesitantly, and told the frog about the ocean, 'A distance of a thousand miles would not be sufficient to extol its vastness; a height of a thousand fathoms would not be enough to plumb its depths. During the time of Yu, after ten years and nine floods its waters were not increased. During the time of Tang, after eight years and seven droughts its shorelines were not diminished. To remain undeviating for an instant or an aeon, neither advancing nor retreating when increased or diminished, this indeed is the greatest joy of the Eastern Ocean.' On hearing this, the well frog was astonished, and lost itself in a daze.

"Now, with your wits unable to understand the limits of dichotomous evaluation (*shi fei*), you still desire to examine the discourse of Master Zhuang. This is like making a mosquito carry a mountain on its back, or a millipede gallop across the Yellow River. You couldn't possibly succeed in such a task. With wits unable to understand the discourse of the ultimate mysteries, you are satisfied with the advantages of a single age. Isn't this to be a frog in a well?" [...]

TRANSFORMATION: LIVING AND DYING WITH TRANQUILITY

The sixth of the *Inner Chapters*, "The Vast Ancestral Teacher," proposes that tranquility comes from acceptance of Circumstance and of the transformations of life and death. This philosophy is similar in many ways to that of the Stoics. The first part of this chapter is devoted to a discussion of the *zhen ren*: the 'genuine person,' or 'person of genuine humanity.' The genuinely human person, the *zhen ren*, is in tune with the cycles of nature, and is not upset by the vicissitudes of life. They are integrated with things, and yet not tied down by them; they are in tune with the cycles of nature, and are not disturbed or harmed by them. This is sometimes expressed with the hyperbole that the *zhen ren* can never be drowned by the ocean, nor burned by fire.

The second part of the chapter hints at the process by which we are to cultivate our genuine and natural humanity. These are meditative practices and psychophysical disciplines—'yogas' perhaps—by which we learn how to nourish the ancestral root of life that is within us. We learn how to return to an axis of stability around which the cycles of emotional turbulence flow, and so are able to maintain equanimity.

This entire process is understood through the metaphor of a potter's wheel, and simultaneously as a whetstone and as a grindstone, on which things are formed, and arise, sharpened, and are ground back down, only to be transformed afresh. With each 'birth' (*sheng* 生) some 'thing' (*wu* 物) new arises, flourishes, develops through its natural (*tian* 天) tendencies (*xing* 性), and then still following its natural tendencies, responding to those of its natural environment, it winds down: enters (*ru* 入) back into the undifferentiated (*wu* 無) from which it emerged (*chu* 出). The truest friendship arises when members of a community identify with this unknown undifferentiated process in which they are embedded, have 'forgotten' differences between self and other, and spontaneously follow the natural developments of which they are inseparable participants.

From Chapter 6, *Da Zong Shi*, "The Vast Ancestral Teacher"

6.1 One who understands what *tian* does and what humans do has reached the utmost. One who understands what *tian* does lives according to *tian*. One who understands what humans do uses what the understanding understands to nurture what it does not understand. To complete one's natural (*tian*) years and not die midway: this is the flourishing of the understanding.

Nevertheless, there is a danger: the understanding (*zhi* 知) has its conditions (*dai* 待) for being correct (*dang* 當), but the conditions remain particularly undetermined (*te wei ding*). So, how can we be sure whether what we call 'natural' is not human, or whether what we call 'human' is not natural? Only with genuine humanity (*zhen ren*) does genuine understanding follow.

What is genuine humanity? The genuinely human of ancient times did not rebel against poverty, were not vainglorious in achievement, and did not make plans for affairs. Being like this, they did not regret making mistakes or take pride in getting things right. Such people as this could climb high without trembling, enter water without getting soaked, or enter fire without getting hot. Such is the ability of this understanding to reach the heights of the way.

The genuinely human (*zhen ren*) of ancient times, didn't dream when sleeping, and had no worries when awake. They did not delight in their food. Their breathing was deep! The breathing of the genuinely human arises from the heels. That of most people comes from the throat: crushed into submission, they retch out their verbalizations. Their addictive desires are deep; their natural impulses are shallow.

Comment: The correctness of understanding (*zhi* 知), or knowledge, is understood through the metaphors of 'dependence' and 'alignment.' "*Dai*" (待) means 'to depend on' or 'to wait for.' Here, "*suo dai*" ('what it depends on') refers to the preconditions for the correct 'alignment' (*dang* 當) of the understanding: its 'matching' (*dang* 當) the actual conditions. Our understanding of what is genuinely natural and what is genuinely human depends on the actual conditions of things. But if these conditions have not yet been settled, if they remain undetermined or indeterminate, then how can we understand where to draw the line between the natural (*tian*) and the human (*ren*)? Is there even a clear line at all? Is it relative? Or is it 'indeterminate' (*te wei ding*)? (This theoretical issue will be taken up in detail in my (SC) discussion of Chapter 2 of the *Zhuang Zi* below) Are there perhaps degrees of humanness or naturalness? The answer given is that we would only know for sure what genuine (the most natural) humanity is when we attain it and embody it: this would be the most genuine type of understanding. This creates a problem of circularity, because we need to have some sense of what to cultivate *before* we achieve it.

But of course, we must have some guiding sense of what it is, however vague, if we are even to be able to name the concept. Genuine humanity, "*zhen ren*," would be the most authentic and natural quality of being human, prior to any and all social and cultural artifices, the ideal of natural humanity which the Daoist tries to recover. This is explained as being thoroughly at one with all the natural circumstances and transformations of the Cosmos, a life of imperturbable tranquility.

The genuinely human of ancient times understood not to delight in living, or to despise dying. They emerged (*chu*) [into life] without rejoicing, and went back in (*ru*) without resistance. They simply went freely and came freely, not forgetting where they began or seeking out their end; they accepted it joyfully and returned it without a second thought. This is what is called not diminishing the way with one's *xin* (heart–mind: emotions and intentions), not assisting the natural with the human. This is called 'genuine humanity.' Being like this, their hearts were oblivious, their faces were tranquil, their brows were open. Cool as autumn, and warm as spring [...]

[...] Thus, in their likes and dislikes they were unified; in their unification and disunification they were unified. In their unification they were followers of *tian*; in disunification they were followers of humanity. When the natural and the human do not defeat each other, this is called genuine humanity.

> *Comment:* The metaphors of emerging (*chu* 出) and entering (*ru* 入) refer to the processes of being born and dying. They connote the emergence of a plant into light and the return into the darkness, from and to the earth.
>
> The heart–mind (*xin*) is seen as the means by which humans seek to add to the natural world. Mo Zi and Xun Zi attribute the human constructs to the cognitive activities (intentions, desires, and plans) of the *xin*. With these, humans seek to improve upon the conditions of the natural world. Such hubris is considered dangerous from a Daoist perspective.
>
> But notice that the most genuine humanity occurs not only when the human does not defeat the natural, or assist the natural, it also occurs when the natural does not overcome the human. There is a balance between the two that comes from the Cosmos itself. Genuine humanity must, after all, be genuinely *human*.

6.2 Living and dying are matters of Circumstance (*ming*). Their having the constant regularity (*chang*) of evening and morning is natural (*tian*), what humans can do nothing about, the conditions (*qing*) of things. They especially treat *tian* as 'father' and seem concerned for it; but how much more should they surpass this! People take their lords as especially exceeding themselves, and would even die for them. How much more should they do so for the most genuine! [...]

The vast mass (*da kuai* 大塊) encumbers me with a physical form, burdens me with a life, eases me through old age, and rests me in death. So, what makes my life good is what makes my death good too.

Now, if we store a boat in a gulley, or a fishing net in a marsh, we might say it is secure. But in the middle of the night a strong person could haul it away, while we sleep unaware. Still, it is appropriate to store the smaller in the larger, though it might slip away. But if you store the whole world in the whole world, then there is no place for it to slip away to. This is the great condition of enduring (*heng* 恆) things.

You manage to seize on a human form and seem happy with it. But if the human form keeps transforming without yet reaching a limit, can its joys be successfully planned? So, the wise wander where nothing can escape and everything is preserved: they find it good to die young and good to die old; they find the beginning good, and the end. Ordinary people emulate this. But how much greater is that which ties all things together, and on which the continuous transformations depend!

> *Comment:* Circumstance (*ming* 命) is what we can do nothing about; it is simply the condition (*qing* 情) of things. The constant regularity (*chang* 常) of the transformations of the natural world, including living and dying: this is just the way the Cosmos is. The Confucians treat *tian* as like a 'father,' but from a Daoist perspective this analogy pales in comparison with the vastness of the Cosmos. Here the term "*heng*" (恆) is used, which means "enduring" and has an explicit sense of 'unchanging permanence.'
>
> The existential lesson to be learned is that we should identify with the whole. When we do so, no transformation can ever count as a loss. From this perspective, the whole endures through the constant transformations.

6.3 Thus, *dao* has its specific conditions (*qing*) and its reliability; without artifice (*wu wei*), without form; although it can be passed down, it cannot be received; it is attainable, and yet cannot appear.

From itself, its own root, before the heavens and the earth, from ancient times it remains steadfast. It inspirits (*shen*) both the spirits and the divine emperor; it produces both the heavens and the earth. It is above the greatest extreme, but is not high, beneath the six directions, but is not deep; produced before the Cosmos and yet is not long-lived; older than the greatest antiquity and yet is not old. [. . .]

> *Comment:* In this passage, an attempt is made to articulate the conditions, or characteristics, of the way. But this attempt runs into paradoxical limits. Insofar as the way is understood as that which produces all things, it cannot be 'located' among them. Metaphorically, it remains 'above,' 'beyond,' and 'prior' to them, and yet cannot literally have these qualities.

This is one of the few passages where a discourse that implies 'transcendence' is explicitly applied to *dao*. In other passages, while *dao* remains subtle and diffuse, it also remains a thoroughly worldly phenomenon.

6.5 Master Si, Master Yu, Master Li, and Master Lai said to each other, "Whoever can take 'no-thing' as the head, living as the spine, and dying as the rump, whoever understands that dying and living, enduring and passing away, form a continuous (*yi* 一) body, we are with them in friendship." The four looked at each other and smiled: with no opposition in their hearts, they became mutual (*xiang* 相) friends. Suddenly, Master Yu became ill, and Master Si went to call on him. Master Yu said, "Magnificent! The formation of things (*zao wu zhe* 造物者) is turning me all constricted and constrained like this!" Crooked and bent, his back stuck out. His chin was hidden in his belly button, with his organs on top. His shoulders were above his crown, and the knobbles on his neck pointed to the sky. His *yin yang* energies were congested, and yet his heart was at ease and without concerns. He hobbled over to see his reflection in the well and exclaimed, "Oh wow! The formation of things is turning me all constricted and constrained like *this*?" Master Si asked, "Do you hate it?" He replied, "Not at all! Why would I hate it? It will gradually transform my left arm into a rooster, and I'll keep watch over the hours of the night. It will gradually transform my right arm into a crossbow, and I'll keep a lookout for roasted owl! It will gradually morph my buttocks into wheels and my spirits into horses. I'll ride them, and won't need a chariot!

"Now, gaining is timely, but losing is what follows: take comfort in timeliness, and settle into what follows; then grief and joy will not be able to enter (to disturb you). This is what the ancients called 'releasing the knots.' But, those who cannot release themselves will be tied down by things. And mere things will not win out against the workings of the Cosmos: that's the way it has always been. What would I hate about it?"

Suddenly, Master Lai became ill, gasping at the point of death. His wife and children surrounded him sobbing. Master Li went to inquire, and said, "Shh! Off with you! Don't disturb the transformations!" He leaned on the door and said, "Magnificent, the formation of things! What are they about to make of you? Where are they about to take you? Will they make you into a rat's liver? Will they turn you into an insect's legs?"

Master Lai replied, "In whatever direction children may go, east or west, north or south, they always follow after the Circumstance set by their father and mother. The relationship of *yin* and *yang* to people is not secondary to that of father and mother. If the latter (*yin* and *yang*) bring my death closer and I refuse to comply, wouldn't that be brash? How could I fault them for that? The vast mass (*da kuai* 大塊) burdens me with a physical form, toils me through life, eases me through old age, and rests me in death. So, what makes my life good is what makes my dying good too.

"Now, if a great smith were casting metal and the metal leapt up and said, 'I really must be made into an Excalibur (a 'Mo-ye')!' the metal smith would surely take it as an inauspicious piece of metal. Now, I have seized on a human form, but if I were to say, 'Only a human! Only a human!' the processes of creative transformation (*zao hua zhe* 造化者) would surely take me to be an inauspicious human. Now, if we take the whole natural world as a vast foundry, and the creative transformations as a great smith, where is there to go that is not acceptable? I will simply fall fast asleep and awaken to a pleasant surprise."

> *Comment:* The Zhuangzian rejection of social structures is sometimes taken to be an individualistic rejection of all social involvement. But in this passage and the next we see two small-scale social communities of people committed to existential authenticity: a life lived in appreciative acceptance of its finitude. Like the Mohists, they emphasize a notion of mutuality (*xiang* 相), though it is understood quite differently. Here it is thought of, not so much as identifying explicitly with the needs of others, as forgetting the difference between oneself and others. Mutuality is not an explicit and deliberate mode of action, but the unconscious presupposition of all interactions.
>
> "*Zao hua zhe*" refers to the processes of creative transformation, and does not name a conscious creator. The explicit analogy in the next-to-last sentence makes this clear: it assumes that the original concept is *not* anthropomorphic. The same is true for "*zao wu zhe*": 'that which creates things.'

6.6 The three Masters Sanghu, Meng Zifan, and Qinzhang had become mutual (*xiang* 相) friends saying, "Who is able to be mutually engaged through not being mutually engaged, mutually act through not mutually acting? Who is able to ascend to *tian* and roam the mists, leap through the limitless (*wu ji* 無極), living in mutual forgetfulness continuously without end?" The three looked at each other and smiled; with no opposition in their hearts they became mutual friends. After some time in silence, Master Sanghu died. Before his burial, Confucius heard about it and sent Zigong to attend the service. One of the friends was weaving out a melody; the other was banging on a drum; in mutual harmony they sang, "Oh, Sanghu! Oh, Sanghu! You've returned now to the genuine (*zhen*), while we still remain human. Oh!" Zigong rushed forward saying, "Pardon me, but is it reverential conduct (*li* 禮) to be singing right next to the corpse?" The two looked at each other and smiled, saying, "What does this one understand about the significance of reverence!"

Zigong went back and reported this to Confucius, saying, "What kind of people are they? They cultivate *nothing*, and set aside bodily concerns. They approach the corpse and sing without flinching! There is no word for them. What kind of person is that?"

Confucius replied, "They are the ones who roam (*you* 遊) beyond the realms, while I wander within. Beyond and within have nothing to do with one another. It was foolish of me to have sent you there to condole with them. Those are the kinds of people who are about to join with the formation of things, and wander (*you* 遊) through the one continuous (*yi* 一) energy (*qi* 氣) of the Cosmos. They treat life as a superfluous appendage, a dangling wart, and dying as bursting a boil to drain the abscess. How would anyone like this be aware of where the order of priority between living and dying lies? Borrowed from different things, but entrusted to the same body; forgetting liver and gall, losing their eyes and ears; turning and returning (*fan fu* 反覆) between end and beginning, not knowing one end from the other; they meander heedlessly beyond the realm of dust and dirt, and go wandering far beyond (*xiao yao*) in exploits free from artifice (*wu wei*). How could they care about how they look to ordinary people, and be taken in by what social conventions deem proper conduct?"

Zigong asked, "So, what method do you, master, rely on?" He replied, "Me? I'm just an ordinary citizen who has been punished by *tian*. All the same, I could share what I have with you." Zigong said, "I dare ask your secret." Confucius replied, "Fish converge in the water; humans converge in the way. Those that converge in the water are nourished just by streaming through the pool. Those that converge in the way: their lives are settled when they do not conduct busy affairs. So, it is said, 'Fish forget each other in the rivers and lakes; humans forget each other in the arts of the way.'"

Zigong said, "May I ask about people who are strange (*ji* 畸)?" Confucius replied, "Strange people may be 'strange' to humans, but are equal to the Cosmos (*tian*). Thus, it is said, 'A noble among humans is a petty person to the Cosmos; while a petty person among humans is a noble to the Cosmos.'"

Comment: Ruists such as Zigong may be flexible in their demonstration of respectful propriety (*li*), but they still remain confined within the bounds of acceptable social conventions. Zigong is not able to appreciate that what he takes to be the weird and disrespectful behavior of the recluses—singing next to the corpse—in fact arises from a profound appreciation of the life and death of their friend. Such 'odd' (*ji* 畸) behavior would be judged petty only from a conventional perspective. In fact, they are 'equal to the Cosmos': the ambiguity is the same in the original: 'on a par with the Cosmos,' or 'considered equal by the Cosmos.'

6.7 Yan Hui asked Confucius, "When Meng Sun Cai's mother died, he wept without tears, in his heart felt no sorrow, and he didn't grieve at her funeral. Despite these three issues, he is renowned throughout Lu for his excellence in funeral ceremonies. How can someone who has such a reputation be entirely lacking in substance? I can hardly believe it."

Confucius replied, "Well now, Master Meng Sun has it, completely! His understanding is surpassing. Simplicity is not easy to achieve; and yet he already had it simplified. Master Meng Sun is unaware of a reason for living or dying; doesn't know whether to prefer what came before or what comes after. [Passage (A): Though his body may be harmed there is no loss to his *xin* (heart–mind); death passes in time but without impinging on his emotions. Master Meng Sun was especially awakened. When others cried, he cried too: but this is just from having the means to do so.]

"We transform (*hua*) into things simply by depending on transformations that we don't understand. However, when you are on the verge of transforming, how do you know that in fact you won't transform? When you are on the verge of not transforming, how do you know you haven't already transformed? You and I in particular are among those who have not yet begun to wake up from our dreams. [...] [Passage (A).] Now, we mutually identify our own 'I'; but how do we know what is the I that we call 'I'? Now, you dream you are a bird and soar into the sky, dream you are a fish and plunge into the depths. But we don't know, is the one who is now speaking the awakened one or the dreamer? [...]"

Comment: The character Confucius, in this passage, does not represent the Ruist approach to the expression of grief, but is expressing a Daoist point of view.

In the *Zhuang Zi*, transformation (*hua* 化) and dreaming (*meng* 夢) often refer to the transformations between living and dying.

I have transposed the passage in brackets (passage (A)) from the last paragraph to the second paragraph, to preserve the continuity of both discussions.

From Chapter 18, §2

When Zhuang Zi's wife died, Hui Zi went to console him. But Zhuang Zi was squatting with his legs apart, banging on a pan and singing. Hui Zi said, "You lived with her and raised children, grew old together until she died. It would be bad enough for you not to be crying, but banging on a pan and singing? Isn't this too much?" Zhuang Zi replied, "It's not like that. When she began to die, how could I not have been affected? But I looked back into when she began, when she was thoroughly without life. Not only did she have no life, she had no physical form whatsoever. Not only did she have no physical form, she had no *qi* whatsoever. In the midst of the primordial confusion, energy arose from a transformation; as the energy transformed, there arose her physical form; as the physical form transformed, there arose her life. Now there has been another transformation and she has died. These belong together like the seasonal transformations of spring, summer, autumn, and winter. When she went to sleep peacefully in the grand chamber, and I followed screaming and crying. Then, I came to the realization that I had not thoroughly understood Circumstance, and that's how I stopped."

From Chapter 24, §6

When Zhuang Zi attended a funeral, he passed by the grave of Hui Zi. Looking back, he said to his retinue, "A man from Ying had a flake of mud as fine as a fly's wing on the tip of his nose, and told Carpenter Shi to chop it off. Carpenter Shi whirled his axe to build up a wind, and released a chop! He sliced the flake clean off without harming the nose, while the man from Ying stood without losing his composure. Lord Yuan of Song heard about it and summoned Carpenter Shi, saying 'I'd like you to try to do this with me!' Carpenter Shi replied, 'Your servant would once have been able to do the 'chop,' but my material has been dead for a long time now.' Since Master Hui died, I have nothing to take as my material; I have no one to discuss things with anymore."

NATURAL POTENCY *DE*

Fullness of potency (*de* 德) is sometimes associated with a relative 'incompleteness' of physical form. The idea is that when potency does not manifest in its usual or ordinary forms, it will find a way to manifest in extraordinary (*yi* 異) forms. Exceptional size or convolutedness are often signs of such potency in nature; and in people it may manifest as unusual physical form and character. From an everyday point of view, such 'oddities' may be considered useless or worthless. But the use of the useless, we have already been reminded, lies in enabling conditions that promote an extended natural lifespan. I begin with some passages from Chapter 4, "In the Human Realm," that touch on the same theme, where such extraordinary people are referred to as *'shen ren'* (神人): people of powerful spirit.

From Chapter 4, "In the Human Realm"

Master Qi of South Bo was traveling through the hills of Shang, when he saw a giant (*da*) tree, quite out of the ordinary: thousands of teams of horses could have been tethered in its shade. Master Qi said, "What a tree this is! It must have extraordinary (*yi*) timber (*cai* 材)." Looking up at its twigs and branches, he saw that they were too knotted and twisted to be made into beams and rafters. Looking down he saw that its trunk was too ruptured to be made into coffins. If you licked its leaves, your mouth would become blistered and sore; if you inhaled them it would make you intoxicated for three days and more. Master Qi said, "This tree must be of no worth (*cai*) to have reached such a vast size. And, yes! People of insightful spirit (*shen ren*) lack 'worth' for the same reason."

In the state of Song, the land of Jing Shi is suitable for catalpas, cypresses, and mulberries. Those that can be grasped between two hands are chopped down by people seeking to make monkey perches. Those three to four handspans around are chopped down by people seeking to make magnificent ridge beams. Those seven to eight handspans around are chopped down by people seeking to make funeral planks for nobles and wealthy merchants. Thus, the danger of having worthy 'timber' is that one will not complete one's natural years, but midway through the path of life, will be chopped down by an axe.

Comment: Cai (材) literally means 'timber,' and in general has a sense of the material or 'stuff' of which something is made. The stuff of which a person is made gives rise to their character and abilities, and so the word also has a sense of 'talent' or 'caliber.' It has a similar significance to *"de"* (德 'potency,' 'virtue'), but is rooted in a more concrete, material metaphor. Two types of 'stuff' are contrasted here: that which is conventionally acceptable and useful, and that which is so strange that it is of no conventional use at all. *"Yi"* (異) means 'different,' but also connotes that which is strange or peculiar, that which does not conform. The Mohists and Legalists value only unity and conformity and are suspicious of difference; the Ruists are more accepting of differences, so long as they can be harmonized, but still make appeals to norms and standards. The Zhuangzian Daoists go further still and embrace more radical forms of diversity: they see in them signs of natural potency.

From Chapter 5, "Signs of the Flourishing of Potency"

5.1 Wang Tai from Lu had been punished with amputation of his feet. His retinue of followers was comparable with that of Confucius. Chang Ji asked Confucius, "Wang Tai is an amputee, and yet his entourage matches yours here in Lu. He does not lecture when he stands up, provides no commentaries when he sits down; yet they go to him empty and return home full. Can there really be teaching without words, or a way to fully form the heart without a [fully formed] body? What kind of person is this?" Confucius replied, "This Master is a sage! As for me, I'm really falling behind and haven't yet gone to him. But if even I would take him as my teacher, how much more should those who are not as good as me! And why stop with the state of Lu? I shall recruit the whole world to join me in following him!"

Chang Ji said, "This man is an amputee, and yet is superior to you, my master. How far beyond the ordinary he is! What is the unique way in which such a person uses his heart–mind?" Confucius said, "Dying and living are of great significance (*da*), and yet they cannot succeed in perturbing him! The heavens may topple and the earth collapse, but he would lose nothing on account of it! He is careful to be without disingenuousness and so does not shift on account of things, because he treats the transformations of things as Circumstance, and sustains (*shou* 守) the ancestral (*zong* 宗)." Chang Ji asked, "What do you mean?" Confucius replied, "Looking at them from their differences (*yi* 異), liver and gall are as far apart as the states of Chu and Yue. Looking at them from their similarities (*tong* 同), the many varieties of things are undifferentiated (*yi* 一, 'one')."

"Now a person such as this does not distinguish whether something is appropriate for the eyes or for the ears, but wanders with the heart–mind into the harmony of their potency. They look where all things are continuous and undifferentiated (*yi* 一), and so do not see any place where they may be lost. This is why he sees the loss of a foot as like dropping a clump of mud."

Comment: Here, sameness (*tong* 同) and difference (*yi* 異) are used in their most general ontological senses. Sameness and difference are relative to the context of comparison. What appears different from the point of view of conventional linguistic distinctions will vanish as one's perspective expands outwards towards the Cosmos. In the same way, what is or is not 'mine' loses its boundaries: the apparent boundaries of any individual picked out from a human perspective vanish from the perspective of the Cosmos. But in the same way, the social differentiations of honorable and base are also erased: all people are equally worthy of respect; a noble can learn wisdom from a criminal. A foot is ultimately of no greater objective value than a clump of mud.

While this may be true from a Cosmic point of view, does it really make sense to recommend that a human should adopt such a non-human view? Should we also regard someone else's losing a foot with the same indifference as we would regard our own? What about someone else losing a head? If not, what kind of ethical reason can a Zhuangzian Daoist give? It seems unlikely that Zhuang Zi is arguing that we should be open to learning anything at all from any criminal whatsoever. What if the criminal is a psychopathic murderer? But it is unclear what Zhuangzian grounds might justify making this distinction. This is the ethical problem raised by the proposal to abandon all evaluations. Are there any constraints to cultivating an attitude of Cosmic indifference, and if so how could Zhuangzian Daoism articulate those constraints?

5.4 Duke Ai of Lu asked Confucius, "In Wei there is an ugly person called Ai Tai Tuo. Men who live with him dream about him and cannot bear to leave him. Women see him and beg their parents, 'I'd rather be this master's concubine than anyone else's wife.' They number by the dozens and are on the rise. No one has yet heard him sing out his own song; all he does is to harmonize with others. He has no official status to come to the aid of those who are facing death, collects no salary to help alleviate their starving bellies. Startling the entire world with his ugliness; harmonizing without singing; his understanding had not gone out into the four realms [i.e., he has no worldly knowledge]; and yet animals mate in his presence! This is surely a peculiar (*yi* 異) kind of human!

"I summoned him and observed him. He really *was* ugly enough to startle the whole world! After he had lived with me for barely a few months, I began to sense the kind of person he was, and before the end of the year I trusted him. The state lacked a prime minister, so I commissioned the job to him. Only after great reluctance did he accept, but half-heartedly as though declining. It was embarrassing for me, but in the end I transferred rule to him. Scarcely any time had passed when he abandoned me and went away. I was devastated as though bereaved, as though I no longer had anyone to enjoy my state with. What kind of person is this?"

Confucius replied, "[...] This Ai Tai Tuo does not speak and yet is trusted, has no accomplishments and yet is made a political confidant, and makes people grant him their states only fearing that he might not accept. This is surely one whose potency is not physically formed and yet whose stuff (*cai*) is complete."

Duke Ai replied, "What do you mean by saying that his stuff is complete?" Confucius replied, "Dying and living, preserving and decaying; depletion and expansion, poverty and wealth; worthiness and unworthiness, slander and praise; hunger and thirst, cold and heat—these are the changes in affairs, and the workings of Circumstance. Day and night they exchange places before us. But since he knows that he cannot peer into their source, he doesn't allow them to disturb his harmony, or let them encroach into the dwelling place of his spirit. [...] This is what it means to say that his stuff is complete." [...]

> *Comment*: Here, the strange person has an extraordinary natural potency, far surpassing that of conventional talent. The paradoxical claim is that genuine social flourishing can be ensured only by a 'leadership' that disdains conventional virtues and values. The best leaders would be those we consider weird and lacking in ability, altogether unconcerned with issues of rulership. This view will eventually be taken seriously by the 'mystically' inclined Imperialists of the Han dynasty (translated in the next chapter).

5.6 Hui Zi asked Zhuang Zi, "Can humans really be without *qing* (情 'distinctive conditions')?"

Zhuang Zi said, "Indeed!"

Hui Zi asked, "But how can humans without *qing* be called 'human'?"

Zhuang Zi replied, "The way gives them their appearance; the Cosmos gives them their bodily form. How can they not be called 'human'?"

Hui Zi retorted, "Since they are called 'human,' how can they be without *qing*?"

Zhuang Zi replied, "This (*shi* 是) is not (*fei* 非) what I mean by *qing*. When I say 'being without *qing*' I mean that humans should not harm themselves with likes and dislikes (*hao wu* 好惡). They should always accord spontaneously (*ziran*) without adding more (*yi* 益) to (the natural conditions of) life."

Hui Zi asked, "But if they don't add more to life, how can they maintain themselves?"

Zhuang Zi replied, "The way gives you your appearance; the Cosmos gives you your bodily form. Don't harm your person with likes and dislikes!

"Now, you are outside of your own spirit, wearing away at your own quintessence (*jing* 精). Leaning against a tree you babble, and at your desk you get lost in a daze. The Cosmos chose for you a bodily form, and yet you squawk on about 'the hard and the white'!"

> *Comment:* The term *qing* (情) is complex, and has no easy equivalent in English. It means both 'conditions' and 'emotions.' In some contexts, it is similar in meaning to *xing* (性) 'dispositional tendencies,' and can be thought of as referring to the distinctive conditions that ground those dispositional tendencies. But it also refers to emotions as the natural conditional responses of creatures to their circumstances. It also refers to our tendency to take pleasure in what is beneficial and to be repelled by what is harmful: our likes (*hao* 好) and dislikes (*wu* 惡), not as a matter of personal taste, but as a matter of basic human motivation. We then approve (*shi* 是) what we like and reject (*fei* 非) what we dislike, and impose these distinctions on our experience of the world. According to Zhuang Zi, here, these predilections should be curtailed, as they are not in keeping with our deepest and most genuine natural tendencies.
>
> Hui Zi is taken aback by what he takes to be Zhuang Zi's claim that the Daoist sage must lack our human dispositional conditions. He argues that you can't have a human without the 'distinctive conditions' of being human. (We must be careful not to presuppose any full concept of 'essence' here, as the text gives us no explicit definition to work with.) Zhuang Zi's response here implies that these distinctive conditions are not fundamental to our nature, but are additions to it. As additions to it, they cause it harm. This implies that what is natural must be left to flourish on its own without human 'assistance.'
>
> Note that Graham translates Zhuang Zi's response differently: "What I mean by '*qing*' is *shi fei* (affirmation and rejection)." Otherwise, his interpretation is largely the same.
>
> The 'hard and the white' is a reference to the logical and ontological distinctions and arguments of the *Ming Jia* (the school of 'language'), of which Hui Zi is traditionally considered to be a representative.

From Chapter 7, "Responding to Emperors and Kings"

7.7 The Emperor of the Southern Ocean was Shu (Swift); the Emperor of the Northern Ocean was Hu (Fleet); the Emperor of the Central Regions was Hun Dun (Amorphous). Shu and Hu would often meet in the Land of Hun Dun, who treated them with great generosity. Shu and

Hu planned to repay Hun Dun's kindness, saying, "All humans have seven holes to see, hear, eat, and breathe, except for this one alone. Let's try and drill some for him." Each day they drilled one hole, and on the seventh day Hun Dun died.

> *Comment:* Hun Dun's name (*hun dun* 渾沌) refers to a kind of primordial indeterminacy (sometimes translated as 'chaos'). Hun Dun, in this anecdote, lacks the sensory openings that would enable them to differentiate sensory qualities and perceive objects. We read in Chapter 5, above (p. 362), that people like the amputee, Wang Tai, "[do] not distinguish whether something is appropriate for the eyes or for the ears, but wander with the heart–mind into the harmony of their potency. They look where all things are continuous and undifferentiated (*yi* 一)." The emperors of the Northern and Southern Oceans evidently don't realize that this is precisely the condition of Hun Dun's liveliness and generosity. The creation of these means of sensory differentiation is also the destruction of Hun Dun's indeterminacy and productive potential.

GOVERNING

Chapter 7 is the last of the *Inner Chapters*, and does not introduce anything new, but closes by returning to a recurring theme from Chapters 1, 3, 5, and 6: that of withdrawing from society. This 'withdrawal' has two functions: the first is to preserve one's 'life'; but the second is to allow society to function naturally, and thus to bring itself to a harmonious completion. Rather than interfering with social interactions, one should allow them to follow their natural course, which, Zhuang Zi believes, will be both imaginative and harmonious. The result of this line of thinking is a paradoxical form of governing (*zhi* 治): refraining from interference and trusting people to flourish naturally. This idea is developed further in the Utopian passages translated in the next chapter. A few related passages from Chapter 28 are translated below.

From Chapter 7, "Responding to Emperors and Kings"

7.2 Jian Wu had an audience with the mad man Jie Yu, who asked, "What did Zhong Ri Shi (Midday Beginning) discuss with you?"

Jian Wu replied, "He told me that when rulers issue structures, models, duties (*yi* 義), and measures from themselves, who would dare not to obey and be transformed by them!"

Jie Yu said, "This is fraudulent potency. Governing (*zhi* 治) the empire that way would be like wading across the oceans or drilling a hole through a river, or making a mosquito carry a mountain on its back. When the wise rulers govern, do they govern the external? They proceed only after aligning themselves, and devote themselves steadfastly only to what they are capable of.

"Birds fly high to avoid the danger of stringed arrows; rodents burrow deep into caves beneath sacred hills to avoid the calamity of being smoked out. And you are more witless than these two little creatures!"

7.3 Cosmic Root was wandering along the southern slopes of Mount Yin. When he reached the upper reaches of the Liao River, he came upon a nameless person, and asked him, "May I ask about acting on behalf of the empire?"

The nameless person replied, "Get away, you boor! How can you ask such a miserable question? I am about to join as a human with the formation of things (*zao wu zhe*), and when satiated, I shall ride the wild and mysterious bird, emerge beyond the six extremes, and wander through the realm of not a thing, to settle in the broad and boundless wilds. Why do you waste my time bothering my heart about governing the empire?"

But he repeated his question. The nameless person replied, "Let your heart wander through the plainness (*dan* 淡), blend your energies with the vast and empty (*mo* 漠), let things follow where they will, and have no place for self-concern (*si* 私). Then the empire will be governed."

Comment: "*Dan*" (淡) means, 'plain,' 'bland,' 'tasteless,' but unlike these English words, it has positive significance in Daoist philosophy. It indicates the subtlety and simplicity of sensory qualities that are so delicate that they are almost imperceptible. For a fuller exploration of this concept, see Jullien (2004).

7.4 [...] Lao Dan said, "In the government of enlightened (*ming* 明) kings, their accomplishments envelop the empire but seem not to come from the kings themselves; their transformations extend to the myriads of things though the people do not depend on them; they make things take delight in themselves, without praising their names. They take their stand in the impenetrable depths, and wander through no thing at all."

From Chapter 28, *Rang Wang,* "Yielding the Throne"

28.1 Yao tried to yield the empire to Xu You, but Xu You wouldn't accept it. So he tried to pass it on to Zizhou Zhifu, but Zizhou Zhifu said, "Make *me* an emperor? I suppose I could do it. But I am developing a seriously worrying illness, and until it's cured (*zhi* 治), I won't have time to govern (*zhi* 治) the empire."

Now, the empire is the most important thing, but he wouldn't allow it to harm his life, much less other creatures. Only one who will not act for the empire can be entrusted with the empire.

> Comment: "*Zhi*" (治) means both 'to bring to order' (or 'govern') and 'to cure.' The precondition of curing, or caring for, the empire is curing or caring for oneself.

28.2 Great King Dan Fu had been residing in Bin, when the Di tribes attacked. He offered them leathers and brocades, but they wouldn't accept; he offered them hounds and steeds, but they wouldn't accept; he offered them pearls and precious metals, but they wouldn't accept. What the Di tribes wanted was territory.

King Dan said, "How could I bear to live with the elders while sending the young to their death? How could I bear to live with the fathers while sending their children to their death? Do your best to live here. What difference does it make whether you are my ministers, or ministers of the Di? I have heard that one should not use the means of nurturing to harm those you nurture." [...]

> Comment: A similar story occurs in the *Meng Zi* 1B15 (p. 149). Notice how the philosophical significance of a story depends on its context. The authorship of the story itself doesn't really matter. What matters is how it is used to make a philosophical point.

28.3 For three generations the people of Yue assassinated their rulers. Prince Sou became anxious about this and fled to the Caves of Cinnabar. But now the state of Yue was without a ruler. They looked for their prince but couldn't find him. They followed his tracks to the Caves of Cinnabar, but he refused to come out. So, the Yue people smoked him out with mugwort, and escorted him back in the royal chariot. As the Prince grasped the reins and climbed into the chariot, he looked up to the heavens and cried, "A ruler? A ruler? Why could you not have left me alone?"

It is not that Prince Sou hated being a ruler, but that he hated the anxieties of being a ruler. Those like Prince Sou would never harm life to gain a state. This is exactly why the people of Yue desired to gain him as their ruler.

DAOIST PHILOSOPHY OF SKILL

The people admired by Daoists of the Zhuangzian school often live on the outskirts of society, away from the dangers of social artifice. Immersing themselves joyfully in the Cosmos, living harmoniously with the natural world, they remain unperturbed by the unavoidable disasters of natural circumstance. By nurturing their natural tendencies, they are thereby able to live their lives to their fullest natural completion. Through cultivating their natural abilities, they recover and develop extraordinary levels of non-verbal embodied skill that are inherent in the make-up of natural creatures.

This sort of skill has a profound significance for Daoist philosophy. It is not just a matter of being really good at things. While one does perfect technique through practice, this does not account for its role in the Daoist conception of a wise and flourishing life. What is more important goes deeper than mere technique. Notice, however, the different answers given regarding whether they have skill, art, or a way.

I begin with the famous story of Chef Ding from Chapter 3, "*Yang Sheng Zhu*" (養生主) of the *Inner Chapters*, 'the principle of nurturing life.' The Lord, Wen Hui, is represented as having descended into the kitchen, to learn from a cook. I end with a story from the *Lie Zi* that has more to say about the nature of embodied modes of 'knowing.'

From Chapter 3 of the Inner Chapters, *Yang Sheng Zhu* (養生主), "The Principle of Nurturing Life"

Our life has boundaries, but knowledge has none. To use what has boundaries to follow what has no boundaries brings danger. To continue after knowledge in this way is simply dangerous. If you act virtuously (*shan* 善), keep away from fame; if you act badly (*e* 惡), keep away from punishment. Follow the guiding channels,[15] and you will be able to protect your person, keep your life whole, nurture what is close to you (*qin* 親), and live your years to the fullest extent.

---

15 Perhaps a reference to the central meridian along the spine in traditional Chinese medicine.

Comment: The term *"zhu"* (主) refers to the central pillar of a building, the main support of the roof. I translate it as "principle," not in the sense of a 'foundational proposition' or 'truth,' but rather as a practice or discipline that is of fundamental importance in life. The practice of nurturing life *"yang sheng"* is the discipline of cultivating the propensities of living processes that lead to good health, and therefore to longevity. But good health and flourishing life are also associated with refined perception and bodily control. So the discipline of nurturing life also results in exceptional levels of skillful interaction with various natural media.

Chef Ding was taking apart (*jie* 解) an ox carcass for Lord Wen Hui. Wherever his hands touched or his shoulders leaned, wherever his feet stepped or his knees stopped, swooping and ringing, he played the blade zinging. Never missing a beat, he danced the *Sang Lin*, to the rhythm of the *Jing Shou*.[16] Lord Wen Hui sighed, "Ah! Excellent! That a technique could reach such heights!"

Chef Ding put down the knife and replied, "What I appreciate is the *way* (*dao*), which has progressed beyond 'technique.' At the beginning when I cut up oxen, all I saw was 'ox'! After three years, I no longer saw an ox as a whole. Right now, at this time, I'm not looking with my eyes, but encountering it with *shen* 神 (spirit): sensory understanding pauses, while the desires of the spirit become engaged; following the natural striations (*tian li* 天理), lunging into the vast cavities, and guided through the vast openings. According with what is simply so (*gu ran* 固然), I don't even sense the sinews, joints, and tendons, never mind the massive bones.

"Fine chefs change their knives yearly, because they 'cut'; mediocre cooks change their knives monthly, because they 'chop.' Now, my knife is nineteen years old, and it has taken apart several thousands of ox carcasses, yet the blade is as though it had just been newly sharpened on the whetstone. The joints have spaces, and the blade has no thickness: when you enter these spaces with what has no thickness, there'll be vast expanses through which the knife-edge may roam, and there'll still certainly be room to spare. This is why after nineteen years the blade is as though it had been newly sharpened on the whetstone.

Comment: While skillful action certainly requires practicing one's technique, the expertise that the Daoists admire goes far beyond the mechanics of technical ability. It also requires cultivation of intuitive sensibility. This is captured in the idea of a 'spiritual sensibility,' embodied as a

---

16 *Sang Lin* (Mulberry Grove) and *Jing Shou* are names of ceremonial songs.

faculty of 'spirit,' *shen* 神, that engages through an embodied awareness of the make-up of things. "*Gu ran*," what is simply so, refers to the brute facts of the ultimate make-up of things: the way they are whether we understand or not.

When magnified, the inner constitution of things manifests as empty channels and spaces. Mediocre cooks have no understanding of this, and hack away at the objects in front of them. Even a good cook will still cut into the tendons. But those who, after years of training, rely on inner sensitivity to the subtlest textures of things, negotiate their way through the empty spaces until the knots are unraveled, and the carcass simply falls apart.

It is interesting to note that while the Daoists are known for extending their concern to the natural world, and including non-human animals in their philosophical discourse, this concern falls short of compassion for the animals that are being hacked apart, cut, or 'unraveled.' Whether this is because of a wholesale rejection of ethical values is unclear. At any rate, this sensitivity to the inner constitution of the animals does not seem to reach their capacity for suffering.

"Nevertheless, whenever I arrive at a knotty place, I watch for what makes it difficult. Timidly, and guarded, my observation lingers, my action slows down; I move the knife with extreme delicacy—and *whoop!* It falls apart: like a clod it drops to the ground.

"I raise the knife and take a stand, look all around, and with a leisurely self-satisfaction, I clean the blade and put it in its sheath."

Lord Wen Hui said, "Marvelous! I hear Chef Ding speak, and from him learn how to nurture life!"

Skill Stories from the Outer Chapters

From Chapter 19, Da Sheng

19.1 Those who have a profound understanding (*da* 達) of the (inner) conditions ("*qing*" 情) of life do not labor over what life cannot affect. Those who have a profound understanding of the conditions of Circumstance (*ming* 命) do not labor over what knowledge can do nothing about. 'Things' are a necessary condition for nurturing the physical form, and yet there are those who have an excess of things whose physical form is not nurtured. Not losing the physical form is a necessary condition for preserving life, and yet there are those who have not lost their physical forms but still lose their lives. The arrival of life cannot be reversed; its departure cannot be stopped. Such a tragedy! Worldly people think that nurturing the physical form is enough to preserve life, but it really isn't. So what is the point of doing worldly things? Even if there is no point, they cannot but be done: there is no evading them.

Now, if you wish to avoid acting for the physical form, it is best to renounce worldly things. Then there will be no entanglements (*lei* 累), and without entanglements there will be level tranquility. With level tranquility, life will continue to renew itself in response to other things. And as life renews itself, one will be almost there. But how can social duties be renounced, and life passed on? If we renounce duties, our physical form will be unlabored; and if we pass on life, our vitality will be undamaged. When the physical form is kept whole and the vitality is renewed, we are continuous with the Cosmos.

> *Comment:* "*Da*" (達) refers to a deep and extensive understanding; it implies a wisdom that is far-reaching and penetrating into all things. The growth of this understanding should ideally match that of the vast and expansive *dao*. The 'inner conditions,' "*qing*" (情), of life are those that enable it to flourish. The entanglements (*lei* 累) are the social duties and family obligations that bind us to our worldly life.

19.3 Confucius was traveling to Chu, when he emerged into a forest clearing. He saw a hunchback catching cicadas with sticks, as though plucking them precisely with his fingers. Confucius asked, "Is this your skill (*qiao* 巧)? Or do you have a *dao*?" "It's that I have a *dao*!" he replied. "After five or six months of practice, if I can keep two balls going (*lei* 纍) without dropping them, then I will lose a small number of cicadas. If I can maintain three, my losses will be only one in ten. If I can sustain five at a time, then it will be as though I pluck them precisely with my fingers. In composing my body, I root myself like a stump; I hold out my arm like a dried branch. In all the vastness of the heavens and the earth, and the multiplicity of the varieties of things, all I am aware of are cicada's wings. I remain unwavering and would not exchange a cicada's wing for all the varieties of things: how would I not succeed?" Confucius turned to his students and said, "He uses his undivided attention, and concentrates his *shen* 神 (sensitivity of spirit); doesn't that describe this hunchback gentleman?"

> *Comment:* The practice that the cicada catcher refers to, "*lei*" (纍), is rather mysterious. Literally, "*lei*" means "to pile up" and so is taken to refer to an exercise of balancing balls vertically. But anyone who has a sense of embodied skill can tell that such a practice will not transfer

to catching flying insects. The term, "*lei*," however, also has a temporal sense of collecting over time: "to connect; to repeat," and so can be understood as referring to the practice of sustaining events continuously. In this case, it would be maintaining the balls in the air at the same time without dropping them.

19.4 Yan Yuan asked Confucius "I once crossed the gushing abyss at Goblet Deeps. The ferryman handled the boat like a demon (*shen* 神)! I asked him, 'Can one learn how to handle a boat?' He said, 'Yes! Excellent swimmers quickly develop the ability. As for divers, they may never have seen a boat before but will know how to handle it.' I questioned him about this but he wouldn't tell. May I ask you what he meant?"

Confucius replied, "Excellent swimmers quickly develop the ability because they forget the water. As for divers, they may never have seen a boat before but will know how to handle it, because they see the surging water of the abyss as a mound, and the tipping of the boat as like a cart slipping backwards. Sliding and tipping in myriads of ways all laid out before him; they cannot enter to disturb his repose. Where would he go and not remain at ease?"

Comment: There is a version of this story in the *Lie Zi*;[17] it's largely the same, but contains a couple of differences. In particular, the ferryman begins by saying that swimmers can be taught, before mentioning excellent swimmers. Confucius then explains that swimmers can be taught because they make light of the water.

When you play for tiles you are skillful; when you play for trinkets, you are anxious; when you play for gold you are witless! The skill is the same, but because you have something at stake you give too much importance to externals. Whenever you overvalue externals, you will be inwardly clumsy.

19.10 Confucius was enjoying the views at Lüliang Falls: curtains of water plunging for 30 fathoms, the current so turbulent for 40 *li*, that turtles, fish, and alligators were unable to swim there. And yet he saw an elderly gentleman swimming in it. Thinking him grieved and wishing to die, he sent his students down to the side of the current to lift him out. They had gone a few hundred steps, when the man emerged, hair streaming over his shoulders, and walked over singing to the side of the pool.

---

17 Graham 1990a, 43.

Confucius followed him and asked, "I thought you were a ghost! But examining you I see you're human. Do you have some *dao* for 'treading' the water?"

He replied, "No, I have no *dao*. I began with (inner) conditions (*gu* 故), grew up with my natural tendencies (*xing* 性), and became complete with Circumstance (*ming* 命). I go under in tandem with the swirls and come out together with the eddies, following the *dao* of the water without imposing myself on it. That is how I 'tread' the water."

Confucius asked, "What do you mean by saying that you began with inner conditions, grew up with natural tendencies, and became complete with Circumstance?"

He replied, "I was born on land and was comfortable on land—these are the inner conditions. I grew up in the water and became comfortable in the water—these are my natural tendencies. What is so without my understanding why it is so—this is Circumstance."

> *Comment:* "*Gu*" (故) refers to the inner conditions, the brute facts about the way things are, without our being able to do anything about them, or understand why they are the way they are. It has the same significance as "*gu*" (固) in other texts. It is similar in significance to "*qing*" (情) and "*ming*" (命), perhaps lying somewhere between.
>
> The explanation of "*xing*" (性) or "natural tendencies," here, is worthy of particular note. It refers, not to the conditions we are born with, as we might expect if we take it to refer to "human nature," but to the conditions we grow up with.

19.11 Woodcarver Qing was carving wood to make a bell stand. When it was finished, those who saw it were astonished by its eerie (*gui* 鬼, 'ghostly') and marvelous (*shen* 神) appearance. The Marquis of Lu summoned him and asked, "What art do you have in making this?"

He replied, "Your servant is merely a worker. What art would I have! Nevertheless, there is one thing (*yi* 一) about it: when I am about to make the bell stand, I do not dare to expend my energies. I make sure to attenuate (*zhai* 齊) in order to still (*jing* 靜) my heart–mind.

"After three days of attenuating, I no longer care for celebration and reward, or rank and salary. After five days, I no longer care about rejection and praise, or skill and clumsiness. After seven days, in stillness I forget that I have four limbs and a bodily form.

"At this time, unaware of the ducal court, my skill is concentrated (*zhuan* 專) and externals slip away. Only then, when I enter the mountain forest, do I observe the natural tendencies of the Cosmos (*tian xing*

天性). When the physical form is at its peak, only then will I succeed in manifesting a bell stand, and only then do I set my hand to it. If not, then I do not continue. In modeling the pattern, I use the cosmic (*tian* 天) to match up with the cosmic [or: "I use nature to match with nature"]. Perhaps this is the reason why the instrument seems eerie and marvelous?"

> *Comment:* "One thing" (*yi* 一), also has a sense of 'unified, integrated concentration'; the same sense as "*zhuan*" (專) that appears in the next paragraph.
>
> "Attenuating" (*zhai* 齊; here, equivalent to 齋), ordinarily refers to fasting, but here refers to a discipline of casting off one's worldly concerns, and sensory distractions. Incidentally, the word for 'celebration' is "*qing*," which is in fact his own name. So, when Qing says that he does not care for celebration, he is also indirectly saying that he places no extra value on himself.

19.13 Carpenter Chui could turn a curve to match compasses and square, his fingers transformed with the things, undetained by his mind. In this way, the vantage point of his spirit (*ling tai* 靈臺) was unified and concentrated (*yi* 一), and unfettered.

When our shoes fit, we forget our feet; when our belts are comfortable, we forget our waists. When the heart–mind is comfortable, the understanding forgets right and wrong (*shi fei* 是非). When our engagements fit comfortably, we have no inward disturbances and do not follow after externals. We begin in comfort without a hint of discomfort, when our forgetting of comfort is comfortable!

> *Comment:* The mysterious phrase, "*ling tai*" (靈臺), can be understood as the vantage point of his spirit: "*tai*" (臺) is a raised observation platform looking out over all directions. "*Ling*" (靈) is similar in some ways to "*shen*" (神), and refers to the swiftness and lightness of a superior intelligence.

From Chapter 13, Tian Dao, "The Dao of the Cosmos"

13.9 What our age values about the way is written in documents: but writing goes no further than speaking. Speaking has value: its value lies in ideas. Ideas follow something, but what they follow cannot be transmitted through words. And yet our era transmits written documents because it values words. Although the age values them, I do not find anything in them worth valuing: it is because you value them, that you negate their value [...]

Duke Huan was studying written documents at the top of the court, while Wheelwright Bian was chiseling a wheel down below. He put down his mallet and chisel, and climbed up into the court. He said to the Duke, "Mind if I ask, what are those words you're studying, sir?"

The Duke replied, "The words of wise people."

"There are wise people?" he asked.

"They're dead," replied the Duke.

"Oh, then what you're studying is just the rotting leftovers of old-timers!"

The Duke said, "I study my written documents and a wheelwright dares to criticize me? You'd better explain yourself, or you die."

Wheelwright Bian said, "Me, I look at it like my work. When chiseling a wheel, if it's loose and lazy then it's smooth but won't take; if it's tight and rushed then it's harsh and won't move. Neither loose and lazy nor tight and rushed, you just 'get it' in your hand and respond from your heart. My mouth can't put it into words: the knack lies somewhere in between. I can't explain it to my child, and my child can't receive it from me. In this way, only after seventy years of practice have I become a mature wheel chiseler.

"Both the old-timers and what they can't 'transmit' are dead. That's why what my lord is reading is nothing more than the rotting leftovers of old-timers."

From the *Lie Zi*

Note: I translate one skill story from the *Lie Zi*, a later Daoist text that shares much in common with the *Zhuang Zi*.

From Chapter 5, "The Questions of Tang"

5.15 Zao Fu's teacher was Master Tai Dou. When Zao Fu began to follow Tai Dou in practicing charioteering, he conducted himself with utmost humility, but Tai Dou told him nothing for three years. He conducted himself with even greater meticulousness until Tai Dou finally instructed him, "An ancient poem says, 'The child of an excellent bow smith must first mend baskets; the child of an excellent metal smith must first mend furs.' First, observe how I run. When you can run as I do you will be able to manage six bridles and drive six horses." Zao Fu replied, "I shall follow as you order."

Tai Dou then set up a path of posts that were only as wide as his feet, placing them at a single pace apart. He set off running and returning without missing a step. Zao Fu followed his example (*xue* 學), and after three days had mastered the skill. Tai Dou sighed and said, "How sharp you are! To have got it so quickly! Everything in charioteering is like this. Just now, in your action, you got it in your feet and responded from your heart.

"Applying this to charioteering, you must control the reins from the point between the bridle and bit, and hasten or slow from where the lips meet; make precise estimates from within your breast and control the joints from within the palm of your hand. Take what you 'get' within your heart and extend it out to harmonize with the horse's intentions. Then you will be able to advance and retreat as straight as a tightrope, and swerve in a perfect radius. When you can extend the road to the utmost distance without wasting strength or energy, this will attest to your having attained the art.

"What you get from the bit, you respond to from the bridle; what you get from the bridle you respond to from your hands; what you get from the hands you respond to from the heart. Then you will see without eyes and urge without a whip. With your heart at ease and your body upright, the six bridles will remain unmuddled, twenty-four hooves will hurl without a misstep; swinging around, advancing and retreating, none will miss a beat.

"Then, you can prevent the wheels of the chariot from leaving the ruts, and the horses' hooves from leaving excess prints. Not experiencing any difference between the precipices of mountain and valley and the levels of plains and marshes: you will see them as the same. This is all there is to my art: you have understood it!"

LANGUAGE, KNOWLEDGE, AND EVALUATION

Chapter 2 of the *Inner Chapters* (often referred to by its Chinese title: the *Qi Wu Lun*) is one of the most complex and intricate of the chapters of the *Zhuang Zi*. The title is usually translated as "Discourse on Equalizing Things," but could also be rendered "Equalizing the Discourses on Things." It is critical of our ordinary categorizations and evaluations, noting the multiplicity of different modes of understanding between different creatures, cultures, and philosophical schools, and the lack of an independent means of making a comparative evaluation. It advocates a mode of understanding that is not committed to a fixed system, but is fluid and flexible, and that maintains a provisional, pragmatic attitude towards the applicability of these categories and evaluations.

Stylistically, it is dense and convoluted, with amusing stories breaking up dense arguments, baffling metaphors and existential poetry juxtaposed without explanation, and often without a sufficiently reliable interpretive context. It appears to be concerned with the deepest and most abstract understanding of ourselves, our lives, our world, our language, and indeed of our understanding itself. The most perplexing sections strain with the paradoxes and contradictions that arise at the limits of language and thought.

According to Guo Xiang's relativistic interpretation, each thing has its own place, its own nature (*ziran*); and each thing has its own value that follows from its own nature. If so, then nothing should be judged by values appropriate to the natures of other things. According to Guo Xiang, the vast and the small are equal in significance: this is his interpretation of the word "*qi*" in the title, "equalization of all viewpoints."

Recently, some Western interpreters (Lisa Raphals and Paul Kjellberg, for example)[18] have focused their attention on aspects of the text that express affinities with the Hellenistic philosophy of Skepticism, according to which we should refrain from making any final judgments that go beyond the immediate evidence, or the immediate appearances. In particular, we should refrain from making judgments about whether it is good or bad for us. When we see that such things are beyond our ability to know with certainty, we will learn to let go of our anxieties and accept the things that happen to us with equanimity (Greek *ataraxia*).

My preferred interpretation is that Zhuang Zi is directly responding to the Mohist insistence on clear *shi fei* distinctions. Rejecting also the Mohist style of discussion, he appeals to an allusive, aphoristic, mythological style of poetic writing to upset the distinctions and blur the boundaries that the Mohists insist must be held apart. Zhuang Zi's position is that this kind of sharp and rigid thinking can result ultimately only in harming our natural tendencies (*xing*), which are themselves neither sharp nor rigid. Rather we should learn to sense what can only be vaguely expressed and thereby recognize the paradoxes of vagueness and indeterminacy that arise from infinitesimal processes of transformation.

Like the cosmology of the *Lao Zi*, the worldview of the *Zhuang Zi* is also one of seasonal transformations of opposites. The world is seen as a giant clod (*da kuai*) around which the heavens (*tian*) revolve about a polar axis (*dao shu*). All transformations have such an axis, and the aim of the sage is to settle into this axis, so that one may observe the changes without being buffeted around by them.

---

18 See their essays in Kjellberg and Ivanhoe, 1996.

From Chapter 2, *Qi Wu Lun*, "Discussions on Smoothing Things Out"

2.1 Nanguo Ziqi (Master Qi, from South End) sat on the ground, leaning with his elbow on a portable scholar's desk. He looked up to the heavens and exhaled, vacant as though bereft of his counterpart (*ou* 耦). Yan Cheng Ziyou stood in waiting before him and said, "What is this! Can one's body (*xing* 形) really be made like withered wood? Can one's heart–mind (*xin* 心) really be made like dead ashes? The one who is now leaning on the desk is not the one who was previously leaning on it."

Ziqi said, "What you wonder about: isn't it sublime? As of now, I have lost Me. Do you understand?

Comment: The theme of counterparts, pairs, or correlates (*ou* 耦) plays an important role in the *Qi Wu Lun*. Counterparts discussed include: something and nothing, living and dying, right and wrong, I and Other, and in this passage, physical form and the heart–mind. We should, of course, be careful not to presuppose that this ordinary pairing must imply a dualism of distinct mental and physical substances.

The body is referred to as 'physical form' (*xing* 形) and implies a visible, tangible, shaped body. "*Xin*" (心) refers to all aspects of our mental life: emotional, cognitive, our desires, meanings, and intentions, and so combines the senses of both 'heart' and 'mind.' For this reason, it is often translated as "heart–mind" as either term alone is insufficient to capture all these senses.

The theme of an invisible, non-tangible breath that impels movement and invigorates phenomena, also meanders through the text in various manifestations: *qi* (energy), wind, emptiness, and here, exhalation (*xu* 噓).

"You have heard the pipes of people, but you won't have heard the pipes of earth; or if you have heard the pipes of earth, you won't have heard the pipes of *tian*."

Ziyou said, "May I ask the crux of it?"

Ziqi said, "When the vast mass expels its breath (*qi* 氣), it is called the 'wind.' This (at first) remains quite unstirred. But when it is stirred up, the myriad hollows become aroused and bellow. Have you really not heard the uproar? In the towering cliffs of the mountain forests there are gigantic trees one hundred spans around; their holes and hollows are like nostrils, mouths, and ears; like sockets, goblets, and mortars, like ponds and pools—surging, and sighing, shouting and hissing, crying and roaring, yowling and growling. They begin singing 'hoooo,' they follow singing '*heeee.*' In a gentle breeze there is a delicate (*xiao* 小) harmony, in a violent storm a magnificent (*da* 大) symphony. When the fierce winds dissipate, the many hollows become empty. Have you really not sensed the quivering resonance?"

Ziyou said, "The pipes of earth are simply the many hollows; the pipes of people are bamboo pan-pipes. May I ask about the pipes of *tian*?"

Ziqi said, "If in blowing the myriad differences, they are made to arise from themselves, all attaining themselves, then who could be one that billows?"

Comment: There is a paradox in this last line: if the cosmic breath gives life, how can it 'make' things be (or end) themselves? If things attain themselves, how can there be one that breathes life into them?

Note: The next section contains a series of fragmented riddles in the form of minimalist poetry. It is deliberately and stubbornly unclear how the fragments relate to one another. The translator is faced with an unfortunate choice: translate them in a fragmented way that renders them close to incoherent, or attempt to make sense of them by finding threads of significance, and grammatical fortuities that create the appearance of fluency. The first preserves the text but alienates an already 'alien' reader; the second inveigles the reader with false promises of clarity, and promises certainty where it simply cannot exist. Most translators choose the latter: to translate the riddles presupposing an already worked out interpretation.

But the text itself tells us, or seems to tell us, that 'great discourse is subtle and diaphanous.' So, I have chosen to tread a middle ground between these translation methods: preserving the enigmatic uncertainty of the original, while attempting some interpretation, either suggested by traditional commentaries, or etymologies, or interconnections between the various passages. But I offer them tentatively and invite readers to construct their own interpretations of these 'subtle and diaphanous passages.'

2.2

Great wisdom (*da zhi* 大知) is broad and open;
　petty knowledge (*xiao zhi* 小知) is transparent.
Great discourse (*da yan* 大言) is subtle and diaphanous (*yan* 炎ª),
　petty discourse (*xiao yan* 小言) is chattery and verbose.

In sleep, the spirits interact.
Upon awakening, the body 'opens,'

and we become connected into the constructs [of the world] and the daily struggles of the heart and mind.

... simple (*man* 縵), deep (*jiao* 窔), secluded (*mi* 密)...

Petty fears are apprehensive;
Great fear is unperturbed (*man* 縵).

Comment: According to traditional Chinese 'folk psychology' (popular understandings of the mind), we have several souls, which separate and wander off when we sleep. Their adventures and interactions become our multiple fragmented and interweaving dreams.

According to the Jin dynasty commentator, Sima Biao, "the body opens" means that 'the eyes open into conscious awareness.'

The text has three rich metaphors juxtaposed with no clear grammatical context: "*man zhe*," "*jiao zhe*," "*mi zhe*." "*Man*" (縵) means 'simple,' 'unadorned,' 'open'; "*jiao*" (窔) means 'deep,' 'hidden,' 'buried'; "*mi*" (密) means 'dense,' 'concealed,' 'quiet.' The particle '*zhe* 者' creates a noun phrase that may be interpreted abstractly or concretely. So "*man zhe*" might mean 'simplicity' or 'the simple ones'; "*jiao zhe*" might mean 'hiddenness' or 'the hidden ones,' and so on. Context would ordinarily clarify how the phrases are intended. But the minimalistic poetic context keeps the meaning wide open.

Note: The following passage is obscure in the extreme: terse grammar, contextless jargon, and juxtaposition of mismatched metaphors. It reads like explanatory comments (which I have indented) attached to a set of sayings. (This sort of intratextual explanatory comment is common in early Chinese texts, and is not unfamiliar in the *Zhuang Zi*.)

"Set off like an arrow by a trigger":
— describes commanding [a dispute over] right and wrong (*shi fei*).
"Restrained as though by a solemn oath":
— describes maintaining the victory.
"Perishing like autumn and winter":
— describes diminishing day by day;
what submerging does to it prevents it from returning.
"Constrained as though tied fast":
— refers to channels of ageing;
none can bring back to brightness the heart that approaches death.

Comment: Disputation over right and wrong (*shi fei*) is discussed in §2.5, below.

Happy or angry,
  Sad or joyful,
    Concerned or regretful,
      Perturbed or intractable:
Attracting and beguiling, these provoke our demeanor.

  Music emerges from emptiness;
  Steam becomes mold.

Night and day replace each other in progression,
  but no one knows where they sprout from.
Enough! Enough! From dawn to dusk we attain them
  —but that from which they arise?

> *Comment:* The cycles and successions of emotions and the cycles and successions of day and night, interrupted with vivid metaphors of the emergence of music and mold from steam and emptiness: time and process form the fundamental presupposition of these verses. The last line emphasizes the place from which the transformations of day and night arise: the reference to dusk and dawn implies that the origins remain within the cycle. But the phrase "dawn and dusk" also has the meaning of 'in a mere instant,' and so evokes the suggestion that the source of such temporal cycles somehow lies in between the moments, and therefore not *within* the cycle in any ordinary sense.

2.3 Without the 'other' (*bi* 彼), there is no 'I' (*wo* 我); without an 'I' there is nothing to choose. This indeed is close to it, but we do not know what makes it so. It is as though there is something genuinely in control, though its traces are quite undetectable. It can function, and we have placed our trust in it, and yet its physical form does not manifest. It has internal conditions (*qing* 情), but it lacks physical form (*xing* 形).

The hundred bones, nine bodily openings, and six organs are all contained in the physical form; but which will we take as the closest and most intimate? Do you delight in them all? Or are there any among them to which you are partial? Do you take them all to be subordinates?[19] Or are subordinates not capable of ordering (*zhi* 治) each other? [If so] do they take turns as ruler and minister? Or is there a genuine ruler among them? When you seek it out, whether you attain its genuine conditions (*qing* 情) or not, this will neither add to nor detract from its genuineness (*zhen* 真).

---

19 Literally, 'ministers and concubines,' neither of whom is a ruler in relation to the other.

Comment: The question here is about whether there is any single aspect of a person that is ultimately in control. If so, would it be one of the many physical parts? Is there some other way, that is consistent and feasible, of distributing control? If there is such a thing, it will genuinely have its own conditions, but these may not be knowable to us. The metaphor of artificial social hierarchies is used to question whether a natural hierarchy can genuinely occur.

The reference to having conditions while lacking physical form invites comparison with the discussion with Hui Zi in §6 of Chapter 5, above (p. 364).

As we endure the physical formation of the body, for as long as we have not died we are simply waiting it out till the end. We exhaust ourselves galloping ahead, cutting and scraping against things, and nothing can make it stop. Isn't this tragic? Slaving away to the end of our lives without seeing our efforts to completion, weary and exhausted, not knowing how to go home. Isn't this sorrowful? People call this 'not being dead'—but why would you want to keep adding to this? As the body undergoes transformations, the heart and mind do so along with it. Isn't this a great sorrow? Human life, is it really as dismal as this? Or am I the one who is dismayed? Is there anyone who isn't dismayed?

2.4 Now, if we follow our hearts and minds as they have developed (*cheng xin* 成心) and make them our authority, then who would be without an authority? But, why would it be necessary for those who understand the exchanges of things (and whose heart–minds choose themselves) to have one? The stupid would also have one in this way. To make evaluative judgments before one's heart–mind is developed would be like going to Yue today and arriving yesterday! This would be to take nothing at all as something. Even the clear-spirited Yu couldn't understand how nothing at all could be something. What am I supposed to do with this!

Comment: The phrase "hearts and minds as they have developed" (*cheng xin* 成心) is complex. It may refer to the maturation of our mental faculties (cognitive, emotional, intentional, evaluative), but it also has a sense of 'prejudgments' or even 'prejudices.'

Only after one makes up one's mind, can one be committed to evaluative judgments. The wise do not do so, and therefore do not make evaluative judgments, but it is only in the process of understanding the changes that their minds spontaneously develop.

The idea that we cannot understand how to take nothing to be something seems to be inconsistent with the interdependence of something
and nothing that we noticed in the *Lao Zi*. This also invites comparison
with §2.8 below (p. 390), where the mutual becoming, and even indis-
tinguishability, of something and nothing is discussed.

2.5   Now, surely speaking (*yan* 言) is not just hot air: those who speak
have their statements. But what they say remains quite unsettled (*te wei
ding* 特未定). So, have they really made a statement? Or have they not
even begun to entertain one? Should we take it as different from the
peeps of fledglings, so that there are indeed disputations over distinctions (*bian* 辯)? Or are there none?

> *Comment:* "Speaking" (*yan* 言) refers to language, speech, or discourse in
> general. It often refers specifically to the doctrines promoted and debated
> by the various schools. "Statements" (*suo yan* 所言), literally 'what is
> said,' refers here to the meaningful content of such discourse. The claim
> is made that this content is exceptionally unsettled (*te wei ding* 特未定).
> Guo Xiang interprets this to mean that so long as philosophical debate
> continues, the disputes (*bian*) remain undecided.
>
> The text, however, goes on to suggest that lack of determination
> implies lack of content. But the continuation of disputes cannot imply
> lack of content. On the contrary, the disputants must still have their
> doctrines in order to continue debating over them. I suggest, then, that
> the lack of determinacy here refers to the indeterminacy of the meaning-
> ful content. Because of the subtlety of worldly transformations between
> things and their counterparts, boundaries become blurred and meanings
> cannot be well-defined. But if meaning is not clearly defined, then can it
> really be said to have meaning?

How did the way become so obscured so that there arose the distinction between the genuine (*zhen* 真) and the artificial (*wei* 偽)? How
did discourse become so obscured that there arose dichotomous evaluative judgments (*shi fei*)? How could the way have gone and not remain?
How could discourse remain and be unacceptable (*bu ke*)? The way is
obscured by the accomplishments of the petty, and discourse is obscured
by glory and honor. This is why there arise the dichotomous evaluative
judgments of the Ruists and Mohists, whereby they affirm what they
deny and deny what they affirm. If you desire to affirm what you deny
and deny what you affirm, then nothing is better than to use clear insight
(*ming* 明).

Comment: The distinction between the genuine (*zhen* 真) and the artificial (*wei* 偽) is the distinction between the natural and the artificial. If the *dao* is what is most genuine, then how can the artificial arise at all? Indeed, how could the most primordial *dao* ever be lost at all? The arising of artificiality is attributed to the 'accomplishments of the petty' (*xiao cheng* 小成), and negation and unacceptability are attributed to 'glory and honor.' The Tang dynasty Buddhist commentator, Cheng Xuanying invites comparison with the *Lao Zi*, in which *ren* and *yi*, humanity and rightness, are blamed for the loss of the way, and in which beautiful words are said not to be trustworthy (Chapters 81 and 18, pp. 303 and 309). But the philosophical question still remains as to how all these artifices could have arisen from a primordially natural and genuine source.

The judgments of the Ruists and Mohists entail evaluative distinctions (*shi fei*) between things, whereby some are affirmed and others rejected. The Ruists and Mohists also dispute with each other over the correct interpretation and application of these distinctions.

On the relativistic reading, the reference to 'affirming what they deny and denying what they affirm' is usually taken to mean that each affirms what the other rejects, and the last line of the passage is taken as an exhortation to recognize the equivalence of all judgments. Guo Xiang interprets the passage differently: both schools affirm that there is *shi fei*, and both deny that there isn't. So we should affirm what they deny (that there isn't), and deny what they affirm (that there is)!

The last line, however, suggests a different interpretation (which I favor): in typical Daoist fashion, it quite explicitly encourages us to affirm what we deny and to deny what we affirm. It asserts that clear insight (*ming* 明) is the means by which we are able to understand such paradoxical discourse. This use of the term *"ming"* is thus in stark contrast with that of the Mohists. *Ming* does not clarify sharp distinctions, but rather allows us to understand how they merge in the course of natural transformations.

No thing is not 'other' (*bi* 彼); no thing is not 'this' (*shi* 是). When they treat themselves as the 'other,' they do not appear; when they affirm (*shi* 是) themselves, they are understood. Thus it is said: the 'other' emerges from 'this,' and 'this' also accords with the 'other.' This is the explanation of the co-production of 'other' and 'this.' However, if they are produced together, they perish together, and vice versa; and their acceptability and unacceptability likewise square off against each other. Affirmation that accords (*yin shi* 因是) must accord with what is rejected, and rejection that accords must accord with affirmation. Thus the wise do not follow (ordinary judgments) but illuminate them against the backdrop of the Cosmic (*tian*). This is what the sage accords with!

> Comment: According to Guo Xiang's interpretation, everything affirms (*shi*) itself and 'others' (*bi*) the other, so everything is both affirmed and othered; but then, nothing is affirmed and nothing othered. The Buddhist commentator, Cheng Xuanying, heartily approves of this interpretation.
>
> Graham takes "*yin shi*" (因是) to be a technical term which he translates "The 'That's it' which goes by circumstance." I render it as "affirmation that accords." It is a flexible mode of categorizing things that Graham contrasts with "*wei shi*" (為是), which Graham translates as "The 'That's it' which deems." I render it as "deeming affirmation." A 'deeming' affirmation is a mode of linguistic attribution as understood by 'realist' ontologies: it presupposes that we refer to objects, and attribute qualities to them, that are independently real.

'This' indeed is 'other'; 'other' indeed is 'this.' (That other there is also one *shi fei*; this here is one *shi fei*.) Are there really 'other' and 'this'? Are there really no 'other' and 'this'? Where 'other' and 'this' fail to meet their counterparts, this is called the axis (*shu*) of the way. When the axis begins to find the center of the wheel, one can respond without exhaustion: then affirmation is an inexhaustible continuum, and rejection is an inexhaustible continuum. Thus, it is said: nothing is better than using clear insight (*ming*).

> Comment: The axis of the way, "*dao shu*" (道樞) is the central axis of the revolutions of the way of the Cosmos. It is described, somewhat counter-intuitively, as the place where counterparts fail to meet. Perhaps this is because the center is the place where opposites dissolve, and so there are no longer any counterparts which could meet.

2.6 To use indicating (*zhi* 指) to illustrate how indicating does not indicate is not as good as using what is not indicated. [For example,] to use a horse to illustrate a horse's not being a horse is not as good as using a non-horse. The whole world (*tian di*) is one indication; the many things are one horse.

> Comment: The term "*zhi*" (指) literally means 'finger'; verbally, it has a basic sense of 'to point'; more abstractly, it means 'to indicate'; by extension, 'what is indicated,' 'what is meant,' and even 'intention' in the sense of one's intended meaning.

The last sentence may also have the sense: 'the Cosmos forms a continuous whole with the finger; the myriad things form a continuous whole with the horse.'

[...] [Passage (B).] Follow (*xing* 行) a path (*dao*) and it is formed; deem (*wei* 謂) a thing and it is so (*ran* 然). How 'so'? They are 'so' where they are so. How 'not so'? They are 'not so,' where they are not so. Things will surely have (some aspect) in which they are so, and (some aspect) in which they are acceptable (*ke* 可). No thing is not so; no thing is unacceptable. [Passage (B): They are acceptable where they are acceptable; and unacceptable where they are unacceptable.]

> *Comment:* "*Ran*" (然) is the most general stative verb for descriptive qualities: 'so,' 'such.' "*Ke*" (可), in its most basic sense, means 'can,' or 'possible'; it has a technical epistemological sense of "acceptable." Both terms are used when affirming the content of a proposition: agreeing that it is correct. The word "*shi*" (是) also performs this function. The three terms are thus functionally equivalent to our logical use of the word "true," though they differ significantly in meaning. Note that I have moved the first sentence of the paragraph to the end, to preserve continuity of thought.
>
> The overall presupposition seems to be anti-realist in spirit: just as a path is created by our walking it, things are not so independently of us, but are made so by our activities (*xing* 行) and our attributions (*wei* 謂). This passage goes on to articulate what may appear to be a radically relativist interpretation of this claim: if things are made so by us, then there is no way that they could not be as we take them to be. In the words that Plato attributes to Protagoras: "humans are the measure of things, of what is so that it is so and of what is not so that it is not so." However, such an extreme relativism neither necessarily follows from the initial claim, nor is it consistent with other central claims in the text (and indeed in this very chapter).
>
> The next passage below, for example, argues for the continuity of opposites through their mutual formation; but their continuity does not necessarily entail their relativity.

Therefore,[20] whether you present a wispy stalk or a solid trunk, a hideous wretch or the renowned beauty Xi Shi, through expansive

---

20 I have rendered "*wei shi*" in the traditional way as "therefore." Graham takes it in his technical sense of deeming affirmation and translates the sentence in the following way: "Therefore when a 'That's it' which deems picks out a stalk from a pillar, a hag from beautiful Hsi Shih, things however peculiar or incongruous, the Way interchanges them and deems them one."

transformations—wily and bewildering!—the way permeates through them as a continuous unity (*dao tong wei yi* 道通為一). In dividing off they are formed; in forming they are destroyed. So, all things are without formation or destruction: they go back and permeate as a continuous unity. Only those with expansive wisdom understand how they permeate as a continuous unity. For this reason, they have no function, and yet take their lodging place in the commonplace. And yet, the commonplace has its function; its function is to permeate; in permeating, it achieves. Come close to achieving and you're almost there. Simply having accorded with this, though we may not understand how it is so: this is the way.

––––––––––

Laboring your clarity of spirit (*shen ming* 神明) to make things into a continuous unity, without understanding how they are the same, is called 'three in the morning.' What does 'three in the morning' mean? The lord of the monkeys was distributing chestnuts. "You will get three in the morning," he said, "and four at night." The monkeys were all furious. "All right then," he said, "four in the morning and three at night." The monkeys were all delighted.

It is not that the words and their fulfillment were deficient, but that joy and anger had a role to play: this indeed is affirming by according with the circumstances (*yin shi*). In this way, a wise person would harmonize them through their evaluative judgments, but from the resting place (at the center of) the potter's wheel (*jun*) of nature (*tian*). This is called practicing both sides.

> *Comment:* Clarity of spirit is "*shen ming*." "*Shen*" (神) means 'spirit' but has epistemological connotations of deep spiritual insight; "*ming*" (明) has the basic meaning of 'bright and clear,' and in epistemological contexts refers to the clear-sightedness itself. In the *Mo Zi*, "*ming*" refers to the clarity of distinctions between dichotomous opposites. In this passage it has precisely the converse connotation: seeing so carefully, that the apparently precise boundaries melt into an indeterminate blur.
>
> In the popular interpretation of this story, the monkeys are being ridiculed here for having a preference between two clearly equivalent choices. But on closer reflection, is there really no practical difference at all between having a small breakfast and large dinner, and having a large breakfast and a small dinner? Rather, what is important is that the wise person should understand how to promote harmony by according with

the circumstances. If the monkey keeper offered none in the morning and seven in the evening, or vice versa, though the total is the same, the choices are most certainly not equivalent. This sort of forced equalization is the result of laboring (or wearing out) clarity of spirit, and proceeds from failing to understand on a deeper level how things are the same (and therefore how they might differ).

I take "practicing both sides" (*liang xing* 两行) to be a pluralist form of practice that acknowledges the pragmatic value of more than one side. It is, however, often interpreted as a more extreme form of radical relativism that recognizes the equal value of all alternative positions.

For commentary on the potter's wheel of nature see §2.12 below (p. 395).

2.7 The people of ancient times: their understanding had reached the pinnacle. Where had it reached? There were those who took it that there had not yet (*wei* 未) begun (*shi* 始) to be (*you* 有) things (*wu* 物): the utmost, exhaustive, unsurpassable! The next best took it that there were things, but that there had not yet begun to be boundaries. The next took it that there were boundaries between them, but there had not yet begun to be the dichotomous evaluative judgments of affirmation and denial.

The elaboration of affirmation and denial is the means by which the way became impaired. The means by which the way became impaired is also the means by which predilections (*ai* 爱) developed to completion (*cheng* 成). In effect then, are there really both developments [of predilections] and impairment [of the way]? Or, are there really neither?

When there are both developments and impairment, this is Music Master Zhao strumming the *qin* (zither); when there are neither, this is Music Master Zhao not strumming the *qin*. Zhao strumming the *qin*, Master Kuang grasping the baton, Hui Zi leaning on his desk: the understanding of the three masters was consummate, and they continued it to the end of their years. Only in their predilections (*hao* 好) did they differ from others. They desired to clarify these predilections. But they were making clear something that was not clear, and so they ended up instead with obfuscating arguments about the 'hard and white.'

Now, Zhao's son also took up the strings to the end, but did so without accomplishment (*cheng* 成). Is this what we call 'accomplishment'? Then even I am accomplished! Is this to be called 'not accomplished'? Then neither I nor anything is ever accomplished! Thus, the dazzling glare of slippery doubts is what the sage steers away from. For this reason they have no function but take their lodging place in the commonplace. This is called using clarity (*ming* 明).

Comment: The term *"cheng"* (成) means 'to form, become, or complete.' It refers in the *Zhuang Zi* to the formation or integration of things, and to the maturation of organic things. In §2.5 above (p. 384) we were told that the way was obscured by the accomplishments of the petty (or petty accomplishments); here we are told that the way became impaired by the completion of predilections (or the development of particular tastes, *"ai"* or *"hao"*).

For "not yet begun to be" (*wei shi you* 未始有) see the comment on §2.8, next.

2.8 Now, here is a statement (*yan* 言)! I don't know whether it belongs to 'this' (*shi* 是) kind (*lei* 類) or not. If a kind and its negation mutually form each other, then there is no way to differentiate (*yi* 異) it from its other (*bi* 彼). Still, let's try and make the statement:

There is a beginning. There is a not-yet-beginning-to-be a beginning. There is a not-yet-beginning-to-be a not-yet-beginning-to-be a beginning. There is something (*you* 有).

There is nothing (*wu* 無). There is a not-yet-beginning-to-be nothing. There is a not-yet-beginning-to-be a not-yet-beginning-to-be nothing. At some point, there is nothing.

But I do not know, of something and nothing, which is really something and which is nothing.

Now I've said something, but I don't know whether what I said really says something or not.

Nothing in the Cosmos is vaster than the tip of an autumn hair, and yet Mount Tai is small; nothing is longer-lived than a stillborn baby, and Peng Zu was an infant.

Comment: This passage is the core of the discussion of the indeterminacy of transformation. The way interdiffuses things to make them continuous and things become their opposites through gradual (and sometimes sudden) temporal processes. The passage focuses on the incipience of change, the 'not yet beginning to be' (*wei shi you* 未始有), and iterates the process. The line between being and not being is blurred through the process of becoming as each morphs into the other.

Commentators sometimes conclude that we can never tell the difference between something and nothing, but this isn't warranted by the argument. While something and nothing may not be clearly distinguished during the process of transition, it doesn't follow that they can never be distinguished.

The text applies this to the production of the statement itself (the text itself) in a performative paradox reminiscent of those of Hui Zi, the 'logician' and friend of Zhuang Zi. The statement itself undermines the clarity of the distinction between what exists and what does not, and thereby undermines the clarity of its own existence.

The Cosmos and I (us) are produced together, and so the many things and I (us) form a continuous unity (*yi* 一). Since we are a continuous unity, how could there also be words (*yan*)? But since we have already described it as "a continuous unity," how could there not be words? One (*yi* 一) plus the words make two; and two plus one makes three. Going on from here, even a brilliant mathematician wouldn't be able to complete it, let alone an ordinary person. So, if by proceeding from nothing to something we arrive at three; how much further will we get if we proceed from something to something! Without proceeding in this way, just judge accordingly (*yin shi* 因是).

The way does not yet have boundaries; statements (*yan* 言) do not yet have reliable applicability (*chang* 常). But with deeming affirmation (*wei shi* 為是) there are dividing lines. There are left and right; there are norms and duties; there are distinctions and disputes; there are arguments and quarrels. This is called decimating potency. Beyond the realm of six harmonies the wise simply remain but do not classify; within the realm of six harmonies the wise classify but do not comment. Regarding seasons and the ages, of the intentions of the former kings, the wise comment but do not dispute. In distinguishing, they have no distinctions; in disputing they have no disputes. How is this so? While the wise embrace them, the common people dispute over them in order to make themselves evident. So it is said: in disputing, there is the unseen. [...]

Comment: The phrase I have translated as "decimating potency" is "*ba de*" (八德), sometimes translated as "the eight virtues." This phrase, however, has a specious clarity that is not in keeping with the tenor of the overall passage. I have taken "*ba*" in its original etymological sense of 'dividing' or 'subdividing into eight parts.' The implication is that potency (*de* 德) is no longer whole, but has been split by the process of *wei shi*, 'deeming affirmation.'

2.11 Toothless asked Royal Grindstone, "Do you know what all things agree in affirming (*shi*)?" "How would I know that?" he replied. "Do you know what you don't know?" "How would I know that?" he replied. "In that case, does nothing know?" "How would I know that?" he replied.

"Still, let's try and put it into words: How do we know that what we call 'knowledge' is not ignorance, and that what we call 'ignorance' is not knowledge?

"Now, let me try and put a question to you: If humans were to try to sleep in a marsh, they would have deathly backaches. But is this true of a fish? If they nested in trees, they'd tremble with fear. But is this true of a monkey? Which of these three knows the correct (*zheng* 正) place to rest?

"People eat varieties of meat; deer eat grasses; centipedes relish snakes; hawks and crows prefer mice. Which of these four has correct taste?

"Apes monkey around with other primates as their mates; elk have relations with other deer; fish tumble around with other fish. Humans consider Mao Qiang and Lady Li to be beautiful; but fish see them and plunge into the depths, birds see them and soar into the heights, deer see them and burst into a gallop. Of these four, which knows the correct beauty in the world?

"As I see it, the sprouts of humanity and appropriateness and the paths of evaluative judgment are so jumbled and chaotic, how would I be able to understand these disputes over distinctions?"

Comment: This passage is taken as the *locus classicus* for the Skeptical interpretations of the *Qi Wu Lun*. Royal Grindstone doesn't assert a Skeptical theory or principle, but simply responds to questions with a plea of ignorance. Arguments that show that correctness (*zheng* 正) is relative to species are used to shake our certainty in our own judgments. Rather than drawing the relativistic conclusion that all judgments are equally good, the Skeptic simply refuses to draw any conclusion at all. This refusal to make any knowledge claim is then applied to disputes over humanistic virtues and evaluative judgments.

Toothless said, "If you do not know benefit from harm, then would the utmost human (*zhi ren* 至人) really also not know benefit from harm?" Royal Grindstone replied, "The utmost human is wondrous (*shen* 神)! Though vast marshes may blaze, they cannot be made to feel hot; though the rivers may freeze they cannot be made to feel cold; though violent thunderstorms may topple rocks from mountains and the winds thrash the oceans, they cannot be startled. One like this rides the energy (*qi*) of the clouds, straddles the Sun and Moon, and wanders beyond the four seas. Dying and living are unable to perturb them, still less the sprouts of benefit and harm."

> *Comment:* "The four seas" is an expression referring to the world of ordinary human interactions, whether small-scale and personal, or on the level of interstate politics. At the end of §2.8 (p. 390), this was referred to as the realm of the "six harmonies."

2.12a Master Startlebird asked Master Talltree, "I heard this from Confucius, that a wise person would not labor after official business, would not pursue benefit or avoid harm, takes no joy in seeking, does not leave tracks along the way: speaks by not speaking, and when speaking says nothing, and wanders beyond the realm of dust. Confucius would have taken this as impetuous talk, but I take it to be the practice of a subtle and marvelous way. What do you, my master, think?"

Master Talltree replied, "Even the Yellow Emperor would be dazzled by this! How would Confucius have the capacity to understand it! As for you, you are getting too far ahead of yourself: you see an egg and expect it to be a rooster to time the night hours with; you see a slingshot and look for a roasted game bird! Let me try some absurd sayings with you; but you must heed them absurdly:

"Traverse alongside Sun and Moon; brace the vault of the Cosmos (*yu zhou* 宇宙). Close them together in a mishmash: through the mutual respect of equal servitude. Ordinary people labor and struggle, and yet the wise are foolish simpletons. Myriads of years will result in a single harvest of pure simplicity. The myriad things are completely so, and will contain each other in this."

> *Comment:* "*Yu zhou*" (宇宙) literally means "eaves and ridge pole" and is a metaphor for the 'vault' of the Cosmos. "*Yu*," the eaves, represent space that extends in all directions, and "*zhou*," the ridge pole, represents time as it extends from past to future.

2.12b How do we know that delighting in life is not a delusion? How do we know that when we hate death we are not like orphans who don't realize that they've returned home? Courtesan Li was the daughter of the border guard of Ai. When the state of Jin first captured her, her tears flowed till they soaked her lapels. Then she arrived at the royal chambers, slept in the royal bed, and had eaten meats of various kinds. After this, she regretted her tears. How do I know that those who have died do not regret their having first begged to continue living?

Those who drink wine in a dream, wake up crying in the morning. Those who cry in their dreams, go hunting in the morning. During a dream we do not know it is a dream. Within our dreams we may interpret a dream. It is only after awakening that we realize it was a dream. And only after a Great awakening would we come to know that this is the greatest of dreams. And yet the foolish take themselves to be awake. So sure in their knowledge of it. Whether lord, or shepherd: so certain of it. Confucius and you are both dreaming, and I, naming your dream, am also a dream. This that I have said is called a 'paradox': you would meet only one great sage in a thousand generations who would understand how to solve it. And that would be in the blink of an eye!

2.12c Suppose that you and I are engaged in an argument (*bian* 辯). You beat me; I do not beat you. Does this mean that you really are right (*shi*) and I really am wrong (*fei*)? If I beat you and not the other way around, does this mean that I am really right and that you are wrong? Is it that one of us is right and one is wrong? Or could we both be right, or both be wrong? If you and I cannot understand each other, then others would surely be in the dark. So who could we call on to make a correct judgment? One who agrees with you? But if they already agree with you, how would they be able to make a correct judgment? One who agrees with me? But if they already agree with me, how would they be able to make a correct judgment? Someone who disagrees, or agrees, with both of us? But if they already disagree (or agree), how can they make the correct judgment? So, if you, I, and others cannot understand one another, are we going to wait for anyone else?

> *Comment:* This passage raises the problem of the 'criterion' in a particularly compelling way. Is it possible to find mutually agreeable criteria to resolve disputes? Mutual disagreement at the deepest levels results in failure to understand one another.

Transforming voices wait for each other as though not waiting for each other. Harmonize them with the Grindstone of Nature (*tian ni* 天倪), according with the grand flowing current. This is the means to use up all one's years to the fullest. What does it mean to 'harmonize them with the Grindstone of Nature'? Affirm (*shi* 是) what you do not affirm; assert to be so (*ran* 然) what you assert not to be so. If the affirmed were really as affirmed, then there would be no argument about the difference between what is affirmed and what is not. If what is so were really as asserted to be so, then there would be no argument about the difference between them.

Forget the years; forget meaning (or: rightness); shake them into the limitless; lodge them in the limitless.

> *Comment:* This passage attempts to articulate a solution to the problem of the criterion; not a direct solution to enable us to find mutually agreeable criteria, but an indirect one of dissolving the problem. Harmonize differences with the Cosmic grindstone: that is, recognize that the transformations of the way will ultimately blend and integrate all things and their counterparts. In the shadowlands between counterparts one may affirm and deny the same thing.
>
> According to the relativistic reading of this passage, affirmations and denials can be made simultaneously if they are relativized to different points of view, perspectives that are equivalent from the perspective of the Cosmos.

2.13 Penumbra asked the Shadow, "Formerly you were walking; now you are still. Formerly you were sitting; now you arise. Why such exceptional lack of stability?" Shadow said, "Do I have something to depend on to be so? Does what I depend on also have something to depend on to be so? Do I depend on snake's scales and butterfly wings? How could I know the reason for things being so, or their reason for not being so?"

> *Comment:* We can search for the reasons that things are the way they are, but we cannot continue infinitely. At some point, we must simply acknowledge the brute fact of Circumstance.

12.14 Once, Zhuang Zhou dreamt he was a butterfly, a fluttering butterfly, doing as he pleased, unaware of Zhou. He suddenly awakened, solidly, evidently Zhou. But he didn't know: was it that Zhou dreamt he was a butterfly, or that the butterfly was dreaming he was Zhou? Thus, between Zhou and the butterfly a differentiation had surely come about: this is what is called the transformation of things.

> *Comment:* We must be careful here not to simply presuppose the epistemological question that Descartes poses in his dream argument: whether the world really is the way we perceive it to be. In this passage,

the transformation between dreaming and waking is taken as a deep metaphor for understanding the transformation of things. And in the context of the dreaming passages above (pp. 393–94), this is taken to be the Cosmic transformation between the limited realm of the living and the unbounded realm of the ultimate awakening.

ENDNOTE

a 炎 literally, 'fiery': perhaps fiery and meaningless (insofar as it extinguishes its own flame). I follow the suggestion of the Ming dynasty commentator, Li Yi, to read it as 淡 (*dan*: flavorless or delicate flavor) and having the sense 'to blend affirmation and denial.' This makes more sense given the Daoist attitude to language: the greatest meaning appears to be without meaning, as the greatest taste appears to lack flavor." See annotation by Li Yi, quoted in Guo 1991.

·11

Zhuang Zi II: Utopianism and Mystical Imperialism, Two Strands of Daoist Thought from the *Outer Chapters*

UTOPIANISM

The *Outer Chapters* of the *Zhuang Zi* contain a strand of Daoist philosophy that promotes abandoning the pursuit of social development altogether and returning to a simpler more natural life, uncomplicated by the hypocrisy of artificially cultivated desires and values. Their ideas can be found interspersed in passages throughout the anthology, but they are especially represented by Chapters 8 to 10 (which Graham attributes to a philosopher he calls the 'Primitivist') and Chapters 28 to 31 (which Graham attributes to a school of Yangists, or followers of Yang Zhu [also known as Yang Zi]). These are beautifully written essays that are savagely critical of the development of social values and social structures, and especially of Confucius and of Ruist values in particular.

These chapters combine the anarchistic ideals of a simple life close to nature that can be found in the *Lao Zi* with practices that lead to the cultivation and nurturing of life. The practice of the nurturing of life mentioned in Chapter 3 of the *Inner Chapters* that leads to 'lasting out of one's natural years' becomes an emphasis on maintaining and protecting *xing ming zhi qing* (性命之情) 'the conditions of nature and Circumstance,' in these later chapters. The Utopian Daoists often appear to be directly critiquing Xun Zi's commitment to transforming and ordering nature through artifice.

From Chapter 8, "Yoked Up Toes"

Yoked up toes webbed together and extra fingers branching out go beyond (*chu* 出) the natural tendencies (*xing* 性) and are extraneous to one's potency (*de* 德). Superfluous appendages and hanging warts go beyond the body and are extraneous to the natural tendencies. Being excessively punctilious about the application of humanity (*ren* 仁) and ideals (*yi* 義), and arranging them alongside the five organs, is not in alignment (*zheng* 正) with the way and potency. Thus, to 'yoke together' toes in the feet is to connect useless flesh, and to 'branch out' extra fingers on the hand is to plant a useless digit. To be 'excessively punctilious' is to 'yoke together' and 'branch out' the natural conditions of the five organs, to be excessively outlandish in the practice of humanity and rightness, and to be excessively punctilious about the function of the senses (of hearing and sight).

> *Comment:* This first paragraph illustrates two ways in which the flow of natural tendencies (*xing*) might get diverted from their natural course, thereby interfering with their natural functioning (*yong* 用). Branches may diverge excessively, as in the case of an extra finger, or they may diminish by converging, as in the case of toes yoked together by extraneous webbing. The metaphor is of natural patterns of flow that may either branch too little or too much. When there is neither excess nor deficiency the patterns are in alignment (*zheng* 正).
>
> The Ruist additions of "humanity" and "rightness" likewise diverge from our natural tendencies, and so are "not in alignment with the way and potency." Now, Meng Zi sees them as arising from our nature, and this is sometimes thought of as similar in spirit to Daoist 'optimism' about human nature, but here we see that it is in fact dramatically opposed. Daoist philosophies do indeed trust our natural tendencies to result in harmonious flourishing, but they do not do so through the development of ethical virtues. It is unclear what underlies this trust: it appears to be a presupposition.
>
> *Note:* "*Chu*" (出) is usually translated to mean that webbed toes and branching fingers 'issue from' nature, but this is not entirely in keeping with the tenor of the subsequent discussion, according to which these things are extraneous to one's nature.

Thus, isn't it the case that one whose sight is 'yoked together' is disordered by the five colors, and dissipated with patterns and decorations, the sparkling and dazzling of green and gold brocade? This is exactly who aesthete Li Zhu was! And isn't it the case that one who is 'excessive' in hearing is disordered by the five tones, dissipated by the six pitches, the sounds of bronzes, stones, strings, flutes, the *huangzhong* and the *dalü* (modes and harmonies)? This is exactly who Maestro Kuang was! And isn't it the case that one who has 'branched out' their humanity has uprooted their potency and blocked up their natural tendencies in order to gain fame and renown, and roused up the world by promoting an unattainable paradigm? This is exactly who Zeng Zi and Shi were! And isn't it the case that one who is 'yoked up' in disputation joins tiles, ties ropes, and chisels sentences, daydreams in the realm of the hard and white, same and different, and wears out finicky phrases and useless sayings? This is exactly who Yang and Mo Zi were![1] Thus, these were all ways of excessive yoking and sideways branching, and not the epitome of alignment for the world.

Those who align with the alignment will not lose the conditions (*qing* 情) of their natural tendencies (*xing* 性) and of Circumstance (*ming* 命). Then, what comes together will not be 'yoked together'; what branches out will not be a superfluous digit; what is long will not be excessive, and what is short will not be insufficient. Although a duck's legs are short, if you stretched them it would fret; although a crane's legs are long, if you chopped them it would grieve. What is naturally (*xing*) long should not be chopped; what is naturally short should not be extended; then there is nothing to reject or be anxious about. This means that humanity and rightness are not the inner conditions (*qing*) of being human. How much anxiety those 'humanity' people have raised!

> *Comment:* The inner conditions (*qing* 情) of natural tendencies (*xing* 性) and Circumstance (*ming* 命) is an expression used by the Utopian writers to refer to the innermost conditions that derive from nature (*tian*), and that condition and promote our natural development. The *qing* are detailed, concrete conditions that ground the *xing*; the *xing* are the dispositional tendencies that are conditioned by the *qing*. Though there is an ontological difference between the two, they hold the same significance in the Utopian philosophy, and so are sometimes used interchangeably.
>
> The discussion here appears to respond directly to Xun Zi's praise of ritual propriety in §19.5b (see p. 196, above).

Now, one whose yoked toes are torn apart will cry; one whose extra branching finger is bitten off will scream. Of these two, one has an excess

---

1 The reference to Yang Zhu here seems to be misplaced.

in number, the other an insufficiency, but in anxiety they are one. Nowadays, the humane people (*ren ren* 仁人) weep and worry over worldly tragedies, while the inhumane (*bu ren* 不仁) people tear apart the inner conditions of their natural tendencies and Circumstance in their gluttony for honor and riches. This means that humanity and rightness are not the inner conditions of being human (*ren qing* 人情). From the three dynasties onward, how clamorous the world has been.

> *Comment:* The excessive additions to nature of the 'humane' people are no different from the deficiencies of the inhumane people in their causing grief and anxiety, by tearing us away from our natural tendencies. Note that this also means that the denial that our natural tendencies include humanity does not entail that they lead to inhumanity, since inhumanity is also presented here as resulting from damaged natural tendencies. But, again, what justifies this confidence that people who follow their natural tendencies will not be inhumane has yet to be made clear.

Now, one who depends on bending hooks and straight lines, compasses, and squares in order to correct things cores away at their natural tendencies; one who depends on knotted ropes, glues, and lacquers in order to strengthen things encroaches on their natural potency. Bowing and bending to ceremony and music, yawning and moaning over humanity and rightness to bring peace to the hearts of everyone: this is to lose one's regular constancy (*chang* 常). The world has its regular constancy. As for (natural) regular constancy: what bends does not use bending hooks, what is straight does not use lines, what is round does not use compasses, what is square does not use a T-square; appendages do not use glue and lacquer, knots and bundles do not use rope.

Now, in the world things all attract each other into existence (*sheng* 生) and yet do not understand (*zhi* 知) from where they come to life; they all attain (whatever they do) in a similar way, but do not understand the means by which they do so. Thus, past and present are not different, without exception. Then, wandering in the realm between the way and natural potency and deliberately acting with humanity and rightness, connecting and binding everything, as though with glue, lacquer, ropes, and cords: this is just to throw the world into confusion!

> *Comment:* The discussion here is reminiscent of Meng Zi's complaint about the damage to our nature caused by the imposition of external norms (p. 117). But, whereas Meng Zi sees humanity and rightness as the natural development of our natural tendencies, the Utopians see

them as disruptive impositions. Regular constancy (*chang* 常) is whatever expresses itself through the development of our natural conditions. What is 'normal' for each kind of thing is whatever is manifested by its natural tendencies. Nothing needs to be altered or made to conform to an external standard of normality.

From Chapter 9, "Horses' Hooves"

Horses' hooves can trample the frost and snow; their manes can withstand the wind and cold; they chomp the grass and drink the water, raise their feet and gallop. These are the genuine (*zhen* 真) natural tendencies (*xing* 性) of a horse. Even if they had ceremonial terraces and magnificent bedchambers they would have no use for them. But then arrives Bo Luo, saying "I excel in governing (*zhi* 治) horses." He singed them, shaved them, cut them, branded them, tied them with reins and shackles, bound them in stables and stalls: and out of ten horses, two or three would die. He deprived them of food and drink, raced them, galloped them, and arranged them in formation. Those ahead were plagued by the bridle pegs and bits, those behind were tormented by the crossed lashing of the whips. And by then more than half the horses died.

Comment: In his "Xing E" chapter, Xun Zi says, "The horses Hualiu, Qiji, Xianli, and Lu'er were the finest horses of antiquity. Even so, they at first had to be reined in with a bit and bridle, and then urged on with a whip" (see *Xun Zi* 23.8, p. 229, above). The Utopian author here provides a vivid and alarming account of what is required for humans to be able to transform horses in accordance with human desires.

The potter said, "I excel at governing (*zhi*) clay. The circular matches up with compasses; the square with the square edge." The carpenter said, "I excel at governing wood. The bends match the bending hook; the straight line echoes the straight edge." But do the natural tendencies of clay and wood desire to match compasses and square edge? And yet generations have honored them saying, "Bo Luo excels in governing horses and the potter and carpenter excel in governing clay and wood." This is also the mistake of those who would govern the world.

———————

My sense is that those who excel in governing the world are not like this. The people have their regular natural tendencies (*chang xing* 常性): they weave to make clothes, and till for food. This is matching (*tong* 同) their natural potencies (*de* 德): they are integrated (*yi* 一) and not partisan. This is called 'natural (*tian* 天) release.' Thus, in the era of utmost natural potency, in proceeding they were firm, and their sight was steady. At that time the mountains had no paths or tunnels, the lakes had no boats or bridges. The myriad creatures lived in flocks, their territories interconnected. Birds and beasts flocked together; trees and grasses grew tall together. And so the birds and beasts could be tied and harnessed for a journey, and you could clamber up and peek into the nests of magpies. So, in the era of utmost natural potency, people lived together with the birds and beasts, and were kin with the myriad creatures. How could there be any sense of noble master and petty folk? Assimilating (*tong* 同) with unknowing (*wu zhi* 無知), one's natural potency will not leave; assimilating with minimizing acquisitive desire (*wu yu* 無欲), this is called 'pure and simple (*pu* 樸).' When pure and simple, the natural tendencies of the people were attained.

But then arrived the sages, spraining and limping over humanity, pawing and crawling after their ideals (*yi* 義), and then the world began to have doubts; indulging in music, finicky and fussy about ceremonious propriety (*li* 禮): and then the whole world began to be split apart. Thus, when pure timber (*pu* 樸) is unharmed, who could make a sacrificial vessel? When white jade [i.e., raw jade] is unbroken, who could make an official jade tablet? When *dao* and its potency (*de*) are not dissipated, why choose *ren* and *yi* (humanity and rightness)? When natural tendencies (*xing*) and inner conditions (*qing*) are not distant, why make use of ceremony and music? When the five colors remain undisturbed, who would make patterned colorations? When the five sounds remain undisturbed, who would respond with the six modes? So, damaging the simple timber to make vessels is the fault of the craftsperson and carpenter. To damage the way and its potency to make humanity and rightness is the error of the sage.

From Chapter 10, "Raiding the Coffers"

[...] A follower of Zhi asked him, "Does a thief also have a *dao*?" Zhi replied, "How could they not have a *dao*? Sagehood lies in shrewdly anticipating the stash within the chamber. Bravery lies in entering first; rightness, in leaving last. Wisdom lies in understanding whether it is feasible or not. Humanity lies in sharing equally. There has been no one in the world capable of becoming a great thief who was not prepared with these five virtues." Observing it this way, an excellent person who does not attain the way of a sage will not be established; and if Zhi does not obtain the way of a sage he will not be able to proceed. The good people in the world are few and those who are no good are many, and so the sages who benefit the world are few, while those who harm it are many.

So, it is said, "When the lips are parched, the teeth are cold. When the wine of Lu is thin, Handan is besieged. And when the sage is born great thieves arise!" Beat up the sages and release the thieves and bandits, and the world will begin to return to order.[2] When the rivers are parched, the valleys are empty, the hills are sparse and the pools are filled. After the sage has died, the great thieves will no longer arise and the world will be tranquil and free of incidents.

But if the sages do not die, then the great thieves will not cease. Though you may double the sages to govern the world, this would only double the benefits to Robber Zhi. Create cups and weights to measure things, and he will take the cups and weights too and steal them all away. Create scales and balances to assess things, and he will take the scales and balances too and steal them all away. Create tallies and seals to insure them and he will take the tallies and seals too and steal them all away. Create humanity and rightness to rectify people, and he will take humanity and rightness and steal them all away too. How do we know that this is so? Those who steal buckles are put to death, while one who steals a state becomes a feudal lord, with humanity and rightness ensconced within his gates. Is this not to steal humanity, rightness, sageliness, and wisdom?

Comment: The Utopian author is worried about sincerity and hypocrisy in cultivating virtues. When we value virtues like humanity and rightness, we simply create more objects of desire, and greedy people will use them to get ahead. The Legalist, Han Fei Zi, as we shall see, was also deeply concerned about hypocrisy and thought that people could not be trusted. This is why he thought that rewards and punishments had to be set up to control their behavior. But the Utopian author points out below that the greatest of thieves at the head of a great state will not be moved by either rewards or punishments.

One who pursues great thievery by overthrowing the feudal lords, and benefits from the theft of humanity, rightness, cups, weights, scales, balances, tallies, and seals, cannot be encouraged with the rewards of carriage and headdress, nor prohibited with the threat of amputation or execution. This will only double the benefit to Robber Zhi and make him unrestrainable. This is the fault of the sages.

---

2 Cf. *Lao Zi* 19 (p. 315).

[...] So, extirpate the sages and get rid of wisdom, and then the great thieves will cease. Flick away the jades and smash the pearls, and petty thieves will not arise. Burn the tallies and break the seals, and the people will be simple and humble. Break the cups and bend the balances, and the people will not be contentious. Savagely destroy the sagely paradigms of the civilized realm (*tian xia* 天下), and you will begin to be able to discuss and criticize with the people. Choose to muddle the six modes, melt away the flutes and zithers, block and deafen the ears of Maestro Kuang, and the people of the world will begin to retain their hearing. Destroy cultural ornaments, disperse the five colorations, glue up the aesthete Li Zhu's eyes, and the people of the world will begin to retain their clarity of sight. Smash to bits the bending hooks and straightening lines and get rid of the compasses and square edges, split Carpenter Chui's fingers and the people of the world will begin to retain their skill. Thus it is said, "Great skill is like clumsiness." Cut away the practice of Masters Zeng and Li, clamp the mouths of Yang and Mo, resist and reject humanity and rightness, and the natural potency of the world will begin to come together in profundity.

[...] When those above are sincerely fond of cleverness (*zhi* 知) and are without the way, then the world will become greatly disordered. How do we know that this is so? The more knowledge (*zhi* 知) there is of bows and arrows, snares, spears, and triggering devices, the more birds will be disordered above. The more knowledge there is of hooks and bait, nets and baskets, the more fish will be disordered in the water. The more knowledge there is of foot traps, pits, nets, and cages, the more the beasts will be disordered in the marshes. The more disturbances there are of clever swindles, trickery of 'hard and white,' sleight of hand between 'same' and 'different,' the more the common people will be confused by argumentation. Thus, the world is constantly in great disorder: the fault lies in coveting cleverness.

Thus, everyone knows to seek what they do not know, but none know to seek what they already know, everyone knows to reject what is bad but none know to reject what is already good: this is why there is great disorder. Thus above there is the confusion (disorder) of the brightness of the Sun and Moon, and below the essence of the mountains and rivers burns away, while in the middle the flow of the seasons are sunk; the wriggling insects, the tiniest creatures, everything loses its natural tendencies. Great is the extent to which coveting knowledge disorders the world! From the three dynasties onward, it has been like this. Neglecting the ordinary people, favoring the laboring sycophants, abandoning tranquility and minimal interference, and delighting in the buzz of plans: the buzzing has already disordered the world.

MYSTICAL IMPERIALISM

A smaller number of passages in the latest strata of the *Zhuang Zi* anthology show distinct signs of Han dynasty eclecticism. It is most evident in the last chapter of the *Zhuang Zi*, "*Tian Xia*" ("The World"), and also in passages from Chapters 11 to 15. Perhaps under the influence of Xun Zi's "Dissolving Beguilement" chapter, Han dynasty scholars surveyed the various competing *dao*s of the pre-Qin period, and attempted to create an overarching *dao* by adopting a syncretistic attitude and choosing what was most valuable from each alternative. In particular, they sought to combine the more 'mystically' inclined philosophies with the more practical ones to create a more complete *dao*. By 'mystical' I mean that they engaged in meditative practices that aimed to cultivate a center of stillness from the perspective of the *dao*. Graham refers to this eclectic strand of Daoist thought as 'Syncretism,' while other scholars (such as Roth 2003 and X. Liu 1994) argue that it is what ancient texts referred to as 'Huang-Lao' Daoism.

We have seen earlier signs of the potential for the development of this political philosophy in the Zhuangzian strand of the anthology, with references to recluses who know nothing of ruling, and prefer to leave the empire flourishing of its own accord (pp. 337, 367); and in Chapter 28 of the *Zhuang Zi*, such reluctant recluses are hailed as the best kind of ruler (p. 368). In the Syncretistic passages, cultivation of one's own inner tendencies (*xing*) is now taken as linked somehow with a special kind of mystical ability to govern, much as nature itself does, by doing nothing (*wu wei*). It is interpreted as a form of 'inner wisdom' (sometimes referred to as 'sageliness within') that is the condition of successful rule. The conditions of 'outer rulership' (or 'kingliness without'), that is, the petty details of rulership, are drawn from other pre-Qin schools, such as Ruism, Mohism, and Legalism, and delegated to those below who serve the ruler.

From Chapter 33, "The World"

33.1 The methods and formulae (*fang* 方) for governing the empire are many: each takes what it has to be unsurpassable. But in which one does what the ancients called the 'art of the way' really reside? We say "There is none in which it does not reside." You ask, "From where does the spirit (*shen* 神) descend? From where does its insight (*ming* 明) emerge?" "Wisdom (*sheng*) has its place of birth; kingliness has its place of completion; and both originate from unifying integration (*yi* 一)."

One who does not depart from the ancestral (*zong* 宗) is called a person of the cosmos (*tian ren* 天人). One who does not depart from the essential (*jing* 精) is called a person of spirit (*shen ren* 神人). One who does not depart from the genuine (*zhen* 真) is called a person of utmost humanity (*zhi ren* 至人). One who reads the signs in the changes and transformations, taking the Cosmos as ancestral, potency as the root, and *dao* as the gateway, is called a sagely person (*sheng ren* 聖人). One who exudes compassion and humanity, taking humanity as benevolence, what is right and appropriate as the pattern, ritual propriety as practice, and music as harmony, is called a ruler of exemplary noble character (*junzi*).

If you follow models (*fa* 法) in making social distinctions (*fen* 分), taking linguistic categories (*ming* 名) as standards (*biao* 表), comparisons for evaluating evidence, and critiques for making judgments: it will be as straightforward as counting a numerical sequence: one, two, three, four... and the hundreds of offices will thereby be ordered by seniority. They take service (to the state) as constant, clothing and feeding (the people) as the central principle of support, propagating, breeding, rearing, and storing as their purpose, so that the aged, the weak, the orphaned, and widowed will be looked after. This is the pattern by which to nurture the people. [...]

The entire world is in great upheaval: the worthy and wise have no insight, ways and potencies are in disunity (i.e., are multiple). Most people in the world latch onto one of them, and examine what is in it with self-satisfaction. This can be compared with the ears, eyes, nose, and mouth: each has its own area of perspicuity and they cannot be interchanged. Similarly, the many schools have a multitude of abilities (skills): each has its merits and appropriate times of application. Still, they are neither complete nor comprehensive. These are the scholars who are twisted to one side (biased). [...] For this reason, the way of inner wisdom and outer rulership is dark and hidden, dense and unmanifested [...]

> *Comment:* Unifying integration (*yi* 一) is the method of the authors of this strand of the anthology. According to this way of thinking, there are many insights from many perspectives (*fang* 方, 'formulae'); but none of them has exclusive validity. Therefore, one's methodology ought to be to learn from each what it is most valuable for, and combine these into an overarching metaphilosophy. This sort of wisdom can be applied most effectively to rulership. This sort of syncretism, or holistic thinking,

becomes typical of Chinese philosophical methodology. The most typical responses in Western philosophy to a competing multiplicity of views, each taking itself to be uniquely correct, tend to be different. A realist will insist that at most one view can be right; the radical skeptic rejects all views as equally unjustifiable, while the radical relativist considers the rejection itself to be unjustifiable.

From Chapter 13, "The Way of the Cosmos"

13.1 The way of the Cosmos is to keep revolving and yet accumulate nothing; thus, the myriad things come to completion. When the way of the Emperor keeps revolving and accumulates nothing, all within the empire will rally together. When the way of Wisdom keeps revolving and accumulates nothing, all within the oceans will be compliant. One who is clear about the Cosmic, thoroughly understanding wisdom, and the potency of the emperor throughout all regions, will act spontaneously.

Obscure and tranquil throughout is the tranquility (*jing* 靜) of the wise. It is not because they say that tranquility is good that they are tranquil. It is because none of the myriad things is able to disturb their hearts that they are tranquil. When water is tranquil it clearly illuminates whiskers and lashes, the level matches the waterline, and great carpenters will adopt their standards (*fa* 法) from it. When the tranquility of water is like clarity, how much more so is the pure [concentrated distillation of] spirit! The heart of the sage is tranquil. It is the reflector of the Cosmos, the mirror of the myriad things. Empty (*xu* 虛) and tranquil, carefree and neutral, quiet and distant, without active control (*wu wei* 無為), it is the equilibrium of the Cosmos and utmost in the way and potency: thus, emperors, kings, and the wise ruler rest therein.

Resting, they are empty; empty, they become full; full, they achieve their right sequence. Empty, they are tranquil; tranquil, they stir; in stirring, they then attain it. Tranquil, they are without active control; without active control their responsibilities of service are discharged (i.e., by others). Without active control, they are at peace; at peace, grief and worry are unable to remain, and through the years they live a long and full life.

Now, one who is empty and tranquil, carefree and neutral, quiet and distant, and without active control, is the root (*ben* 本) of the many things. Understanding these and facing south is to be a ruler as was Yao; understanding these and facing north is to be a minister as was Shun. Residing in these from above is the potency of emperors and kings; residing in these from below is the way of profound (*xuan* 玄) wisdom and pristine (*su* 素, simple) kingliness. Retire with these and wander through rivers and oceans, and the scholars of the mountain forests will be compliant. Step forward with these to pacify the age, then one's achievement will be great and one will be renowned for having unified the empire.

Tranquil, one is wise; active, one is king. Without doing anything one is honored; simple and plain, and yet no one in the empire will contend for illustriousness.

Thus, one who is illuminated and clear about the potency of the world is called the great root, the vast ancestor, and is one who harmonizes (*he* 和) with the Cosmos. And so to smoothly regulate the empire is to harmonize the people; harmonizing with the people, this is the joy of being human. Harmonizing with the Cosmos, this is the joy of the Cosmos.

Master Zhuang said, "My teacher! My teacher! It grinds down the myriad things, but this is no crime; it bestows lavishly throughout the myriad ages, but is not 'humane'; it is senior to high antiquity and yet is not long lived; it encompasses and embraces the whole world, carves out the myriad forms and yet is not skillful; this is what is called the joy of the Cosmos. So, it is said, 'Those who understand the joy of the Cosmos, their living is the functioning of the Cosmos, their dying is the transformation of things. Tranquil, their potency merges with yin; in movement, they billow together with yang.' So, one who understands the joy of the Cosmos grudges nothing cosmic, rejects nothing human, has no ties to things, no duties to the spirits of the departed. Thus it is said, 'In activity, they are as the Cosmos; in tranquility, they are as the earth; with a concentrated (*yi* 一) heart–mind settled, they rule as king over the empire. The ghosts do not haunt; the spirits do not make weary; with a concentrated heart–mind settled, the myriad things are compliant.' These words are applied to the world with emptiness and tranquility, and extended to all things: this is what is called the joy of the Cosmos. The joy of the Cosmos is used by those of wise heart to nurture the empire."

13.2 Now, the potency of emperors and kings takes the Cosmos as ancestral, takes the *dao* and *de* (potency) as the central mainstay, and *wu wei* (being without active interference) as the regular and constant. Being without active involvement, there will be surplus in putting the empire to use. With active involvement (*you wei* 有為) one's application in the empire will not suffice. This is why the ancients honored being without active involvement. Those above are without active involvement, but if those below are also without active involvement, then above and below have the same potency. And if those above and below have the same potency there will be none to act as minister. Those below are actively involved; but if those above are also actively involved then those above and below will have the same way. And if those above and below have the same way, then there will be none to act as ruler. Those above must be without active involvement and put to use those below; those below must be actively involved and be put to use on behalf of the empire. These ways cannot be exchanged.

Thus, the ancient kings (who ruled) over the empire, although their understanding fell upon the whole world, they did not plan for themselves. Although their distinctions (*bian* 辯) carved out the many things, they did not explain (*shuo* 說) themselves. Although their abilities exhausted all within the seas, they did not act on their own behalf. The heavens do not give birth and yet the myriad creatures transform, the earth does not rear and yet the myriad creatures are nurtured. Emperors and kings are not actively involved and yet the empire succeeds. Thus it is said, "Nothing is more marvelous (*shen* 神) than the heavens, nothing more prosperous than the earth, nothing is greater than the emperors and kings." And it is said, "The potency of emperors and kings accompanies the Cosmos (heaven and earth). This is the way of straddling the Cosmos, riding the myriad creatures, and putting the human herd to use."

13.3 The root lies above! The branches lie below. The essential lies in the central mainstay; the details lie with the ministers. The deployment of the three armies and the five armaments is a branch of potency. The inculcation of reward and punishment, benefit and harm, and the five punishments is a branch of education. The meticulous comparison of ceremonies and laws, measures and numbers, forms and titles, is a branch of government. The sounds of bells and drums, and the display of feathers and banners, belong to the branch of music. Mourning garments and funeral vestments belong to the branch of sorrow. These five branches follow only after the turning of the concentrated spirit and the movement of the art of the heart–mind.

Among the ancients were those who studied the branches, but they were not ranked ahead. The ruler comes first, the minister follows; the father comes first, the child follows; the older brother comes first, the younger follows; the elders come first, the youth follow; the man comes first, the woman follows; the husband comes first, the wife follows. Honor and lowliness, first and last, are the practice of the world. Thus, the wise person adopts the imagery from therein. That the heavens are honored and the earth lowly is the placement of the clarity of spirit. That spring and summer come first and autumn and winter next, is the ordering of the four seasons. That the myriad creatures arise, the sprouts taking on different forms, the taking of life upon the harvest, is the flow of the transformations and changes. Thus, at the utmost spirit of the Cosmos is the sequence of honor and lowliness, before and after: how much more so should this be of the human way! The ancestral temples promote those who are close; the imperial pavilions promote the honorable; the village communities promote by seniority; the practice of official business promotes by worthiness: these are the sequences of the great way. To discuss the way but reject its ordering is to reject the way. How can one who discusses the way reject the way, and choose the way?

13.4 Thus the ancients who were clear about the great way first clarified the Cosmos, and then the way and potency. When they had clarified the way and potency, humanity and rightness were next. After humanity and rightness, social distinctions and duties were next. After social distinctions and duties, forms and titles were next. [...] assignments were accorded next [...] inference and assessment were next [...] approval and disapproval (*shi fei* 是非) were next [...] reward and punishment were next [...] When rewards and punishments were clarified, the unintelligent and the wise took their appropriate places, the noble and base stepped into theirs. The humane, the virtuous, and the unworthy received their posts according to their conditions: they were necessarily assigned according to ability and accorded with their titles. This is how one serves those above, nurtures those below, governs things, and cultivates oneself. Understanding and planning are not used: one must go back to the cosmic. This is the great serenity, the pinnacle of government.

Thus, the History says, "There are forms and there are titles." The ancients had forms and titles, but these were not what they put first. When the ancients discussed the way, forms and titles were raised after the fifth step; rewards and punishments after the ninth. To rush into a discussion of forms and titles is to fail to understand what is fundamental (the root). To rush into a discussion of rewards and punishments is to fail to understand the beginning. Those whose doctrine upsets the way, or whose explanations oppose the way, may be put in order by others. How can they order others! Those who rush to discuss forms and titles, rewards and punishments, understand the tools of governing, but they do not understand the *dao* of governing. They can be put to use in the empire, but are inadequate to the task of utilizing the empire. These are the argumentative scholars, the one-sided people. The ancients had the meticulous comparison of ceremonies and laws, measures and numbers, forms and titles. But they were the means to serve those above, not the means to nurture those below.

PART IV

Fa Jia: The School of Law (Legalism)

12

Han Fei Zi

INTRODUCTION

Legalism

In attempting to regulate any social group, one's first thought might be that a set of rules that everyone is required to abide by is necessary for social order. But for the rules to be effective, they must be backed up with the authority to impose negative consequences for failure to conform. The larger the society, the more complex and structured these rules become, till eventually they become codified as laws (*fa* 法) and punishments. Legalism is a philosophy that justifies this type of social control. Early Legalist thinkers included Shang Yang (390–338 BCE), Shen Buhai (400–337 BCE), and Shen Dao (350–275 BCE). They explicitly articulated many legalistic principles on which traditional societies had been run.

As the Warring States period was drawing closer to its dramatic finale, Han Fei Zi articulated a detailed philosophy in favor of such Legalist government, drawing on concepts articulated by these earlier thinkers, and on his own individual insights. He was motivated by a genuine concern for the well-being of the people of the state, and yet he was deeply cynical about human nature. He believed that people are motivated by selfish desires and fears, and ultimately can't be trusted to live well together. Nevertheless, these same selfish desires and fears also provide the key to controlling the people, as we can appeal to their desire for rewards and their fear of punishments. The types of punishment prevalent at the time were notoriously brutal: exile, branding, castration, mutilation, and execution.

Like the Mohists, the Legalists also believe that a society must be unified by a single set of goals, maintained by a unified set of laws and standards (*fa* 法) that apply equally to everyone. They must be clearly articulated, and their conditions must be precisely measurable, if rewards and punishments are to be weighed correctly without exception. Note that "*fa*" refers not only to laws as we understand the term, but also more generally to objective and universal models and standards. What is important is the objectivity and universality that they embody. This also entails cultivating a spirit of public-mindedness in the people, to prevent special interest groups from pursuing and promoting their own private benefits, and to prevent collusion with foreign states. Other concepts include the leverage that comes from a position of influential status (*shi* 勢), that is, one's strategic position or elevated status. But more generally Legalism can be seen as the art of control, in which the emphasis on law is one aspect. Han Fei sometimes uses the term *wei* 威 (awe-inspiring power) to imply both influential status and the threat of punishment.

Despite Han Fei Zi's high-minded ideals, his cynicism regarding human nature and the extremes of oppressive government he promoted resulted in tyrannical forms of government. Several centuries before Han Fei Zi, Confucius had already witnessed the result of such tyrannical states, and was profoundly unimpressed, promoting rulership by virtue as the only authentic means of achieving a genuinely flourishing society.

The Life and Death of Han Fei Zi

Han Fei Zi lived from 280 to 233 BCE, and the story of his life is an interesting one. Briefly put, he was a prince in the state of Han, and made efforts to advise his ruler, but was ignored. When the powerful state of Qin, which was soon to conquer all of China and bring the Warring States period to a close, attacked the little state of Han, the King of Han sent Han Fei Zi as an envoy to Qin. The King of Qin was aware of Han Fei Zi's writings and was favorably disposed toward Han Fei Zi and his philosophy. Indeed, the state of Qin had been implementing Legalist policies for some time. However, one of the King's ministers, Li Si, slandered Han Fei Zi, who was then imprisoned. Li Si then had poison sent to Han Fei Zi, which he drank. (Li Si, who is a famous Legalist in his own right, met a similar end.) The King of Qin later regretted his treatment of Han Fei Zi, but it was too late.

It is worth noting that while the other philosophers covered in this book lived long lives, Han Fei's life was cut short by the treachery of another Legalist, who was in turn a victim of treachery. It is also noteworthy that the Qin dynasty, which adopted Legalism as its governing philosophy, lasted only 15 years (from the unification of China in 221 BCE, which marks the end of the Warring States period, until its fall in 206 BCE). The Qin dynasty was superseded by the Han dynasty, which in time adopted Confucianism as its official philosophy. The Han dynasty is regarded as a "golden age," though the full story is more complex. But before one gets carried away by the relative success of Confucianism over Legalism, it should be noted that, official designations notwithstanding, the Han rulers actually employed a syncretistic mix of Confucian and Legalist philosophies, as has typically been the case through the rest of Chinese history.

Han Fei Zi and Xun Zi

Han Fei Zi is recorded as having been a student of Xun Zi, though it is not at all clear how close or substantial this relationship was. Han Fei Zi can reasonably be presumed to have been influenced by Xun Zi (see *Xun Zi* 22.3e, p. 215, for a particularly Legalist-sounding passage). And Xun Zi did acknowledge that Legalist regimes had some significant merits (see the final comment to Chapter 14, p. 435, below, for more detail on Xun Zi's attitude toward Legalist regimes). Further, Han Fei Zi's analysis assumes that people are basically selfishly motivated, which may remind us of Xun Zi's perspective on innate dispositions. However, while Xun Zi thought of people as having naturally selfish dispositions, he also believed in character reformation. Indeed, Xun Zi focuses on achieving such reformation. And since a fair degree of success in this regard is expected, Xun Zi does not assume that most everyone will act selfishly, as Han Fei does. Though they both appeal to the metaphor of bending a person into shape, Xun Zi sees this bending as autonomous effort on the part of the learner to cultivate him/herself, whereas Han Fei is thinking mostly of coercion. After all, if most people are selfish and not amenable to reform, then the only practical way to regulate a society is by intimidation and manipulation.

FUNDAMENTALS OF LEGALISM (FROM CHAPTERS 43, 7, 6, AND 5)

The fundamentals of Han Fei Zi's Legalist philosophy include law (*fa* 法), method (*shu* 術), the "two reins" of punishment and reward, and the leverage that comes from *shi* 勢 (influential status, power and authority). Passages explicitly discussing influential status are translated in the second half of this chapter ("Defense of Legalism, and Criticism of Confucianism and Mohism," p. 426), below, as they are integrated into the defense of Legalism and criticisms of Ruism and Mohism. Suffice it to say here that 'influential status' (*shi*) refers to the power or purchase arising from one's social position. Influential status is closely related to awe-inspiring power (*wei* 威), and thus to the authority to issue rewards and especially punishments. These rewards and punishments are issued according to a method that ensures that accomplishments correspond to proposals, that activities correspond to duties, and that rules and commands are adhered to.

From Chapter 43, "Deciding [between] Law [and Method]"

In this chapter Han Fei Zi briefly describes what he means by "*shu*" 術 (method) and "*fa*" 法 (law), arguing that they are both indispensable for rulers.

[The Indispensability of Both Method (Shu 術) and Law (Fa 法)]
A questioner asked, "Regarding the doctrines of these two schools, that of Shen Buhai and of Gongsun Yang, which is most critical for the state?"

I answered him saying, "These cannot be [comparatively] measured. If a person does not eat for ten days, he or she will die. If freezing conditions prevail and one wears no clothes, one will also die. If one asks, 'which is more critical for humans, clothes or food?'—it's not that only one is indispensable; both are tools for nurturing life. Now, Shen Buhai speaks of *shu* 術 (method), and Gongsun Yang emphasizes *fa* 法 (law).

"*Shu* (method) involves awarding official positions on account of reliability, requiring that results conform to the established descriptions [that is, what has been proposed], firmly grasping the handle of life and death [i.e., the power to execute], and testing all ministers' abilities. These are what the ruler grasps.

"Law (*fa*) includes: rules and commands promulgated to officials in the bureaucracy, the certainty of punishments in the mind of the common people, reward and survival for taking great care about the law (*fa*), and punishments applied for the violation of commands. This is what ministers take as their teacher. If the ruler lacks method (*shu*), there will be degradation from above. If ministers lack law (*fa*), there will be chaos from below. These are both indispensable. Both are tools of emperors and kings."

From Chapter 7, "The Two Reins"

Strictly speaking, Han Fei's metaphor is of two "handles." However, his usage corresponds nicely with English idioms involving reins, such as "the reins of power." These two reins are the power to impose punishments and to issue rewards. Han Fei Zi argues that it is crucial for the ruler to keep these two mechanisms of control in his own hands. He must neither delegate these powers, nor allow his ministers to influence him in the distribution of punishments and rewards. However, while these powers are to remain with the ruler, he must not use them whimsically or according to his publicly visible personal likes or dislikes. Rather, punishments and rewards must be administered objectively according to whether or not the recipients' actions corresponded with the duties implied by their titles, or to specific approved proposals. In other words, there is a method (*shu* 術) to handling the two reins, as briefly described in Chapter 43, above.

Enlightened rulers guide and restrain their ministers by means of two reins, and that is all. These two reins are punishment and beneficence. What does "punishment and beneficence" mean? I say: execution and mutilation are punishments; celebration and reward are beneficence. Those who conduct themselves as ministers dread execution and penalties, and they covet reward and celebration. Thus, if a ruler personally wields his punishments and beneficence, all ministers will fear his awe-inspiring power (*wei* 威), and flock to him to secure his benefits.

But the treacherous ministers of this age are not like this. A minister who hates someone is able to appropriate [the rein of punishment] from the ruler and accuse the person. Likewise, they are able to appropriate [the rein of beneficence] and reward someone they love. Now if the power and profit of reward and punishment do not issue from the ruler, but instead they carry out rewards and punishments upon the advice of their ministers, then all the people of the country will fear the ministers and slight the lord. They will flock to the ministers, and abandon their lord. This is the calamity that results when the ruler lets go of [the reins of] punishment and beneficence.

A tiger is able to overwhelm a dog by means of his claws and teeth. But if the tiger relinquished his claws and teeth, and allowed the dog to use them, then, on the contrary, the tiger would be overwhelmed by the dog. [Likewise,] the ruler uses punishment and beneficence to control the ministers. But if a ruler relinquishes punishment and beneficence and allows ministers to use them, then, on the contrary, the ruler will be controlled by the ministers. [...] When a lord is coerced, restrained, obstructed, or deceived, it coincides with the forfeiture of punishment and beneficence, and allowing his ministers to wield them. There has never been a case when [such a ruler] was not in mortal danger.

A ruler who intends to prevent treachery examines the match between forms (*xing* 刑) and descriptions (*ming* 名), that is, between what is said and what is done.

> *Comment:* Form, or manifestation (*xing* 刑), here means results or accomplishments, which are supposed to tally with what was proposed in words. The word "*ming*" 名 has the basic meaning of 'name,' but is also used to refer to linguistic descriptions in general. It can also be used in the sense of a 'title,' as we shall see further below.

Ministers put forth proposals, and the ruler gives them assignments based on their proposals, focusing exclusively on the assignment and holding them responsible for its achievement. When achievements match assignments and assignments match proposals, they are rewarded. When achievements do not match assignments and assignments do not match proposals, they are punished. Thus, if the ministers' proposals are great but their achievements are meager, they are punished. One isn't punishing the meagerness of the achievement, but the mismatch between the achievement and its description. [Likewise,] if the ministers' proposals are meager, but the results are great, they are still punished. It's not because one isn't pleased by great accomplishments, but because the harm of not matching descriptions [with results] is regarded as exceeding the [benefit of] great achievements. This is why they are punished.

In former times, Marquis Zhao of Han got drunk and fell asleep. The attendant responsible for caps saw that the ruler was cold. So he placed a garment over the ruler. Upon awakening, [the ruler] questioned his attendants saying, "Who supplied this garment?" The attendants answered, "The Cap Attendant." Accordingly, the ruler blamed both the attendant responsible for garments and the one responsible for caps. He blamed the Garments Attendant for neglecting his assignment. And he blamed the Cap Attendant for exceeding his authority.

Comment: More literally, the Cap Attendant "exceeded the duties stemming from his position" (越其職), thus his actions did not match the "title"—that is, the name of his position, which implies certain duties and not others. When one is allowed to take responsibility for tasks that are not assigned, this is a kind of usurpation of authority, which Han Fei Zi regarded as dangerous even for trivial violations.

It's not that [the ruler] didn't dislike the cold. It's that he regarded the harm of encroaching on the duties of another's office as more severe than the cold. Thus, when enlightened rulers train their ministers, the ministers may not exceed the responsibility of their office in their achievements, and may not make proposals that they fail to meet. For exceeding the responsibilities of one's position results in the death penalty, and failure to match [proposals with results] will be punished. This ensures that efforts will be directed toward the duties attending their position, and that their words will be honest and upright. And so ministers will not be able to band together to form [dangerous] cabals that work together [for their own purposes].

For rulers there are two calamities. [On the one hand,] if one appoints the worthy (*xian* 賢), one's ministers will exploit worthiness in order to take advantage of their lord. [On the other hand,] if one promotes arbitrarily, then affairs will be mired in difficulties and not succeed. Now, if a ruler is fond of worthiness, the ministers will adorn their conduct in order to meet their ruler's desire. And so the quality of the ministers will not be apparent. If the quality of the ministers is not apparent, the ruler will lack the wherewithal to differentiate between ministers. [...] Thus, if rulers reveal their dislikes, then the ministers will hide their motives; if rulers reveal their likes, the ministers will feign having abilities [...]

Thus it is said, "Rid oneself of likes and dislikes, and the ministers will be unadorned." If one's ministers are unadorned the great ruler will not be deceived.

Comment: By getting rid of (or at least concealing) one's desires, the ruler ensures that the ministers will not be able to manipulate the ruler. They simply make proposals, and fulfill assignments. In effect, the ruler favors only a very narrow quality in his ministers, namely, being good at producing the specific result that had been proposed. This avoids the pitfalls associated with promoting either the incompetent or, perhaps more dangerously, promoting those 'worthy' in a more general sense.

From Chapter 6, "Having Measures"

This chapter stresses the importance of following objective laws as opposed to making subjective judgments or pursuing self-interested schemes. Laws are to be followed strictly by everyone, which suggests that not even the ruler is above the law.

———————

No state is always strong or always weak. If the laws and standards (*fa* 法) upheld are strong the state is strong, and if the laws upheld are weak the state is weak [...]

In the present age, if one is able to repudiate private (*si* 私) corruption and promote public (*gong* 公) law, the people will be secure and the state will be well ordered. If one can discard private actions and practice public law, then the military will be strong and enemies will be weak. Seek out those who govern with laws and measures and promote them to positions above the ministers; then the ruler will not be deceived by lies and fabrications. Seek out those who have a balanced power of judgment in their understanding of distant affairs; then the ruler will not be deceived about the relative importance of situations across the empire.

Now, if you promote those who are praised for their ability, then ministers will distance themselves from their superiors and instead pally up with subordinates. If you recommend for office according to political factions, then the people will cultivate alliances and will not seek employment in accordance with law. Now, when an office loses those with ability, the state will fall into ruin. If you administer rewards on the basis of reputation, and punishments on the basis of slander, then—since people are fond of reward and repulsed by punishments—they will be lax in their civic actions, and instead will pursue private schemes and pally up with subordinates for mutual benefit.

If they forget their sovereign and associate instead with foreign agents in order to promote their own members, then the subordinates will have scarce means to serve their superiors. With factions that have foreign contacts, the greater the associations and the more numerous their members, and though they commit great misconduct, they will have extensive means of covering it up. So, loyal ministers will face peril and death though they are without fault, while foul and corrupt ministers will take ease in personal profiteering though they lack any achievements. If loyal ministers face peril and death though they are faultless, then virtuous ministers will go into hiding. And if foul and corrupt ministers enjoy safety and profit though they lack achievement, then the foul and corrupt ministers will advance. This is the root of decline.

In this way, the ministers spurn the law and emphasize the practice of private alliances, and trivialize public law. Multitudes will head for the gates of the powerful, while not even one will turn up at the court of the ruler. They will hatch hundreds of plots for the convenience of private family connections, but not one will make plans for the state of the ruler. Although the subordinates are numerous, it is not out of respect for the *ruler*; and although the official positions are filled, it is not for service to the *state*. In this way, though the ruler has the title of 'ruler,' in reality the responsibilities are delegated to the households of the ministers. Therefore, I humbly say, in the court of a lost state there are no people.

That the court has no people does not mean a decrease of numbers in the imperial court. It is that the ministerial households serve one another for mutual benefit, and not for the enrichment of the state. The higher-ranking ministers in service respect only one another, and not the ruler; the lower-ranking ministers use their income in order to nurture their alliances, and do not take on the responsibilities of their office. The reason for all this is that the ruler does not judge from above according to the law, but trusts the subordinates in their actions.

Therefore, the enlightened ruler entrusts the selection of personnel to the *law*, and does not promote them himself; allows the *law* to appraise achievement, and does not make his own judgment. In this way, those who have ability will not remain in obscurity, and those who fail will not be able to embellish their failings. Promotion cannot be achieved through reputation alone, and discharge from office will not result from hostile criticism alone. So relations between ruler and ministers are clearly defined and easy to administer. And this is possible only if the ruler is scrupulous about the law.

Comment: Note the fundamental contrast between public interest (*gong* 公), which is impartial, and private interests for personal or factional benefit (*si* 私). Note that this also applies to the decisions of the ruler: everything must be decided according to objective laws and standards, and never according to personal judgment.

When the worthy act as ministers, they face north, swear oaths of allegiance, and have utterly undivided hearts. In the imperial court, they will not shirk low office, and in military service will not shirk difficulties. They accord with the actions of their superiors, and follow the laws of the ruler. With an empty (*xu* 虚) mind (*xin* 心) they simply await orders, and make no judgments (*shi fei* 是非) of their own. Though they have mouths, they do not speak on their own behalf; and though they have eyes, they do not see what is profitable for themselves. They completely submit to the control of their superiors.

A minister can be compared to a hand: above, it tends to the head, below, it tends to the feet. It never fails to provide relief from cold or heat, and even if the deadly sword of Mo Ye were to attack the body, it would not fail to parry the blow. [In the same way,] the ruler makes no private use of wise and worthy ministers, or of able personnel; and the people do not cross the borders to make alliances, or have connections with distant territories. When the noble and base do not transgress boundaries, and when the foolish and the wise stand in appropriate balance, this is the height of government [...]

The law of the former kings said, "There must be none among the ministers who should wield power, none who distribute benefits: they must follow the instructions of the king. There must be none who do despicable things: they must follow the path of the king." In ancient times, the people of an orderly age upheld the public law, and rejected private scheming. They concentrated wholeheartedly on following the practice, and awaited their appointments.

A ruler who tried personally to inspect all the officials would have neither the time nor the strength to do so. Though the superiors might use their eyes, the subordinates will beautify their appearance; if they use their ears, the subordinates will beautify their tones; and if they use their intellect, the subordinates will make beguiling speeches. The former kings took these three means to be insufficient; so they set aside their personal abilities, and followed laws and measures in order to carefully calculate rewards and punishments. Thus, the former kings maintained the essential, so their laws were minimalistic and inviolable, singularly controlled throughout the world. The clever could not use their deceits; the dangerous could not use their flattery; the wicked could rely on nothing. For thousands of miles, no one would dare be fickle in their statements; and of the officials in the court, no one would dare to hide excellence or embellish faults. Court officials flocked to their service, whether working together or earnestly as individuals, none dared overstep their duties. Thus, governing was unhurried with time to spare, because of the way in which superiors relied on the authoritative power of their status (*shi* 勢).

Now, the ministers encroach upon their rulers—just as the terrain gradually shifts direction—making the ruler lose his grip, until he is unaware of having turned from east to west. For this reason, the ancient kings established the compass to grasp the points of sunrise and sunset. Therefore, the enlightened ruler does not allow the intentions of the ministers to wander beyond the law, and does not allow special favors within the law. No actions whatsoever may contravene the law. Law is the means to oppose wrongdoing and expel private interest. Strict punishments are the means by which to ensure that commands are followed and inferiors are punished.

Authority cannot be delegated, and control cannot be shared. If authority and control are shared, then all manner of wickedness will become evident. If the law is not trusted, then the practice of the ruler will be in danger. If punishments are not decisive then wickedness cannot be overcome.

Now, it is said that skillful carpenters can judge a line with their eyes alone, and yet they still prioritize measuring with compass and square edge. The wisest of people can successfully manage their affairs with precision, and yet they still prioritize the precedents of the laws of the former kings. Thus, when the plumb line is straight, crooked wood can be chiseled straight; when the level is balanced, bumps can be planed flat; when the balances are well strung, heavy and light can be adjusted; when measures are set up, greater and lesser quantities can be adjusted. Therefore, when laws and standards govern a state, all that is needed is to support them and implement them.

Laws make no exceptions for nobility, just as the plumb line does not bend into a curve. What the laws introduce, the wisest cannot argue their way out of, and the strongest cannot dare to fight. When punishing errors, the greatest ministers cannot escape; when rewarding excellences, the lowest commoners cannot be passed over. Thus, in correcting the failings of the superiors, when interrogating after the iniquitous conduct of subordinates, when bringing order to disorder, when resolving the twisted, and amending animosities: there is nothing to compare with laws and standards as guidelines for unifying the people. When subordinating the officials and commanding the awe of the people, when holding back wanton indulgence and laziness, and preventing lies and hypocrisy, there is nothing to compare with law.

When the punishments are heavy then no one will dare to replace the noble with the wretched; when laws and standards are cautiously determined, then superiors will be respected without attempts at encroachment. When superiors are respected in this way, then the ruler will be strong, and will be able to maintain the essentials. Thus, the former kings respected (law) and passed it down (to posterity). But if the ruler is lax about the law and adopts private schemes, then there will be no differentiation between superior and subordinate.

From Chapter 5, "The Way of the Ruler"

In this chapter Legalist methods are framed in Daoist terms.

———————

Dao 道 is the beginning of the myriad phenomena, and the guiding thread of evaluative judgments (*shi fei* 是非). For this reason, the enlightened ruler attends to beginnings, thereby knowing the source of the myriad phenomena [that is, knowing how things come about]. He rules according to this thread, thereby knowing the first indicators of accomplishment and of ruin. Thus, empty and still, he waits, commanding that terms (*ming* 名) be self-designated, and that affairs be self-determined. Being empty, he knows the proper conditions of fullness [i.e., of results]. Being still, he knows the standards of movement [i.e., the activities of his ministers]. Those who make proposals set their own terms (*ming* 名). Those who conduct affairs manifest their own results (*xing* 形, literally, "form"). When results and terms are found to cohere, the lord has no business interfering, for [affairs] have returned to their proper conditions.

Thus it is said, "A ruler should not reveal his desires. If a ruler reveals his desires, ministers will endeavor to carve and polish themselves accordingly. A ruler should not reveal his intentions. If a ruler reveals his intentions, ministers will endeavor to present themselves as uniquely qualified." Thus, it is also said, "Discard fondness; discard distaste. Only then will ministers reveal their unadorned selves. Discard wisdom; discard tradition. Only then will ministers cautiously ready themselves." Thus, possessing wisdom, but not using it to formulate plans, cause the myriad things to know their own place. Possessing worthiness, but not therewith conducting affairs, observe the motivations of ministers and subordinates. Possessing courage, but not using it to show aggressiveness, make one's assembled ministers exhaust their combativeness [in competition with each other]. In this way, one discards wisdom and yet has brilliance, discards worthiness and yet has achievements, discards courage and yet has strength. All one's ministers keep to their duties; the various officials have their routine tasks; all are employed according to their abilities. This is called the practice of regularity.

Thus, it is said, "So reposed, seeming to reside nowhere in particular. So translucent, no one can determine his position." The enlightened ruler minimizes active control (*wu wei* 無為) from above. His ministers are fearful and cautious below. The *dao* of the enlightened ruler involves utilizing the wise, fully employing their deliberative efforts, while he, on this basis, manages affairs decisively. Thus, the ruler does not exhaust his wisdom. The worthy display their talents, and the ruler assigns responsibilities to them accordingly. Thus, the ruler does not exhaust his abilities. If there are achievements, the ruler gets credit for their merit. If there are faults, the ministers bear the blame. Thus, the ruler's reputation is not diminished. In this way, though not worthy, he directs the worthy; though not wise, he regulates the wise. The ministers take up the hard work, the ruler takes up the success. This is the essential practice of the worthy ruler.

The way (*dao* 道) resides in being unobservable. Its use resides in being unknowable. Empty and still, have no affairs. From darkness observe flaws [in others]. See, yet be unseen. Hear, yet be unheard. Know, yet be unknown. Knowing where their words are heading, make no allowances and do not revise, but examine whether they match the results. If you have a single person for each office and do not allow communication, the myriad things will all be done to the fullest. Cover tracks, conceal beginnings, and subordinates will not be able find the source. Discard wisdom, cut off ability, and subordinates will not be able to discern one's intentions. Maintain your decision and examine whether [the results] accord with it. Carefully take hold of the [two] reins, and firmly grasp them. Do not let others covet them—cut off all hope, smash any thought. [...]

The way of the ruler of people is to take the still and retreating as most precious. They do not take control of affairs themselves and yet discern the clumsy from the skillful; they do not themselves make plans or stratagems, and yet discern fortune and misfortune. Therefore, without making proposals, they excel in responding. They do not commit themselves to anything, yet they excel in increasing. Proposals that have been accepted are held fast as a contract. Affairs that have accumulated are grasped as a tally. Rewards and punishments arise from agreement between the tally and the contract. Thus, the various ministers make their proposals; the ruler assigns their tasks according to their proposals, and holds them responsible for their achievement. If the achievement matches their task, and the task matches the proposal, they are rewarded. If the achievement does not match the task, or the task does not match the proposal, they are punished. The way of the enlightened ruler does not permit ministers to make proposals and fail to match them.

Thus, when enlightened rulers issue rewards, like the moistening of a timely rain, the people are benefited from their largess. When they issue punishments, terrifying as the crash of thunder, even spirits and sages cannot be inattentive. Thus, the enlightened ruler does not skimp on rewards, and does not waive punishments. If one skimps on rewards, then the work of effective ministers will deteriorate. If one waives punishments, then treacherous ministers will find it easy to do wrong. For this reason, those having genuine achievements, however distant and lowly, must be rewarded; those who have, in fact, overstepped, however near and dear, must be punished severely. If the distant and lowly are sure to receive their reward, and the near and dear do not escape punishment, then the distant and lowly will not be remiss and the near and dear will not be haughty.

DEFENSE OF LEGALISM, AND CRITICISM OF
CONFUCIANISM AND MOHISM
(FROM CHAPTERS 46, 49, 50, AND 14)

In the sections below, Han Fei Zi contrasts the purported effectiveness of his Legalist methods with those of Mohism and Confucianism, especially the latter, often emphasizing the importance of influential status (*shi*). These selections also provide glimpses into Han Fei Zi's view of human nature, and reveal his extremely instrumentalist perspective.

From Chapter 46, "Six Antithetical [Types of People]"

In this chapter, Han Fei Zi criticizes six types of people, and praises their opposites. For example, he criticizes those who avoid difficulties and risks, as well as those who study and develop their own ideas rather than simply following the law. But Han Fei Zi's case against these types of people is not what makes this chapter interesting. The sections translated below are chosen for what can be gleaned about Han Fei Zi's view of human nature and his application of utilitarian reasoning, as well as the sharp contrast with the Confucian idea of benevolent governance, which involves modeling appropriate conduct so as to inspire the development of personal integrity in others.

[Utilitarian Justification for Legalist Policies]

[…] There is a proverb of old which says, "Governing is like washing one's hair. Although there will be hairs lost, it is necessary to do it." Those who grudge the sacrifice of the loss of a hair while forgetting the benefit of the growing hairs do not understand weighing (*quan* 權) [the relative importance].

> Comment: Meng Zi also mentions the need for weighing the relative importance of competing concerns (see *Meng Zi* 4A17, p. 130). But Meng Zi also repeatedly indicates that there are things that simply should not be done (see *Meng Zi* 3B1, 6A10, 7B31, 4B8, 4B28, pp. 130, 121, 127, 131, 127), indicating that there are limits to the application of utilitarian cost–benefit analyses. Han Fei Zi, however, seems willing to take utilitarian expedience to an extreme, especially in the realm of politics.

Piercing boils is painful. Taking medicine is bitter. If on account of bitterness and fatigue one does not pierce boils and take medicine, then the body will not survive and one's illness will not end. […]

Now, scholars all try to persuade rulers to eliminate the profit-seeking mind, and pursue the way of mutual care. This is asking for rulers to surpass parents in familial affection. This half-baked theory of kindness is deceptive and misguided. Thus, enlightened rulers do not accept it. In the orderly governing (*zhi* 治) of sages, laws (*fa* 法) and prohibitions are carefully attended to. If laws and prohibitions are clear and evident, officials will govern well. If rewards and punishments are certain and impartial, then the common people will be productively employed. If the people are productively employed and officials govern well, then the state will be rich. If the state is rich, the military will be strong, and the work of the hegemonic king will be complete. […]

[On Human Nature and Utilitarianism]

An enlightened ruler's governing (*zhi* 治) of the state involves increasing the scope of those protected and enhancing the severity of the punishments of offenders. He controls the common people with laws and prohibitions, and does not depend on them restraining themselves with personal integrity. A mother's love for a child is twice that of a father. But a father commands his children to do things ten times better than a mother. Government officers do not love the common people, and they command them better than 10,000 fathers. Mothers amass love and yet their orders amount to little. Government officers make use of awe-inspiring power (*wei* 威) and sternness, and the common people pay heed and obey. The records of sternness and of love can easily be distinguished.

Moreover, what parents ask of their children is to be secure and profitable in their activities. In their personal conduct, they desire them to avoid crime. What the ruler and superiors expect from the common people is, in the face of difficulties, to apply themselves to the death, and in times of peace to exhaust their strength [in the service of the state]. Parents apply deep love and intimacy toward their children aiming for their security and profit (benefit), yet they are not heeded. [In contrast,] a lord, with his lack of love or [concern for the people's] benefit asks for the people to work themselves to death, and yet his commands are carried out. The enlightened ruler understands this. Thus, rather than nurturing a heart of kindness and love, he increases the power and authority (*shi* 勢) that arises from awe-inspiring might (*wei* 威) and sternness. Thus, mothers handle their children with deep love, and children develop many faults from the policy of love. Fathers have weaker love, 'instructing' with a bamboo rod, and children develop many merits as a result of applying sternness.

Now, consider how families manage their livelihood. [One family] endures hunger and cold together and mutually strives with arduous labor. Even if they encountered the hardships of military service and the distress of hunger and famine, the family with warm clothes and fine food would surely be this one. [In contrast, suppose another family] practiced mutual charity, thereby [acquiring] clothing and food, or showed favor and affection by sharing idle leisure and amusements. In days of hunger and years of famine, the family who would marry off wives and sell children would surely be this one. Thus, the way of law is to suffer first and later benefit; the way of humanity (*ren* 仁) is to first be joyful and later be reduced to poverty. The sage, assessing (*quan* 權) their relative weight, produces what is the greatest benefit. Thus, he uses the mutual endurance [achieved by] law, and discards the mutual charity of the humane person (*ren ren* 仁人).

Comment: Here Han Fei Zi clearly articulates a utilitarian justification for draconian political policies. One may ask: are there other considerations besides utilitarian that ought to come into play here?

From Chapter 49, "Five Vermin"

In this chapter Han Fei rails against another set of people: scholars, orators, independent swordsmen, those that shirk military service, and merchants/craftspeople, whom he calls the "five vermin." But this chapter also covers more significant topics. The sections translated below contrast Han Fei Zi's Legalist philosophy with certain aspects of Confucianism and Mohism. Han Fei Zi criticizes the notion that a political system resting on benevolence or ethics can achieve order. Rather, he argues, it is only the Legalist methods, such as leveraging influential status (*shi* 勢), as well as using law and the two handles of rewards and punishments, that will reliably produce a properly compliant citizenry.

[The Impotence of Loving Care]

Now, both Ruists and Mohists claim that the former kings cared impartially (*jian'ai* 兼愛) for the whole world, looking on the common people as though a father or mother.

> *Comment:* Strictly speaking, it is only the Mohists who advocate *jian'ai*, and Meng Zi and Xun Zi reject Mohism. However, while the term "*jian'ai*" may be inappropriately applied to Confucians, it is nevertheless true that Confucians taught that the relation between the ruler and the people ought to be like that of parents and children, that rulers ought to rule with humanity, striving to do their utmost for the people.

How do they show that this is so? They say, "When the Minister of Crime issues punishments, the lord cancels his musical performance. When hearing a report of an execution, the lord weeps." This is how they promote the former kings. Now, if the relation between ruler and minister being like that of father and son ensures order, this implies that there is no turmoil between father and son. [However,] in natural human affection no one surpasses parents. All [parents] are loving, and yet this does not necessarily achieve order [in the family]. Even if there was profound love, how would this dispel unruly behavior? Now, if the former kings' love for the common people did not exceed parents' love for their children, and children are sometimes unruly, then how did the common people become orderly? Moreover, if in using law (*fa*) to implement punishments the rulers wept, this is expressing humanity (*ren* 仁); but it is not regarded as order. Those who, weeping, do not wish to punish are humane (*ren*). But it is the necessity of punishment that is *law* (*fa*). Since the former kings upheld the law and ignored their tears, the incapacity of humanity (*ren*) to achieve order is perfectly clear.

[The Rarity of Fondness for Appropriateness and Humanity]

Further, the common people will surely submit to power and authority (*shi* 勢), while few are able to embrace appropriateness (*yi*). Confucius was a sage of the world. With his cultivated conduct and enlightening way (*dao*), he traversed the lands within the seas. Yet, within the seas, there were only seventy people who became devoted adherents, espousing his humanity (*ren*) and valorizing his appropriateness. For those who value humanity (*ren*) are few. And those capable of appropriateness are rare. Thus, out of the whole wide world, only seventy people became devoted adherents, and only a single person[1] exhibited humanity and appropriateness.

> *Comment:* Confucians would reply that the example of a few exemplary persons would inspire others to improve themselves, and that norms of ritual propriety provide a means for such cultivation of character. While there seems to be *some* degree of truth in this, one may reasonably wonder whether Confucians are too optimistic in this regard. Similarly, one may wonder: Is Han Fei Zi too pessimistic about human morality? Is he too optimistic about the efficacy of law and awe-inspiring power?

[The Relative Efficacy of Shi 勢 (Influential Status, Power and Authority)]

Duke Ai of Lu was an inferior ruler. But when he faced south as ruler of his state, of all the people within his borders, none dared not to serve him. The common people surely submitted to his *shi* 勢 (power and authority). Power and authority truly makes it easy to cause people to submit. Thus, Confucius remained a minister, and Duke Ai remained a lord. Confucius did not embrace [Duke Ai's] appropriateness, he submitted to his power and authority. Thus, Confucius would not have submitted to Duke Ai on account of appropriateness, yet Duke Ai relying on his power and authority made a servant out of Confucius.

Now, scholars try to persuade rulers not to ride on their power and authority, which is sure to succeed, but rather that by applying themselves to conduct exhibiting humanity and appropriateness they can become kingly. This would require rulers to reach the level of Confucius and for all the people of the age to fall into line. This is certainly not an effective method.

---

1   Presumably referring to Confucius himself, or perhaps Yan Hui.

Comment: Similarly, Han Fei Zi elsewhere writes: "If Yao and Shun lacked the enticement of honors and rewards and threat of punishments and penalties, if they relinquished power and authority and cast away law, and instead went door to door making their case and arguing with people, they would not have been able to govern three families."[2]

[The Relative Ineffectiveness of Non-Legalist Methods]

Now, there are children of poor character. The parents get angry with them, but they do not reform. The neighbors chastise them, but they are not moved. Teachers and elders instruct them, but they do not change. The use of the parents' care, the neighbor's conduct, and the teachers and elder's wisdom—these three forms of edification are applied to them, and yet they are never moved. They never reform a single leg hair. When an agent of the district office sends soldiers, extending the reach of public law, to threaten disobedient people, only then out of fear and apprehension will they modify their circumstances and change their behavior. Thus, the care of parents is not sufficient to educate children. One must surely wait for the district office's stern punishment. The common people are sure to be spoiled by care, and be attentive to awe-inspiring power (*wei* 威). [...]

So, rewards should be ample and reliably awarded, so that the common people covet them. Punishments should be heavy and inescapable, so that the common people fear them. And the law should be unequivocal and fixed, so that the common people understand it. Thus, the ruler bestows rewards without exceptions, and delivers punishments with no reprieves. If he supplements his rewards with praise, and accompanies his punishments with aspersions, then the worthy and the unworthy will both fully exert themselves.

From Chapter 50, "Prominent Schools"

Han Fei Zi here once again argues for the superiority of Legalism over Ruism and Mohism. First, he argues that there are disputes and inconsistencies *within* Ruism and Mohism in addition to the inconsistencies *between* them. Han Fei Zi argues that by taking them all as legitimate one ends up following an incoherent set of doctrines, which can only result in disorder. Then he argues that it is really power, exercised in Legalist fashion, that reliably produces order. In the final section translated below, Han Fei Zi argues that winning over the hearts and minds (*xin* 心) of the people is not an adequate strategy because the people do not understand

---

2 *Han Fei Zi*, Chapter 40, "Critique of *Shi* (Power and Authority)," 難勢第四十.

what is good for them. So, instead, the ruler must impose unpopular policies on the people—making them toil in the fields, requiring military service, imposing taxes, and punishing the deviant—all ostensibly for their own benefit.

[The Inefficacy of Legitimizing Inconsistent Theories]
The most prominent schools of thought of our time are Ruism and Mohism. The pinnacle figure in Ruism is Kong Qiu (Confucius), that of Mohism is Mo Di (Mo Zi) [...] After [the death of] Confucius and Mo Zi, the Confucians divided into eight [schools], and Mohists diverged into three. What was accepted and what was discarded was not the same among them, and each called themselves the genuine Confucians and Mohists. Confucius and Mo Zi cannot come back to life, so who shall we get to decide which of the contemporary schools [is authentic]. [...]

> Comment: In this and similar ways, Han Fei also calls into question the connection between the schools of thought as they are being articulated in his time and the authority on which they supposedly rest.

When the Mohists inter their dead, they wear winter clothes in the winter and summer clothes in the summer. They use three-inch-thick wood coffins, and wear mourning clothes for three months. Rulers of our times regard this as frugal and accept it as a legitimate ritual practice.

The Confucians impoverish their families to bury their dead. They wear mourning clothes for three years, and suffer such great deterioration that they need to walk with a cane. Rulers of our times regard this as filial and accept it as a legitimate ritual practice.

But if one legitimates the frugality of Mo Zi, one should not legitimate the extravagance of Confucius. And if one legitimates the filial piety of Confucius one should not legitimate the impiety of Mo Zi. Filial piety, impiety, extravagance, and frugality are all included in Confucianism and Mohism. And those above regard it all as legitimate ritual practice. [...]

> Comment: Next Han Fei Zi criticizes the teachings of Qi Diao and Song Zi. Qi Diao (who is presumed to be a member of one of the schools of Confucianism) is described as advocating standing strong against crookedness. Song Zi, on the other hand, is said to advocate the avoidance of conflict. And yet, once again, the rulers regard it all as legitimate. From all this Han Fei Zi derives the following conclusion.

Conflicting schools of thought cannot stand together and produce order. While simultaneously accepting varied schools and blunderingly following contradictory theories, how could there be no disorder? [...]

Comment: Xun Zi expressed a similar idea, writing: "One who [tries to] travel two roads [at the same time] will not reach one's destination. One who serves two lords will not please [them]" (*Xun Zi* 1.6).

[The Importance of Power]

If your powers are many then others will come to your court. If your powers are few, then you will go to the court of others. Thus, the enlightened ruler devotes himself to power. In a strict household, there is no violence and boldness. But kind mothers have spoiled children. From this we know that awe-inspiring power (*wei* 威) and position of authority (*shi* 勢) can prevent the outbreak of violence, while virtue (*de* 德) and generosity are not sufficient to put an end to disorder.

When a sage orders a state, he does not depend on others doing him good; he uses their inability to do [him] wrong. If depending on others to do him good, he will not find ten within his borders. If he uses their inability to do wrong, then the whole state can be made to fall in line. Those who produce order use the masses and discard the few. Thus, they do not strive for virtue (*de* 德), they strive for law (*fa* 法). [...]

Comment: The Legalist "method" involves arranging things so that the ruler cannot be undermined.

[The Common People Do Not Know What Is Best for Them]

Nowadays, those who do not understand order are sure to say: "Win over the hearts and minds (*xin* 心) of the common people." If the desire to win over the hearts and minds of the common people were sufficient to produce order, then Yi Yin and Guan Zhong [wise ministers of old] would have been of no use, as one could simply listen to the common people. [However,] the wisdom of the common people is ineffectual, as their hearts and minds are like those of infants. If infants do not have their heads shaved, they will have bellyaches. And if they do not have boils cut, those will gradually worsen. To shave a head, or remove a boil, one person must hold the infant while a caring mother treats it. And yet the infant will cry and howl incessantly. Infants do not understand that undergoing a minor pain will bring about a great benefit (*li* 利).

The superiors urge the tilling of fields and the cultivation of crops, and thereby ensure ample production for the common people. And for this the superiors are regarded as cruel. They elaborate penalties and provide weighty punishment, thereby to prevent depravity. And for this the superiors are regarded as severe. They levy taxes in coin and grain to fill granaries and arsenals, so as to save the hungry in time of famine and ready the army for mobilization. Yet for this superiors are regarded as greedy. They ensure that everyone within the state's borders understands the need for defense and that no one shirks his personal responsibility, and combine their forces to fight fiercely in order to capture enemy prisoners. Yet for this superiors are regarded as violent. These four are the means to order and security, and yet the common people do not know enough to be pleased.

From Chapter 14, "Traitorous, Robbing, and Murdering Ministers"

This excerpt reinforces the point made above: despite their merits, Legalist policies will be criticized by the ignorant masses.

Sages scrutinize the facts related to right and wrong and discern the conditions of order and chaos. Thus, in their governing (*zhi* 治) of a state, they establish clear and precise laws, put stern punishments on display, to thereby rescue all from the chaos of life, and eliminate the misfortunes of the world. They ensure that the strong do not mistreat the weak, the many do not oppress the few, the aged are sustained, the young and orphaned grow to maturity, the borders are not encroached upon, rulers and ministers have mutual affection, fathers and sons rely on each other, and there is no worry about dying [in war] or being taken prisoner. This is the epitome of great achievement. But stupid people do not understand. They regard it as oppressive.

The stupid firmly desire order and yet detest the means by which order is achieved. They all detest danger yet rejoice in what produces danger. How do I know this? Stern punishments and severe penalties are what people detest, and yet they are the means by which the order of a state is achieved. Taking pity on the people, and lightening punishments and penalties, is what the common people rejoice in, and yet it endangers the state. Sages who make the state's laws are sure to go against [the opinions of] the age, and yet accord with the way and potency (*dao de* 道德). Those who understand this are in agreement with what is [truly] appropriate, but in disagreement with common opinion. Those who do not know it are in disagreement with what is [truly] appropriate, but in agreement with common opinion. If, throughout the world, those who know it are few, then what is [truly] appropriate will be slandered.

Comment: Xun Zi, who is reputed to have been Han Fei Zi's teacher, gives some degree of credit to those he calls "hegemons" (*ba* 霸), who may be inferred to follow Legalist practices. Xun Zi writes, "They open lands for cultivation, fill storehouses and granaries, and facilitate equipment usage. They carefully recruit and select scholar-officials of talent and skill, and then gradually lead them forward with honors and rewards, and correct them with severe punishments and penalties. In matters of life and death, and when the continuation or annihilation of lineages is at stake, they defend the weak and prohibit violence" (*Xun Zi* 9.8). Here Xun Zi seems to confirm what in this chapter Han Fei Zi asserts. However, Xun Zi cautions that there are problems with this approach to governance. In the following quotation, Xun Zi refers to the state of Qin, which would ultimately win the battle of the Warring States and unify China under the short-lived Qin dynasty led by the so-called "First Emperor," Qin Shi Huang, who adopted and implemented Legalist policies. Before all that happened, Xun Zi wrote, "The state of Qin is in this category [of being extremely well ordered (*zhi zhi zhi* 治之至)]. Nevertheless it is in fear. Despite having numerous positive qualities concurrently and in the greatest possible degree, if one measures it by the success and fame of a true king, it is far inferior. Why is this? Because of the dearth of Confucians (*ru* 儒). Thus it is said, 'Pure, a true king; mixed, a hegemon; otherwise one will be annihilated'" (*Xun Zi* 16.6). Legalist doctrines achieve compliance through coercion, and dismiss the importance of "win[ning] over the hearts and minds of the common people" (see *Han Fei Zi*, Chapter 50, p. 431, above). But can that ever truly be either successful or proper? Perhaps it is fitting to end by wondering whether Confucius had been right all along when he said: "Lead (*dao* 道) them with [Legalistic] government (*zheng* 政), keep them in order with punishments, and the common people will avoid trouble but have no sense of shame. Lead them with virtue (*de* 德), keep them in order with ritual propriety (*li* 禮), and they will develop a sense of shame and furthermore will reform themselves" (*Analects* 2.3, p. 94).

Bibliography

Ames, Roger T., ed. 1998. *Wandering at Ease in the Zhuangzi*. Albany: SUNY P.

Ames, Roger T. and David L. Hall. 2001. *Focusing the Familiar: A Translation and Philosophical Interpretation of the Zhongyong*. Honolulu: U of Hawai'i P.

———. 2003. *Dao De Jing "Making This Life Significant": A Philosophical Translation*. New York: Ballantine Books.

Ames, Roger T. and Henry Rosemont Jr. 1998. *The Analects of Confucius: A Philosophical Translation*. New York: Ballantine Books.

Bai, Tongdong. 2012. *China: The Political Philosophy of the Middle Kingdom*. New York: Zed Books.

Behuniak, James. 2004. *Mencius on Becoming Human*. Albany: SUNY P.

Bell, Daniel A. 2008. "Just War and Confucianism: Implications for the Contemporary World." In *Confucian Political Ethics*, ed. D. Bell, 226–56. Princeton, NJ: Princeton UP.

Chai, David. 2008. *Early Zhuangzi Commentaries: On the Sounds and Meanings of the Inner Chapters*. Saarbrücken: VDM Verlag Dr. Müller.

Chan, Alan. 1991. *Two Visions of the Way*. Albany: SUNY P.

Chan, Wing-tsit. 1963. *A Source Book in Chinese Philosophy*. Princeton, NJ: Princeton UP.

Chen, Daqi 陳大齊. 1954. *Xunzi Xueshuo* 荀子學說 [Xunzi's theory]. Taipei: Chung-hua Wen-hua Publication Committee.

Chen, Jingpan. 1990. *Confucius as a Teacher*. Beijing: Foreign Languages P.

Chong, Kim-chong. 2003. "Xunzi's Systematic Critique of Mencius," *Philosophy East and West* 53.2: 215–33.

———. 2017. *Zhuangzi's Critique of the Confucians: Blinded by the Human*. Albany: SUNY P.

Cook, Scott, ed. 2003. *Hiding the World in the World: Uneven Discourses on the Zhuangzi*. Albany: SUNY P.

Coutinho, Steve. 2004. *Zhuangzi and Early Chinese Philosophy: Vagueness, Transformation and Paradox*. Aldershot: Ashgate.

———. 2014a. *Introduction to Daoist Philosophies*. New York: Columbia UP.

———. 2014b. "Zhuangzi." In *Berkshire Dictionary of Chinese Biography*, vol. 1, ed. Kerry Brown, 149–62. Great Barrington, MA: Berkshire.

———. 2014c. "Conceptual Analyses of the *Zhuangzi*." In *Dao Companion to Daoist Philosophy*, ed. Xiaogan Liu, 159–91. Dordrecht: Springer.

Csikszentmihalyi, Mark and P.J. Ivanhoe. 1999. *Religious and Philosophical Aspects of the Laozi*. Albany: SUNY P.

Cua, A.S. 1985. *Ethical Argumentation: A Study in Hsün Tzu's Moral Epistemology*. Honolulu: U of Hawai'i P.

———. 1998. *Moral Vision and Tradition: Essays in Chinese Ethics*. Washington, DC: Catholic U of America P.

———. 2005. *Human Nature, Ritual, and History: Studies in Xunzi and Chinese Philosophy*. Washington, DC: Catholic U of America P.

Dubs, Homer. 1973. *The Works of Hsuntze*. Taipei: Ch'eng-wen.

Duyvendak, J.J.L. 1924. "Hsün-tzu on the Rectification of Names," *Toung Pao* 2.23: 221–54.

Eno, Robert. 1990. *The Confucian Creation of Heaven: Philosophy and the Defense of Ritual Mastery*. Albany: SUNY P.

Fingarette, Herbert. 1972. *Confucius: The Secular as Sacred*. New York: Harper Torchbooks.

Fraser, Chris. 2016. *The Philosophy of the Mozi: The First Consequentialists*. New York: Columbia UP.

Gardner, Daniel K. 2007. *The Four Books*. Indianapolis, IN: Hackett.

Goldin, Paul Rakita. 1999. *Rituals of the Way: The Philosophy of Xunzi*. Chicago: Open Court.

———, ed. 2013. *Dao Companion to the Philosophy of Han Fei*. New York: Springer.

Graham, A.C. 1989. *Disputers of the Tao: Philosophical Argument in Ancient China*. La Salle, IL: Open Court.

———. 1990a. *The Book of Lieh-tzu: A Classic of Tao*. New York: Columbia UP.

———. 1990b. *Studies in Chinese Philosophy and Philosophical Literature*. Albany: SUNY P.

———. 1992. *Unreason within Reason*. La Salle, IL: Open Court.

———. 2001. *Chuang-Tzu: The Inner Chapters; A Classic of Tao*. Indianapolis, IN: Hackett.

Guo, Qingfan 郭慶藩. 1991. *Zhuangzi Ji Shi* 莊子集釋. Taibei: Guan Ya Wenhua 臺北: 貫鴉文化.

Hagen, Kurtis. 2007. *The Philosophy of Xunzi: A Reconstruction*. Chicago: Open Court P.

———. 2011. "Xunzi and the Prudence of *Dao*: Desire as the Motive to Become Good," *Dao: A Journal of Comparative Philosophy* 10.1 (March): 53–70.

———. 2016a. "Would Early Confucians Really Support Humanitarian Interventions?," *Philosophy East and West* 66.3 (July): 818–41.

———. 2016b. "Project for a New Confucian Century." In *A Future without Borders: Theories and Practices of Cosmopolitan Peacebuilding*, ed. Eddy M. Souffrant, 168–89. New York: Brill-Rodopi.

Hall, L. David and Roger T. Ames. 1987. *Thinking through Confucius*. Albany: SUNY P.

———. 1995. *Anticipating China: Thinking through the Narratives of Chinese and Western Culture*. Albany: SUNY P.

———. 1998. *Thinking from the Han: Self, Truth, and Transcendence in Chinese and Western Culture*. Albany: SUNY P.

Hansen, Chad. 1983. *Language and Logic in Ancient China*. Ann Arbor: U of Michigan P.

———. 1992. *A Daoist Theory of Chinese Thought: A Philosophical Interpretation*. New York: Oxford UP.

———. 2009. *Laozi Tao Te Ching on the Art of Harmony*. London: Duncan Baird.

Huang, Chun-chieh. 1993. "'Rightness' (*i*) versus 'Profit' (*li*) in Ancient China: The Polemics between Mencius and Yang Chu, Mo Tzu, and Hsün Tzu," *Proceedings of the National Science Council, Part C: Humanities and Social Sciences* 3.1: 59–72.

Huang, Yong. 2012. *Confucius: A Guide for the Perplexed*. London and New York: Bloomsbury Academic.

Hutton, Eric L. 2014. *Xunzi: The Complete Text*. Princeton, NJ: Princeton UP.

Inoue, Tetsujirū and Kanie Yoshimaru 井上哲次郎, 蟹江義丸共編, eds. 1970. *Nihon Rinri Ihen* 日本倫理彙編, vol. 6. Kyoto: Rinsen Book Co.

Ivanhoe, Philip J. 2000. *Confucian Moral Self Cultivation*, 2nd ed. Indianapolis, IN: Hackett.

———. 2003. *The Daodejing of Laozi*. Indianapolis, IN: Hackett.

———. 2013. *Confucian Reflections: Ancient Wisdom for Modern Times*. New York and London: Routledge.

Jullien, François. 2004. *In Praise of Blandness: Proceeding from Chinese Thought and Aesthetics*. Cambridge, MA: Zone Books, MIT P.

Kaltenmark, Max. 1969. *Lao Tzu and Taoism*. Stanford: Stanford UP.

Kjellberg, Paul and Philip J. Ivanhoe, eds. 1996. *Essays on Skepticism, Relativism, and Ethics in the Zhuangzi*. Albany: SUNY P.

Klein, Esther. 2011. "Were There *Inner Chapters* in the Warring States?," *T'oung Pao* 96: 299–369.

Kline, T.C., III, and Philip J. Ivanhoe, eds. 2000. *Virtue, Nature, and Moral Agency in the Xunzi*. Indianapolis, IN: Hackett.

Knoblock, John. 1988–94. *Xunzi: A Translation and Study of the Complete Works*. 3 vols. Stanford: Stanford UP.

Kohn, Livia and Michael LaFargue. 1998. *Lao-tzu and the Tao-te-ching*. Albany: SUNY P.

———, eds. 2001. *Daoism and Chinese Culture*. Cambridge, MA: Three Pines P.

LaFargue, Michael. 1992. *The Tao of the Tao Te Ching*. Albany: SUNY P.

Lai, Karyn. 2017. *An Introduction to Chinese Philosophy*. Cambridge: Cambridge UP.

Lai, Whalen. 1993. "The Public Good That Does the Public Good: A New Reading of Mohism," *Asian Philosophy* 3.2: 125–41.

Lau, D.C. 1970. *Mencius*. New York: Penguin.

———. 1979. *Confucius: The Analects*. New York: Penguin.

———. 1996. *Tao Te Ching*. Hong Kong: Chinese UP.

Lau, D.C. and F.C. Chen, eds. 1996. *A Concordance to the Xunzi*. Institute of Chinese Studies Ancient Chinese Texts Concordance Series. Hong Kong: Commercial P.

Legge, James. 1960. *The Chinese Classics*. 5 vols. Hong Kong: Hong Kong UP.

Li, Chenyang. 1999. *Tao Encounters the West: Explorations in Comparative Philosophy*. Albany: SUNY P.

———. 2004. "Zhongyong 中庸 as Grand Harmony: An Alternative Reading to Ames and Hall's *Focusing the Familiar*," *Dao: A Journal of Comparative Philosophy* 3.2 (June): 173–88.

Li, Puqun. 2012. *A Guide to Asian Philosophy Classics*. Peterborough, ON: Broadview P.

Littlejohn, Ronnie L. 2015. *Chinese Philosophy: An Introduction*. New York: I.B. Tauris.

Liu, JeeLoo. 2006. *An Introduction to Chinese Philosophy: From Ancient Philosophy to Chinese Buddhism*. Malden, MA: Blackwell.

Liu, Xiaogan. 1994. *Classifying the Zhuangzi Chapters*, trans. Donald Munro. Michigan Monographs in Chinese Studies 65. Ann Arbor, MI: U of Michigan P.

———, ed. 2015. *Dao Companion to Daoist Philosophy*. New York: Springer.

Lloyd, Geoffrey and Nathan Sivin. 2003. *The Way and the Word: Science and Medicine in Early China and Greece*. New Haven: Yale UP.

Machle, Edward J. 1993. *Nature and Heaven in the Xunzi: A Study of the Tian Lun*. Albany: SUNY P.

Mair, Victor, ed. 1983. *Experimental Essays on Chuang-tzu*. Honolulu: U of Hawai'i P.

McCraw, David. 2010. *Stratifying Zhuangzi: Rhyme and Other Quantitative Evidence*. Language and Linguistics Monograph Series. Taiwan: Academia Sinica.

Moeller, Hans-Georg. 2004. *Daoism Explained*. Chicago: Open Court.

———. 2006. *The Philosophy of the Daodejing*. New York: Columbia UP.

Najita, Tetsuo, ed. 1998. *Tokugawa Political Writings*. New York: Cambridge UP.

Ni, Peimin. 2004. "Reading *Zhongyong* as a *Gongfu* Instruction: Comments on *Focusing the Familiar*," *Dao: A Journal of Comparative Philosophy* 3.2 (June): 189–203.

———. 2016. *Confucius: The Man and the Way of Gongfu*. Lanham, MD: Rowman & Littlefield.

Nivison, David S. 1996. *The Ways of Confucianism: Investigations in Chinese Philosophy*. Chicago: Open Court.

Olberding, Amy. 2011. *Moral Exemplars in the Analects*. Abingdon: Routledge.

———, ed. 2013. *Dao Companion to the Analects*. New York: Springer.

Peerenboom, R.P. 1993a. Law and Morality in Ancient China: The Silk Manuscripts of Huang-Lao. Albany: SUNY P.

———. 1993b. "What's Wrong with Chinese Rights? Toward a Theory of Rights with Chinese Characteristics," *Harvard Human Rights Journal* 6: 29–57.

Perkins, Franklin. 2014. *Heaven and Earth Are Not Humane*. Bloomington, IN: Indiana UP.

Rosemont, Henry, Jr., ed. 1991. *Critics and Their Critics*, vol. 1 of *Chinese Texts and Philosophical Contexts: Essays Dedicated to Angus C. Graham*, ed. Henry Rosemont. La Salle, IL: Open Court.

———. 2012. *A Reader's Companion to the Confucian Analects*. Honolulu: U of Hawai'i P.

Roth, Harold, ed. 2003. *A Companion to Angus C. Graham's Chuang Tzu: The Inner Chapters*. Monographs of the Society for Asian and Comparative Philosophy. Honolulu: U of Hawai'i P.

———. 2004. *Original Tao: Inward Training (Nei-yeh) and the Foundations of Taoist Mysticism*. New York: Columbia UP.

Schwartz, Benjamin I. 1985. *The World of Thought in Ancient China*. Cambridge, MA: Harvard UP.

Sellman, James. 2001. "Introduction to the Quanxue Chapter of the *Shizi*," *Asian Culture Quarterly* 29.1: 61–68.

Shen, Vincent, ed. 2013. *Dao Companion to Classical Confucian Philosophy*. New York: Springer.

Shun, Kwong-loi. 1997. *Mencius and Early Chinese Thought*. Stanford: Stanford UP.

Slingerland, Edward. 2003. *Confucius: Analects with Selections from Traditional Commentaries*. Indianapolis, IN: Hackett.

Stalnaker, Aaron. 2004. "Rational Justification in the *Xunzi*: On His Use of the Term *Li* 理," *International Philosophical Quarterly* 44.1: 53–68.

Tu, Wei-ming. 1976. *Centrality and Commonality: An Essay on Chung-Yung [Zhong Yong]*. Honolulu: U of Hawai'i P.

————. 2012. *Confucius: The Embodiment of Faith in Humanity* [e-book]. Washington, DC: World and I Online.

Van Norden, Bryan W. 2007. *Virtue Ethics and Consequentialism in Early Chinese Philosophy*. Cambridge: Cambridge UP.

————, trans. 2008. *Mengzi: With Selections from Traditional Commentaries*. Indianapolis, IN: Hackett.

————. 2011. *Introduction to Classical Chinese Philosophy*. Indianapolis, IN: Hackett.

Wagner, Rudolf. 2003. *A Chinese Reading of the Daodejing*. Albany: SUNY P.

Wang, Robin. 2012. *Yinyang: The Way of Heaven and Earth in Chinese Thought and Culture*. Cambridge: Cambridge UP.

Watson, Burton, trans. 1963. *Hsün-tzu: Basic Writings*. New York: Columbia UP.

————. 1964. *Chuang Tzu: Basic Writings*. New York: Columbia UP.

————. 1968. *The Complete Works of Chuang Tzu*. New York: Columbia UP.

————. 2003a. *Han Feizi: Basic Writings*. New York: Columbia UP.

————. 2003b. *Mozi: Basic Writings*. New York: Columbia UP.

Wen, Haiming. 2009. *Confucian Pragmatism as the Art of Contextualizing Personal Experience and World*. Lanham, MD: Lexington.

Yan, Xuetong. 2011. *Ancient Chinese Thought, Modern Chinese Power*. Princeton, NJ: Princeton UP.

Yearley, Lee. 1980. "Hsün Tzu on the Mind: His Attempted Synthesis of Confucianism and Taoism," *Journal of Asian Studies* 39: 465–80.

Ziporyn, Brook. 2003. *The Penumbra Unbound: The Neo-Taoist Philosophy of Guo Xiang*. Albany: SUNY P.

————. 2009. *Zhuangzi: The Essential Writings with Selections from Traditional Commentaries*. Indianapolis, IN: Hackett.

————. 2012. *Ironies of Oneness and Difference: Coherence in Early Chinese Thought, Prolegomena to the Study of Li*. Albany: SUNY P.

From the Publisher

A name never says it all, but the word "Broadview" expresses a good deal of the philosophy behind our company. We are open to a broad range of academic approaches and political viewpoints. We pay attention to the broad impact book publishing and book printing has in the wider world; for some years now we have used 100% recycled paper for most titles. Our publishing program is internationally oriented and broad-ranging. Our individual titles often appeal to a broad readership too; many are of interest as much to general readers as to academics and students.

Founded in 1985, Broadview remains a fully independent company owned by its shareholders—not an imprint or subsidiary of a larger multinational.

For the most accurate information on our books (including information on pricing, editions, and formats) please visit our website at www.broadviewpress.com. Our print books and ebooks are also available for sale on our site.

broadview press
www.broadviewpress.com

This book is made of paper from well-managed FSC® - certified
forests, recycled materials, and other controlled sources.